Max Linder circa 1921, Witzel, courtesy of Museum of Modern Art

The Rise and Fall of Max Linder:

The First Cinema Celebrity

Lisa Stein Haven

Filmography by Catherine Cormon

Orlando, Florida

The Rise and Fall of Max Linder: The First Cinema Celebrity
© 2021 Lisa Stein Haven. All Rights Reserved.
No portion of this publication may be reproduced, stored, and/or copied electronically (except for academic use as a source), nor transmitted in any form or by any means without the prior written permission of the publisher and/or author.

Published in the USA by
BearManor Media
1317 Edgewater Dr. #110
Orlando, FL 32804
www.BearManorMedia.com

Cover design by Marlene Weisman
Cover photo courtesy George Eastman Museum

Softcover Edition
ISBN: 978-1-62933-712-8

Printed in the United States of America

Table of Contents

Part I: Biography   1

Preface and Acknowledgments   3
Chapter 1: Auspicious Beginnings (1883-1905)   9
Chapter 2: A Screen Comedian (1905-1912)   27
Chapter 3: World Fame and World War I (1913-1916)   63
Chapter 4: America, the Land of Opportunity (1916-1917)   93
Chapter 5: America Revisited (1919-1922)   129
Chapter 6: Decline and Departure (1923 – 1925)   169
Epilogue   203
Bibliography   207
Index   215

Part II: Filmography   229

Preface   231
Acknowledgements   235
Abbreviations   237
Filmography   241
Cross References   373

Dedication

To Maud Linder and Georg Renken, who dedicated their lives to Max Linder's legacy

Part I: Biography by Lisa Stein Haven

Preface and Acknowledgements

The life and legacy of French silent film comedian Max Linder, born Gabriel Leuvielle, despite his daughter Maud's efforts, has been forever tainted by his unfortunate ending. His story must be viewed through the lens of the mania that lead to this ending, even though its cause can never be adequately understood. It must be told in consideration of the fact that "Max Linder" was a stage name, and perhaps a character that Gabriel Leuvielle truly wished to extricate himself from, well before late October 1925. His story, therefore, like that of many screen celebrities, cannot be completely ascertained by this telling, because Linder and his publicity agents were adept at subterfuge—at telling a life story that the public wanted to hear--not one that was necessarily authentic. Therefore, I have given little credence to periodical biographies of Linder, even those from his own lips. What I have attempted to write here is one version of Gabriel/Max's life and film career, augmented by images whenever possible, in hopes of reaching an American/English audience who have never before been provided this information at this level of intensity. Despite the fact that most English-speakers have been unable to read Maud Linder's books about her father, I hope to provide a nod to and an amplification of her original work, filling in gaps and providing enhancements to what she has already provided, where possible.

I did not have the privilege of meeting Maud Linder. By the time I contacted her, she was not well, and was separated even from her friends by the medical care providers she had chosen. Having learned about her from others, I understand that she would probably not have approved of this project, but I have written it with the goal of at least making her take notice. Due to this and other circumstances, I have not had the privilege of accessing the newly formed Institut Max Linder at the Institut Lumière in Lyon, France, so the artifacts and documents portrayed in Maud's books and in her films have not been available to me. Therefore, I cannot say that this is the definitive book on Max Linder, as I had originally hoped. Instead, I hope it will be one very good book among many more on Linder in the years to come. I don't visualize myself being in competition with French film scholars who may write those books in any way.

I only started this project, because I recognized an important gap in film history: Max Linder had been written about only in a few short pieces since several biographies came out in French in the 1960s. Upon Maud Linder's death in October 2017, however, he became a hot property once again, a phenomenon that was long overdue. At that point, I already had two years of research completed and was facing a summer of trying to end that research as much as possible, under the new circumstances. I applaud and heartily wish to thank those French scholars who continued to support my efforts beyond this point and beyond the formation of the Institut Max Linder.

My sincerest thanks go first and foremost to Catherine Cormon for joining me on this wild ride. She has been an incredible partner on the project, and I can't imagine what it would be like—what the book would be like—without her. Because she has allowed the inclusion of her magnificent filmography, I will not be attending to each and every one of Linder's existing films in my chapters. Also, while I do include some information about analysis and interpretation of Linder's character and certain films, my purpose here is to compose a life story first. Many excellent interpretations and critiques of Linder's work already exist.

A special thanks to Marlene Weisman for the beautiful cover she designed!

I tip my proverbial hat to the writers and scholars who came before who worked hard to put Linder's story in print, such as Charles Ford, Jean Mitry, René Jeanne, Frank Bren and, most recently, the very gracious Snorre Smáre Mathiesen, whose short bio just appeared about two years ago, but clearly showed me the work I needed to do. This project would not have been possible, however, without the support and initial prodding of Steve Massa, the author of the very well-written chapter on Linder in his *Lame Brains and Lunatics*. Steve has been unflagging in helping me with research available at his institution, providing contacts at other institutions as well as general moral support. I really can't thank him enough. Brian Anthony, too, helped, having spent 20 years fostering a relationship with Maud Linder. His insight and generosity are greatly appreciated.

Other dear colleagues providing much-needed support are Kate Guyonvarch and Arnold Lozano, always helpful and supportive (Kate especially helped with discerning French handwriting!), Uli Ruedel, who has been a huge motivator on this project, Rob Arkus, who selflessly provided any video help he could, Ono Hiroyuki, who donated his Linder information from Chaplin's man, Kono, the late David Shepard, who told me it was "about time" for this project, when he wrote a reference for me to support a grant application in the last months of his life, and David Robinson, who graciously offered his work on Linder and his English translation of an important Linder essay from *Chaplin: The Mirror of Opinion* (1983). Thanks to Jean-Paul Woodall, Christophe Pavillon and Dominique Dugros for providing companionship, hospitality and expertise during my tour around France in summer 2018 and support afterward. Dominique is by all accounts an official research assistant/translator for the book. He often sent me articles on Linder that he'd found and was happy to translate them. He also provided the reading of Linder's military document from the proper French military context that I include in the project. And he has assisted Catherine Cormon in translating film notes from the French for the filmography. Thanks to

Camille Kolebka, her husband and family for allowing us to access the Leuvielle yard and property during our visit to Cavernes and for providing the incredibly informative "history of the house's origins" document they had received when they purchased the property (Christophe Pavillon made this happen!). Thanks to Arnie Bernstein for hosting me in Chicago and providing his expertise and companionship in that city. Thanks to Jorge Finkleman for providing research support. Jack Theakston pointed me in the right direction regarding the genesis of particular gags.

Thanks to scholars Andrew Shail, Jean-Claude Seguin and the late Georg Renken for sharing their work on Linder. Georg Renken's invaluable maxlinder.de website (no longer available except on archive.org) was the best research repository on Linder anywhere, and I hope it somehow gets reincarnated. He was also very gracious answering Linder questions when needed. Thanks also to those scholars who wrote reference letters, which helped me to receive two large internal Ohio University grants, the Baker Fund grant and the Ohio University Research Council grant, without which this project would not have been possible: Yuri Tsivian, Charles Wolfe, Frank Scheide, Arnie Bernstein, and, again, Steve Massa. My university (OU) and my colleagues there, especially Billie Mautz, Angela Richcreek, Dev Poling, Hannah Nissen and Carma West, have provided unfathomable support as well—with these grants, helping me to arrange travel and much more.

The following archives and archivists have played important roles in the project, by providing much-needed materials: Ashley Swinnerton of the MoMA Film Study Center, Serge Bromberg and Eric Lange of Lobster Films, Béatrice De Pastre, Eric Le Roy, and Daniel Brémaud of the Centre national du cinéma, Céline Ruivo, Monique Faulhaber, Véronique Chauvet and Laure Marchaut of the Cinémathèque français, Stéphanie Salmon, Stéphanie Tarot and Robin Lamoreaux of the Fondation Jérôme Seydoux-Pathé, the staff of La Bibliothèque nationale de France, Arts et spectacles, Francesca Bozzano and staff at the Cinémathèque de Toulouse, the staff of Archives de la Gironde (Bordeaux), the staff of Archives des Alpes-Maritimes (Nice), Georg Wasner and Roland Fischer-Briand of Österreische Film Museum,

Nicole Meystre-Schaeren and Eléonore Rinaldi Lecciso of Archives de Montreux, Aldijana Bećirović and Kristina Höch of Filmarchiv Austria, Ulrike Polnitzky, Bildarchiv und Grafiksammlung of the Österreichisches Nationalbibliothek, Gabriela Avila, St. Augustine College (Chicago), Leslie Martin of the Chicago Museum of History, Sophia Lorent of the George Eastman Museum, Matej Strnad and his staff at NRA, Prague, Agnès Bertola of the Gaumont-Pathé archive, Paris, and the staff of the New York Library of the Performing Arts.

Thanks to my colleague Mike Nern for serving as a stalwart editor of the project and providing his wisdom in that regard. Last but not least, I'd like to thank my husband, Mark Haven, for allowing me to travel where I needed to and for as long as I needed to and for giving his tacit support for whatever project I pursue.

All translations are mine unless otherwise noted.

Archival Collections
AUT-FAA-Wie: Austria - Film Archiv Austria – Wien
AUT-ÖFM-Wie: Austria - Österreichisches Filmmuseum – Wien
AUT-ON-Wie: Austria - Österreichische Nationalbibliothek - Wien
BNF: Bibliothèque Nationale de France, Paris
BNF-A: Bibliothèque Nationale de France, Arsenal, Paris
CZE-NFA-Pra: Czechia - Národný Filmový Archiv – Praha
FRA-ADAM-Nic: France – Archives départementales des Alpes-Maritimes - Nice
FRA-ADLG-Bor: France – Archives départementales de La Gironde - Bordeaux
FRA-CF-Par: France - Cinémathèque Française – Paris
FRA-CdT-Tou: France - Cinémathèque de Toulouse – Toulouse
FRA-CNC-Par: France - Centre National de la Cinématographie - Paris / Bois d'Arcy
FRA-FJSP-Par: France - Fondation Jérôme Seydoux-Pathé - Paris
FRA-GPA-Par: France - Gaumont-Pathé Archives - Paris

FRA-Lob-Par: France - Lobster Films – Paris

UK-BL-Lon: United Kingdom – British Library Archives and Manuscripts - London

USA-CHM-Chi: United States of America - Chicago Museum of History – Chicago (IL)

USA-GEM-Roc: United States of America - George Eastman Museum - Rochester (NY)

USA-MoMA-New: United States of America - Museum of Modern Art - New York (NY)

USA-NYPL-PA-New: United States of America – New York Public Library of the Performing Arts – New York (NY)

Chapter 1: Auspicious Beginnings (1883-1905)

This story begins with a house—a house that came with Suzanne Baron into her marriage to Marcel (Jean) Leuvielle and became the Leuvielle mansion, a house that still sits at the intersection of Avenue du Port and Route des Valentons in Cavernes (58 Chemin des Cavernes now), a village just outside of Saint-Loubès, France in Gironde and used to include about 35 acres of vineyards in addition to the buildings. The Dordogne river is down the lane, about a block and a half walk. A document entitled "Origine Antérieure" (literally "previous origin," but really a history of the house's previous owners and the way it was transferred) created in 1985 and the property of the present owners Camille Kolebka and family states that Suzanne Baron was gifted the house November 25, 1871, by Matthieu Carteyron and his wife Jeanne Bertrand, when she was still a minor, upon Jeanne Bertrand Carteyron's death the same year. Her parents, Gabriel Baron and Jeanne Carteyron Baron sponsored the transfer. Upon her marriage, Suzanne and her husband Marcel Leuvielle then listed their four children, Maurice, Gabriel (Max), Gérard Laurent and Marcelle Crabit as each owning a fourth of the estate. It outlines the death of Marcel (Jean) Leuvielle on November 19, 1938, with the house and acreage passing to Suzanne and her remaining children. Max's daughter Maud is listed as the recipient of his share at this time. Jean Marie Pierre and

Marcelle Crabit took the property over on November 19, 1951, paying a sum of 60,000 francs per year to Suzanne and also attending to her needs from the pharmacist. Suzanne died on April 20, 1958, with the inheritors now listed as the Crabits, Gérard, Maurice's two children (he died early from syphilis) and Maud. On October 23, 1958 the property passed out of the Leuvielle family entirely when the Crabits sold it to the Lecuillier family.

The Leuvielle house in Cavernes, photo by Lisa Haven

The Leuvielle family spent 87 consecutive years in this house and their lives continue to be stamped upon it. Along with it, they owned vineyards, both near the property and at other locations in the area, amounting to 14.4 hectares (35.58 acres), suffered under the phylloxera infection of vines and survived, suffered the loss of their second-born and moved on, but, according to her own account, failed to deal lovingly or fairly to his only child.

As of 1866, Cavernes was listed as a "village", with only 55 houses and a population of 498 inhabitants. Vineyards and houses were located along the river Dordogne, on alluvial and marsh soils, which transmitted different qualities to the wine than wines grown on the hillsides. The proximity of the river Dordogne also permitted flooding of the vines in order to fight phylloxera, an insect that destroyed leaves and vines with its larvae.

Cavernes, France with the Leuvielle house in the bottom left corner

The best source of the family history is Maud Linder's own, in her book *Max Linder était mon père* (1992), from which the reader can access the information with her own particular bias, given that she was an ostracized family member for most of her life. For instance, she described the old farmhouse as having no running water or toilet facilities and that cooking was done in the kitchen fireplace. It's interesting to think of young Gabriel, born December 16, 1883 growing up here. As dark, dingy and melancholy as it was to young Maud, it must have been the location of play and fantastical imaginings for the frail Gabriel, who became acquainted with every kind of domesticated beast and with the French countryside, its marshes, its rivers and streams. The port of Cavernes, just down from the Leuvielle house, is a ghost of its former self at this point, but still on view is the village square green just in front of it that hosted a festival each year (yes, "a jour de fêtes") in the summertime, an event at which Gabriel supposedly got the initial stirrings inside him that would become the acting and writing bug, possibly through viewing and enjoying Le Grand Guignol, which he later acted out with his sister and which would eventually transform his life and redirect it away from his rural upbringing.

Linder's birth certificate is interesting if only for its several-page description of the sanctity and legality of the Leuvielle marriage, as if it had to prove that son Gabriel was legitimate. He was born at 8:00AM at home in Cavernes to parents married on August 10, 1880, "le fils légitime de Jean Leuvielle." The sex of the baby was delineated and two "witnesses" signed off on the record, Jean Jerôme Ernest Chicou and Jules Edouard Délu, upstanding citizens of Saint-Loubès.[1]

Perhaps the story of young Gabriel's predilection for sickness and his experience with cholera and a baker's oven are well known. Some truth lies at least in the practice of tending sick babies in a low-temperature oven—at the baker's—because no one would have had their own oven at the time. His mother Suzanne seems to have supported this story with her own version in Maud Linder's book in which she relates that she stayed by her son's side until old Dr. Rouge exclaimed that the child was saved. Linder himself often joked that he had an important oven in his life.

True enough, however, was the fact that despite their best efforts at curing the grape vines by flooding them with 20 centimeters of water from the Dordogne, as recommended, the Leuvielles and their neighbors found that while the phylloxera temporarily disappeared, mildew from the water set in, so they were no better off. In 1887 then, Jean and Suzanne left their two boys, Maurice and Gabriel, with their maternal grandmother, Jeanne Baron. Answering an ad for experienced vintners, the two arrived in Rochester, New York and spent a year there learning about more hardy breeds of grapes and sharing their own expertise. They rented an apartment at 55 South Street, which is now an industrial region on the Genesee River's edge. Their third child, Gérard, was born in New York on April 21, 1888,[2] and turned out later to be their only child interested in taking over the family wine business. In any event, the three Leuvielles came back on the boat that year with luggage stuffed with American money (wages were three times that of France) and/or

American vines, which were much more phylloxera resistant. Their financial troubles disappeared after that point.

Maurice Leuvielle, equipment captain for France, soccer, Haven collection

Two years after this sojourn, the Leuvielles' final child, a girl they named Marcelle, was born on June 8.[3] Patriarch Jean could now concentrate on his healthy vines. He was growing vines in the "palus" or marshlands, which would have yielded less-fine wines than those grown on the coast, but in 1898, as an example, he was producing an average of 85 barrels per year of wine of four different types.[4]

Linder's father is well-portrayed by the story he related to Robert Florey in 1922:

> My father was a mad smoker; he would light a cigarette in the morning and transmit the fire from that cigarette to the others he smoked until evening. He never stopped. One day he fell ill. The doctor said that if he didn't quit, he was lost. He didn't stop and

smoked more. My mother reproached him, too, "I would like to see you not smoke." Said my father, "you smoke as much as I do." There was only one way to keep him from smoking. I proposed it. "Well, I smoke, but I make a point of quitting when I want to, while you wouldn't be able to," I said to my father. We bet who would be the first to stop, and for 15 days we closely watched each other. After a month we had neither of us smoked. My father did without cigarettes and recovered. Since then, I no longer smoke!

Linder's upbringing and the closeness of his nuclear family becomes clear with this story, one of the type rarely available in print.[5]

Gabriel Leuvielle at eight years old, Haven collection

Gabriel, who claimed himself in an interview that he was referred to as Max his entire childhood, although the name Maximilien is not a part of his name, was not interested in being a vintner or in any other form of earning a living outdoors. Linder's parents enrolled him at the Lycée de Talence at 2 avenue de Thouars[6] outside Bordeaux at a young age, due to his inattention in the local St. Loubès schools. Talence, at that time, was a boy's boarding school, founded on April 16, 1860. In his early teens, Linder was separated from his family and his country home and learning how to form relationships and discovering what his true interests really were. He began to learn fencing at Talence, a skill that he would use again and again in his acting career. He lead his fellow inmates in hijinks as daughter Maud related, in one case leading a group to jump from the roof of the school into a reservoir of the school's potable water.[7] He also impressed a family friend, Dr. Henry Ducan, the mayor of St. Loubès at the time, who convinced the staff at Talence to hook the boy up with Adrien Caillard, a renowned diction teacher.

Lycée de Talence, Bordeaux, Haven collection

Boys in art class, Lycée de Talence, Haven collection

He could have stayed at Talence until graduation but moved over to the Société de Sainte-Cécile to take advantage of Caillard's tutelage in 1902. Sainte-Cécile's (later the Conservatoire municipal de Bordeaux) was located in downtown Bordeaux at 124 rue du Docteur Albert Barraud, right next door to the Palais-Galien, which is a first century AD amphitheater ruin from the Roman city of Burdigala. He attended full-time beginning in the fall of 1902, with his parents now in agreement and paying his way. Both the school (renamed and repurposed) still exist and although it is not remarkable in itself, the ruin is. Walled off from the public now, the ruin is so attractive that one can easily imagine a young Gabriel (Max) creating scenarios in and among the crumbling bricks and stones and beginning his lifelong habit of flirting with and wooing the opposite sex. It wouldn't be surprising to find out that this ready-made set served as an occasional location for classical drama performed by Sainte-Cécile's students. Linder found his calling at Sainte-Cécile's, being hired while going to school there in his first stage role. Much like Ohio University in Athens, Ohio has its repertory theatre in Cape Cod, Massachusetts, Saint-Cécile's (or really Bordeaux's) was the Théâtre des Arts de Bordeaux in Biarritz and Linder was given his first role there, due to a lucky break—three of the young actors scheduled to star in a show's premiere lost their lives in a freak accident. Linder was able to take one of their places for the first night only, because he knew the role by heart. This was during his first year at Saint-Cécile's. The second year, July 7, 1903, Linder was listed as performing Percinet in Edmond Rostand's *Romanesques*, Legougé's *Par droit de conquête*, and L. Manuel's *Les Ouvriers* for his competitive examinations. His role as Percinet won him a second in comedy; the first prize was not given out that year.

Palais-Galien ruin, photo by Lisa Haven

St.-Cécile's today, photo by Lisa Haven

He landed a spot (small roles only) in the Théâtre des Arts de Bordeaux for 1903-4. Mr. Grandey, who had given him a chance for one night in Biarritz had been replaced by Mr. Bachelet. He also had parts in *Le Barbier de Séville*, *Les Précieuses ridicules*, and *Les Fourberies de Scapin*.[8] According to Frank Bren (whose source was Maud Linder) Linder's father asked him to take a pseudonym at this time, in order not to implicate the family name in any way and he chose first "Lacerda," and then "Linder." The genesis of "Linder" is different depending on who tells the story. According to Bren (Maud), Max was walking with his sister Marcelle down the streets of Bordeaux when they saw the name "Linder" in a shoe shop window. Linder also told this version to reporters when asked. Others say he adapted it from "Lender," namely from Marcelle Lender, a famous theater actress at the time. Whichever is true, this was the name that stuck.

Adrien Caillard, Linder's first arts teacher, had left Bordeaux for new horizons, namely the Ambigu-Comique theater in Paris.[9] This gave Linder the excuse he wanted to go there himself and his parents agreed, even providing him a sort of allowance. Linder's goal by this time was to enter the Paris Conservatoire and become part of the company of the Comédie française. First thing's first. Linder auditioned for the Paris Conservatoire for the first time in autumn 1904, with unhappy results. His judge, Louis Leloir, was a professor at the conservatoire but also in the company at the Comédie française. He told Linder, "What is it you wanted me to teach you? You're nothing but an old ham!" Linder was defeated at these auditions two more times, in 1905 and 1906. It was not to be. But Caillard was able to give his former student a balm of sorts—a last minute part as the captain of a sinking ship in the Ernest Morel play *Le Tour du monde d'un enfant de Paris*. Because he had not fully mastered the part and due to the fact that the costume didn't fit his small frame, René Jeanne noted succinctly that Linder "averted total disaster thanks entirely to the fall of the curtain." This is also the first time his pseudonym "Max Linder" appeared in print (in the cast list). Then, with Caillard in the cast, Linder joined the company of *Le Crime d'Aix* in the small part of Payardel, meaning he hadn't totally been counted out after the Morel play debacle. This was a play in five acts and eight tableau by Albert Pujol, which centered around a sensational assassination scene.[10] December 19, however, he was given the opportunity to display his fencing prowess when a contest played out on the Ambigu stage, Salle Berlier versus Salle de l'Ambigu, with Linder representing the latter: "The two winners were Mr. Max Linder from the Ambigu hall, and Mr. Olivier from the Berlier hall."[11] On May 26, 1905 Linder and Caillard participated in another fencing contest put on by the Association des artistes dramatiques at the Vélodrôme Buffalo where they represented L'Ambigu: Caillard came in first and Linder second.[12] Linder revealed to journalist Javier Bueno that he traded fencing lessons for a place in the Théâtre des Variétés with the famous actor Le Bargy[13] and he would find other occasions to trade this skill for something he wanted, not to mention using it in his own films now and then.

Max Linder as Caulaincourt in *La Belle Marseillaise*, 1905

Linder's stage appearances throughout 1905 were small parts but many, including in *La Conquête de l'air* by Camille Audigier and Paul Géry, premiering January 16, 1905 as "Santa Fé":, *Les Deux orphelines* by Adolphe d'Ennery and Eugène Cormon, premiering January 20, 1905, *Paillasse*, by Adolphe d'Ennery et Marc Fournier, premiering February 14, 1905 as "Beaumesnil," *La Belle Marsellaise*, by Pierre Berton, premiering March 3, 1905 as "Caulaincourt." René Jeanne, renowned theater scholar, having seen this production, noted that this play was an historical drama set the day after "la machine infernale" affair and showed the adventures of the Chouans' conspiracy against the authority of the First Consul: "Max Linder played the role of a handsome soldier in the entourage of Bonaparte: an intelligent portrayal in a dapper gold uniform."[14] This was followed by *Les Aventures de Thomas Plumepatte*, by Gaston Maro, premiering May 19 1905 as "Maxwel," *La Fleuriste des halles*, by Henry Demesse, premiering June 15 1905 as "Joseph," *La Bande à Fifi*, by Gardel-Hervé and Maurice Varret, premiering July 11, 1905 as "Ildefonse," *Crime d'un fils*, by Maurice Lefèvre, premiering September 8, 1905 as "Tom Bluff," *Le Régiment*, by Jules Mary and Georges Grisier, premiering October 6, 1905 as "Poplard," *Les Deux orphelines* (again) by Adolphe d'Ennery and Eugène Cormon, premiering October 31 1905 as "Du Presles," and *La Grande Famille*, by Arquillière, premiering November 22 1905 as "Rondet". This final play ran until February 1906 and allowed Linder a rare review in *Le Journal du Dimanche*: "M. Linder is quite nice and flirtatious as the second-lieutenant Rondet [d'Issenes aus Nevers]."[15] Jeanne remembers this as Linder's longest role so far—of about 100 lines—one that kept him on stage a lot, even when he wasn't speaking.[16] Also another of these was a cinema-theater production (his first), Henri Demesse's *La Fleuriste des halles*. The production presented filmed dream sequences together with real-time acting on the stage. For this to work safely, the projector had to sit outside the back of the theater in a courtyard, housed in an iron box (along with its operator!).

As Jeanne stated (and he knew Linder personally), "without the theater, cinema would not have had Max Linder, and that would have been regrettable." Jeanne understood well that Linder was at least as invested in his theater career as he was his film career, even if he didn't always receive the reviews he desired. When he was between film projects, he made sure he was on the stage, even if (and sometimes this was preferable to him) he had to come up with his own sketch in order to do so. More important, and often overlooked, is the fact that Linder became super-famous before 1914 because of his perfecting of the cinema-theater event. At such an event, a clip of one of his films would be shown, then he and his company of actors would act out the rest live onstage. It was this invention (not Linder's own, but originating with the production of *L'Auvergnate* by M. Meynet and Marie Geffrey on September 29, 1899) that drew him huge crowds across Europe and into Russia, 1912-13. Linder may not have been the first master of the cinema-theater production, but he became one of the best.

Linder, second from left as second-lieutenant Rondet,
in *La Grande famille* (1905)

In 1906, Linder's theater career continued with *Pour sa patrie*, by Marquis de Castellane that premiered on March 2, 1906 as "L'abbé de Pradt", then *La Tourmente* by Maurice Landay, premiering on March 30, 1906 and *La Goualeuse* by Gaston Marot and Alevy, premiering on April 12, 1906. On June 4, Linder signed a three-year contract with Madame Réjane at her theater,[17] now known as Le Théâtre de Paris, located at 15 rue Blanche. Linder later announced that he was offered a better deal by Le Théâtre des Variétiés and so moved there for the three years.[18] Beginning November 6, Linder was heralded for his performance in the first act of *Miquette et sa mère* at Variétés and that only then did he sign a contract with Fernand Samuel, the director of the Variétés.[19] The first act, was actually *La Main droite*, a short curtain-raiser written by André Barde, which Linder performed in with Carpentier and Mademoiselles Frémaux and Marius to great reviews.

The next step in Linder's evolution was to be small parts in films. Jean-Claude Seguin Vergara has presented information to the effect that, yes, Linder claimed that he premiered in film with the Pathé Brothers, but he reminds us that "brothers" is plural and that besides Charles based at Vincennes and Joinville, there was also Eugène, Édouard and Théophile (this has since been corrected by Frank Kessler as brothers Jacques, Émile and Théophile, with the first, Jacques, never having been involved in the film business. Eugène and Édouard were cousins, not brothers[20]). Théophile, the rogue brother, was placed in charge of the business in Germany, but in fact, he was also making films himself. Seguin used the two unpublished Suzanne Pathé memoirs as evidence that, indeed, Linder made films for Théophile, thereby making it impossible to say which of his films was first and when it was shot (and where). Suzanne Pathé did mention that her father's films were weak and not well-done, so she offers the possibility that many of them were re-shot at Joinville. With this theory, Linder's first films may have had the same titles and the same plots but were shot twice by two different teams.[21]

Théophile Pathé incorporated his company, La Société de Théophile Pathé frères, March 28, 1905, along with his cousins Eugène and Édouard. The company's goal was "the manufacture, sale and purchase of cinematographic devices, films, raw materials and all accessories related to the industry."[22] His daughter Suzanne remembered when he was looking for actors that "he had noticed the play of a young man whose mimicry skills had struck him [Linder]. When the curtain lowered on this last act of the play, he went and persuaded the young man to come and try his luck the next day at our shooting theater, Avenue Gambetta, for six francs from the stamp, free transportation and lunch paid."[23] She noted that Linder was used in her father's filmmaking often, because he worked hard and took direction well, but Linder finally succumbed to the rewards brother Charles promised him and "defected" to Joinville.[24]

This is certainly in the same small window of time that Linder began his onscreen career, but it has been hard to prove Suzanne Pathé's assertions given no physical evidence. Some have argued, however, that Théophile Pathé also printed postcards, like the ones Linder posed for around that time. Maud Linder includes the four Linder postcards in her book *Les Dieux du cinéma muet: Max Linder* (1992) and Linder himself admitted posing for them in a later interview. The only clue to the postcards possibly being a Théophile Pathé enterprise is the "bee in flight" symbol, which the company utilized, and which is found on the cards.

Max Linder and May, cigarette card, 1905, Haven collection

Whether or not Linder began with Théophile or not, he ended up with Charles Pathé and that's where he stayed. His first effort was *Première sortie*, which premiered on August 5, 1905. Similar to other comics, like Buster Keaton, Harold Lloyd and even Chaplin, Linder's screen character of the dapper dandy did not appear fully formed onscreen until about a year later. In the meantime, Linder took any part, no matter how small—on screen and onstage, if only because his 150-franc salary as a stage actor was nicely supplemented by the 20 francs a day pay for appearing onscreen.

Notes for Chapter 1

[1] *Ans 1883, Actes de l'etat civil, Commune de St.-Loubès, Registre de Naissances,* **FRA-ADLG-Bor.**
[2] Gérard would have been born an American citizen in this case. One wonders if he ever considered that fact.
[3] Life story information paraphrased from Maud Linder, *Max Linder était mon père*, Paris: Flammarion, 1992: 36-51.
[4] Pierre Bardout, *Saint-Loubès en Entre-Deux-Mers: Éléments de son histoire des origins à 1914*, Bordeaux: Centre de Recherche et de Documentation Pédagogiques, 1975: 121-122.
[5] Robert Florey, *Deux ans dans les studios Américains*, Paris, Publications Jean-Pascal, 1922, p. 230.
[6] The school buildings still exist as they did when Linder attended, but are now referred to as Lycée Victor-Louis after a famous architect.
[7] Maud Linder, *Max Linder: Les Dieux de cinéma muet*, Paris: Èditions Atlas (1992), p. 15.
[8] Georg Renken, "Chronicle," *maxlinder.de*, 2019.
[9] *L'Intransigeant*, May 29, 1904, p. 3.
[10] Edmond Stoullig, *Les Annales du théâtre et de la musique*. Paris: Librairie Paul Ollendorff, 1905, p. 326-328.
[11] *L'Humanité*, December 20, 1904, p. 3.
[12] *Gil Blas*, May 27, 1905, n. p.
[13] Javier Bueno, *Caras y Caretas (Buenas Aires)*, April 12, 1913, n.p.
[14] René Jeanne, "Max Linder et le Théâtre," *Revue d'histoire du théâtre*, Vol.2, April-June 1965, p. 167.
[15] *Le Journal du Dimanche*, December 3, 1905, p. 781.
[16] René Jeanne, "Max Linder et le théâtre," *Revue d'histoire du théâtre*, Vol.2, April-June 1965, p. 167.
[17] *Le Gaulois*, June 4, 1906, n. p.
[18] *La Correspondencia de España*, October 4, 1912, n.p.
[19] *Le Figaro*, November 14, 1906, n.p.
[20] Frank Kessler, "Pathé vs. Pathé, Exhibit A: Reading an Archival Document," *Film History*, Vol. 25, Issue 1-2, 2013, p. 123.
[21] Jean-Claude Seguin Vergara, "Max Linder," *grimh.org*, 1999-2020, available at https://www.grimh.org/index.php?option=com_content&view=article&layout=edit&id=2716&lang=fr#2
[22] Jean-Claude Seguin Vergara, "Max Linder," *grimh.org*, 1999-2020, available at https://www.grimh.org/index.php?option=com_content&view=article&layout=edit&id=2716&lang=fr#2
[23] Suzanne Pathé, *Souvenirs*, p. 369. Manuscript owned by Nouchka Pathé, granddaughter of Suzanne Pathé.
[24] Suzanne Pathé, *Souvenirs*, p. 373.

Chapter 2: A Screen Comedian (1905-1912)

Pathé Frères, Joinville-le-Pont, Haven collection

Charles Pathé was the founder of Pathé Frères, only bringing brother Émile into the business after the 1895 start date of the company. Initially Pathé sold only bootlegged Edison kinetoscopes (not protected in Europe). He then threw in with Henri Joseph Joly in an attempt to replicate the Lumière cinématographe but the two men had a disagreement that ended their business relationship and Joly's machine didn't work well anyway. By December 1897, however, Pathé connected with an interested manufacturer, Claude Grivolas, in Chabot, and financier of the Crédit Lyonnais, Jean Neyret. The three men were able to incorporate at that point, becoming the Compagnie générale des cinématographes, phonographes et pellicules. Brother Émile was soon to take over the second in the list, phonographs, and had quite a success with that in the years to come. Film was more difficult. Ferdinand Zecca was Pathé's first "filmmaking" employee and would become a manager in the future.

At this time, there were literally no cinemas or venues for showing film to the public beyond fairgrounds and outdoor spectacles, but this would quickly change, as old theater venues retooled to become houses well-geared for such performances. In 1902, Pathé collected the funds to build the first house of glass studio in Vincennes, right outside the far reaches of Paris, near the Bois de Vincennes and its nearby castle. Two years later, he would add an additional such building at Vincennes and begin building two more at nearby Joinville-le-Pont, right on the riverbank. This area later grew to include several major factory buildings for different aspects of film processing. Pathé also built a facility at Montreuil about the same time.[1]

By 1905, the Pathé company had divided up film genres between particular directors, allowing each to then form his own unit of technicians and actors. Linder first worked (and would often work with) Louis Gasnier, although he had the experience of working with many directors before he took over the helm in 1910. His close friend, Armand Massard, wrote the scenario already for his second film, *Rencontre imprévue* (1905).

G.-Michel Coissac reports that it was Lucien Nonguet, an acquaintance of Linder's at the Variétés that was the first to suggest to him to try the pictures. His version states that being young and full of himself, Linder approached Charles Pathé one afternoon in Vincennes and was offered the aforementioned 20 francs a day for film work.[2] Linder himself is noted as reporting it was Louis Gasnier, not Nonguet, but the pay was the same.[3] For two years or so, it is clear that Linder was taking any role he could get—often in films that don't feature him at all, adding to the difficulty in identifying extant films during this time. During this period, he took parts as small as the Jewish jeweler in *Pour un collier* (1907) and as diverse as Polichinelle in *La Légende de Polichinelle* (1907). Linder's only stage effort in 1907 was *La Revue de centenaire* by Paul Gavault, P. L. Flers, and Eugène Héros, a three-act play in which the main parts were played by Albert Brasseur, Georges Guy and Max Dearly. Linder played personal secretary Eugène de Beauharnais. It premiered March 7, 1907 and ran for 114 performances. Linder was also engaged with his new toy, performing in film and, later in the year, perfecting a persona, which would serve him well.

Linder as Eugène de Beauharnais in *La Revue de centenaire* (1907), Haven collection

Pour un collier (1907) with Linder far right,
courtesy George Eastman Museum

Linder continued his contract with Variétés in the 1907-8 season, appearing as Serguigny in Alfred Capus's *Les Deux écoles* starting January 3, 1908 and at the same time, a short piece entitled *Passez muscade!* by Georges Lignereaux and Maxime Bertrand at the same venue, in which Linder played Lucien Verdier, one of his rare true comedy roles on the stage. On March 4, 1908, Linder (as Lender) was the only star mentioned in a performance of a cinema-theater program at the Omnia theater in Amiens. Georg Renken notes that this was the first time Linder was labeled a screen actor in the press. The report mentioned that the house was packed, and that Linder deserved great popularity: "if his name appeared on the programs. It will come."[4] April 24, the play *Le Roi*, by Gaston-Arman de Caillavet, Robert de Flers and Emmanual Arène premiered and ran 350 performances. Linder played William Touret but was also the second for Max Dearly in the role of "Blond." He received more than one notice of his work in this play over the months, but being such a small role, one wonders how much his screen popularity was affecting this fact.

Max Linder as The Dandy, courtesy Museum of Modern Art

With a performer like Max Linder, who eventually adopts a persona for his screen (and sometimes stage) work, scholars would be hot to try to trace the development of that persona through the actor's career. Eve Golden provides one of the most lyrical descriptions of this persona: "Max, the dapper but hapless boulevardier in impeccable morning coat and silk topper."[5] Charles Ford suggested the character,

> flirtatious, careful of his person, ignoring the scruffy and hating him even by intuition, Max Linder is a gentleman properly dressed in a jacket, pin-striped pants, a top hat, varnished shoes

with gaiters and white gloves, holding in his hand a strangely conquering and casual cane. It has often been said that it was not a princely elegance but rather a bourgeois, situated exactly at the level necessary to be appreciated by the crowds. He was no longer a tramp escaped from some asylum at night, but a son of a good family who knew the customs of the beautiful world, who sought their votes and intended to amuse them with his misadventures. The dandy, the "gandin," had to face many pitfalls, thwart many plots of fate, he got out of each scabrous situation with an unalterable good humor and a comical casualness, which invariably rallied all his sympathies.[6]

Richard Abel's contribution to this description is also important to note:

His character is [ ] stabilized into that of an impeccably dressed young bourgeois--in frock coat, tie, and vest, with either striped or black trousers, spats, a top hat and cane. Consistently inhabiting well-appointed apartments, fully equipped with servants, as [Georges] Sadoul points out, Max rarely ever worked; instead, he either courted young women (not always unmarried), frequented restaurants and nightclubs, or indulged in various sports. In other words, he now epitomized the leisured bourgeois rentier or young man living on an allowance and pursuing a life of "decadence."[7]

Ford believed that what Linder had brought with him from the theater onto the silent screen was a knowledge of audiences. He perhaps felt some advantage in the world of mimicry and pantomime over the authority of "the word" onstage, so that his rather lackluster stage reviews morphed into enthusiastic screen ones very quickly. Unlike other screen comedians, Linder was not schooled by the vaudeville stage, but by observing human nature. Dmitri Tiomkin, the pianist, remembered this uncanny ability when he accompanied Linder in St. Petersburg, Russia in 1913: "Except for Chaplin, I have never known another comedian who had such an objective view of his art. Linder was sensitive and responsive to any audience and could talk audience psychology with the intellectual perception of a professor."[8] He developed the "course poursuite" (chase scene) used ubiquitously in slapstick films (only after him, that is)—a strategy for which Mack Sennett was to adopt and become famous. Linder, though, also took time to react and respond non-verbally to situations and events in the storyline as would have been normal human behavior.

Some scholars name *Le Pendu* (1906) as the first film in which Linder uses the persona he has created. Certainly, *Les Débuts d'un patineur* (1907) is pretty much all "Max." He remembered that "it cost me a lot more than it brought back to me as it was the first time I put on skates, I took a great divet from the lawn; I tore my pants off, flattened my top hat that cost me twenty-five francs and lost a pair of gold cufflinks!"[9] In fact, Ford asserts that it was this film and its success that caused the most-respected Pathé comic of the time, André Deed, to blow town for Rome and thereby leave a big hole in the line-up of comedians—a hole which Linder could then easily fill.[10]

Le Pendu (1906) was based loosely on a popular song of the day by the same name, by Mac Nab, which sports a sketch of a hanging man on the sheet music title page, facing away from the viewer, his bowler hat on the ground all but covering some sort of (suicide?) note. It is a sort of ballad of a garçon who comes to be hanging in the forest of St. Germain, because his young lady has refused his hand. Passersby suggest calling the police, just in case the young man was not yet dead. However, the police keep passing the buck, until finally a commandant accepts the responsibility. The hanging man has become a shade of blue by this time. The young man is saved, his parents notified and all ends well—enough. Certainly, this is almost moment to moment the same as the second part of Linder's film. The first part, where he is rejected by his love and her parents is amplified. The original song was probably a criticism of police bureaucracy, but Linder's amplification of its comedic possibilities worked well. He achieves this by making visible to the audience the hook on his coat, which allowed him to hang without really placing his life in danger. Otherwise, he would have been dead by the time anyone decided to save him. One report noted that the song was played as background to the film's premiere on December 14, 1906, thereby firmly linking the two. In this film, as importantly, Linder has created his relatable dandy character, a persona he inhabited in many a film from then on. So, "Max, the dandy" can be considered born in December 1906, meaning that he became a more well-inhabited persona starting in 1907, one that, like Chaplin's later Little Tramp persona, showed a discernible evolution over time.

Le Pendu by Mac Nab sheet music, Haven collection

By June, he received fan mail from as far away as Hungary, from which one young female aristocrat offered to marry him, enclosing a ring and a portrait. Linder denied the gift of a ring but turned her down flat, saying he preferred Parisian women and the city itself.[11] Linder also remained in the papers due to his fencing prowess, having won another contest (with zero touches) June 30, the prize being his portrait painted by artist Frédéric Regamy. By July 5, Regamy was on the train to Paris in order to interpret Linder in pastels.[12]

Légende de la Polichinelle (1907) with Linder at the left, courtesy Cinémathèque francaise

Meanwhile, Pathé Frères was doing what it could to make its players and staff into a happy and loyal family. A "fête du théâtre" was celebrated July 4 with Mrs. Pathé presiding at the Cirque d'Hiver theater,[13] where a combination of new Pathé films and in-person sketches were featured.[14] Ferdinand Zecca noted that the "fête du travail," as he termed it, included everyone: all workers from both Joinville and Vincennes, including their families, to the tune of 2000 people.[15] This audience demanded that Linder perform a poursuite of sorts and so this manifested as an actor shown on film who picked up a telephone, received a message and then hurriedly left for the theater. He was forced to move through a lively and energetic theater crowd to make it, and arrived at the theater in tatters, where he entered in person onstage and "took up the tale of adventures."¹⁶ This actor was Linder and it was his first cinema-theater or film-sketch experience. He would continue using variations on this plot (additions, subtractions and transformations) for more than seven years. André Deed outlined the philosophy behind the film-sketch idea or "Film joué"¹⁷ as it was termed in France in an article for *Ciné Journal* in 1912. It had five requirements: 1) a special film created for the introduction, usually at the location of the performance, 2) a two-act play presented live on the stage, usually by three actors 3) pieces of film throughout (he mentions 1100 kilos worth!) that depict action such as explosions, scenes in the water, catastrophes, etc. 4) special music to accompany the films, and 5) these scenes being followed by five turns (vaudeville or music-hall) to round out the night and guarantee success.¹⁸

Un Drame à Séville (1907), courtesy of George Eastman Museum

June 5, 1908 is the date Georg Renken gives for Linder's first appearance in print as part of a certain film, that film being *L'Obsession de la belle-mère* (1908). This print appearance in *Gazeta de Noticias* (Rio de Janeiro) preceded any such mention in Europe by a full year. There was still some onus connected with a bonified stage actor admitting that he appeared in films and Linder only made that admission in print after it came out in Rio, on June 9 in *Comoedia*. Different information comes from Andrew Shail, who believes that a poster in Maud Linder's collection for *Le Petit jeune homme* (1909), which features Linder's full name, is the first incidence of film-star marketing in history.[19]

Un Drame à Séville (1907), courtesy of George Eastman Museum

Linder was later to explain some details about his filming process, after he was directing, writing and acting. His first lady interviewer shared some details about the way a film was generally created, Linder telling her that he first came up with a situation, studied its possibilities and then began directing and shooting it, with changes and new ideas popping up along the way. He explained to her that there was no time to write anything down, since he was expected to film two or three films a week (50 a year).[20] Another interviewer, Mr. Bonnat achieved some details about location shooting:

—Tell me something about how [a film's] made.
—That's horrible, because, my friend, I think out by myself and I plan myself. Sometimes I'm lying down and toying with an idea when I start to see clearly the matter, bang, jump out of bed, wrap myself in a gown and on the spot start to unfold the matter. When I have finished one, I have to start thinking about another.

---How many movies do you have to do?

—Fifty. That is almost one a week. I have hired six actors, cast them, explaining what to do and then to work. We talk about the films we make, saying what comes to mind when appropriate. Meanwhile, the camerman works and everything goes smoothly.

—And on the street?

—That's hard, but I liken it to a battle plan. Simply, when the commanding general knows to pave the way for the troops, things keep running smoothly. The first thing to take care of is that the public does not realize that we are there when it comes to doing something on a street. Just imagine that this is an incident that takes place in the Place de l'Opéra in Paris, because the passing public would not notice a possible filming. Everything has been agglomerated when the flow is interrupted and officers would take us to the police station before we had accomplished our purpose. Instead, I tell the cameraman to be there at a certain place at a specific time. The artists that we engage have the same information, and to the second bang! we appear in the place altogether. When officers and the public want to approach us, the film has already been made.[21]

Rue Louis Besquel, Vincennes, France, Haven Collection

The neighborhood in and around the Vincennes factory was especially desired as a location for exteriors. Rue du Donjon, Rue du Bois, and especially Rue Louis Besquel can be seen in many films. Roland-François Lack has identified 14 houses on this street, many designed by Georges Malo, as appearing in Linder (and other) films.[22]

Les Plaisirs du soldat (1907), courtesy Fondation Jérôme Seydoux-Pathé

By September 18, Linder was reported near death (a mistake that the media made more than once). A friend of Linder's, M. Rouzier-Dorcières stated that the actor was at home in Saint-Loubès very ill, but two days later, Linder's father, Jean Leuvielle, assured all that his son was doing much better. No explanation was ever given about what illness had brought him down. By the 24, Linder himself wrote the press that he was becoming better every day, giving his audiences much heart.[23] Yet an actor named Reusy had to replace him as "Tournet" in *Le Roi*, which was still running in Paris. Linder had called off due to this illness until the first week of March 1909. Amazingly, when the Variétiés launched a road company of *Le Roi* January 9, 1909, Linder, sick at home in Saint-Loubès accepted playing the larger Dearly part, "Blond," to a home audience of Bordelais and received even better reviews: "Mr. Max Linder, specially hired, will create the extraordinary role of police officer Blond. Max Linder is no stranger to the people of Bordeaux, who applaud him in the most successful fantasies of cinematography, where his spiritual humor, his acrobatic prowess, his delicious fantasy marvel.²⁴ Another reviewer found his performance as "Blond" stunning. However, he lasted only two weeks playing the role in Bordeaux. He was reported to have acted the part for a couple of days at the Théâtre des Célestins in Lyon, which began March 10, 1910, probably because he had just officially returned from "bed-rest" March 8.

By June 9, he was launched in a balloon over the Vélodrôme at Parc-de-Princes for a charity event, "Fête de *Comoedia*," which doubled as a scene in his film *Le Voleur mondain*, in which he plays famous French jewel thief, Arsène Lupin. *Comoedia* noted the film's appeal:

> Mr. Max Linder and the artists of the Pathé house outdo themselves. Arsène Lupin steals a bicycle, jumps into a broken cab, rushes into a car, finally, when his pursuers reach him, he flees in a balloon. This possible funny scene earned Max Linder a monster ovation. The applause crackles from all sides, when, majestically and daringly, the spherical soars into the air.²⁵

Deux grandes douleurs (1908) courtesy Fondation Jérôme Seydoux-Pathé

Retour inattendu (1908) Haven Collection

Linder's stage achievements in 1909 are few, for he has by now (actually in June) given up his contract with *Variétés*, who intended to start the season again with *Le Roi*. Linder had decided to put his stage career on the back burner and concentrate on Pathé, which on June 18, granted him a new contract with a "high" salary. He, therefore, relegated his stage appearances to two, first playing himself for one night in a charity event for breastfeeding mothers, October 12, in a piece entitled *La Chance du mari*, by Gaston-Arman de Caillavet and Robert de Flers. Later that month, October 28, he premiered at Le Cigale in *Et aïe donc!*, a revue by Rip and Paul Ardot, that was praised for its music, costumes and sets—all very sumptuous. The revue was comprised of 11 tableaux: 1) Luna-Park, Ville d'eaux; 2) Contrôle modern-style; 3) Dans l'Arkansas; 4) Et aïe donc!...; 5) l'Amour fantaisiste (grand défilé); 6) l'Inauguration; 7) les Nihilistes; 8) les Tuileries; 9) l'Amant de la lune; 10) Champ de courses d'amour; and 11) Bacchus est roi! (Apothéose). Linder played both "Le roi" and "Cyrano" in different tableaux, but only until December 1, when Fernal took over his parts.

His first film under the new contract was *Aimé par sa bonne* (1909) which was released on July 24 in Innsbruck, Austria at the Theater-Kinematograph. As would be Linder's usual formula, this film centered on Max, the young dandy, who is about to get married, but who is also sought after by his maid. When she finds out that he is to attend a dinner at the house of his fiancée, the maid spikes his drink with too much gripe water—a mixture of bicarbonate of soda with certain herbs, commonly given to babies with digestive problems. Of course, the resultant situation this places Max in becomes the true center of the fun. Around the time of the third film in this series, *Le Petit jeune homme*, released on August 13, Linder is always named alongside his films in Europe, almost a full year after he was named in the Brazilian papers.

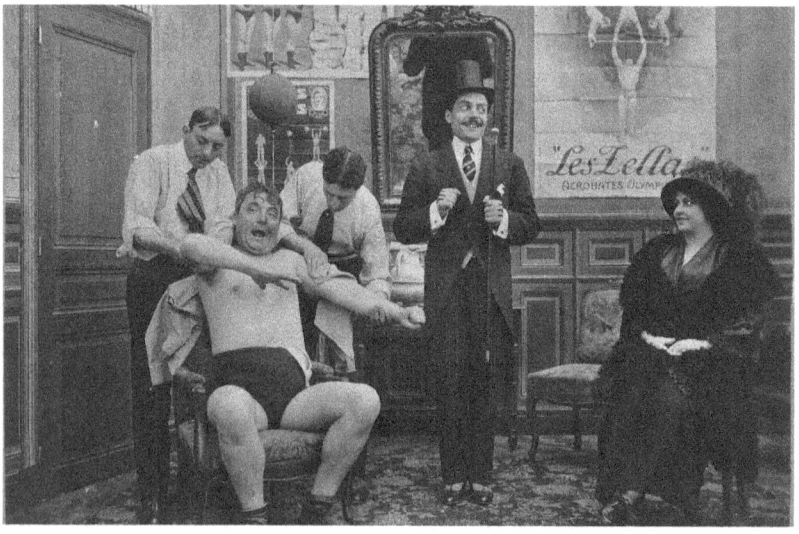

Avant et après (1909) courtesy Fondation Jérôme Seydoux-Pathé

In an article penned by Armand Massard, whom Linder met at Pathé and would be a lifelong friend, Linder's continued prowess with the sword was well-documented. For the fifth year in a row he had won "des Artistes," and this year also "Joe Bridge."[26]

Production at the Pathé plant in Joinville-le-Pont came to a screeching halt in late March, when the Seine flooded, reaching the eaves of most of the factory's buildings. Linder was portrayed as a sort of hero during the tragedy, the papers noting that "Max Linder was one of the last to leave and waded three-quarters of a mile through water up to his waist when he finally left the factory, remarking " 'If this keeps on, we will have to play our parts in bathing suits!'"[27]

Joinville-le-Pont in the 1911 flood, Haven Collection

At the time Linder made *Les Effets des pilules* (1910)[28] and it was released July 10, he had reached the height of his career at Pathé, with his inept dandyish man-about-town character now both recognizable as Max Linder and labeled as such in advertisements across Europe. Also, with the film just previous to this one, *Max est distrait*, Linder is believed to have finally taken the directing helm away from Pathé's Lucien Nonguet and Louis Gasnier, a position he was soon to adopt permanently. This one-reeler contains a spin or two on several Linder comedy standards, such as marital discord, accidental infidelity and the duel (here in the multiple). With a scenario by Linder himself, the film provides further evidence of his fascination with the effects of chemical alteration on human behavior and also, the blurry and intransigent line between life and death, that also occurs in films such as *Le Pendu* (1906),

Le Duel de monsieur Myope (1910), *Max a un duel* (1911), *Max et Jane veulent faire du théâtre* (1911), *Le Duel de Max* (1913), and others.

Les Effets des pilules (1910) courtesy Fondation Jérôme Seydoux-Pathé

Also, in July, articles about Linder, especially one entitled "Max Linder, The Inimitable" in *The Film Index*, began to appear in the American press. The writer rattles on about how beloved Linder was in America and how it might take a golden bridge from France over the ocean to get him to visit that country, but he also noted how versatile Linder was in his silent film portrayals: "Now we can see him as the man of the world, and then again as the timid lover, and still again as a ferocious bandit. He can be funny—oh, so funny! And then again he can make his audiences sob and weep when the occasion calls for it."[29]

His stage appearances this year were both film-sketches. One included another revue, this time at the Olympia, called *Cocher! à Olympia*. Premiering April 2, the revue had 22 acts (or tableaux). In Linder's, he performs essentially the same act he had offered at the Pathé company occasion at Cirque d'Hiver a couple of years previous. October 20, the Olympia launched another revue, entitled *Vive Paris!* written by Maurice Millot. Linder performed in a sketch with Tom Pender titled *Jeffries contre Johnson,* which was a parodic interpretation on skates of the (white) James Jeffries vs. the (black) Jack Johnson prize fight, held on July 4, 1910. This was also a film-sketch performance, beginning with film of Linder at a prizefight, itching to try the sport himself.[30]

Une Bonne pour monsieur, un domestique pour madame (1910)
courtesy Fondation Jérôme Seydoux-Pathé

November 8, Linder was admitted to the hospital and later operated on for acute appendicitis. He later told the tale that this ailment had been precipitated by an accident on the stage of the Olympia in the skating sketch: " 'I slipped and fell. . . .then from the blow I was told of the peritonitis and had to have this terrible operation. My belly was opened on three or four sides.'"[31] Linder was attended at the l'Hôtel-Dieu. His friend Armand Massard provided a blow-by-blow description of the emergency:

> Last night, an automobile ambulance came to pick him up at his home, on the boulevards. To carry him on a stretcher to the car, it was necessary to cross the sidewalk between a double onlooker

hedge, which was not slow to crowd. On his berth, in spite of the blanket pulled up high on his chest, and a cap over his eyes, his poor head, thinned by suffering, appeared pale on the pale pillow. ... Then it was towards the operating room, through Paris, a slow, terribly painful journey. Each jolt corresponded to a more acute pain, a more lamentable cry. At half past ten, his condition having worsened from hour to hour, he was carried on the operating table. Before he fell asleep, he said in a weak voice to the surgeon (a friend hastily called at the last minute, who showed admirable dedication and zeal): "I am not afraid. . . . I'm used to 'surgeons.' You know, if you had brought a cinematographer here, and this was the last scenario I played, you could have sold the film to M Pathé for a large price!"

Complications from the operation meant he would be out of commission for eight months, even though there appeared several press releases on December 31 that he was back on the job.[32] Near the end of that period, July 6, 1911, Linder was operated on once again (for the third time), by Dr. Di Chiara. The star wrote a "letter" to *Comoedia* that he was not near death, as the press was reporting and in a foreshadowing move (one even he didn't realize), he noted "When I die . . . I will tell you."[33]

In 1911, Linder was starting to be featured in newsreels, the first of which was *Pathé Journal #91*, released in Germany on January 14. This bit of film showed Linder being released from the hospital after his appendicitis debacle. But his second appearance in a newsreel, *Pathé Journal #144: La Rentrée de Max* happened all the way at the end of that year, after Linder had spent much of his recovery at Arcachon, in southwest Gironde, not far from the Leuvielle family estate. Again, as in 1908, he also traveled back home to Cavernes and decided to make use of the location for a film. He was well-known enough now that he thought he could put over a film that was autobiographical and he was right. The players were his parents Jean and Suzanne and his sister Marcelle, his sidekicks a recalcitrant horse and a dog. Out of this mélange he created *Max Linder en convalescence* (1911). He also shot parts of *Max cherche une fiancée* (1910) while he was recovering in Arcachon. Linder must have enjoyed the place, because he spent summer 1911 there as well, renting the Villa Elizabeth at Avenue Nelly-Deganne. His first film following his return was *Voisin, voisine* (1911) released July 28.

L'Ingénieux attentat (1910), courtesy Fondation Jérôme Seydoux-Pathé

Max en convalescence (1911) courtesy Fondation Jérôme Seydoux-Pathé

That autumn, Linder was feeling well enough and flush enough to look for an apartment in a prime section of Paris, even buying an advertisement in *Le Journal* that ran November 18. The ad read "I am looking for a pretty, small apartment, modern. Proximity Champs-Élysées, Madeleine, Bastille. 2000 francs. Write Max Linder, Hôtel Brébant." The one he chose was located at 113, Quai d'Orsay, on the bank of the Seine. He would reside there for many years. Leo Faust describes the apartment and its furnishings:

> In front of the house splashes the Seine, and in the distance, on the other bank, diagonally opposite, gleams the typical structure of the Trocadero.
>
> An old maidservant-type Dutch cleaning woman, led me into a little coquet salon, yellow satin and dark red mahogany.... In the field of paintings Linder seems to be an admirer of pointillism. On the wall hung several paintings, all in the pointillist style, with lots of bright ocher-yellow and hard blue colors, but on the whole, quite clever in their genre. Furthermore, I discovered such a beautiful library cabinet with bound Shakespeares, Lamartines, Victor Hugos. But the most atypical item was on the yellow satin sofa, which was tastefully built in a corner, a very big teddy-bear![34]

1912 was a banner year for Linder, one in which he released 32 (known) films and appeared in at least three film-sketch productions. Starting the year in Chamonix, a place he would spend many days and months of relaxation over the years and the place he would meet his future wife, Linder formed a bob-sled team and won a local contest February 7. March 24, he appeared at the Olympia in the first of three film-sketches, this one written by himself. His intent was charitable, in that he pledged all funds raised from the event to the military for the purchase of a plane. Just a few weeks later, Linder signed a contract to tour Europe for three months, presenting his film-sketches in each location. His salary would be 60,000 francs. Then May 1, he was part of "Fête annuelle: Syndicat des exploitants de cinématographe de la Côte

Max at home in Paris, courtesy Fondation Jérôme Seydoux-Pathé

d'Azur," at which patrons toured the Pathé studios on Rue de Turin after a reception at the Hôtel Cecil and experienced films and photographs there, then on to Monte Carlo for aperitifs. Breakfast the next day was held at Cecil followed by a visit to the city. That night there was a gala in honor of the airplane again, with Linder and Robinet guaranteed guests.[35]

June 6, Linder arranged another charity event (this time to benefit the *Courrier cinématographique*) at the Brasserie Cinéma Rochechouart, at which he performed another film-sketch, which amounted to a compilation of a couple of past ones. In it, Linder is supposed to box Nick Winter (Georges Vinter in character as the famous policeman) but doesn't show. While his second, Winter's second and the referee wait, Linder is called on the phone, the scene appearing on film (as has been done before). Linder still arrives in tatters, but then begins to box. Both seconds are knocked out and then both "boxers" consider themselves to be the winner. This was followed by a series of films to round out the night. The event raised 500 francs.

July rolled around and it was time for Pathé to attempt to sign Linder once again. This time, he demanded a million francs for three years and Pathé was forced to raise the price of his films about 20%. His salary was believed to be about 100,000 francs per year the contract before, meaning that he would be receiving about 250,000 francs per year. With this raise in pay, he was able to purchase a yacht, which he christened "Film" and launched at Arcachon about August 10, entering the boat in a regatta just two weeks later.

Linder's big European tour began in September 1912 and his frequent co-star, Stacia Napierkowska was his stage partner on much of the trip. About this time an article appeared that boils down the depth and breadth of Linder's popularity:

> But who is *Max Linder?* Max Linder actor, comedian and bon vivant, who every day performs in some of the world's five continents before many hundred thousand spectators. Five continents know the name, elegant shape, the way of his hair and moustache. And when the name is displayed on the participants list, rapture rumbles throughout the viewers, because Max Linder is easy for fun, to laugh, always been in good spirit and brightens everyone, when he shows up on the white sheets. We can say without hesitation: *Max Linder today is the most popular actor.* The most popular comedian at this time and never had any mimic had more viewers, than his pulling faces.[36]

The pair's arrival in Barcelona was preserved for posterity by *Pathé Journal #183*. Before his performances began, Linder drew a crowd outside of the Hotel Cólon where he was staying. He ventured out one day to get permission to film in the city, received it, then began filming. An afternoon edition of the paper recounted the process:

Max took off his overcoat and was dressed in a jacket torn everywhere, with an undone tie and broken hat. He made his way out of the station, for which he demanded the assistance of an urban man and a policeman, who were to arrest him and who immediately offered to help him. [He had arrived at the station from Paris without a ticket.]. Max desperately left the platform, the aforementioned law enforcement officers caught up with him, and they all rolled on the ground.

From there he moved to the boulevard de Santa Monica, where another piece of film was shot, Max fleeing at full speed, from the drinks kiosk to the book market, to chase the police.

The third piece of film was shot by Max in Plaza de Cataluña, where he simulated the theft of a donkey, which he mounted and went to the Novedades theater, which he entered, doing a singular cartwheel as he went up the curb. The one who owned the donkey pounced on Max, and, forming a group, along with several policemen, they all entered the theater.

In the Plaza de Cataluña and in front of Novedades, the work of Max Linder was witnessed by more than 1,000 people.[37]

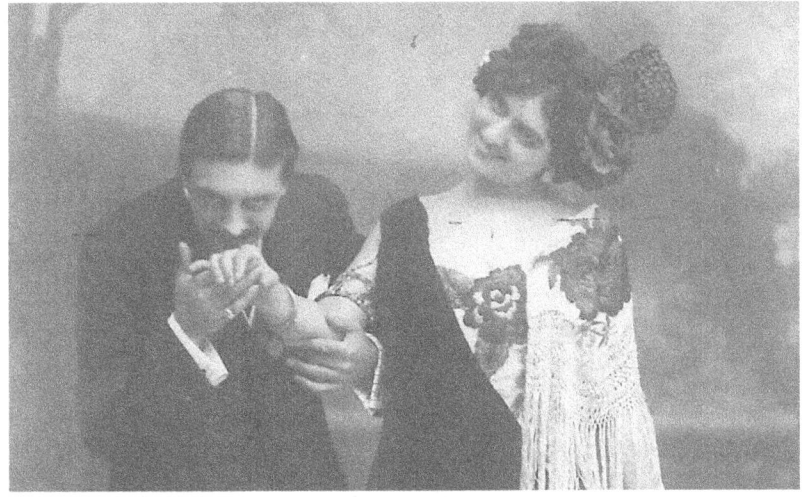

Linder and Señorita Villars, Barcelona, 1912, Haven collection

These scenes would be used as a sort of introductory bit of film for the night's performance.[38] Their first appearance took place September 20 at Teatro Novedades in Barcelona, where the evening consisted of a premier showing of *Mariage au téléphone* (1912) and a newish film sketch *Pédicure par amour*, a title of one of Linder's 1908 films, which was written by Charles Decroix. This time and for this sketch both Linder and his friend Armand Massard are credited as writers. *Ciné Journal* describes the evening in a little more detail, noting that it had 13 acts (tableaux) and featured, in addition to Napierkowska, Mari Marini, Esther of Aragon, Jane Lise, Miss Celia Galley, Angelina Villard, and more, and included "The Dance of the Bear," and "Oriental Dances," as well as the Linder film elements.[39] September 25, Linder was guest of honor at a lunch banquet given at the restaurant "El Tibidabo," then given a tour of the Rabassada, a grand hotel that had recently been expanded to include a casino and amusement park. September 28 before an audience of 10-30,000 people, Linder performed a bullfight at the Barcelona arena, most of which was recorded, either for his film *Max toréador* (1912) released the next day or for one of two *Pathé Journal* newsreels featuring the star-as-bullfighter not released until November 15. Napierkowska and others of Linder's company watched in horror from the President's box as Linder showed off what had been a quick study of matador moves, killing a bull.

Despite this success, Linder received fairly negative reviews in Barcelona, with one writer noting that "the only artistic thing is the dance of the bear, danced exquisitely by Mlle. Napierkowska,"[40] another that his performance left a lot to be desired and that he and Napierkowska, showing that they were fatigued, simply suspended the performance before it was over.[41] In Madrid a few days later, he told A. R. Bonnat about it, saying first that his experience in Spain so far had been "bad." He explained this as due to a difference in expectation: "The press has treated me very badly. Sure: they had counted on a comedy in three acts and have encountered a show that gives twenty five minutes."[42] His last performance there was September 29.

Linder in the arena, Barcelona, courtesy Fondation Jérôme Seydoux-Pathé

Linder and Stacia Napierkowska, courtesy Fondation Jérôme Seydoux-Pathé

Madrid was next. Linder and party arrived in the city by October 2 but didn't begin their run at the Gran Teatro until October 7, due to a railway strike. This gave the star time to try to counteract the damage possibly done by Barcelona reviews. First, he printed a *mea culpa* in the papers:

> My dear friend: I just came to your beautiful and charming city. I would be very grateful to you if you would offer to be my interpreter close to the public and the press in Madrid to dedicate my first salute. I wish, if possible, to plead to the newspaper editors to insert this letter, for the public to realize that I am not perfect, nor do I pretend to be a great actor of comedy or drama, but simply an artist of the cinema. My work, my *vaudeville* and the *sketch*, I have the honor to present, are like me, completely cinematic, that is to say, with no claim of any kind. My desire is to just have fun and to make the people of Madrid laugh. Yours faithfully, Max Linder.[43]

Spanish magazine commemorating the tour, 1912, Haven collection

Second, and he may have done this as a matter of course anyway, Linder employed a claque in the audience, not unnoticed by the press: "Such is the candid grace of this fable that the public found it very pleasing and applauded willingly. The indiscreet cheering of the claque put Max Linder's success at risk for a moment. This claque of the Gran Teatro must learn not to be so deliriously excited when there is no reason."[44] Third, and this may have been directed by the Gran Teatro itself, additional acts were performed, including Miss Aguilar, who sang a selection from *The Barber of Seville*, a zarzuela by Giménez, not from Rossini's opera, Mr. García Romero, Miss Maria de la Paz, who delighted with La Riojanica, from Caballero, Carmen Fernández, beautiful and singing very well in different genres and, finally, the Chimenti, Italian duettists.

They again presented *Pédicure par amour*, followed by the film *Max boxeur par amour* (1912). The very next performance, Linder again had an accident. One viewer remembered that Linder was called from a box near the proscenium and decided to attend the young men there who called him by trying to jump into the box, instead of accessing it in the normal way. He misjudged the distance and hit the box with his knees, then fell to the floor. The audience thought it was all part of the act until they saw Linder limping, with a blood stain on his trousers. A Dr. Ruiz Albéniz in the audience rushed to attend Linder and examined him backstage. Linder had suffered a minor dislocation of his knee and he was in shock.[45] Still, he attempted to go onstage the next night anyway, omitting a couple of the show's more dangerous features. After this performance, he came down with a fever, which laid him up for a week or so in the Ritz hotel where he was staying. Linder was able to attend a meeting with Spain's most accomplished fencing champion on October 12 but did not perform there again. He and his company arrived in Lisbon, Portugal three days later and probably bid a relieved farewell to Spain, which had been a land of bad luck for them.

Linder's stint in Lisbon only lasted four days (October 19-22) and took place at the Theatro da Republica, where his film *Entente cordiale* (1912) became part of the show. One reporter recounted that a crowd was waiting for Max at the Rocio station by 2:30 in the afternoon and he didn't arrive there until 4:50:

> a penetrating hiss announces the arrival of Max Linder. While some rush to meet the carriage where it appears at the hatch, others climb on benches, or on unloading cars. A round of applause roars. With enormous difficulty, Max Linder is preparing to descend. He wears a light belted overcoat and a travel beret covers his head. He looks with curious eyes at the sensation he produces in the crowd and his mouth opens in a kind smile. He greets with his hand and manages, after serious efforts, to set foot on the asphalt.[46]

Kyrelor, bandit par amour (1910), courtesy of Fondation Jérôme Seydoux-Pathé

Linder's entourage arrived then at the Hotel de Inglaterra, but soon after calming the crowds of reporters and fans inside the building's atrium, it was discovered that his co-star was across town at the Grand Hotel on Avenide and that his rooms were there also. Linder arrived ahead of the crowds (his driver savvily took a street behind the hotel to get them there) and he soon settled in for a rest, just barely having recovered from his accident in Madrid.

As in Barcelona, Linder attempted to shoot some film in the streets of Lisbon to use as an introduction to his performance. This time, the effort was more difficult because of the crowds and crowds of admirers. One reporter related, " 'In Paris,' he tells me, 'I do what I want. Nobody notices. Anytime I do the most extravagant things in the middle of the boulevard and everyone leaves me alone.'" But Linder is mollified later by the adulation he receives from regular people in a regular neighborhood, " 'I found in Lisbon what I didn't find in Madrid or Barcelona; typical and curious things. Then the color of this whole city compared to the gray of Paris! ... It is a charm and I am very satisfied.'"[47] There seems to be less information on what the Portuguese audiences thought about Linder and Napierkowska's performances and more on their lives and time spent touring around the city. One item being reported, however, was that America had courted the Linder troupe and that he would be taking his company to America in January 1913—at either the Palace in Chicago[48] or at the Metropolitan Opera in New York.

Max Linder contre Nick Winter (1912), courtesy Fondation Jérôme Seydoux-Pathé

He followed this with a 15-day stay at the Ronacher Theater in Vienna beginning November 15, this time with partners Léonora and Jacques Vandenne, ending on the 30. He notified the press that he planned to arrive a couple of days early, so that he could film his "arrival" for the show, this time via balloon, which also caused a variation onstage later, when he arrived by climbing down a rope from high above. For this performance Stacia Napierkowska was replaced by English actress Mademoiselle Léonora. One viewer provided that

> the equally famous and popular cinema comedian of the Pathé Frères company is currently in Vienna, where he lets all sparks of his delicious talent explode in a humorous sketch in the Ronacher establishment. The traction that Max Linder's appearance has on the Viennese audience proves once again that the cinematograph also offers the best propaganda for acting skills and that real talents can also conquer the masses by storm through cinema art. We shall come back to Max Linder's guest performance in Vienna in detail, so it should only be mentioned today that the sketch in which Linder appears, the "corn surgeon out of love", brings up extremely delightful confusion scenes, and that the sketch is preceded by a cinematographic shot of Linder showing us the great perils under which the "highly anticipated" Linder finally comes to the Ronacher Theater.[49]

Vienna's crowds were highly appreciative of the performance, both the filmed and live parts, with the first night completely sold out, making the visit a success for all. His last days in Vienna, Linder attended the evening's screenings at two theaters, Hellos-Palast-Kinematographen-Theater and the elite Kleine-Buhne.[50] Unlike the Portuguese press, the Viennese reported little on the "real" Max Linder, concentrating only on his performance and its merits.

By December 2, he was in Berlin at the Wintergarten Theater, in what was supposed to be a two-week run. His popularity there, however, forced an extension a further two weeks until December 31. For his twice nightly performance, he has now pretty much settled on the filmed entrance via balloon, followed by *Pédicure par amour* and the bear dance with whatever female partner was along; in Berlin she was again Léonora. The director of the theater usually engaged the other acts for what truly was a vaudeville/music hall type of evening. At the Wintergarten,

> these included Sahary-Djeli, the oriental dancer, followed by the Zanfrellas, who brought a wonderfully equilibristic novelty. On a high, very small rotating pedestal, both partners, a gentleman and a lady, perform their peculiar tricks on a darkened stage, but the two equilibrists are within a circle of light so that their silhouettes within this circle are visible on the back wall of the stage. Since the performance of the Zanfrellas is very excellent and great care is also taken with the beauty of the silhouettes, the number offers a double pleasure.[51]

Next was Lipinsky's 40 comedy dogs in "Drunken Adventures," followed by the Shelveys (contortionists), Wieland the juggler, the cycling act of Fred St. Onge and Miss Efestco and the Schwarz family in a burlesque on "The Broken Mirror." The premiere performance was sold out—the Wintergarten had some 4000 seats—and Linder himself received 15 curtain calls and dozens of flower bouquets each evening, in appreciation from the audience. One reporter suggested that the star might be popular there simply due to the fact that he had a German name (Linder) and many were wondering who his historic German ancestor was. In reality, it is likely that they simply liked the semi-grotesqueness of the *Pédicure par amour* sketch.[52] Another viewer provided an important point in his assessment of the performance,

> The language (the piece brings a French dialogue) distracts from its indescribably expressive facial expressions rather than underlining one or the other. Quite apart from the fact that the foreign word remains incomprehensible to wide circles, the cinema also offers technically much better viewing options

than the stage. The facial expression and the gesture remain visible to all viewers in the movie theater, in the theater, actually only in the front rows. So, it happens that the real Max Linder has nothing new to say to us today, because we could see his idiosyncrasies much more clearly in the cinema than on stage. And we understand that this comedian could never have become popular without the film. Still, it was a good idea to bring Linder to Berlin: he showed the importance of film as an interpreter of foreign individuals. And that should be the permanent win of this guest performance.[53]

Linder would not have made it as a stage actor, for his expressions were not visible to the last rows of the audience; film is the optimal vehicle for demonstrating the talent of foreign actors.

Un Pari original (1912), courtesy Fondation Jérôme Seydoux-Pathé

During this time, about December 7, Linder was approached by two different German film companies with offers to lure him away from Pathé. They offered him 1.5 million francs for three years and an additional 10,000 francs to buy him out of his present contract.[54] He hinted that he might say "yes," extending his Berlin run for two weeks due to his popularity, but also possibly to mull the offer over or to make sure that the news reached Paris and Pathé, before he returned home to hit them up for another raise.

Notes for Chapter 2

[1] Richard Abel, *The Ciné Goes to Town: French Cinema 1896-1914*, Berkeley, CA: U of CA P, 1994, p. 19-22.
[2] G.-Michel Coissac, *Histoire du cinématographe: De ses origines à nos jours*, Paris: Éditions du "Cinéopse," 1925, p. 414.
[3] Charles Ford, *Max Linder*, Cinéma d'aujourd'hi 38, Paris: Éditions Seghers, 1966, p. 103-4.
[4] *Comoedia*, March 4, 1908, n. p.
[5] Eve Golden, *Golden Images: 41 Essays on Silent Film Stars*, Jefferson, NC, McFarland & Co., Inc, 2001, p. 76.
[6] Ford, p. 23-24.
[7] Richard Abel, *The Ciné Comes to Town: French Cinema 1896-1914*, Berkeley, CA: U of California P, 1994, p. 240.
[8] From an article about Dmitri Tiomkin from *Films in Review*, November 1951 quoted in Jack Spears, *Hollywood: The Golden Era*, London, Thomas Yoseloff, 1971, p. 86.
[9] Coissac, p. 415.
[10] Ford, p. 19.
[11] "Max Linder," *Comoedia*, June 9, 1908, n. p.
[12] George Dubois for *La Culture physique*, July 1, 1908 and "Espada," *Le Rappel*, July 5, 1908, n.p.
[13] Pathé Frères had recently purchased the venue and remodeled it for screening films.
[14] "Pathé Frères Celebrate," *Variety*, July 18, 1908, n. p.
[15] MS Ferdinand Zecca, n. d. Fonds Maurice Bessy, **FRA-FJSP-Par.**
[16] "M. Charles Pathé," *Kinematograph and Lantern weekly*, July 23, 1908, n. p.
[17] Catherine Cormon refers to the film portion of these performances as "films raccordés," or "connected films" in her filmography here.
[18] André Deed, "Dernière heure: A propos du film joué au "Ciné-Théâtre," *Ciné Journal*, April 6, 1912, p.23.
[19] Pamela Hutchinson, "Fame at last—was this the world's first film star?," *theguardian.com*, November 22, 2019, available at https://www.theguardian.com/film/2019/nov/22/fame-at-last-was-this-the-worlds-first-film-star.
[20] Encarnación Osés, "Una Interviú con Max Linder," *El Cine*, September 28, 1912, n. p.
[21] A. R. Bonnat, "Chismorreo: Hablando con Max Linder," *La Correspondencia de España*, November 4, 1912, n. p.
[22] Roland-Francois Lack, "Où est Max," thecinetourist.net, available at https://www.thecinetourist.net/wheres-max.html.
[23] "Max Linder mourant," *Comoedia*, September 18, 1908, "Max Linder va mieux," *Comoedia* September 20, 1908 and "La santé de Max Linder," *Comoedia*, September 24, 1908 respectively, all n.p.
[24] *La Petite Gironde*, January 19, 1909, n. p.
[25] *Comoedia*, June 14, 1909, n.p.
[26] Armand Massard (EGO), "Silhouettes sportive: Max Linder," *La Presse*, June 14, 1910, n.p.
[27] "[Max Linder, the famous comedian]," *The Film Index*, April 2, 1910, n. p. Also, remembered in "An Infant Industry Restless in its Crib," *The Moving Picture Word*, March 27, 1920, p. 2112.
[28] Thought lost, this film was discovered in the archives of Gaumont-Pathé by Georg Renken in February 2017.
[29] "Max Linder, The Inimitable Celebrated and Versatile Pathé Artist," *The Film Index*, July 16, 1910, p. 3.
[30] "Olympia, Paris," *Variety*, November 12, 1910, p. 19.
[31] *La Correspondencia de España*, October 4, 1912, n. p.

[32] "Pictures," *Variety*, December 31, 1910, p. 17 and Pathé ad, "Max Sends Compliments," *The Film Index*, December 31, 1910, p. 2.
[33] "La Santé de M. Max Linder," *Comoedia*, July 25, 1911, n. p
[34] Leo Faust, "Max Linder," *Nieuws van den dag voor Nederlandsch-Indië*, November 30, 1914, n.p.
[35] "Syndicat des Exploitations de Cinématographe de la Côte d'Azur," *Ciné Journal*, April 27, 1912, p. 5.
[36] "A mozi kedvencei," *Délmagyarország*, October 27, 1912, n.p.
[37] "Max Linder en Barcelona," *El Imparcial*, September 22, 1912, n. p.
[38] "Pelicula de Max," *Diario de Tarragona*, September 20, 1912, n. p.
[39] "Au Pays des Hidalgos: Barcelona en Fièvre," *Ciné journal*, September 21, 1912, n. p.
[40] "Música y Teatros," *La Vangardia*, September 21, 1912, n. p.
[41] "Max Linder en Barcelona," *El Imparcial*, September 22, 1912, n. p.
[42] A. R. Bonnat, "Chismorreo: Hablando con Max Linder," *La Correspondencia de España*, November 4, 1912, n. p.
[43] "Gran Teatro: Una carta de Max Linder," *La Correspondencia de España*, October 4, 1912, n. p.
[44] Caramanchel, "Los Teatros" *La Correspondencia de España*, October 8, 1912, n. p.
[45] "Max Linder, Lesionado," *El Globo*, October 9, 1912, n. p.
[46] "Max Linder Chegou...," *A Capital*, October 16, 1912, n. p.
[47] "A Rua: A Baixa em revolução," *A Capital*, October 18, 1912, n.p.
[48] The tour was to start January 27. Napierkowska's agent, C. M. Ercole, made the arrangements with Martin Beck, "Max Linder Coming Over," *Variety*, October 4, 1912, p. 4.
[49] "Max Linder in Wien," *Kinematographische Rundschau*, November 17, 1912, n.p.
[50] "Max Linder in Wien," *Kinematographische Rundschau*, December 1, 1912, n.p.
[51] "[Der Wintergarten,]" *Vossische Zeitung*, December 4, 1912, n. p.
[52] Being of German ancestry myself, I make this observation from personal experience only. No disrespect is attended.
[53] "Max Linder im Berliner Wintergarten, *Erste Internationale Film-Zeitung*, December 7, 1912, n.p.
[54] "Max Linder's Erfolg in Berlin," *Lichtbild-Bühne*, December 14, 1912, n.p.

Chapter 3: World Fame and World War I (1913-1916)

In January 1913, there was no sign of Linder traveling to America any time soon. He told Javier Bueno, who asked if had any desire to go there, "yes, I would like to go, especially to Argentina, to Buenos Aires, but until now, proposed contracts have not yet been agreed upon."[1] Instead, he would be going to Budapest for about 15 days and then to Russia.[2] Linder somehow felt obliged to always let the press know how much he was being paid—4000 francs per night in Budapest, for instance. After Bueno's article, it seems as if South America, too, kind of woke up to Linder, with one Brazilian article even claiming him as having been born in Para, Brazil. Many assumed from Bueno's report that he would be visiting South America that year—Argentina and Brazil at least—but this did not happen either.

What did happen was that Linder's popularity had reached a sort of acme. He attended a boxing match at the Cirque d'Hiver on January 8 but caused more excitement by his presence than did the match between Georges Carpentier and Marcel Moreau—and this was Paris! So, by July, he decided to rent the Olympia theater and advertise the first "Saison de Max" (Season of Max) for five weeks beginning July 6. Expecting a performance similar to what he had provided on his world tour, many ticket-buyers were disappointed. The show featured nine Pathé films, only three of which were Linder's: *Max toréador* (1913), *Max Linder pratique tous les sports* (1913) and *Les Vacances de Max* (1913), with two long intervals and no Linder! John Cher, reporter for *The Bioscope* in Paris, conveyed his disgust, not with the films, but with the theater management:

> There were two intervals, and only nine films in all exhibited. As someone in the audience remarked; the "entr'actes" constituted the major portion of the entertainment. To wait, as it seemed to me, some thirty minutes for absolutely no reason whatever, in a semi-lighted hall, with not even a little Tzigane orchestra or advertisement slides to while away the time, is not the sort of thing to cause amusement, or to induce one to revisit the place. Such a show is a disgrace to Olympia - the music hall - and the moving picture industry, and one calculated to do great harm to all exhibitors in the city, destroying, as it does, the desire to see the moving pictures.[3]

Linder on a Pathé Frères set, film unidentified, courtesy Fondation Jérôme Seydoux-Pathé

But this didn't seem to sour Cher on Linder; indeed, he was a big fan and continued to be. On August 21, Cher reported a "Linder sighting" at Gare St. Lazare, with Linder, in a raincoat and sunglasses over his shoulder looking dejected and gloomy. No one seemed to recognize him! But all Cher had to do was wait a bit. In fact, Linder was scheduled to perform in one of his film-sketch performances at the Alhambra Theatre in Paris premiering August 30, which opened the venue's season. *Variety* had reported on January 24 that Linder was already negotiating this deal, to the tune of $1352 weekly (23, 322 francs).[4] It was titled *C'est le tango qui est la cause de ça* (*Blame it on the tango*), but the sketch again was *Pédicure par amour*. However, there were modifications for the Parisian audience. Linder's introductory film this time included him having problems with his car and ending, as before, arriving by balloon. The *Pédicure* sketch was the same, except that his leading lady was Hilda May and her father was George Gorby. The bear dance was replaced by a tango (Linder and May), thus the title. Cher eagerly attended and noted that people were standing six deep in the aisles as well as packing the seats. Linder and company received many curtain calls as well.[5] But then, September 2, he had another accident on stage. This time, he fell from the rope as he was moving down it to make his entrance. He finished the show, but cancelled performances on September 3 and 4. Georg Renken asserts that about this time Linder considered and eventually hired a double for the more dangerous aspects of his work. In fact, Charles de Rochefort, son of an aristocratic French family that ignored their wishes and sought a career in films, worked with Linder on several Pathé films, claiming he was Linder's double on *Max pratique tous les sports* (1913). He also claimed to have worked on *Max se marie*, *Max et la belle-mère* (1911) and *Max chez le commissaire*, but only one of these titles actually exists.[6]

During the spring months of 1913, before this performance, Linder had been in Monaco filming what would become *Le Hasard et l'amour* (1914), in which he operates a hydroplane, and *Max à Monaco* (1914). He was also working on his first comedy feature, *Duel de Max* (1913), which was five reels—about an hour—in length. However, because Linder used the mirror scene, which became more famous for him in his American film *Seven Years Bad Luck* (1921), it could not be shown in its complete form in most European countries where the Schwarz brothers held a copyright on the sketch. So, it was released on July 25 in two forms: a shortened form without the mirror scene and the full-length version, which could be shown in the UK. In 1920, Pathé was finally able to re-release the film in Europe in its longer form.

Max et l'inauguration de la statue (1913), courtesy Fondation Jérôme Seydoux-Pathé

Voisin, voisine (1913), courtesy Cinémathèque français

Linder and company set off for Budapest the second week of November, to premiere their show November 14 at the Royal-Orpheum theatre. *C'est le tango qui est la cause de ça* was the tour's show throughout, with Lucette Darbelle and Georges Gorby as co-stars. The hot air balloon entrance to the stage was utilized, *Pédicure par amour* enacted, and the tango danced. Hungarian reviewers liked the show and touted it as a family show that was geared to pleasing no particular social class of people.[7] Amidst the fun, Linder was greeted by a marshal at the door of his room at the Ritz, demanding payment of 1000 francs in recompense for his failure to show up for a performance at the London Hippodrome. In fact, he would never perform in person in London. The show's final performance in Budapest was November 30. Then they were off to St. Petersburg, still the preferred city of the Romanovs, so Russia was at this point the type of place it would never be again after 1917. Darbelle would be replaced by Mary Mitchell for the remainder of the tour.

Arriving at the Warsaw station on December 3, Linder and party were greeted by a thousand well-wishers, who grabbed their French hero and carried him on their hands over the heads of the crowd. The cameramen of *Pathé Journal* captured the moment in a short newsreel that had its premiere on January 14, 1914. Linder visited the Zon theatre, where he would be playing December 4-14. The first two performances were sold out. Near the end of the run, one writer reported that, unknown to anyone, Linder had switched out his secretary for himself in the first part of the performance in which the introductory film is played and he enters the stage via rope, as if from a balloon. If true, this may have been another example of his using a double:

> A few days ago, thanks to missteps of a watchman, a journalist friend of his came suddenly into the dressing room of Max Linder and was dumbfounded with surprise, because at the same time as one Max Linder lowered himself on a rope on the stage, another sat in the dressing room.
>
> "What is it, Mr. Linder?"
>
> "Very simple," replied the artist, lazily yawning. "Today I'm in a bad mood, tired, completely unable to laugh, and contractually obligated." So, he adapted his secretary.
>
> "But what about the public?"
>
> "As you can see, they are very happy, and do not suspect anything."
>
> "And if all is exposed?"
>
> "No one would believe it. Everybody will think that this is one of the Linder tricks." At this time, the work of the double was over, and bursting into the dressing room was the sweaty, tired secretary, strikingly similar to his patron, dressed in exactly the same suit, boots and tie like the real Linder.
>
> "Successful? No one noticed?" Max Linder asked of his secretary.
>
> "Went off perfectly, Maestro..."
>
> "Well, I'm going to bow, — the real Linder sighed and set aside a cigar and went to the ramp.[8]

Renken mentions that parts of the show from this point made it into Linder's later film *Coiffeur par amour* (1914), however, since one of the Muscovite reporters noted that the sketch Linder performed was so-named, it is possible that the company tweaked the *Pédicure par amour* sketch in order to remove the more "grotesque" elements like the corn surgery, to raise it to the level of higher art—or at least a more palatable one. Linder's pianist at the venue was Dmitri Tiomkin, a young pianist who would one day write film scores in America, like ones for *The Guns of Navarone* (1961) and *High Noon* (1952). He remembered, "I sat at the piano and improvised all through his act. He was brilliant and unpredictable, and ad-libbed frequently. He never did the same act the same way twice."[9]

Linder attending a banquet in his honor, St. Petersburg, Russia, courtesy Fondation Jérôme Seydoux-Pathé

Unlike Chaplin's Little Tramp character, Linder's "dandy" did not appeal to the world's intelligentsia. Many reports during the tour would contain lines like "and the intellectuals sighed," or "the intelligentsia rolled its eyes" or something in that neighborhood. Yuri Tsvian does mention, in his account of the tour, that Linder spent an evening at "The Stray Dog" (Brodyachaya Sobaka) in St. Petersburg, meeting Futurist poet Vladimir Mayakovsky there, who had begun to adopt at least Linder's top hat as part of his dandyish costume. This evening, Mayakovsky was wearing a yellow jacket with broad black stripes. As Tsvian relates from Georgi Ivanov's memoir, Linder was not in the mood to be performative, or even nice. Linder walked in stiffly with a strained smile on his face. Having answered the [welcoming] cheers with a reserved bow, he bowed again and sat down, without taking off his white kid gloves. The patrons of the club thought he meant to demonstrate a magic trick or two, but Linder was in no mood to perform and responded curtly. He only wished to talk about the Hermitage's collection of Rembrandts—if he could find a empathetic ear.[10]

A Russian magazine commemorating the visit, Haven Collection

Perhaps Linder would get a second wind in Moscow, where he was to perform from December 16 to the 21. As in St. Petersburg, Linder was hoisted over the heads of his adoring public (this time college students) upon his arrival at the Nicholas station and was somehow saved by the director of the Zona theater, Mr. Bryansk. Linder and his new partner, Englishwoman Mary Mitchell, expressed their interest in Moscow and seeing its sights, with Linder especially desiring to shoot some film in front of the Kremlin.

December 18, Linder subjected himself to the whims of the Muscovites who wanted to mark his visit with photographs and films. They seated him in a Russian sleigh, upholstered in red velvet and drawn by a troika (team of three horses) and transported him first to the Kuznetsk bridge. Next, the procession headed for Red Square and Linder was directed to speed towards the Execution grounds and Old St. Basil's church. Then, it's through the Spassky gate to the Kremlin. He refused to allow a photo-op at the Tsar's Bell, but allowed one at the Tsar's cannon, although he refused to place his head in the barrel. On to the monument of Emperor Alexander II and then to the Grenadier palace.[11]

Russian tango sheet music, Haven collection

After his performance on December 18, Linder was invited to a big banquet in his honor, which was attended by 100 locals from all areas of business. A roaring success, the event didn't break apart until 3:00AM. On the 20th, Linder was invited to the Letuchey Mishi (the Bat), better known as the Chauve-Souris, by Nikita Balieff, which became very popular in New York, Los Angeles and other big cities where the touring company played. In honor of his French guest, Balieff introduced Linder, then changed the night's program to a selection of Russian folk songs, which everyone was persuaded to join in singing. Soon, Linder found himself up on stage reciting one or two famous French monologues.[12] Linder's final night of performances, he claimed he was too exhausted to do two shows, even though they were sold out. During his final performance that night, he reverted to *Pédicure par amour*, then debuted a trick in which he appeared in three places in the house, the gallery, the hatch and the orchestra—obviously using his doubles as much as possible! He then performed the tango with Miss Mitchell, then showed one of the short films he had made on location in Moscow, *Max Linder and Mrs. Prokhorov* (1913)[13] in which he: "fell in love with Moscow merchant Prokhorov's wife, after a series of quid pro quo scenes, Max escapes from the home of the jealous Prokhorov and everything ends in a common scuffle."[14] His last day in Moscow, he was to finish another short film entitled *Max and the Russian girl student* (1913)[15] before leaving on the train that night. Many Muscovite children were greatly disappointed that Linder was leaving and they hadn't been able to see him, because they had no money for his "performances" or even for the cinema. A young male student wrote a poem lamenting this, comparing their sadness at Linder's departure to the death of Tolstoy. A girl also wrote a letter pleading with the star to visit them at school. It was never sent (but did make the papers!). Also, gossip was spreading among the children that if a person saw Linder on the street, he was not friendly but gloomy and "no jumping!"[16] That night, December 21, Linder arrived at the station to leave on the 8:00PM train and was again carried hand by hand over the heads of the crowd to the train car. He spoke a few words in Russian, was kissed by a Russian lady and waved his handkerchief to all as the train pulled out of sight.[17]

Four Russian postcards, Haven collection

He had decided earlier in the day not to shoot the final scene with the young Russian girl, because he thought it would be more impactful for her simply to be unable to part with him. The film consisted of the young girl riding around to all the sights of Moscow in a troika with Linder, with a fond farewell at the end. Linder, obviously going for a bit of Bohemian romance in the film, wanted to dress the girl in a tattered embroidered coat and a head scarf, known as a kokoshnik, but he was overruled. She wore a tattered coat and no overshoes, instead. In the alternate ending, the girl, Miss Carron, a young Frenchwoman, traveled on to Kiev with the party and had her final scenes shot there.

Linder played only one performance in Kiev, although he was booked for more. For the only time on the tour, the house was nearly empty the second night and the performances then cancelled. When Linder asked about this, he was simply told that the ticket prices were too high. He responded by demanding that the prices be lowered, but this did not happen. This could also have been due to the fact that the first performance was on Christmas Eve—meaning that the residents of Kiev had other plans or had already spent their money on the holidays. Those who had bought tickets for subsequent performances were not refunded and the managers of the Tsirk theater (Linder's venue) left town. To add insult to injury, Linder reported that a Crédit Lyonnais check for 20,000 francs had been lifted from his luggage between Moscow and Kiev.[18]

Linder was to arrive in Odessa on the last day of the year, giving his first performance that evening. The papers reported that he was again carried from the train on the hands of strangers—until it came to light that this was all staged by a theater company working in the "Theater of Miniatures" or Kleinkunst tradition.[19] Renken reports that the performances took place in the Gorodskom Teatre for five nights (this included a two-night extension due to popularity) and the crowds and general welcoming of Linder and company nearly equaled that of Moscow. Finally, the tour ended with two nights at the Fiharmonja theater in Warsaw, Poland, were Linder was also swarmed and his performances sold out. A Pathé camera crew shot his arrival, which appeared about January 13, 1914. The chances are good, however, that the person they filmed was not Linder, because he had been "kidnapped" from the train and held for ransom by a Polish producer named Mordka Towbin and a Linder double met the crowds. Aleksander Hertz, the producer with whom Linder was officially booked, had to promise that ticket sales for the Linder shows would be split with Towbin. When the agreement was reached, Linder was transported to his hotel.

The only description of this performance suggests that Linder arrived in his usual way, by filmed balloon ride, but then suggests that the skit was replaced by his little film *Max and Mrs. Prokhorov* (1913),[20] even though Renken suggests it was still *C'est le tango qui est la cause de ça*. With Linder's growing level of exhaustion at each stop, it would not be surprising if this was the case. Tired, but still thinking film, Linder stopped at Berlin on the way back to Paris, January 14, in order to shoot some of the scenes—at the Brandenburg Gate and other places—that can be found in *Max professeur de tango* (1914).

In March, Linder and Max Aghion launched a revue piece they had written at Gaité Rouchechouart called *Elle est de....* It starred Made Andral, Castel, Marius Reybus, and Dave Loty, who played "Max Linder." This might have signaled that Linder was no longer interested in performing onstage in any capacity, but in fact, it just meant that he had found another way to make money. The sketch was not well-received and closed within a month.[21] A description of the show sounds very much like a mixture of film clips and onstage action, similar to what Linder had performed himself on his tour. John Cher, the reporter for *The Bioscope*, described "the first act of the revue is a very clever mixture of stage and screen scenes. The episode commences on a train; there is a wife returning to her husband, and an amorous traveler. ...The pictures show a most exciting chase through the principal streets of Paris, and, of course, the trio arrive at the Gaité Rochechouart, whereupon the screen rises, and the artistes come rushing pell mell into the hall."[22] The revue began at this point.

June 11 Linder appeared himself in the *Revue de Marigny* in a sketch entitled "Député" (Deputy), which again combined film and stage elements. Its scheduled premiere date of June 6 was postponed only the day before. Parts of this sketch were new to this type of performance transmission and others hearken back to Linder's past sketches. It began with Linder receiving a message that he must attend a political meeting in a nearby town, but his young wife will not allow him to go without her. Still in person, the audience saw the pair lugging heavy baggage out of their apartment and on to the station. Then the film portion began at the station, where the wife latched onto Linder's neck and was swept away with him onto the train. At his destination, Linder tried to send his young wife back home, but failed. He packed her into his trunk at this point and moved onto his appointment, at the home of an angry uncle. The stage then took up the action and much mayhem ensued, as Linder tried to keep his uncle from finding the wife, first in his bed, then in his suite's bathroom and finally, in the same bathtub his uncle used and attempted to use while the wife was hiding in it.[23] Some of this plot was taken from the Linder short *Les Vacances de Max* (1913). He reportedly made $116 a day for these performances.[24] Also added to the *Revue de Marigny* June 11 was Irene Bordoni's very successful Linder impersonation sketch, "Les sosies de Max Linder," for which even Linder expressed his admiration.

It wasn't long after his film debut in 1914 that Charlie Chaplin's Little Tramp had his imitators, on film, on stage and amongst his rank-and-file admirers. Linder's imitators started to appear only a year or so before, with Irene Bordoni's act being one of the first and one of the most-beloved. She first took the stage in costume as Max December 12, 1913 in a two-act play called *Si j'ose exprimer ainsi*. Another impersonator, but not so successful, was André Sechan in the film *Comment il manqua son mariage* (1914) as "Maxi."

Sometime in 1914, Linder began to rent a villa in Varenne-St. Hilaire, a suburb (about seven miles away) of Paris and spent time relaxing there. In the summer of 1914, the few months before the onset of the Great War, Linder was interviewed in Varenne and hosted friends there on occasion, seemingly without any hint of what was to come. During one interview, Linder again bragged about his salary, noting in detail the amount he was making at Pathé and also what he had made on the tour. He also claimed, a claim disputed, that he was offered 20,000 francs in salary by Pathé right off of the Variétés' stage (when actually, he received 20 francs a day).²⁵ Actress Gaby Deslys was a visitor at "the villa" that summer and got into some trouble there. The *New York Times* reported in mid-July that Linder, in order to celebrate Bastille Day, had invited his friends to his villa. Linder, Deslys, her dancing partner Pilser and four others were nearly drowned on the Seine, due to the fact that the dock outside of Linder's villa collapsed as they tried to board a boat in order to cross to the other side of the river to better view the fireworks.²⁶

André Sechan as "Maxi"

Linder on location in Chamonix, France, 1914, courtesy Fondation Jérôme Seydoux-Pathé

He had talked about returning to some of his tour venues in 1914, but this never materialized. And then the war stepped in (on July 28, with France entering the war on August 2), took Linder by the lapels, shook him up, shattered him, and then set him loose on a ravaged landscape, formerly known as France. Austria-Hungary still had a few Linder films on the shelves waiting to be shown, when war was declared, such as *Max asthmatique* (1914), *Max et sa belle-mère* (1914) and *Max au couvent* (1914), which were released, but without any advertising. Pathé closed its Berlin office the day after war was declared. The final Linder film to be screened that summer was *Max à Monaco* (1914).

Linder volunteered for service right away. There have been many versions and perspectives on his Great War service. The one presented here refers only to his military record, begun in 1903, contained in the collection of the Archives de Gironde in Bordeaux. Dominique Dugros offers his contextualization and analysis of the document, which is presented here without critique. Others may have different ideas. Linder was referred to by both his birth name, Gabriel Leuvielle, and his stage name, Max Linder, on the document. His randomly assigned number was 119. He was given an exemption with no explanation in 1904 and then he tried to enlist for the war's duration September 17, 1914 in Paris in the 17th district at the 19th squadron of the "Train des équipages militaires," or automobile group. He then reported for duty on September 18. Linder was assigned to the auxiliary service. A stomach disruption resulted in a decision by the Military Governor of Paris on proposal by the Special Reform Commission of the Seine district, n°5 to remove him on December 5, but he was maintained in the auxiliary service by the 3rd Special Commission of Paris until March 25, 1915. Another decision to relieve him (by the military governor of Paris) was dated April 2, 1915 due to parvi-abdominal weakening (hernia), due to surgery (previous appendectomy). General bad state. Reformed n°2 (ailment not a result of service) by the 3rd Special Commission of the Seine district dated April 28, 1915 for pulmonary bacillus disease, right area. He was transferred to the 13th Artillery on September 18, 1914 (which is out of chronological order).

Filming *Max et sa belle-mère* (1914) in Chamonix, courtesy Fondation Jérôme Seydoux-Pathé

As Dugros explains, this part of the record states every detail of the soldier's career (campaigns, injuries, acts of bravery, military decorations). If there is no mention at all of Linder's battles or trips to the front, it seems that it's because he probably never left his barracks. Men with fragile health, who consequently could not be sent to the front but could be called up for military service in order to be militarily or non-militarily employed, according to their professional skills, were assigned to the auxiliary services, after examination, commissions, etc. A man who belonged to the auxiliary services was assigned to a regiment. He was enlisted like all the other men but was not assigned to a fighting unit. He was, therefore, considered "on the field" (since he had been called up to fight against Germany) without being in the fighting service. Those men's serial number records clearly state that they were "on the field" against Germany or "Campagne contre l'Allemagne aux armées" as Linder's own document states. Finally, Linder was enlisted in the 19th squadron of the "train des équipages militaires," based in Vincennes, conveniently near the Pathé studios. This squadron was controlled by the Military Governor of Paris, who also commanded the 13th Field regiment. As he was not enlisted in the fighting services, Max was enlisted in the squadron and in the regiment as a reservist.[27]

As Mark Twain has said, "the report of my death has been exaggerated." Interestingly, three days before he showed up for service, Linder was reported dead by the German newspaper *Rigasche Zeitung*. Four days later, other papers were carrying the story, which related that Linder was hit and run over by a car on September 2 during a military operation. American papers didn't pick up the story until the beginning of October and by then he was described as having died at the battle of the Aisne.[28] The *New York Times* reported Linder as saying, before he joined his company, " 'I am a fatalist. What is to be will be. When I am to die, I will die, whether on the battlefield or in my bed at home.'"[29] The German papers insisted that he was of German ancestry and this belief became so entrenched that a year later he was forced to show his birth certificate to the press, à la Barack Obama.[30] He was convalescing with stomach troubles later in the year, about November 6, but it had nothing to do with a battle. October 4, the retractions began to appear. Linder had supposedly "called" from the hospital at the front to correct the reports. One report asserted that it had been a case of mistaken identity; Linder had handed his camera over to a Parisian journalist friend who was killed by a stray missile and buried as "Max Linder" due to the nameplate on the camera.[31] By June 1915, when he had been relieved of service permanently for bad health, he stuck to the story that he had in fact been seriously injured and had a scar to show for it (probably his appendix operation scars!). Linder had received approval from Pathé to have his military company filmed, with himself in uniform, probably to dispel any remaining idea that he had died in service. The film (a *Pathé Journal*) was released May 16 in Turin, Italy. Linder spent about three months in the hospital, recuperating from pulmonary problems either at Buffon or Contrexéville in Paris (or both). His secretary, Albert Petit, later shared that upon leaving the hospital, Linder only weighed 90 pounds, down significantly from his usual 135.[32]

Russian card with Linder in "costume," with the words, "At the urgent request of the people, I live again. Max Linder," Haven collection

What should be the most reliable source about Linder's military career is provided in an essay by Émile Massard, son of Armand Massard, and grandson of the subject of the essay for *La Liberté* in 1923. If true, it's quite a story. Massard, Sr. (Armand's father) was charged with driving an emergency vehicle on a mission with General Berdoulat at the Aisne. The headquarters of the 6th army on the road from Paris to Soissons via Villers-Cotterets was no problem, but from Soissons to Reims, he encountered "the Bosche" (the Germans) on the other side of the Aisne. Outside Soisson, Massard lost his driver, who ran for cover, so he then joined Linder in the other car. They arrived safely at Chassemy, where Armand was, with 287 French in a trench. Both Massard, Sr. and Linder were chewed out by the colonel for having made the trip at all. However, they accomplished their mission at Braisne and had to return the same way, this time in the dark. No headlights were allowed, although Linder tried to shine them anyway and was again reprimanded. Massard, Sr. worried at what Linder's response would be when they got stopped by a sentry, and he soon found out. Every French guard was to call out "Qui vivent?" The answer was to be "La France," but Linder answered with his own name and was taken aback when the guards responded with laughter. Linder also didn't know the passwords. He was supposed to say "Caen," and hear the response "Cambronne." The two men made it back to Soisson, but the road to Viller-Cotterets was a problem; "the path was smashed, ruts of 50 centimeters crisscrossed the ancient Roman road." With an improvised lantern, Massard, Sr. attempted to light the car's way, with Linder driving. He went two times into a ditch. At 5:00AM, they finally arrived in Viller-Cotterets. Both men were given housing tickets, but Linder just lay down on the ground—the reason for an upswing in his pulmonary problems that would cause his hospital visit and his release from service. Massard, Sr. touted Linder's bravery that night anyway: "All the same, my brave Max had bravely shown this energy, this endurance, this beautiful mood, which are the characteristics of the French race, and that Max Linder embodies like a good Frenchman, and the great artist that he is."[33]

Max pédicure (1914), courtesy Fondation Jérôme Seydoux-Pathé

After his discharge, Linder was able to film what was really a patriotic film, much like what Chaplin, Pickford and others would be producing in the States: *Deux août 1914,* which was released April 14. Although it is technically a comedy, Linder does a great job here of depicting the drastic change from a time of pleasure and joy—an endless summer—to a time of war and a never-ending one at that. The difference in tone between the two parts of the film is palpable and ably catches the atmosphere of the times. Again from Ouchy-Lausanne, which is the location Linder departed from to begin his next tour, he wrote Léon Madieu (head of Pathé's Board of Directors) about taking a look at this film and also *Max entre deux feux* (1917), hoping for his approval.[34]

Le Pendu (1914), courtesy Fondation Jérôme Seydoux-Pathé

Mid-May Linder planned another cinema-theater tour for himself, in the second year of fighting. His venues this time would be only in Italy, a country that played little if any role in the war. He headed for Turin first, moving on to Milan, Florence, Genoa, Rome and ending in Naples the first part of June 1915. The French military had released him even from auxiliary service by April 2, so Max was free to leave the country after that—and return to civilian life. This trip he would perform in *Député*, traveling with co-stars Germaine Ryser, Émile Rouvière and Louis Gauthier. The first stop was Turin, with performances May 16 and 17 at the Teatro Alfieri, then on to Milan, May 19 through 23 at the Del Verme theater. Linder mentioned to the press that he would next travel to Florence and on to Genoa, but little has been found in the way of evidence to support that claim. He did, however, appear in Rome from May 27-31 at the Teatro Nazionale and received some press there. The description of one night's performance indicates that Linder's "evening" had taken a decidedly patriotic turn:

The talented artist was, as always, very happy in his own special stage play and aroused great cheers, which at the end of the funny sketch took an enthusiastic nature, when he presented himself dressed as a French soldier next to an Italian soldier. It shouted from everywhere: long live France, long live Italy and the Marseillaise and the national anthem sounded, the clapping audience listened standing. Then a large laurel crown with golden berries was offered to Max Linder between massive, prolonged ovations, while he, advancing to the fore, handed to a representative of the Italian Red Cross an envelope containing the amount which he offered personally and what turned out to be a thousand and two hundred lira.[35]

Indeed, Linder had made the tour on his own dime, and all the proceeds from his performances were to benefit the Italian Red Cross. Rome may have been his last stop, for although he mentioned Naples as part of the tour, no evidence of that stop has been uncovered.

Max au couvent (1914), courtesy Fondation Jérôme Seydoux-Pathé

By September, Linder was again in Lausanne, Switzerland trying as best as he could to continue his film career amidst the turmoil. He was able to complete *Max victime de la main qui étreint* (1915), a parody of *The Mysteries of New York* (1914), a film Louis Gasnier directed in America for the Pearl White series, at that location. He stayed at the beautiful Beau Rivage hotel, an accommodation he would retreat to again and again over the years to come. At the same time, his former employer, Pathé Frères, announced they would be attempting to ship more Linder films to America during the war, and spend more money there advertising them,[36] but wouldn't actually release any until February 25, 1917.[37] A letter from Linder to Charles Pathé written while in Lausanne is important to include in its entirety due to all that it provides in the way of telling details about how Linder operated—here with Mr. Pathé, whom he'd worked for since 1905 and whom he still refers to as "vous." It becomes all the more ironic, given this polite pronoun, at how much Linder demands:

> September 5, 1915
> Ouchy, Lausanne
>
> Dear Mr. Pathé,
> I accept the condition of 45 francs per meter of negative during the duration of the war, that is to say until the signing of the peace treaty, therefore, the films which would not have been seen at that time by you, which would not be finished, would be outside this contract and would remain my property.
> I would like a film, which I intend to call "Max médecin malgré lui," which I have not yet finished and for which I have a lot of work to do, to enter this new war treaty.
> I would like you to give instructions so that I can have three days a week to shoot on the Rue du Bois; this is essential to make my "Interiors."
> I would also like my negatives to be paid in cash.

Receive, Dear Mr. Pathé, the assurance of my most sympathetic feelings. Max Linder

(in handwriting is the following) I had to leave immediately for Switzerland because I had a terrible bowel attack. As soon as I get better, I will write to you about a good cameraman for myself.[38]

Max and his secretary in his home study, courtesy Fondation Jérôme Seydoux-Pathé

In October, he wrote a caustic letter to Mr. Madieu, complaining of the quality of the film (blank film) that he had been sent from Pathé, noting that it was badly scuffed: "The film I want to make here comes at a very high cost, so I cannot undertake this work if I do not have an absolute guarantee on the quality of the film." Linder assured Madieu that he was determined to make films in Lausanne despite his health problems but needed good quality film: "Send Eastman!"[39] Then in November, another letter to Madieu demonstrated that he was working several Pathé managers against each other to try to get a better deal: Charles Pathé, Léon Madieu and Ferdinand Zecca. In despair, Linder had sent his "good cameraman," Mr. Almard, back to Paris to choose the film himself. He had arrived back in Lausanne with 2000 meters and then two more shipments arrived—1000 meters each—one from Zecca and one from Madieu. Now, Linder was writing because he didn't want to be charged for the extra. Also, he asked Madieu to allow him to pay only 25 centimes per meter of film, instead of the 45 centimes his new contract with Mr. Pathé demanded (and which he had already signed).[40]

Back in France, December 21 was a planned "Journée du Poilu" or Day of the Soldier. All cinemas in the country were supposed to donate their day's earnings to the war effort. In Paris, the Gaumont Palace celebrated the day with the Garde Republican Band playing and stars such as Rigadin, Prince and Linder handing out programs.

1916 was less eventful in the life of Max Linder—that is until the news hit in late August that he had resigned from Pathé and would be heading to Chicago to join the Essanay Studios there by the end of the year. It seems it was a matter of money. Pathé offered him only 12,000 francs per film for 15 films; Essanay reportedly was offering much more (some reports claiming 2 million francs). France was tired and war weary. Linder was sick, both physically and spiritually. It was time to try his luck in the new world.

Linder poster with the A. Barrère caricature in Creil, France, Haven collection

As mentioned before, Pathé hoped to ship more Linder films to America. By March 17, 1917, these films were still being waited upon. However, some of them included re-issues and some new films that Linder completed before he left for Chicago. New films included *Max et l'espion* (1917), a two-reeler, *Max et le sac* (1917), *Max, médecin malgré lui* (1917), *Max devrait porter des bretelles* (1917) and *Max entre deux feux* (1917). This last was filmed on location in Lausanne, Switzerland. Whenever Linder was nearing a mental or physical breakdown, he fled to either Switzerland (Chamonix or Lausanne) or the French Riviera (Nice or Monte Carlo). Such was his state when he filmed *Max entre deux feux*, which was most likely filmed in 1916.

For this period of recuperation, Linder had taken his sister Marcelle with him, whom he cast as one of the two women vying for his affections in the film. In true Max Linder dandified fashion, he arrives at the Côte d'Azur and decides to woo two women, hopefully without either of them finding out. Max is successful for a while, but, of course, his ruse is soon discovered. The ladies decide to engage in a duel to decide who will be Max's true love, but Max himself hides high in a tree to observe the proceedings and ends up being the receiver of the gunshot—instead of either of the two women.

The reviewer in *The Moving Picture World* (June 30, 1917) spent more ink proclaiming the beauty of the Riviera setting, rather than the success or failure of Linder's comedy: "When it comes Max gets over a full share of laughs." Certainly, Linder appearing in a Pathé film in the spring of 1917 must have been a bit confusing for audiences, since headlines were busy reporting his activities in America, working under contract to Essanay. Today, the film is mostly anecdotal, due to the appearance of sister Marcelle alongside her brother (and cast as his possible amour!).

Notes for Chapter 3

[1] Javier Bueno, "Una Entravista con Max Linder, *Caras y Caretas*, April 12, 1913, n. p.
[2] *The Bioscope* for February 27, 1913 announced that Linder's Russian plans had been formalized, even though he wasn't to leave for that country until much later in the year.
[3] John Cher, "Parisian Notes," *The Bioscope*, July 17, 1913, n. p.
[4] "Linder Negotiating," *Variety*, January 24, 1913, p. 2.
[5] John Cher, "Parisian Notes," *The Bioscope*, September 4, 1913, n. p.
[6] Charles de Rochefort, *Secrets de vedettes*, Paris, Éditions Kergema, 1947, p. 47-51.
[7] "[Max Linder első föllépte...]," *Budapesti Hírlap*, November 16, 1913 and Max Linder!, *Szinházi élet*, November 9, 1913, n.p.
[8] "Videl li Peterburga Maksa Lindera?," *Russkoye Slovo*, December 16, 1913, n. p.
[9] From an article in *Films in Review*, November 1951 and quoted in Jack Spears, *Hollywood: The Golden Era*, London, Thomas Yoseloff, 1971, p. 186.
[10] Georgi Ivanov, "Marinetti i Linder," *Segdonia*, No. 95, April 5, 1931, p. 5. Cited in Yuri Tsvian, "Russia, 1913: Cinema in the Cultural Landscape," *Griffithiana*, XXVII, No. 50, May 1994, p. 133.
[11] " 'Gastrol' Maksa okolo tsar-kolokola," *Ranneye Utro*, December 19, 1913, n. p.
[12] "Linder v Moskve," *Ranneye Utro*, December 21, 1913, n. p.
[13] *Maks Linder I G-Zha Prokhorova* (1913).
[14] "Maks Linder v Moskve," *Stol. Molva*, December 22, 1913, n. p.
[15] *Maks I Kursistka* (1913).
[16] "Maks Linder v Moskve," *Stol. Molva*, December 22, 1913, n. p.
[17] "Ot'yezd Maksa Lindera," *Russkoye Slovo*, December 23, 1913, n. p.
[18] "[Maksa Lindera likstas ...]," *Latwija*, December 29, 1913, n. p.
[19] Tsvian's essay contains a great discussion of this tradition: Yuri Tsvian, "Russia, 1913: Cinema in the Cultural Landscape," *Griffithiana*, XXVII, No. 50, May 1994, pp. 124-147.
[20] "Maks Linder w Warszawie," *Kurier Warszawsk*, January 9, 1914, n. p.
[21] It premiered on March 27 and ended on April 23, 1914.
[22] John Cher, "Parisian Notes," *The Bioscope*, April 16, 1914, n. p.
[23] Burns Mantle, *Chicago Tribune*, July 12, 1914, n. p.
[24] "[Max Linder is booked]," *Variety*, June 5, 1914, p. 19.
[25] In an interview with *Moving Picture World* during a visit to America in 1914, Charles Pathé reported that Linder, in the early days with Pathé, earned $5,000 to 6,000 a year, but now made $40,000 to $60,000. "Charles Pathé's Views," *Moving Picture World*, January 24, 1914, p. 390.
[26] "Gaby Deslys's Escape," *New York Times*, July 16, 1914, n. p.
[27] Email communication with Dominique Dugros, August 20, 2018.
[28] "Movie King Killed, *The Washington Post*, October 1, 1914, n. p.
[29] "[No news that has come]," *New York Times*, October 11, 1914, n. p.
[30] "[Depuis quelques temps]," *Le Journal*, April 17, 1915, n. p.
[31] "[The story of Max Linder's death,]" *The Sunday Times*, November 29, 1914, n. p.
[32] "Max Linder is Now with Us," *The Moving Picture World*, November 26, 1916, p. 1144.
[33] Émile Massard, "Max Linder au volant," *La Liberté*, July 7, 1923, n. p.
[34] Max Linder, Ouchy-Lausanne to Léon Madieu, Paris, May 1915, Madieu Collection, **FRA-FJSP-Par.**
[35] "La serata di Max Linder al Nazionale, *Il Messaggero*, June 1, 1915, n. p.
[36] "Pathé May Import Linder," *Variety*, September 17, 1915, p. 20.
[37] "Pathé-Linder Comedies," *The Dramatic Mirror*, February 24, 1917, n. p.
[38] Letter Max Linder, Ouchy-Lausanne, to Charles Pathé, Paris, September 5, 1915, Madieu Collection, **FRA-FJSP-Par.**

[39] Letter Max Linder, Ouchy-Lausanne to Léon Madieu, Paris, October 21, 1915, Collection Madieu, **FRA-FJSP-Par.**

[40] Linder also snuck in a complaint that Mr. Zecca always answered him through his secretary, not personally, which he found offensive. Letter Max Linder, Ouchy-Lausanne to Léon Madieu, Paris, November 6, 1915. Collection Madieu, **FRA-FJSP-Par.**

Chapter 4: America, the Land of Opportunity (1916-1917)

What must Linder's spiritual and mental state have been like for him to accept a deal with the infamously curmudgeonly George K. Spoor of Essanay Studios in Chicago, Illinois and to thereby gamble his entire possibility of success with American audiences on that deal? Surely, he had read or heard reports of Spoor's miserliness when it came to film production, refusing up until the time of the Linder deal to even consider producing a feature film of any kind. And if not that, surely Linder had heard of Charlie Chaplin's departure from the company, a loss from which it would never recover. The promise of a $260,000 ($5,000 a week) contract for 12 films cannot have meant that much to Linder, who by all accounts was never in financial trouble throughout the decline of his career post-World War I and yet, a letter dated January 3, 1916, from Linder to Charles Pathé describes the fact that Keystone had recently offered Linder $140,000 a year for two years including all production costs—a deal Linder fervently hoped would push Pathé to offer him more (Pathé would later offer $300,000, but perhaps without production costs included).[1] So, money must have indeed been the deciding point.

Max Linder and George K. Spoor in Chicago,
courtesy Chicago Museum of History

George K. Spoor was a typical American rags-to-riches businessman, starting with a newspaper kiosk in Chicago and moving into the film business via theatre ownership, the Phoenix Opera House in Waukegan, to be exact. After teaming up with a gentleman named Edward H. Amet, who invented a usable projector, and despite the constant haranguing of Thomas Edison's rights lawyers, Spoor soon founded a film rental company in Chicago. He followed this up by founding a film shorts production company in August 1907, then quickly teamed up with G. M. Anderson, who was soon to become "Bronco Billy," an early pioneer of the Western film genre.[2] The result shortly thereafter was the Essanay Film Manufacturing Company, which eventually occupied space in the northern suburbs of that city on 1333-1345 W. Argyle Street. Anderson, a Midwesterner, soon tired of the dearth of western-like locations in the Chicago area and moved out to Niles, California where he set up another studio branch in 1912. Forward-thinking Anderson was also the one to suggest and press for the hiring of Charlie Chaplin, who was looking for a new film contract after the end of his Keystone tenure. Anderson got

Chaplin a one-year contract for $1250 a week and a $10,000 bonus, even though stingy Spoor refused to meet the young Englishman upon his arrival in Chicago and put off paying the bonus for some time. Chaplin moved to continue his work at the Niles studio after just three months in chilly Chicago.[3]

Essanay studios, Chicago, courtesy Chicago Museum of History

As Smith and Selzer in *Flickering Empire: How Chicago Invented the U.S. Film Industry* report,

> Spoor and Anderson, however, were . . . a study in contrasts. Anderson had movie star good looks and an affable personality, while Spoor was a heavyset, business-like man who has been described as "unsmiling." When Charlie Chaplin went to work for Essanay in 1915, he found that the two men frequently engaged him in a sort of "good cop, bad cop" routine. Somehow, though, their partnership worked. It would span a full ten years, and the production of approximately two thousand movies, an eternity in the tumultuous, rapidly evolving era of the early film industry.[4]

Flash-forward a year and Chaplin's film contract was again at an end. This time, he had financial wizard and half-brother Syd Chaplin negotiating a new contract for him. It would not be with Essanay. John Freuler of Mutual Film took home the prize, leaving Essanay without its biggest money-making star. Around this time, Spoor also lost the partnership of Anderson as well, meaning that Linder was not to experience even the seemingly more balanced management style provided by the Spoor/Anderson contrast, for Anderson departed months before Spoor even considered signing Linder, notably to a contract worth $185,000 more than Chaplin's--even considering the bonus—and not even a year following Chaplin's departure.

All of these were factors in what proved to be the studio's demise, although Chaplin claimed it was mostly the fault of Thomas Edison's Motion Picture Patents Company.[5] Spoor shut Niles in early 1916, before he decided to sign Max Linder in a last-ditch effort to save the company.

However, before considering a contract with Linder, "Essanay [found it necessary to combine] with the most powerful remaining MPPC studios to form a new distribution company, V-L-S-E (Vitagraph, Lubin, Selig, Essanay), and later K-E-S-E (Kleine-Edison-Selig-Essanay), the aim of which was to release features exclusively."[6] Linder's films would be produced by K-E-S-E. Linder's French countrymen, however, were hoping he would stay in France and continue making films there. A writer, initials J. P., in *La Rampe* for the June 8, 1916 issue, made a compelling statement for all:

> *Le Film* announced in its last number that Max Linder has been engaged by an American house [film company] due to "a million" per year. But Max Linder, who has not signed anything yet, will probably stay in France; a large house, of which I hope I will soon be able to tell you the name,[7] it seems, has engaged the happy Max to a much more handsome salary... For a French house that is rare, certainly, the sacrifice is great, may not that be a very nice gesture to prevent our big stars from emigrating from France, and believe it well, however exorbitant, this price is not terrible

if we think of the conditions that we would impose the foreign houses to "pass" later, some bad comedy or even, if necessary, to get us back for the price of gold the best films that Max Linder would have shot at home. This serves as an example, that the goal is always a French scenario, shot in a French house, by French artists; at whatever cost, we will still save money.

Spoor's luring of Max Linder to a supposed 12-film contract in 1916 is the stuff of film publicity legend. H. A. Spoor, a close family member, and Essanay's European representative, allegedly left his office in London and found Linder recouping in a war hospital in Contrexéville, France from a gunshot wound to his lung, talked him into the $260,000 contract about July 31, 1916 and shipped him over several months later, after Linder spent some time recouping in Switzerland and getting himself and his team organized.[8,9]

Two cable communications from Linder to a colleague he calls Rastally, but was really actor/director Amédée Rastrelli,[10] included in the collection of the library of the Cinémathèque française, show us that Linder seemed to wield enough power over Spoor to assist Pathé confederates in negotiating their American contracts, at least initially. The first cable, dated October 10, 1916 from Linder to Rastrelli located at the time in Penmarch (Brittany) states:

> Essanay offers you 80 dollars per week for America. The dollar converts to 5 francs 90 centîmes. Respond immediately if you accept so that I can retain your place on the boat *Espagne* leaving the 28th for Bordeaux. It is impossible to negotiate by talking. Respond 'yes' or 'no.'

But Rastrelli's situation was not settled until Linder was already in Chicago with his 46 pieces of luggage. On December 2, 1916, Linder sends this message: "Spoor accepts. Rastrally (*sic*), depart immediately second class. You will be given 500 francs."[11] Perhaps Rastrelli had demanded more than the

$80 a week and finally got it. His first Essanay film was not released, however, until Linder was totally out of the picture.¹²

Essanay Max Linder Comedies.

Max in military garb, publicity postcard for Essanay, Haven collection

The papers were heralding the deal as early as August 2, 1916, a good two months before either of these letters.¹³ The *Chicago Examiner* reported Linder's salary as $400,000 for a one-year contract, signed that day, a figure which was corrected in subsequent reports.¹⁴ A French columnist for *La Rampe* (initials KIN) from another perspective, offered "Let us hope that our Max knows how to remember sometimes that times are hard for the poor world and that there are hundreds of comrades in the black hole."¹⁵ It was noted elsewhere that Linder "succeeds Charlie Chaplin," so this dark cloud hung over the whole affair from the beginning. Reports quoting Linder himself usually contained this caveat: "The [French] government is thinking of passing a new law requiring the return of discharged soldiers, and it may be that in a year's time, they will call for me again."¹⁶ Most reports also noted that Linder was donating half his Essanay salary to his mother country, much needed during the continuing devastation of the war and by those "comrades in the black hole."

Essanay spared no ink paving the way for its new comedy star. Linder left Bordeaux October 29 on the S. S. *Espagne* for New York harbor. Arriving three days late on November 9, 1916, due to the ship having rammed another unidentified boat in the Bay of Biscay, Linder was greeted by Essanay president George Spoor and M. W. Colwell, personal publicity representative. Spoor mentioned to Linder that he had been waiting in New York since Monday. Linder was accompanied by his long-time valet, Albert Petitmaître (referred in subsequent reports simply as "Albert Petit"), who would also act as his interpreter in most situations. The *New York Telegraph* offered this representation of Linder explaining the ship's tardiness to the welcome party:

> "I was asleep," he remarked, "and at first I thought we had been torpedoed. Yet I was calm. I opened my cabin door and saw, just across my passageway, a man very much affrighted and wearing pajamas just like mine. Then I was affronted and stepped forth. But it was not another man. It was myself in a glass."[17]

He would use much of this in the film he was about to make (and the recurrence of the mirror gag in his films suggested it was one of his favorites), but whereas he is quoted in other reports as donning pink pajamas during the crisis,[18] he opted for a set of red ones for the screen—obviously for better contrast.

Spoor and company had arranged with a local hotel to put on a luncheon for Linder that would be accompanied by menus in the French language, but, of course, no one thought to train the waiters in the language (or so it was reported), with one waiter being quoted as responding to Linder's order in French with "Come again, cap; I ain't been here long enough to get next to that lingo."[19] Even so, the celebration was short-lived and Spoor, Linder and company took the 20th Century Limited to Chicago that night.

Max Linder publicity photo, courtesy Museum of Modern Art

As *Cine-Mundial* reports, Linder was besieged by 112 journalists and photographers once he arrived in Chicago to start work. Despite this bombardment, he was the epitome of grace, commenting that "The Americans have better conditions for comedy than the European ones, because their natural vivacity adapts better to joy and laughter. The United States has given the world some of the most marvelous cinematographic artists I've ever enjoyed."[20] For his initial film at Essanay, *Max Comes Across* (1917), which began production the first week of December, Linder took inspiration from his long voyage to America on the S.S. *Espagne* during war time, the pre-eminent danger of the ship sinking, as well as the usual joys and tribulations of any luxury steamer ride. Obviously, Linder was not pleased with the "four scenarios" waiting for him in Chicago, about which he is quoted as saying: "'The average motion picture manuscript,' thinks Max, 'makes excellent waste paper.'"[21] The Chicago History Museum archive holds a signed contract for one of these scenarios. Editor of *The Press* [Philadelphia] Richard J. Beamish received $50 for one entitled "Professor Max" that was never used.[22] So, Linder seems to have followed that adage "write about what you know" and came up with a scenario based on his recent voyage. Certainly, such a journey was rife with opportunities for gags and comedy, a fact not lost on him. He would also act as his own director. The suggestion that Chaplin stalwart Leo White was to help him in this regard soon went by the wayside.[23] A fire at Essanay on December 4, right as Linder was getting started, might have been a bad omen. Linder was in his dressing room being interviewed at the time: "His first concern was for his picture, and he hurried his valet out of the plant with the clothes which had already been registered in scenes and then continued the interview."[24,25] *The Chicago Tribune* reported differently, that despite no command of the English language, Linder was directing the responding firemen in their efforts to douse the fire.[26]

Upon his arrival in the windy city, Linder had begun to order the S. S. *Espagne* be reproduced board for board and nail for nail in the largest of the Essanay studios available, Studio A. Spoor again acquiesced to Linder, this time to the tune of many thousands of dollars. Linder's set of the lounge on board, complete with grand piano, used the set-on-rollers technology that Charlie Chaplin would later make famous in his Mutual film *The Immigrant* (1917).[27] *Essanay News* reported that

> The ceiling is encrusted with mercury lights which shower a dazzling brilliance on the interior. One enters through the port side of an ocean liner. He comes upon a deck complete, even to

the anchor chains. There is a row of luxurious cabins; further on a large dining salon; and then a big lounging room, lavishly furnished as befits an ocean liner.

The lounge room has been prepared for the after-dinner musicale. There is a piano in the center. Surrounding it are passengers aboard the boat, pretty girls and handsome men in evening dress. . . . Alas, the sea is running high. The boat rolls and the lounge room tilts dangerously from one angle to another. The basso sings on oblivious to the disorder, but Max is having trouble with his piano. It rolls with the boat's motion away from him, then, getting a good start, as the floor tilts back, rushes at the little pianist, knocks him off his stool, and passes over him.[28]

This method of set design may seem costly but is part and parcel of Linder's desire to "get it done." One witness noted that "his sets are some of the most complete ever constructed in the film industry. Every one is a 'solid,' no canvas enters into their construction. For instance, it took a week to build one small set. Max finished his scene in it in two hours. Preparation is his by-word."[29]

Linder Essanay set with Leo White as his double, courtesy George Eastman Museum

Max Comes Across (1917), courtesy Chicago Museum of History

Mal de mer and other steamship-life antics complicate the plot, which involves the ship being bombed, Max in his scarlet pajamas not believing the emergency due to a joke between himself and his shipboard friend, played by Ernest Maupain, and other such antics. A steamship was rented and placed on Lake Michigan to film some of the fun on deck, but, being wintertime in Chicago and on Lake Michigan, Linder found the day's filming a bit chilly:

> The day Linder chose for the filming of the pajama scene the thermometer registered two below zero, and the wind on Lake Michigan was moving at about thirty miles an hour. But on the big steamer chartered for the purpose, Max and his company, the latter also clad in night attire, cavorted about the deck for fully fifteen minutes. Toes were frozen and pneumonia threatened, but nevertheless good scenes were obtained. And what is a frozen toe or pneumonia to a good comedy scene in the motion picture industry?[30]

Other such antics in the film included a love interest for both men, played by "unknown" Martha Early (later Ehrlich),[31] who soon changed her name to Martha Mansfield and would star in all three Linder Essanays. She signed a long-term contract with Myron Selznick in May 1920, after achieving even greater fame as John Barrymore's leading lady in *Dr. Jekyll and Mr. Hyde* (1920).[32] She is perhaps best known for the fact that her costume caught fire on the set of *The Warrens of Virginia* (1924). She tragically died from the burns several days later.[33]

Because this was his first film for Essanay and in America, Linder's method and work demeanor seemed especially interesting to the media, as compared with run-of-the-mill filmmaking. Of course, it was Linder's relationship with the English language that writers placed at the top of their list of items of focus. Upon his arrival, Linder had made the statement that he would master the language in exactly three months, but when that time had passed, it was clear that he would be relying on two interpreters instead (perhaps he was already thinking of returning to France and didn't want to spend the energy required). On the set of his first Essanay film, one writer noted that Linder seemed to be shouting orders in every language *but* English, creating an atmosphere where "all is confusion."[34] Martha Mansfield offered a similar perspective on this problem and on Linder as a director in general: "[Linder] was a natural born, funny, unrestrained comedian. And as he could not speak a word of English and I spoke little French, it was indeed difficult trying to act when I hadn't the least idea what it was about or what it was that I should do."[35]

A *Motion Picture News* reporter noted Linder's "European scheme of production," which, he claimed,

> forms an interesting contrast with American methods. Max assembles his picture as he goes along, subtitles and all. When he completes two or three sets, he utilizes any studio delay to cut and trim his scenes. Thus it is soon possible for him to have complete continuity in several one, two and three hundred foot

strips. When he has photographed his last scene, he merely has to insert it in the proper space and his picture is complete.[36]

The press covered Linder's off-screen life less, but a glimpse of it here and there can provide a little information. He stayed at a prominent Chicago hotel, which went as far as building a toboggan run for him just outside. Unfortunately, however, his feet being too small for men's shoe sizes in Chicago, he was unable to indulge in ice-skating, another favorite sport. His military exploits led to an invitation from the U. S. government to speak about his experiences at the Ashburn Flying Field right outside Chicago in Ashburn, Illinois.[37] His first studio visitors were opera stars Lina Cavalieri and her husband, Lucien Muratore, who happened to be appearing with the Chicago Opera company in December 1916. The couple resided in Paris and the three had been friends for some time. The two opera stars also viewed a "photodrama" in which both appeared[38] during their visit.[39]

Max's first Essanay film was completed by January 5, 1917, in just about the one-month time period Linder had promised Spoor. Foreign film distributors from countries like France, Germany, England, Russia and even China had already made deals with Spoor regarding the Linder films,[40] but North America was another matter. The amalgamation of several distributors Spoor had signed onto, Kleine-Edison-Selig-Essanay, would be releasing the film. Spoor and his partners set in motion several schemes to try to ensure the film's success. The first of these was to develop an entire publicity corps for just the Linder productions. E. R. Pearson, formerly branch manager of first the General Film Company and then Pathé and World, was hired to lead a team of 31 salesman in the effort. K-E-S-E provided $100,000 and an additional $25,000 for advertising in the trade press.[41] Most of this amount likely went to the rank-and-file theater owner, for the print ads for the film promised that "Essanay will pay half of your advertising in newspapers on Max Linder comedies."[42] All publicity efforts that traveled through the mail were adorned with a sticker of Linder's smiling comedy face (the Linder grin) in order to add just another level of familiarity and recognizability to the actor's image.[43]

Max Comes Across (1917) set, courtesy of Chicago Museum of History

Another scheme was to preview the film in New York City. The film's wrap party was held in the Essanay studios (Chicago) on the afternoon of January 5, 1917,[44] where just such a preview screening was announced as scheduled for Tuesday morning at 11:00 on February 6 at the New York Roof Theatre. Four days later, the Strand Theatre announced that it had contracted for the comedy just hours after the preview screening, thereby paving the way for everyone else to follow suit.[45,46] Yet another strategy was having a novelization of the film's story appear in one of the most important fan magazines, *Motion Picture*, that featured the story (as written by Edwin M. La Roche) in its April 1917 issue. Of course, many intriguing images from the film were interwoven with the text, including three large photos of Linder's rubber face in one of its over-the-top expressions. In the novelization, much is made of the atmosphere in which Linder and his companion, Maupain, boarded the ship—an atmosphere haunted by the torpedoing of another liner shortly beforehand. They are portrayed not as courageous, but afraid only of appearing unmanly in the eyes of the other. In fact, Linder's later "saving" of those aboard occurs purely by accident.⁴⁷ It seems likely that this written adaptation of Linder's plot could only have contributed to the film's failure at the box office, if it had any effect at all.

Of course, exhibitors were always encouraged to come up with their own schemes to persuade movie-goers. Titusville Pennsylvania's Princess Theatre advertised that "In order to introduce Max Linder to the public, the first 100 adults entering the theatre at the matinee will be admitted free. Also, five passes will be given out. The ones holding the lucky number will be admitted free to see Linder each time shown. Come early and see who will be the lucky one. Doors open 2:30 p.m."⁴⁸ These schemes seemed to work for the first Linder film, for it was reported in late February that 150,000 prints had been distributed (a gross exaggeration) and that ads for Linder films had appeared in every newspaper of size in America.⁴⁹ Of course, merchants didn't want to be left out of this possible windfall as evidenced by one Broadway café concocting the "Max Linder" cocktail, for which K-E-S-E promised to provide the recipe upon request.⁵⁰

Max Comes Across (1917) opened on February 26, 1917 in the following Chicago theaters: the two Jones, Linnick and Schaefer loop theaters, the McVicker's and the Rialto for one-week runs. It opened the same day at the Strand in New York City.⁵¹ Despite the hype and the reporting of so many prints of the film in distribution, the film did not do well at the box office. The reviews don't reflect this in all cases, but Linder's decision to make a comedy film about a ship being torpedoed was simply not a good idea given the times. The ship he traveled on, S. S. *Espagne*, had only had a brief scare created by its ramming of another boat at night. Of course, there was the sinking of the R. M. S. *Lusitania* in May 1915, perhaps the best-known example, but by 1916, ocean liners being torpedoed was a common occurrence, due to World War I, and became a legitimate fear. In 1916, both the S. S. *Cymric* and the S. S. *Sussex* had been torpedoed, and just after Linder's arrival in New York, the HMHS *Brittanic*, an ocean liner that had been converted into a hospital ship, went down with more than a thousand passengers, although only 30 of those lost their lives.⁵² Making any sort of comedy about this situation was ill-timed. One reviewer picked up on this mistake noting, "It is unfortunate that a disabled passenger ship should have been decided upon as a motive for a goodly portion of the attempted comedy. At this time it is difficult to find merriment in antics, no matter how funny in themselves, that arise from this source."[53]

Although they mostly overlook this blunder, reviews of the film were overwhelmingly negative anyway. A review by Peter Milne suggests that Linder's first film for Essanay was a dud. "*Max Comes Across*," he writes "is handicapped by practically a total lack of story. To cover up this deficit each episode of the picture has been lengthened until the humor of it is considerably diluted." Milne notes that "Mr. Linder is still saturated with the continental idea of humor which doesn't always score with our own country."[54] Linder was to learn this difficult lesson, but much too late for the success of his Essanay contract. Julian Johnson, who wrote the column "The Shadow Stage" for *Photoplay*, came out strongly against this film and the two Essanay films to come, writing, "This is the vitalized portrait of a man struggling to be funny; working desperately to be funny; creating laughs from nothing, instead of letting laughs spring at ease from laughable situations"—this, despite seeing the film amongst 4,000 people at a New York theater laughing uproariously. "Linder today," he writes, "seems to me an affected, serious man who looks tremendously old when he permits his countenance a reposeful moment."[55] *Billboard*, however, mentioned that "One reel is a disappointing thing to show Max up in, however, for his first American picture. Everything he does is good, clean, broad comedy, but one reel is just about half enough."[56] In an even kinder review, James M. McQuade in *The Moving Picture World*, however, notes that "The services of Max as a pianist at a special concert aboard ship affords one of the most mirthful incidents during the voyage. A storm comes up and the piano slides backward and forward across the salon, with Max either in hot pursuit or in quick retreat; but he always contrives to stick to the piano stool, although in its mad gyrations it is sometimes turned upside down."[57] His French audience didn't see the film until much later,[58] but found his comedy much the same:

This is the first film that our French comic has given us since the war. We find Max pretty much the same as he left us, but, on the other hand, we see in his scenario an Americanism that is perhaps only a concession to his audience. But this is not to displease us since pushing the comedy to the extreme, Max Linder does not commit the mistakes of taste found in many comedians. (Of course, I'm not talking about Charlie Chaplin.) . . . .[The film's comedy scenes] are varied and pleasant and Max has lost none of his qualities of expression.[59]

As Boisyvon mentions in this review, Linder had, even in this one-reeler, escaped many of the pitfalls common to other comedians that separated the great from the mediocre in that avocation. Linder's arrival in New York in November 1916 demonstrated immediately how he intended to set himself apart from his American competitors, and probably especially Chaplin. It must have been fun for American readers to see that Linder's eyes were insured for a million dollars,[60] or that he drank little alcohol and mostly just warm water with lemon.[61] But Linder wanted Americans to focus more on two aspects of his persona that he kicked into high gear upon his arrival—his love of fashion, the fashionable and looking fashionable (he supposedly contributed to Chicago's economy by purchasing 50 pairs of shoes in the first few weeks of his residence) and his dedication to military service during the present war. His dapper appearance, both on and off the screen, helped to separate himself from the "costume" of most lowly comedians, Chaplin included. He could easily develop that aspect of his persona by equating it with simply being French and thereby persuading his American audience that the French gentleman is nothing if he is not well-dressed and that Europe herself was not yet starving and devastated; it was still the place where tradition, aristocracy and good taste prevailed. Second, he had to firmly convince his audience that he was a patriotic Frenchman, that he had sacrificed himself for the good of France, despite the fact that he was a screen star—creating a stark contrast here between himself and Chaplin, who most felt was hiding out from the war in California and receiving a truckload of envelopes containing white feathers as a reward. So, to this end, photos of Linder were either of Linder the French soldier, who brought along his one-legged German shepherd "Wah"[62,63] as a tangible piece of evidence of his military service (and who starred in the first two of Linder's Essanays[64]) or Linder, the nattily dressed French dandy and great connoisseur of women. Stories about Linder, like the one in *Photoplay* in February 1917 by Gordon Seagrove, also concentrated on one of the other of these topics for reinforcement, quoting the valet: " 'He will wear three pairs a day at least and of the forty-six trunks full of clothes he will select at least three suits a day. One must dress. Mr. Max Linder believes this.' "[65]

Linder and his three-legged dog, Wah, courtesy Museum of Modern Art

Although Linder announced that he began his second Essanay film, *Max Wants a Divorce* (1917) on January 8, 1917 in Chicago, there is some indication that he had negotiated for a possible move to the warmth of California well before this time: "it is rumored that, on account of the weather conditions, the Linder Company may later be installed in a special studio in California."[66] He again occupied Studio A, had the sets built by this date and also claimed to be the author of the scenario, one that would be well-known to most viewers, since it was a typical French farce-type plot, in which a young bachelor is promised (this time) $3,000,000 if he remains a lifelong bachelor. Unfortunately, he had already just married and spends the film trying not to show the world this fact, despite the machinations of his new wife. With a nice twist at the end, the film is easily labeled a comedy instead of a tragedy and all is well for both Max and his new bride, ably played by Martha Mansfield. Ernest Maupin and "Wah" also star.

Max Linder K-E-S-E ad, Haven collection

Essanay was still trying very hard to keep up appearances. It held the Reel Fellows' Studio Ball in the studios on Saturday, February 11, an event that "shatters all records of moving picture balls."[67] Twenty-one hundred people attended, including stars, film administration and fans and all the studios were made available for the event, with Studio C featuring a 15-piece orchestra that played dance numbers named for Essanay hits and Studio B demonstrating the intricacies of film production, with Bryant Washburn and company showing off their talents in a story currently in production. Thirteen Essanay players either made a speech or entertained the group in some manner. Linder gave a speech in French. "Wah" was also in attendance and became a popular participant.[68] It seems clear that Linder was still "all-in" at this point and at least attempting to be an engaged part of the Essanay company.

Max Wants a Divorce (1917) with Martha (Early) Mansfield, courtesy Museum of Modern Art

Max Wants a Divorce set showing cameras,
courtesy Chicago Museum of History

Already with this second American film, however, the publicity efforts on the part of Essanay and the media in general had died down, although Essanay did continue to go halfsies on advertising with exhibitors. *Essanay News* wrote only about the flood of mail received about Linder's marital status, stating "Max is not married, and so far, has given no intimation that he will ever marry,"[69] and about oddities on set, such as the $50,000 pearl necklace[70] and a "live skeleton" used in the film. The film premiered on March 26, 1917, also at the Strand in New York City. Reviews of this film were mixed, but generally good. Edward Weitzel in *The Moving Picture World* noted that "the speedy French comedian never worked faster nor more amusingly than in *Max Wants a Divorce*."[71] A *Variety* reporter stated that "The comedy should be a welcome addition to any program as the slapstick work is not overdone and fits in with the development of the piece. The fly in the amber is the recurrence of that tiresome but apparently everlasting pie in the face incident."[72] Louella Parsons, in her relatively new position as film critic/gossip at the *Chicago Herald* offered that "The second Max Linder comedy, *Max Wants a Divorce*, has made its appearance and was greeted with continuous and hearty laughter."[73]

Max Wants a Divorce (1917), courtesy Museum of Modern Art

Max Wants a Divorce (1917) with Martha (Early) Mansfield, courtesy Museum of Modern Art

It's no surprise that Linder had the same opinion of the Chicago weather as Chaplin before him, but despite his weakened condition overall, managed to stay in the city to produce his second film, moving to California for the third. The official word on the move was printed in the *Essanay News* in early March, that upon completion of the second film, Linder took lock, stock, company of players[74] and 46 suitcases (and "Wah") out to Los Angeles, leaving Chicago on March 6,[75] where a studio in Culver City had been arranged for his use in filming number three: "In a farewell speech delivered from his private car, Max explained that conditions in Chicago for the production of motion pictures are ideal. His transfer to the coast was made necessary by the crowded conditions at the Essanay studios."[76] Linder also left Essanay Chicago a note on studio stationery, recently discovered in the Chicago History Museum's Essanay studios archive, in which he referred to those left behind as "friends" and thanked them for their "many kindnesses." His salutation "Believe me" may be the most telling phrase in the note, however.[77]

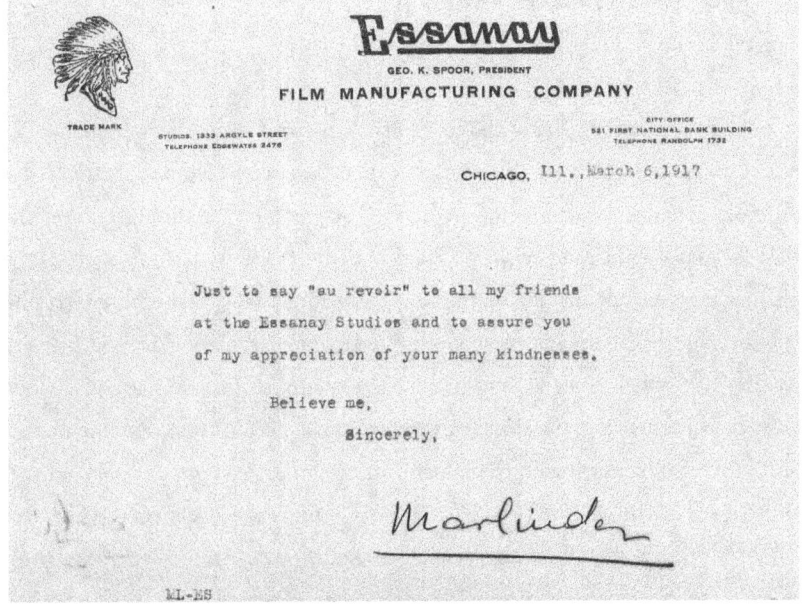

Linder's cable to his Essanay co-workers, courtesy Chicago Museum of History

The *Essanay News* continued to capitalize on its star's experiences in an attempt to promote the next as yet unnamed film. On the train to Los Angeles, it quotes Linder as reporting "The vastness of this great country is amazing. Why it required a longer time to cross some of the states than it does to cross entire nations in Europe."[78] At a whistle stop in Arizona, Linder was introduced to a group of cowboys, supposedly exclaiming that he thought such characters existed only in wild west shows. The *Chicago Tribune's* film critic, Mae Tinee, noted the comedian's departure with this ditty, with no explanation as to why she seems to be ridiculing him for a German accent:

O, our Max LinDER he took a CHOO-choo,
All on the big RailWAY,
O, our Max LinDER he took a CHOO-choo,
He's gone a-VAY,
He left us last ni-ight for CalifornYEE,
Beat it with his trunks forty-VUN, forty-THREE,
Three special cars and a VAL-ay,
He's gone a-VAY.[79]

Although Essanay had tried to set up an in-print rivalry between Chaplin and Linder, the falsity of this story became clear when Linder reached Los Angeles, where he was greeted by about 100 people.[80] Although a specific date is unknown, Linder visited Chaplin at the Lone Star studios, probably within a few days of arriving on the west coast about May 9,[81] because Chaplin was among the invited guests at Linder's welcome party a few days later given by Essanay officials, even speaking a few words of greeting to his fellow comedian before the attendees. A three-minute piece of film documents the studio visit; Chaplin was in the midst of filming *The Adventurer* (1917) at the time (his last Mutual film) and part of the meeting takes place on the film set. The pantomime each man engages in for the film was probably the way they were actually communicating with each other, for neither man understood the other's language. The last few minutes involve some hijinx at Linder's car, with Albert Austin assisting. This would not be Linder's only visit to the Chaplin studios.

Linder and Charlie Chaplin, Lone Star Studios, *The Adventurer* (1917) set, courtesy Roy Export, S. A. S.

V. R. Day was the manager of the Essanay studios in Culver City, where Linder would make his final Essanay film.[82] Grace Kingsley reported that "The Essanay Company, at Culver City, is contemplating securing more land, especially as most of the present area is being used for the Max Linder pictures.[83] "Securing more land," really meant renting it, because the so-called Essanay Studios Culver City were actually the studios of the Culver City Film Company (later Master Films) located at Durango Avenue and Exposition Boulevard.[84] Essanay's leasing of this studio property began and ended in 1917 and was mostly done in order to accommodate Linder. Many have commented that this final Essanay film, to be titled *Max in a Taxi* (1917)[85] showed its star to be ailing and in very poor condition. It is all the more ironic then that some of the stunts he used in the film were especially difficult and physically demanding. It's the story of a young dandy, who, after a wild night out with his friends, in which he sets one friend's pants on fire (among other things), his father bans him from the house and cuts off his funds. Max finds an invitation to a party at a wealthy home, cleans himself off after being outside for four days, and attends the party, where he downs a bunch of pastries in order to ease his hunger.[86] In the midst of this exercise, Max is taken to meet the daughter of the house, played by Martha Mansfield, and they dance, Max still with his cheeks loaded with sweets. After ending the afternoon successfully, he decides to get a job and chooses driving a taxi, even though he has no experience. Of course, while he is out and about learning how and how not, he runs into the mother and daughter he had recently met and demonstrates his inability to drive the car, ending up smashing it to pieces and being thrown up onto the power lines, where he is finally saved by the daughter. This plot summary is supported by a review in *The Bioscope* appearing in the July 19, 1917 issue, but at least two other very different summaries suggested perhaps that more than one print version existed, or that information was being released in such a way that moviegoers were kept in the dark about some of the most important gags.[87] Linder himself "writes" a piece for *Motion Picture Magazine* that failed to run until October 1917 in which he compares one suspenseful scene to the danger of the battlefields he had experienced in France:

> I had conceived what you might call a "thriller" as a scene in my third Essanay comedy, *Max in a Taxi*. Having been disinherited by my wealthy father, the scenario directed that I lie down in front of an onrushing express-train, thus to doff my life-burdens. The train was to rush down upon me; all would be over—but no! Within ten feet of where I lay was to be a switch, which the audience had not perceived. And, even as the engine's pilot stretched forth to snuff out my life, the train suddenly was

to strike the switch, swerve to a side-track and whizz past, leaving me and my life-burdens intact.

The scene was filmed without a flaw. I lay down upon the track; the huge express-train rushed up to within ten feet of me. The switch opened and it swung to the left and past. Yet during the fleet second of the action, the terrible horror almost paralyzed me—what if by some unforeseen accident the switch refused to open? Here was death which I could see hurtling directly at me. I could not escape it.[88]

Another perspective on this same scene is offered in the *Salina Evening Journal*: "A special train was employed for the scene, and it was figured no rehearsals would be required. However, the first trial did not suit the comedian, so the train had to be sent back to its starting point for another trial. Five times the scene was repeated before it proved acceptable to Max. The cost of this few feet of film was enormous, but necessary."[89]

Max in a Taxi (1917)

K-E-S-E offered the same deal to exhibitors—to pick up half of their advertising costs, as they had done for the previous two Linder films. Previews of the film were screened in New York and Chicago (Jones, Linick and Schaefer's theaters) the second week of April,[90] with the film then being released on April 23.[91] Reviews seemed to run the gamut. Julian Johnson, in his *Photoplay* column "The Shadow Stage," equated what he perceived as the film's failure with Linder's illness: "Max Linder is very ill, we're told, so in consideration let's call his latest comedy, *Max in a Taxi*, a sick man's attempt at expression. For that's about all it amounts to. It is heavy and laborious."[92] However, Hanford C. Judson of *The Moving Picture World* thought differently, writing out right that "Max Linder is an artist." "His mind rollicks," Judson notes, "and one can't help laughing, for it is so spontaneous and unexpected. He has an inexhaustible supply of jollity and no sour rind to make us pay for laughter with puckered lips. It is a free out-giving—funny, warm and human."[93]

By the date of the third film's release, Linder was indeed gravely ill. Reports of both his condition and his situation with Essanay and his 12-picture contract were erratic and unsubstantiated at best, although a letter he wrote to Chaplin on April 20, 1917 provides some information:

> On account of work too hard for my health I am ill again. The doctor advises me to stop working for several months. As he ordered me to go to bed every night at 9, I cannot ask you to dine with me, but I should be delighted if you would call for lunch . . . as soon as you can. I have to observe a very severe cure. What a shame I cannot take yours. I am certain I should be cured at once. The too short time I passed the other day at the Garrick made me forget all my trouble. All my congratulations to you. I consider your picture as most remarkable on any point of view."[94]

Linder seemed to be suffering from his war wounds, specifically those to his lungs (the "tuberculosis" word is mentioned in more than one report).

He was even released from a court summons for speeding in late April, from the court of Justice Hinshaw, due to his condition.⁹⁵ So, being accustomed to spending periods of time in sanitoriums in Switzerland to get himself up to speed again, Linder entered one in northern Arizona the first week of May, probably the Castle Hot Springs resort in Hot Springs, Arizona, about forty miles north of Phoenix, a location patronized only by the elite, seeking cures to everything from obesity to every possible bronchial affliction imaginable. One report stated that he was, at this time, "fatally ill" and not expected to recover and that he had given up his Essanay contract.⁹⁶ In fact, George K. Spoor made an announcement to this effect on May 8.⁹⁷ It's important to note that Spoor had just laid off 50 employees at his Essanay Chicago studios and was contemplating releasing future films at Pathé.⁹⁸ Linder, however, was back in Los Angeles (at his house at 803 Rodeo Drive, Beverly Hills⁹⁹) by May 26, and the press was reporting that a fourth scenario had already been written with production on the film beginning soon,¹⁰⁰ with no mention of a broken contract. However, Linder was back in the care of another facility again by early June, this time closer to Hollywood, probably the Pottenger Sanitorium in Monrovia, California.¹⁰¹ He allowed a picture of himself there to be printed in *Photoplay* magazine, but it didn't appear until the July 1917 issue. The *Jackson [Michigan] Citizen Patriot* reported that Linder was nearly out of danger again by August 19,¹⁰² but by then he was almost back in his homeland. His departure for home was announced July 30. Linder was given permission to travel by his physician.¹⁰³ However, he was still telling the press that he would continue his Essanay contract when he returned in February 1918.¹⁰⁴

It seems likely that George K. Spoor was more than disconcerted at his experience producing Linder. Production costs plus Linder's extravagant salary most likely tolled the death knell for his company. In fact, as has been mentioned, the company folded within a year of Linder's departure and Spoor noted many years later that his company had lost $87,000 in the deal. Even though critics such as Ivan L. Gaddis succinctly compared Linder with Chaplin, noting that "The screen Linder is a Beau Brummel who produces mirth by working downward from a pinnacle of immaculateness: the screen Chaplin, in vulgar parlance, is a bum who gets his laugh by working upwards,"¹⁰⁵ Linder, in fact, had not become another Chaplin and he had not, for himself, recreated the furor over his films that he had experienced in France before the war. Because Chaplin was at least planning the building of his new studio at La Brea and DeLongpre in the second half of 1917, the reality of his continued success could not have been lost on his new French friend. Linder had no ill feelings towards Chaplin, however, as indicated by the fact that Chaplin saw the Frenchman off at the station August 9.¹⁰⁶ Chaplin had already presented Linder with a photo of himself famously inscribed "To my esteemed friend, Max Linder. From his disciple, Charlie Chaplin." Linder now presented Chaplin with three photos of himself, one inscribed "To the King of Directors," one to "The King of Artists," and one to "The King of Friends." The two then proceeded to mimic each other for the film cameras and Linder began his journey home.¹⁰⁷

One of Linder's photos signed to Chaplin in 1917, courtesy Roy Export, S. A. S.

Another of Linder's photos signed to Chaplin in 1917, courtesy Roy Export, S. A. S.

Notes for Chapter 4

[1] Linder also notes in the letter that "I just tried to make three films but given all the difficulties that I encountered in the studio, I have given up working." These films must have included *La Tulipe merveilleuse* (1915) and/or *Deux août 1914* (1916). TS Letter Max Linder to Charles Pathé from Paris January 3, 1916, **FRA-FJSP-Par**.

[2] Michael Corcoran and Arnie Bernstein, *Hollywood on Lake Michigan*. Second edition. Chicago: Chicago Review Press, 2013, 14-15.

[3] William Grisham, "Those Marvelous Men and Their Movie Machines: Chicago's Film Pioneers Delighted Audiences with One-reelers More Than 50 Years Ago and Turned Our Town into the Country's Movie Capital," *Chicago Tribune Magazine*, December 7, 1969, p. 44.

[4] Michael Glover Smith and Adam Selzer, *Flickering Empire: How Chicago Invented the U. S. Film* Industry, London: Wallflower Press, 2015, p. 76.

[5] Charles Chaplin, *My Autobiography*, London: The Bodley Head, 1964, p. 166.

[6] Smith and Selzer, p. 151.

[7] One source suggested this was Pathé and that they had offered Linder 1,800,000 francs ($300,000). (Charles Bernard, "La Rampe du Cinema," *La Rampe*, August 24, 1916, n.p.)

[8] James S. McQuade, "Chicago News Letter," *Moving Picture World*, August 19, 1916, p. 1228.

[9] Linder also made several films for Pathé during this convalescence, including *Max entre deux feux* (1917), *Max et le sac* (1917), *Max et l'espion* (1917), *Max médecin malgré lui* (1917) and *Max devrait porter des bretelles* (1917).

[10] **FRA-CF-Par**, Max Linder archive has documentation that Rastrelli along with E. E. Violet, Linder's director for *Max, der Zirkuskönig* (1924) were active in the Max Linder Reunions held in the 1940s in Paris.

[11] **FRA-CF-Par.**

[12] Amédée Rastelli made five films for Essanay in 1917, including *Hard Luck* (1917) and *A Depot Romeo* (1917). Back in France, Rastelli wrote and directed several Fritzigli films for Export Union. Most likely, Linder met him at Pathé where he starred in several shorts, the last in 1912.

[13] Charles Bernard, the manager of Linder's Ciné Max Linder at the time, reported in *La Rampe* in the August 24, 1916 issue, "About Max, it should be made clear about his commitment to America. Some newspapers talk about the "Keystone," others cite various famous brands, there are even some who dispute the US commitment and give a figure of 1,800,000 francs offered by Maison Pathé. The truth is this: Max Linder signed with "Essanay" for a year, with facultative renewal, at will, for a second year. He will shoot 12 films a year without having to worry about scenarios, artists, or staging. Finally, the contract is in round figures (that's the word) of 2 million a year."

[14] "Max Linder Coming" **USA-NYPL-PA-New**, *Moving Picture World*, George Kleine Scrapbook.

[15] "La Rampe du Cinema: Au Bout du Film," *La Rampe*, August 10, 1916, p. 11.

[16] "Max Linder, Famous" **USA-NYPL-PA-New**, *New York Telegraph*, Kleine scrapbook.

[17] **USA-NYPL-PA-New** Kleine scrapbook.

[18] "Max Linder Starts" n.p. **USA-NYPL-PA-New**, Kleine scrapbook.

[19] "Max Linder, to Eat" np. **USA-NYPL-PA-New**, Kleine scrapbook.

[20] "Arreglos Completos Para Linder," *Cine-Mundial*, January 1917, p. 39.

[21] Longacre, "Just for Fun," *Motion Picture News*, January 13, 1917, p. 424.

[22] Contract between Essanay Film Manufacturing Company, Chicago, Illinois and Richard J. Beamish, Essanay Studios collection, **USA-CHM-Chi**.

[23] Steve Massa, *Slapstick Divas: The Women of Silent Comedy*, Albany, GA: BearManor Media, 2017, p.536.

[24] *Exhibitor's Review*, February 1917, **USA-NYPL-PA-New**, Kleine Scrapbook.

²⁵ *Essanay News* ("Essanay Stars Fight Blaze," 12-12-1916, p. 3) reported that Linder, along with other stars present during the fire, grabbed buckets and had the blaze put out by the time the fire brigade arrived.

²⁶ "Real Blaze in Film Plant," December 5, 1916, p. 17, **USA-NYPL-PA-New**, Kleine Scrapbook.

²⁷ Jack Theakston alerted me to the fact that in A. Nicholas Vardac's *Stage to Screen: Theatrical Method from Garrick to Griffith* (Benjamin Blom, NYC, 1968), he offers several instances of innovations on the stage that became precursors to the ship-on-rollers idea. In a staging of G. B. McCutcheon's *Brewster's Millions* at the New Amsterdam Theatre, beginning December 31, 1906, the special effects man, Frederick Thompson, unsuccessfully according to one critic, "attempted to put upon the stage the spectacular scene of a solid, three-dimensional yacht laboring in a great storm" (p. 85). It seemed to "'hardly be a part of the play'". The film version of *Treasure Island* (1915) may then have been the first such attempt on film, showing "the *Hispaniola* adrift and rocking like a channel craft" (87), with better results and better reviews.

²⁸ "Essanay's Fun Factory," **USA-NYPL-PA-New**, Kleine Scrapbook.

²⁹ "Linder Comedy," *Moving Picture World*, p. 4209, **USA-NYPL-PA-New**, Kleine Scrapbook.

³⁰ "Linder Finishing First" n.p., **USA-NYPL-PA-New**, Kleine Scrapbook.

³¹ Featured in the June 1917 *Picture Play* with an illustration in the portrait section, the caption reads that "Martha Early was born in Mansfield, Ohio and is seventeen years old. For the last two seasons she has come into the limelight as a musical comedy actress of exceptional promise, playing at the Century Theater, New York."

³² At this time, Mansfield was characterized as "the daughter of the United States in every sense of the expression." Born in New York, Mansfield grew up in Mansfield, Ohio, from which she took her stage name, and started her career on Broadway right out of high school. ("Myron Selznick Signs Martha Mansfield to Long Term Contract for Photoplays," *Moving Picture World*, May 15, 1920, p. 969.)

³³ Steve Massa, *Slapstick Divas: The Women of Silent Comedy*, Albany, GA, BearManor Media, 2017, p. 536.

³⁴ "Essanay's Fun," **USA-NYPL-PA-New**, Kleine Scrapbook.

³⁵ C. Blythe Sherwood, "A Mansfield of the Follies," *Motion Picture Classic*, June 1919, p. 76.

³⁶ "Linder Comedy," *Moving Picture World*, p. 4209, **USA-NYPL-PA-New**, Kleine Scrapbook.

³⁷ "Linder to Lecture," *Cleveland Plain Dealer*, November 20, 1916, p. 4.

³⁸ Probably *The Shadow of Her Past* (1916), distributed by Pathé in the States. Husband Muratore wrote the script for the film.

³⁹ "Lina Cavalieri Guest," *Essanay News*, December 16, 1916, p. 1.

⁴⁰ "Max Linder, Celebrated," p. 987, **USA-NYPL-PA-New**, Kleine Scrapbook.

⁴¹ "Big Linder Comedy," p. 1016, **USA-NYPL-PA-New**, Kleine Scrapbook.

⁴² *Dramatic Mirror* 2/17 ad, **USA-NYPL-PA-New**, Kleine Scrapbook.

⁴³ Muckley, n.p., **USA-NYPL-PA-New**, Kleine Scrapbook.

⁴⁴ "Title," p. 386, **USA-NYPL-PA-New**, Kleine Scrapbook.

⁴⁵ Exhibitors were in the habit of accepting the Strand's booking as "a safe guide."

⁴⁶ "Linder Comedies," *NY Saturday Review*, n.d., n. p., **USA-NYPL-PA-New** Kleine scrapbook.

⁴⁷ p. 80-81.

⁴⁸ "Max Comes Across" ad *Titusville [PA] Herald*, March 12, 1917, p. 4.

⁴⁹ "Linder Series Booked," *Moving Picture* World, p. 1229, **USA-NYPL-PA-New**, Kleine Scrapbook.

⁵⁰ "Here's a Real Rib Tickler Named after Film Star," *Cleveland Plain Dealer*, January 7, 1917, p. 5.

⁵¹ "Thousands See Linder Comedy" *Essanay News*, March 10, 1917, p. 1.

⁵² "The Sinking of the *Lusitania* at 100: Passenger Ships in World War I," *U. S. Naval Institute News*, May 7, 2015, at https://news.usni.org/2015/05/07/the-sinking-of-the-lusitania-at-100-passenger-ships-in-world-war-i.

⁵³ **USA-NYPL-PA-New**, Kleine Scrapbook.
⁵⁴ **USA-NYPL-PA-New**, Kleine Scrapbook.
⁵⁵ May 1917, n.p., **USA-NYPL-PA-New**, Kleine Scrapbook.
⁵⁶ "*Max Comes Across*" n.p., **USA-NYPL-PA-New**, Kleine Scrapbook.
⁵⁷ James S. McQuade, review of *Max Comes Across*, *Moving Picture World*, February 24, 1917, p. 1207.
⁵⁸ This review dates from November 16, 1919.
⁵⁹ Boisyvon, n.p., **USA-NYPL-PA-New**, Kleine Scrapbook.
⁶⁰ "Max Linder's Eyes" *Essanay News*, **USA-NYPL-PA-New**, Kleine Scrapbook.
⁶¹ "Lemon and Water," *Essanay News*, January 27, 1917, p. 3.
⁶² "Reel," *Chicago Evening American*, **USA-NYPL-PA-New**, Kleine Scrapbook.
⁶³ It is my contention that the dog's name was probably "Roi," (King), which when pronounced correctly in French sounds like "Wah," with a rolled "r" at the beginning. It makes more sense to me that the dog, a German shepherd, should have this name and if Linder noticed the mistake in the press, he probably just went with it, knowing that the unusual name would elicit greater publicity.
⁶⁴ "Linder's Dog of War" *Exhibitor's Herald*, **USA-NYPL-PA-New**, Kleine Scrapbook.
⁶⁵ Gordon Seagrove, [no title] *Photoplay*, February 1917, p. 99.
⁶⁶ No title *Picture-Play*, **USA-NYPL-PA-New**, Kleine Scrapbook.
⁶⁷ "Reel Fellows' Ball" *Motion Picture News,* March 3, 1917, p. 1411.
⁶⁸ "Reel Fellows' Ball" *Motion Picture News*, March 3, 1917, p. 1411.
⁶⁹ "'Max Wants Divorce': But He's Not Wed" *Essanay News,* Mar. 10, 1917, p.1.
⁷⁰ "50,000 Necklace" *Essanay News,* March 24, 1917, p. 3.
⁷¹ April 17, 1917, p. 115, **USA-NYPL-PA-New**, Kleine Scrapbook.
⁷² *Variety*, Mar. 23, 1917, n.p.
⁷³ Ad for *Max Wants a Divorce* (1917), *Motion Picture News*, Apr.14, 1917, p. 2312.
⁷⁴ It's interesting to note that Martha Mansfield traveled with the troupe in the company of her mother.
⁷⁵ An intriguing note in a piece in *Essanay News* entitled "Max's Friends to See Him in United States (December 16, 1916, p. 3)," suggested that Linder had had his time in Chicago filmed for his friends' entertainment back in France. Since these films have never been found and there is virtually little to no footage of off-screen Max or of Max directing, I can only hope this film turns up at some point.
⁷⁶ "Linder at Work in Culver City," *Essanay News*, March 24, 1917, p.1.
⁷⁷ **USA-CHM-Chi**, Essanay Studios collection.
⁷⁸ "Max Feels as if He Circled the Globe," *Essanay News,* March 24, 1917, p.1.
⁷⁹ "Max He's Gone A-Vay" *Essanay News* March 24, 1917, p. 3.
⁸⁰ "Linder at Los Angeles," *Variety*, March 10, 1917, p. 26.
⁸¹ One source notes, "Linder's first act upon reaching Los Angeles was to pay an official call at the Chaplin studio." ("Max Linder is now a Californian," *Photoplay*, June 1917, n. p., **USA-NYPL-PA-New**, Kleine Scrapbook).
⁸² "V. R. Day," *The Moving Picture World*, May 19, 1917, p. 1133.
⁸³ Grace Kingsley, "Studio: Fine Arts Changes," *The Los Angeles Times*, March 18, 1917, p. 29.
⁸⁴ Julie Lugo Cerra and Marc Wanamaker, *Images of America: Movie Studios of Culver City*, Charleston, SC, Arcadia Publishing, 2011, p. 122.
⁸⁵ The title of the film was announced in several venues around April 7, 1917, including in "Third Max Linder Comedy," *Motography*, April 7, 1917, p.742.
⁸⁶ This scene causes a flash-forward to Chaplin in *A Dog's Life* filmed a year later in which Charlie downs a similar number of pastries on brother Syd's lunch cart.
⁸⁷ "Taxicab Farce is Linder's Next Essanay," *Motion Picture News*, April 14, 1917, p. 2339, notes a variation on the plot that made up the final film: "Max is in love with a beautiful society girl. He has everything framed up to marry her when the stock market hits his fortune and leaves

him without a nickel. Max's hotel throws him out, holding his baggage. All he has to wear is what is on his back—a suit of evening clothes. Max leaps into a taxi, dons the chauffeur's long coat and cap and is sitting at the wheel, when his girl and her mother catch sight of him. He tells them he owns the machine. Complications develop rapidly when Max's girl desires a ride and he is unable to drive. She does, however, and then there is more trouble, finally winding up with the arrest of Max for theft of the machine just as he is about to marry the girl. Eventually all comes out happily." In his review of the film, Hanford C. Judson offers yet another ending to the film (and he at least *saw* this version): The aunt and the "princess," as Judson calls her "stop in front of [the princess's house] and leave Max who can't get away. There is plenty of fun left for next morning when they find Max still there" (Review published in *The Motion Picture World*, May 5, 1917, p. 811). It's worth noting as well, that *Essanay News'* description of the film matches that of *The Bioscope* ("Linder's Third Essanay Film Is Proving Big Money-Getter," May 1917, n.p., **USA-NYPL-PA-New**, Kleine Scrapbook.

[88] Max Linder, "It Reminded Him of Battlefields," *Motion Picture Magazine*, October, 1917, p. 61.

[89] "Max Linder Likes Blondes," May 5, 1917, p. 6, **USA-NYPL-PA-New**, Kleine Scrapbook.

[90] "Third Linder Comedy Gets Trade Showings," *Motion Picture News*, April 21, 1017, p. 2494.

[91] "*Max in a Taxi* Acclaimed His Greatest Film at Record Runs," *Essanay News*, April 21, 1917, n. p., **USA-NYPL-PA-New**, Kleine Scrapbook.

[92] Julian Johnson, "The Shadow Stage," *Photoplay*, July 1917, p. 135.

[93] Hanford C. Judson, Review of *Max in a Taxi*, *Moving Picture World*, May 5, 1917, p. 811.

[94] Linder refers here to viewing Chaplin's *The Cure* (1917), which was released on April 16. MS Letter Max Linder to Charlie Chaplin, April 20, 1917, Max Reinhardt archives, **UK-BL-Lon**, MS88987/2/18.

[95] "Wounds Win Release," *Los Angeles Times*, April 19, 1917, p. 2.

[96] "Max Linder Fatally Ill," *Wellington [Kansas] Daily News*, May 8, 1917, p. 3.

[97] "Postpone Linder Comedies," *New York Telegraph*, May 8, 1917, n.p. **USA-NYPL-PA-New**, Kleine Scrapbook.

[98] "Max Linder Very Ill," *Variety*, May 4, 1917, p. 20.

[99] MS Letter Max Linder to Charlie Chaplin, April 20, 1917, Max Reinhardt archives, **UK-BL-Lon** BL, MS88987/2/18.

[100] "Viva Max!" *Motography*, May 26, 1917, p. 1101.

[101] Guy Price in "Los Angeles," noted that "Max Linder is improving at Monrovia," *Variety*, August 3, 1917, p. 34.

[102] "Film Flashes," *Jackson [MI] Citizen Patriot*, August 19, 1917, p. 19.

[103] "Comedian Will Go Home," *Los Angeles Times*, n. p., **USA-NYPL-PA-New**, Kleine Scrapbook.

[104] "Again Rumored That Linder Will Resume Work," *Motion Picture News*, August 11, 1917, p. 993. Also, "Comedian Max Linder Sails Home to Paris, *Motion Picture News*, September 1, 1917, p. 1432.

[105] "Linder Versus Chaplin," *Motion Picture Magazine*, July 1917, p. 4.

[106] This send-off must not have been expected, for Linder sent a telegram to Chaplin, which stated: "Dear Charlie, before leaving America I send you a hearty handshake. Max Linder," Max Reinhardt collection, **UK-BL-Lon**.

[107] "Max Linder Goes Back to Dear Old France," *Hanford Kings County Sentinel*, August 16, 1917, p. 10.

Chapter 5: America Revisited (1919-1922)

A letter from Linder to Charlie Chaplin from Ouchy/Lausanne, where Linder was continuing his convalescence, dated May 15, 1918, demonstrates that the two kept in touch and that Charlie was in some small way trying to entice his friend to return to the States and try again.[1] Linder had received, in a letter from Chaplin, photos of the new Chaplin studios, which he claimed appeared "built with a comfort and luxury unknown up to the present time." One of the reasons Linder had given his American friends for leaving was that he was building a new cinema in Paris, and he again used this excuse for not returning promptly, for construction "will not be terminated before the end of August." He would then return to California in September at the earliest: "It is impossible for me to tell you anything about my plans as I have received up to the present moment no official proposition from any American company. Most probably I will come there without contract. Besides, I intend to work in the same way as you do, that is to say, I will make a few pictures, eight at most."[2]

In the same letter, Linder mentions that he had just completed a lengthy interview in which he "eulogized" Chaplin in the French magazine *Le Film*, an essay that David Robinson translated in its entirety for his book *Chaplin: The Mirror of Opinion* (1983). This essay makes clear Linder's strong feelings of respect for and devotion to Chaplin, probably due to his receipt of a friendly welcome at the Chaplin studios the year before and the time the two men had spent in each other's company since. In his response, Linder mentions that rather than Chaplin's professor, as the press noted, he was Chaplin's student, having learned many things from watching him work (and being one of very few people, at the time, to be invited on set):

> Until seeing Charlie at work, I never fully realized how unimportant is the amount of film used and the number of times a scene is shot. In France, we count the number of meters shot as if there were some set relation to the length of the finished film. In reality there is a relation only to the quality of the film and the care taken by the director. I will cite some figures to give a precise idea of the quantity of the film used. To make a film of 1,800 feet, Chaplin spent two months. He used more than 36,000 feet of negative; that is to say that every scene was shot twenty times. That represents, with trials, alterations, retakes, some fifty rehearsals.[3]

Linder and Chaplin in 1921 at the Chaplin studios, Hollywood, courtesy Roy Export S. A. S.

In fact, although other scholars have gotten it wrong, Linder and his agent had attempted to acquire an American contract as early as January 1918, when an ad testifying to Linder's health and listing his American credits appeared in the January issue of the *Motion Picture Studio Directory and Trade Annual*, along with the usual alphabetical listing of Linder's attributes as an actor. The ad, strangely, lists the following credits, the final two of which have been misinterpreted as Essanay films planned but not made: *Max Comes Across, Max in a Taxi, Max Wants a Divorce, Max the Heartbreaker, Max Plays Detective*. Clearly, Linder had included two of the Pathé films he made before coming to the States in November 1916, which were released during his tenure with Essanay: *Entre deux feux* (1917), in English *Max the Heartbreaker*, and *Max et l'espion* (1917) or *Max Plays Detective*. Perhaps Linder felt no one would check up on him, and five films seemed better than three. His agent T. E. Letendre, based in New York, failed to get Linder any offers with this ploy, so he turned again to France.

Ciné Max Linder program, Haven collection

Ciné Max Linder was at times referred to as "Cinemax," a term Linder claimed to have coined, but which caused great consternation among his viewing public and, especially, Georges Lordier, owner of a similarly named house, whom Linder took to court in the summer of 1914. This was his first theater in Paris. As Georg Renken reports, the theatre was built in 1912 and originally named the Kosmorama. It then became the "Topical" Cinema Pathé-Journal, the theatre's name when Linder purchased it on October 10, 1913. After renovations, it opened as the Ciné Max Linder on December 17, 1914 and premiered Linder's own *Très moutarde* (1914). *La Presse* noted that "The Ciné Max Linder will be the only establishment in Paris to screen the new sensational films of the "King of the Screen,"[4] meaning the first run of his films.

The *Essanay News* for April 21, 1917 reported that the theatre had been bombed by Zeppelins during an air attack on the capital. Whether or not this was true, Linder was planning what was to be a major renovation of the structure, at least a month and a half before he arrived in America the first time.[5] Linder himself reported that he had sold this first Ciné Max Linder in April 1918 to the Omnia Company, keeping 25% interest for himself.[6] The coverage on the theater is nothing if not confusing, for many reports even refer to it as Linder's studio, where he had produced a few films during his long hiatus from America. Linder did appear onstage there, however, in a sketch or two during this time.[7]

24, Boulevard Poissonnière, the first theatre's address, is the same location of the second one, whose renovations cost, in one report, "in the neighborhood of $1,500,000 and will be constructed along the lines of American theatres." One report noted that this second "monstrously-sized" theater was built on the site of a former and celebrated English café.[8] Florence Lawrence, however, in an article for the *Los Angeles Examiner*, reported that the new theatre would cost only $240,000 and accommodate 1000 moviegoers. She mentioned that Linder hoped to feature American film artists, such as Douglas Fairbanks, who, at the time, was little known in France: "The house will combine many unique architectural features, including fountains, quaint lighting arrangements and an entrance which will lead the spectator away from the screen to find his seat. . . . It will be beautiful in color scheme, with its pale cream marble, mauve velvet curtains and gold frames and paneling." According to Renken, it re-opened on May 14, 1919.

It is clear that Linder spent most of 1918 trying to secure backing for filming *Le Petit café*. His letters to Henri Diamant-Berger while convalescing in Ouchy/Lausanne focus on his attempts to assure Diamant-Berger that his films had drawn big audiences in the States, i.e., that his producing a film for Linder would be money well-spent, and that he was perfectly healthy.[9] In one passage, Linder compliments Diamant-Berger on the Easter issue of his magazine *Le Film*, saying that it rivals any such volume in Italy or America, but then chastises Diamant-Berger for a photo of himself appearing in the April 29 issue: "Permit me to tell you that I was stupefied to see my head in your April 29 issue. My God! How I have aged!!!!!."[10] He also mentioned that he would be visiting "Monsieur Pathé" on his return to Paris from Lausanne,[11] perhaps in order to stir up the idea that Diamant-Berger might face some competition. Linder chose Tristan Bernard's play written in 1912, *Le Petit café*, as his subject, although no information exists as to why and how this was chosen, except that it probably helped Linder to engage Bernard's son Raymond as director, a situation with which Bernard, Sr. was very pleased. Linder noted in an interview that "it is not convenient [to film] in France where everything is lacking, where everything has to be improvised or replaced."[12] The *Exhibitors Herald* noted in 1920 that "although the original stage part was played by John E. Young at the New Amsterdam theatre in New York, it is said that the star character fits the talents of the French comedian to perfection."[13] With Diamant-Berger producing, Pathé was convinced to release the film under its banner, noting that it was termed "a special attraction."[14] It was previewed at the Ciné Max Linder on November 15, 1919 and then released at the Omnia-Pathé on December 19, 1919. Because of Pathé's distribution monopoly, it did not premiere in the United States until well after Linder's return there, June 6, 1920.[15]

Max as Albert Loriflan in *Le Petit café*, courtesy Museum of Modern Art

Although Tristan Bernard's popular play had not found its way onto film until Linder's incarnation in 1919, it is clear that its plot may have inspired Mack Sennett in his 1915 *Tillie's Punctured Romance*, in that both films feature a mountain-climbing wealthy patriarch who falls to his death and a "missing" heir, who learns of his/her legacy while working as a lowly waiter/waitress. Linder plays this missing heir, Albert Loriflan, who with another derelict pal played by Henri DeBain, finds a job at Le Café Philibert (with Philibert played by Jean Joffre). With American actress Wanda Lyon as Yvonne, Philibert's daughter, ignored--her beauty and charm right under his nose--dalliances both old and new begin to haunt Albert at his place of business. A one-night-stand with Edwige the violinist, played energetically by Flavienne Merindol, results in several humorous encounters, the final such with the rejected Edwige presenting her many children to Albert in hopes of gaining his sympathy and "love." When Albert finally receives his inheritance, after his father's lawyer and Philibert join together in an attempt to pinch it from him, the lowly waiter transforms into a well-dressed man about town in his off hours, resulting quickly in a romance with well-to-do Bérangére d'Aquitaine (played by Andrée Barelly in scenes shot at the Pavilion in Paris's Bois de Boulogne). She later discovers him sweeping up at the café, confronts Albert there, then leaves him in disgust. Albert and Yvonne discover each other at last and he realizes that he doesn't need money to be a rich man after all.

Wanda Lyon as Yvonne, *Le Petit café* (1919),
courtesy Cinémathèque français

Perhaps Linder waited to pursue this story until a good five years after Charlie Chaplin's *Caught in a Cabaret* (Keystone 1914), in order not to repeat, gag for gag, Chaplin's particular success with that story—one of a waiter who masquerades as a wealthy gentleman in order to woo women above his class. It is clear that Linder, having become good friends with Chaplin, intended the film to, if the audience made the correlations from *Caught in a Cabaret* or *Tillie's Punctured Romance*, be an homage or at least a nod to his young counterpart, because the first scene of the film is an out-of-context Linder imitation of Chaplin's Little Tramp—mugging the camera in what might be a personal message to Charlie himself.

Le Petit café (1919) Linder with Andrée Barelly,
courtesy Cinémathèque français

Bernard makes frequent use of the iris-out in the film, a common practice, but perhaps more notable is his use of Max Linder "narrating" on the same frame with the printed titles as well as Linder "narrating" at the bottom of the frame with actors and action taking place at the top. And, several years before Chaplin's *Woman of Paris* (1923) and the American works of Ernst Lubitsch, Bernard effectively communicates one of Albert's overnight adventures (with Edwige) by focusing the camera on his broken umbrella—left outside her house when they arrive in the dark and shown still in that same position the next morning.

G. de LaPlane interviewed Linder for *La Rampe* shortly before the film's premiere (19 October 1919), who had this to say about the production:

> I simply wanted to profit from the summer by filming in France. Diamant-Berger offered me a role I have wanted to play for many years, so I accepted. Convinced that the example must be set by the stars, I strove to realize the will of the author and director during three months of friendly collaboration. I have rarely encountered a more attractive role for an actor than that of "Albert" in *Le Petit café*. I am happy to have been able to bring it to the screen.

Le Petit café (1919) with Linder, Andrée Barelly, Flavienne Merindol, and Armand Bernard, courtesy Cinémathèque français

Louis Delluc reviewed the film in both *Paris-Midi*[16] and *Le Siècle*, arguing that if a person liked the stage version, he would like the film version. "You will laugh again," he writes. While he commends the company itself — and Bernard the director — he has much more to say about Linder:

> We will notice a real effort in the play of certain lighting and the choice of natural settings. If we don't see everything, if we are unaware of such details worth remembering, the fault will be Max Linder's. He is so dazzling that one wonders if it is not a comedy whose title is Max Linder, all of whose characters are named Max Linder, whose actors are all the unique and innumerable Max Linder. We have never seen him expend so much verve and energy. What fireworks! Humorist, acrobat, dancer, juggler, mime, jeune premier, what isn't he? This is a role tailor-made for the triumph of all his brilliant gifts. Finally!

Le Petit café (1919) program, Haven collection

French reviewers overall wanted to claim this film and Linder's performance in it as a return to the fold, as if his work in America signaled a sort of defection. One such reviewer, Henri DeBain, who had played the *plongeur* beside Linder in *Le Petit café*, talking to Vincent Gédéon in 1923, noted that this particular film pleased him because it was a sophisticated film devoid of the usual slapstick *trucs* (devices).[17] In a similar vein, L. D. in "Ceux que tournant . . . Max Linder," published in *La Liberté* that "There is nobody in the world, by the way, who does not know the elegant jacket, the striped trousers with their impeccable crease, the essentially chic top hat of Max. Max is a 'type.' But today Max Linder turns on the famous *Petit café* which will allow him to deploy in front of the public, which cherishes him, new aspects of his talent." Yet, Linder continued to make plans to return to America.

The *Exhibitor's Herald* reported this intention to return to America to make films as early as February 1918,[18] and so did *The Moving Picture World* in both February and March 1918,[19] but as has been described, one thing and another caused Linder to change these plans. Even though Linder had received a note from M. Pichon, French minister of the Foreign Office, that his name had been put forward for the Légion d'Honneur medal for his service in the Great War,[20] on November 11, 1919 he finally left Le Havre aboard the S. S. *France* bound for New York City, registering as Max Linder Leuvielle and listing his next of kin as his father Marcel in Saint-Loubès, Gironde.[21] He would not be greeted in New York this time by a welcoming party from a film company who had so eagerly hired him, for, as he mentioned in the letter to Charlie Chaplin, he intended to produce his own pictures and thereby to make films "the American way." In an interview he provided to the press in Paris November 9 before boarding ship, Linder had much to say about his motivation and justification for returning to America to make films at this point in time:

> "I am quitting Paris to go to America because the United States understands the tremendous scope of the possibilities of the film, whereas Europe has not progressed a step in the development of

the screen art since I first appeared on the film fifteen years ago....It is a fact that there is not a single 'movie' studio in Paris today. The French methods are antediluvian, the theaters are dingy, and there is absolutely no modernism, imagination or initiative."[22]

Harsh words, indeed. Clearly Linder had not brokered a deal in France of the magnitude that he desired.[23] Or perhaps it was the fault of French workers and their new attachment to Bolshevism. Linder suggested as much in an interview with Edwin Schallert six months after he arrived in America: "It was impossible to have satisfactory workmen at the studios. That's why I am here in America. Since the war, everyone in France sticks out his chest and says, 'I will not work; I have been a soldier, that is enough.'"[24] Unfortunately, although he was able to wrangle a deal or two with production companies once in Hollywood, he had not foreseen the fall of the French franc and ended up paying double the amount he had envisioned on what would be his final trip to the States.[25]

Linder arrived with his business manager and secretary in Hollywood, then, the second week of January 1920, establishing himself initially at the Beverly Hills Hotel, almost two years after he had begun talking about a return to the States to work. Some reports offer that Linder arrived with only his interpreter and business manager, others with someone termed "Mrs. Linder," but identity unknown.[26] Finding out that any suggestion Syd and Charlie Chaplin had made about working at the Chaplin studios had been forgotten or promised only lightly in the first place, Linder then turned to countryman Maurice Tourneur, who offered to share his studio space at Universal.[27] In fact, Tourneur had just relocated to Universal in January 1920 in order to allow more than one unit to film at a time.[28] Linder was also able to get Robertson-Cole interested in distributing, with his contract demanding four 5-reel films a year.[29] So, with those hurdles surmounted, Linder formed his own production company, Max Linder Productions, and began work on his first American-made 5-reeler, initially entitled "The Broken Mirror." By June, after a change of cameraman to Charles Van Enger due to the loss of a considerable amount of film by the previous one,[30] what became *Seven Years Bad Luck* was previewed in Los Angeles in August (it had been completed by mid-month) and finally premiered on February 19, 1921 at Chicago's State-Lake theater.

Seven Years Bad Luck (1921) with Alta Allen, Haven collection

As one reporter notes, "The central theme of the picture shows a man trying to escape from the jinx which has been laid upon him by a broken glass. Naturally, this gives opportunity for a large play upon all sorts of superstitions."[31] One of the most notable slapstick elements of the film is the "mirror scene," a tried-and-true vaudeville/music hall gag that Linder had employed once before in his *Le Duel de Max* (1913), one that cost him then due to copyright infringement and one that would cost him once again with this film, in the Schwarz Brothers' 37th court case on the issue. Of course, the gag found its way into many other films and television shows regardless, including The Marx Brothers' *Duck Soup* (1933), Chaplin's *The Floorwalker* (1916), and Bugs Bunny's *Hare Tonic* (1945), among many others. Other notable elements of the film include fun with zoo animals (with Linder supposedly bitten on the arm by Lucille the lion[32]), train stations, swimming pools and county jails, combined with Linder's adroit portrayal of various offbeat characters, that aid in disguising him throughout his trials.

Linder's company included Charles Dorian (on loan from Tourneur) and Al Davis, assistant directors, although Wilton Welch, an Australian who got his start with Jesse Lasky, was added to the directing team in mid-July.[33] The cast was comprised of Thelma Percy (after Alta Allen), Alta Allen, Betty Peterson (the Maid), Lola Gonzales (terpsichorean dancer), Harry Mann (the Chef), Chance Ward, Ralph McCullough, Hugh Saxon, Cap Anderson, F. R. Crayne and Pudgy the dog.[34] Manager Harry Caulfield lasted only the one film, for he is reported to have left for the east coast by October 30.[35] Jessie Robb, writing in *Motion Picture World* (May 7, 1921), noted that the film was "custard pieless and free from the ordinary slapstick and suggestive vulgarity of most so-called comedies. Much of the fun is subtly achieved."[36] In *Motion Picture News* (May 7, 1921), J. S. Dickerson commented that "'Seven Years' Bad Luck' is unadulterated farce of a quality that seldom reaches the screen in more than two-reel lengths and presents Max Linder in a role eminently suited to his talents."[37] *Chicago Tribune* critic Mae Tinee gushed:

> The most polished of the comedians in this "Seven Years's Bad Luck," written by himself, he proves to be also both adroit and amusing. As I remember, the comedies I saw him in a number of years ago did not impress me especially. This one, which has some unique comedy situations and some really clever acting, did.[38]

Exploitation strategies for the film ranged from reminding the filmgoer that "at one time Linder was the one real comedian of the films and bill him as the original" (sounds familiar) to offering free admission to anyone willing to risk seven years bad luck by breaking one of the cheap mirrors set up in the theater's lobby or offering "Horseshoe Matinees," at which the theater owner promised to pay the war tax for any child bringing a horseshoe to the theater, which, after serving as lobby[39] decoration during the film's run, could be sold as scrap iron (a pricey commodity at the time) when no longer needed.[40]

Robert Florey photo, *Seven Years Bad Luck* (1921) location shot, Haven collection

Linder began what would become a two-year tradition, inviting a gaggle of film folk, Chaplin and Tourneur among them, to his home for Christmas night. The first such party (Christmas parties always doubled as birthday parties for Max, being born on December 16) wasn't reported in the press until January 21, 1921, but its description suggested that Linder spared no expense to entertain his new friends: "At a loss for proper wines, he seized upon a large quantity of two-year old red and white wines, labelled the bottles "Chateau Yquem 1879," and various other famous vintages and had his butler serve a different vintage with each course. And it took three courses, it is said, for the connoisseurs to wake up!"[41] By the time of Linder's second Christmas in California, he was able to offer his guests the gustatory gifts of his own personal chef.

By the time *Seven Years Bad Luck* (1921) proved a hit at the cinemas, Linder had hired a new publicity director, Clarke Irvine, stolen from the employ of Tourneur, to take over what had become a big job.[42] Still working to get his *Seven Years Bad Luck* (1921) released, Linder began negotiating (reported as early as August 1920[43]) with Alain Valabrégue and Maurice Hennequin for rights to a popular French farce, *Coralie et Cie* (*Coralie and Company*), which they had written in 1901. He ran into problems immediately because it became clear that Cines, an Italian film company, had already obtained such rights from the authors.[44] Correspondence between Valabrégue and Linder shows this to be true. However, it also shows again Linder's skill in negotiation. In a letter to Valabrégue dated September 18, 1920 on Max Linder Productions stationary, Linder writes:

> I wrote to my friend M. Massard three months ago to ask M. Hennequin (because I believed you to be always in Lausanne) if it would be okay for me to buy *Coralie et Cie*. Two months later, I received a letter from Massard, saying that *Coralie* had been sold to Cines.
>
> You know, dear friend, also as well as I, that the play is impossible to put on in America as is. So, I have asked an American author to collaborate with me in order to make the play playable here.
>
> This author has made a very decent play and actually, I have paid him $2000 for his work. Naturally, after I received the letter from Massard, I told him that *Coralie* had been sold to Cines but that I did not despair at being able to buy it.
>
> The American author who, like me, has been waiting for three months for a response from the Italian company, has just written to me that he could no longer wait and that he was willing to give me back my $2000 and sell the idea that he had found, thanks to your play, to Christie's Comedies.

I was completely disheartened, for you and for me. For you, since the author in question can sell an idea he had found in *Coralie* and you cannot touch a centime of the rights. For me, who has worked more than two months on the subject, it is obvious that is going to be put on, very probably, by another, because, my dear friend, copyrights do not exist here. A person steals ideas without a scruple.

I will ask M. Whippel,⁴⁵ the American author in question, to kindly wait an additional two months; therefore, dear friend, here is what I propose to you: If you can arrange with the "Cines," I agree to pay you for your part, 20,000 francs and 20,000 francs for Mr. Hennequin's share which will make the sum of 40,000 francs to have the authorization, for the world, to write an American version of the play *Coralie et Cie*.

I ask your complete discretion regarding the conditions of this business proposition.

I hope to receive a response as soon as possible.⁴⁶

Be My Wife (1921) location photo, Linder and Alta Allen, Haven collection

By October 29, Linder was able to respond to Valabrégue with his thanks: "I am very happy that you have learned that I can purchase *Coralie et Cie* in Italy."[47] However, it is obvious that Valabrégue had offered Linder another script in addition, which he refused, saying that it was a rare French play that could be Americanized in such a way as to be successful. Linder had, however, his much-desired green light, and began work on his second project, with a working title of, first, "Too Much Pep" and later, "Who Pays My Wife's Bills?" before he settled on simply *Be My Wife*.

Initially, the American public indicated some concern that the story would be too bawdy for them. In late January 1921, Linder addressed this issue in a *Los Angeles Times* article: "The one possible reason for such rumors concerning 'Too Much Pep' is the fact that the story was suggested to me by a famous Parisienne farce which, in its original form, might have justified any comments made upon it. But I have changed the situations so completely and have so entirely revised the plot that there is no semblance left."[48] If a comparison is made of the original play and Linder's finished film, it is clear that he and his co-writer did change many aspects of the play. The first reel of the film is not in the play at all except for the fact that a married couple is introduced, Jules and Lucienne, who are very much in love. The one conflict they seem to have is that Lucienne's aunt, Laure, dislikes Jules very much and seems to be dead set on breaking the two up. In the film, the couple is Max and Mary, who are not yet married in reel one and Max must resort to subterfuge to marry the girl despite her aunt's efforts to marry her to someone else, Archie. In the play, Archie is Ernest, and his role is mainly to inform the husband about Coralie & Co., and the fact that although it is indeed a high end fashion house, it is also a place where married women "hook up" with married men—not their own. Ernest explains this to Jules (Max): "The clients of Coralie & Co., married women for the most part, desire to deceive their husbands in total security, in an annex of the fashion house that gentlemen of the 18th century referred to as the little house. A discreet, pretty, secret place where one can surrender to the games of love without fear."[49] In the Linder version, the fashion house converted to as much a speakeasy as a rendezvous place for married people, although it is Mary's misunderstanding regarding Max and Mrs. Dupont's "rendezvous" that leads to trouble. Clearly, Linder wanted to focus the audience's attention as much on the set conversion (the annex of the play simply becomes a magic trick of sorts in the film—changing from fashion house to speakeasy and back with the press of a button) as on the fact that married people were meeting there hoping to commit adultery.

Under the auspices of Max Linder Productions and initially a Robertson-Cole project, *Be My Wife* was filmed in the early months of 1921 at Universal City and completed in mid-May. Grace Kingsley reported back in December 1920 that Linder had seen Viora Daniel as Roscoe Arbuckle's leading lady in *Life of the Party* (1920) and immediately sought to sign her for this film, probably noting what Maude Cheatham reported that "with her beauty, her vivid imagination, her sweet girlish enthusiasm, and hopes, Viora Daniel promises to become a favorite twinkle."[50] In fact, he succeeded in borrowing her from Famous Players Lasky for the role of Mrs. Dupont.[51] Daniel herself offered to interviewer "Irma" that "Max is so romantic looking, with talkative eyes, that she's brushing up on her French so she can talk to him without an interpreter. She says she just knows she's going to want to talk to him about great souls and things like that."[52] The film also featured character greats such as Lincoln Stedman (Archie) and Caroline Rankin (the aunt), with Linder's 'wife' again played by Alta Allen (*Seven Years Bad Luck*). Others included Charles McHugh,[53] Madame Rose Dione and Pal, the pit bulldog. Charles van Enger photographed.

Linder, as usual, was involved in all aspects of this production, including the women's gowns at Coralie & Co., which he is reported to have designed himself. Grace Wilcox reports in *It* magazine (in a pejorative French dialect) Max discussing his foray into fashion design:

> So when I want 'vamp' stuff—I make ze 'vamp' dress of black and ze hat too; when I want ingenue—zen I have ze fluffy ruffles; when I want heavy—I make heavy dress—you know—but always I have everysing so simple as possible—but different—sometimes

not much—sometimes—more—often—almost nuzzing—but you see here some pixtures of Max gowns--.⁵⁴

Willis Goldbeck described the Linder set as dark, bleak as only a deserted studio stage can be bleak:

> The corrugated iron roof seemed to send a chill thruout the great barn-like structure. Some distance ahead, just beyond the jumbled wreck of what appeared, in the scant light to have been a bedroom, I caught the green gleam of a Cooper-Hewitt, showing faintly through chinks in a plaster wall. I stumbled on and came presently out into a big set, the modiste shop."⁵⁵

Goldbeck was ordered to interview Linder in the studio canteen, where he waited and soon watched as Linder pulled up in his bright "yellow and nickel" monster sedan,⁵⁶ driven by an African-American chauffeur—alone, always alone.

Linder, orangutans and Mr. and Mrs. Joe Martin,
courtesy George Eastman Museum

Guillermo J. Reilly interviewed the French star in the Café des Beaux Arts in Hollywood about this time. Reilly noted that Linder took credit for performing the San Vito, better known as "the shimmy" for the first time on screen, even though young Jackie Coogan (and others) had performed it long before onstage. Linder told a story about a party Chaplin had thrown him upon his arrival in Hollywood the second time. Chaplin had hired a small jazz band and Mae Collins was acting as the hostess. At one point in the evening, each guest had to perform a dance solo to the beat of the music already playing: Chaplin's was a classical slow step, Linder danced to a flute, in a "convoluted and timely Spring Song." Chaplin then asked guests to present an original charade. Linder's scene was entitled "The Invisible Fear," and took place in "The Suicide Club."[57] In this telling improv performance, the Club announced that any cowards who wanted to commit suicide and lacked the courage to do so could come to the rescue of their partners. In other words, no one could cross back over the threshold of the club in any form other than that of a corpse. Reilly reported that this scene got so rowdy and there was so much loud screaming of the suicides, that Linder, at least, lost his voice for the remainder of the night.[58]

Betwixt and between filming, Linder found himself entertaining or being entertained when duty called. He attended the Moving Picture Star Ball on March 5, the first such event in San Francisco, organized by Eugene H. Roth and the San Francisco Advertising Club to facilitate interest in northern California as an ideal spot for filming and studio location. Twenty-five or thirty film stars were invited, among them Roscoe Arbuckle, Charles Murray, Leatrice Joy, Mary Miles Minter, Bebe Daniels, Douglas MacLean and many others, all transported the day before the event by two special Pullmans. Greeted by city officials, the stars were then part of a parade through downtown San Francisco, a reception at the St. Francis Hotel, and an evening banquet. The ball took place the next day.[59] On March 9, Linder was one of many stars recorded as attending the premiere of the season, *The Four Horsemen of the Apocalypse* (1921) with Rudolph Valentino.[60] Later that month, H. C. Witwer recorded his experience at the Haworth studios interviewing

Sessue Hayakawa for *Picture-play*, noting that when he challenged Hayakawa to a bit of jujitsu, Linder, visiting the set, tried to coach the star. Indeed, Witwer was defeated.[61] In late April, Linder was to entertain Prince Albert of Monaco at his home, the prince being in town to receive an award for his undersea research.[62] It is clear that Linder made every effort to be part of this community, despite the fact that his English had not improved.

Linder with General Davis and Major Eichelberger,
courtesy George Eastman Museum

About this time as well, Linder appeared in several "Snapshots" short films that featured stars in occupations other than those on the set. The first of these for Linder was titled *Federated Screen Snapshots No. 1*, released in June 1921, which included a section on Linder entertaining his two operatic friends Lina Cavalieri and Lucien Muratore. Other stars included Roscoe Arbuckle, Ben Turpin, Jesse Lasky, Cecil B. DeMille and others (an interesting compilation).[63] Produced by Jack Cohn and Lewis Lewyn for Federated Film Exchanges of America, Inc., the film was supposed to be the first of a series, touted as "the fan magazine of the screen."[64] A similar film found recently in the New Zealand Film Archive and entitled *Hollywood Snapshots* shows

Linder doing acrobatics at his home, which is visited by a traveler looking for immorality in Hollywood, one Hezekiah, who also visits Carter DeHaven, Owen Moore, Viola Dana and others. Produced by Hodkinson Films, this short is believed to have been released shortly after the industry's hiring of Will Hayes, sometime in early 1922.

But nearing the end of filming, Linder was concerned with more important matters. First was the preview screening, which took place at the Rosemary theatre in Ocean Park on April 22. Linder and Charlie Chaplin snuck in the back way of the theatre and were gladdened to be met by immediate laughter.[65] The film was still entitled "Who Pays My Wife's Bills" at this point. By May 20, it was reported that Linder was on his way to New York to personally screen the film for Robertson-Cole.[66] However, he had been courting Sam Goldwyn in a big way and so, it is likely that he traveled with the film to show it instead to Goldwyn and Company, which he did the evening of June 7 at Aeolian Hall on W 43rd Street.[67] In fact, he parted ways officially from R-C on May 23, claiming that he was unhappy with the manner in which his first film was distributed. It was announced then in the press in August 1921 that Linder had successfully signed with Goldwyn to distribute this and future projects. *Be My Wife* then premiered on November 6, 1921 at Godard's Theatre in Sacramento, California.[68]

On the way to New York, where he was to "vacation" for two weeks at the Biltmore following his business dealings, Linder stopped at Chicago and was feted by R-C salesman H. R. Phillips, who took him to the new and amazing Tivoli theatre, where he received an extensive behind-the-scenes tour by manager Balaban.[69] In New York, Linder and his manager, Clarke Irvine, visited boxer and countryman Georges Carpentier at his practice venue on Long Island one afternoon.[70] Linder also attended an AMPA (Associated Motion Picture Advertisers) luncheon given in his honor, held at the Café Boulevard.[71] French director Léonce Perret and his wife Valentine hosted a dinner in honor of two of their countrymen, Linder and Abel Gance, at that time most famous for *J'accuse* (1919), where the future of French films in America was discussed.[72] Linder was back in Los Angeles July 3.

Linder with Abel Gance in New York, Haven collection

Reviewers across the board praised Linder for adapting his style to American audiences in this second film by eliminating his habit of over-expressing and over-gesturing. Laurence Reid noted that "Being a pantomimist first, last, and always, he has succeeded in repressing the exaggerated gesture, so that his expressions have developed an eloquence heretofore lost." Most also mentioned that the film was uneven, having really three different plots and climaxes, with too many wordy title cards in the first of those. However, all remarked that the film's highlights included the wedding scene rodent gag, Linder's fighting himself in a mock burglary attempt in another scene and the Coralie dress shop set that had the ability to quickly transform itself from a speakeasy into said dress shop through a complex network of sliding panels and trap doors.

Linder had "previewed" his ideas about the third film to the press in New York during his vacation. Generally, he described that it "started in a far eastern capital, and with many beautiful women, atmosphere and the principals, moves westward to New York and Atlantic City, thence across to Los Angeles for the windup."⁷³ Of course, this very vague description never materialized. Instead, Linder decided to film a parody⁷⁴ of his friend Douglas Fairbanks's film *The Three Musketeers* (1921). He would even convince Fairbanks to let him film on the same sets. But the press suggested that Linder waited until Fairbanks left the country to announce the project, as if Fairbanks would have somehow disapproved.⁷⁵ Another publicity ploy, no doubt. Goldwyn was to distribute the film, which was initially entitled "The Last of the Musketeers." By the end of November, Linder had hired Vincent Bryan to help with the scenario.⁷⁶

Linder and Douglas Fairbanks fencing, Haven collection

Filming started in December but was abruptly halted around the holidays because Linder was suffering from a bad case of "klieg eyes," or actinia conjunctivitis, a serious eye malady brought on by too much and too close exposure to the Klieg lights most studios relied on. Linder held his second annual Christmas/birthday party at his home near Christmas and this time a picture of the Hollywood glitterati attending made the papers, where all can see Linder adorned in dark sunglasses. He wouldn't be able to return to filming until late January 1922.⁷⁷ Robert Florey reported interviewing Linder at his California home, a new one located on Argyle Avenue, where the house sits up against a hill (or mountain, as Florey describes) and overlooks the city. He had to climb up so many steps to get to the front door, he wrote, that he felt hot and tired: "The panorama became magnificent and the vegetation and its plot splendid; the citrus trees, the oranges, the eucalyptus were immense and confused amongst the palms and the figs; it was all a tangle of tropical trees pushing upward in total freedom." He could even see the Pacific Ocean from the huge veranda.[78]

Linder's Christmas party with (l-r) Georges Jomier, Barbara Bedford, John Gilbert, Patsy Ruth Miller, Leatrice Joy, Charlie Chaplin, Linder, Bessie Love, Ruth Wightman Morris, Gaston Glass and Gouverneur Morris, courtesy of Roy Export, S. A. S.

Again, Linder made the most of his time off, performing a burlesque fencing match for the *Los Angeles Examiner's* benefit for poor children in December,[79] and spending lots of time with Charlie Chaplin,[80] whom the press was hounding about a possible engagement (to Mae Collins?), even though he had just received his divorce from Mildred Harris. Chaplin probably needed the company of a sworn (at this point) bachelor, to throw the press off the scent and, living as he did on Temple Hill Drive, he was a close neighbor of Linder's, as Jack Spears suggested. Spears had claimed (a claim that now possesses more merit) that the two men often spent time in the evenings creating and discussing gags and the day's filming work.[81] Robert Florey noted in a 1922 interview with Linder the French star's affinity for his English/American friend: "We have, Charlie and I, the same nature, a similar character. However, I want to be cheerful and react; I exercise how to be cheerful and happy every morning; I sing loudly, I whistle, I dance. . . and I'm sad, sad. . . infinitely!"[82]

Robert Florey and Linder in costume, courtesy Museum of Modern Art

In March 1922, the two were photographed as attending the premiere of Von Stroheim's *Foolish Wives* (1922) at the Mission theater in Los Angeles.[83] And on April 3, Charlie and Max attended the first day of shooting on Fairbanks's new effort *Robin Hood* (1922).[84] And, indeed, Chaplin was again one of Linder's guests at the aforementioned Christmas party. Others were Bessie Love, Ruth Wightman, Patsy Ruth Miller, Barbara Bedford, John Gilbert, Leatrice Joy, Gouverneur Morris, Gaston Glass and Georges

Jomier,⁸⁵ the personal chef Linder had hired for himself. About the same time as this holiday merrymaking was going on, Linder's former secretary, Norwood Smith, was convicted of forging checks using the star's name and bank account. Smith faced counts on two particular checks, one for $875 and another for $173. Linder claimed he was out about $1750. In fact, Smith was found to have forged at least 25 checks in total.⁸⁶ Although Linder had Albert Petit at his side this trip as well, he could not protect his employer from the threat of such crimes.

Cinémagazine cover, 1921, Haven collection

In February, Linder celebrated 18 years in the business with Clarke Irvine at a fine luncheon. Irvine recounted the event to the press, noting that Linder claimed 363 films to his credit by this time, 303 of which he had directed. Among his ambitions—bringing his mother to America to retire, making more films and going on a world tour—was a portentous one indeed—to make a loving marriage.⁸⁷ Within a year, he would be very near achieving that one—an act he would regret.

Linder and Jobyna Ralston, *The Three Must-Get-Theres* (1922), Haven collection

Back on the set, Linder moved quickly in the filming of his third effort. It follows the plot of the old and well-known Dumas tale but is more about burlesquing the Fairbanks effort than anything else. All the characters have parodic names: Knockout Dart-in-again, Porpoise, Walrus and Octopus, Duke of Roquefort, Cardinal Richie-loo, Lord Poussy Bunkumin and such. In the cast were some old stalwarts, like Caroline Rankin, but Linder also engaged new blood-- Bull Montana, Jobyna Ralston, John J. Richardson, Charles Mezzetti, Clarence Wertz, Harry Mann, Frank Cooke, and Fred Cavens, who held a dual-role as assistant director and the character of

Bernajoux, and Jean de Limur as Roquefort, a Frenchman who would soon prove his importance to Chaplin during the upcoming *Woman of Paris* (1923) project. Harry Vallejo and Max Dupont photographed. This version allowed Linder to show off his fencing skills, a sport he had excelled at since he was a young man looking for stage work in Paris. In fact, many of the scenes are overwhelmed with it. The parodic moments are too many to list, but highlights include the "lovely" Queen Anne, played here by Rankin as opposed to Fairbanks's Mary MacLaren, the use of anachronisms, such as jazz bands, cars and trucks, a typewriter, telephones (and not just located in the usual places, but on trees!), and the scene in which Richelieu is stroking the arm of a chair as he waits for the Musketeers to be apprehended on their way to England Linder converts to him (here Richie-loo) stroking a monk's bald head—bald except for four long hairs, each of which the cardinal plucks out as a musketeer is captured (except for the last one, of course). Linder chose to trade D'Artagnan's yellow horse for a mule in his version, another obvious moment of burlesque, but his particular mule, named Jazbo, got out of Linder's control at one point, throwing the actor straight up into the air. Linder took ten days to recover his health (and probably his pride).[88]

Fairbanks's set is not featured in Linder's film like it is in its predecessor. There are no long allées of trees that the horsemen ride up and down, and no emphasis on the rich paintings or decoration of Louis XIII's palace. These are not Linder's foci. He wants the audience to focus on the comedy, the tiny bits of business like the horse eating his hat or the hesitancy of that same horse to leave his beloved cow behind when Dart-in-again wants to go to Paris to seek his fortune. Also, important for the comedy must be the title cards. Knowing this and still not in command of the English language, Linder brought Thomas N. Miranda on board for this duty in early May.[89] The film was ready in late May and previewed at the Dome Theater in Ocean Park. Soon thereafter, Linder joined with the Allied Corporation,[90] a newly formed European arm of United Artists, to distribute it. This came about purely by happenstance. Linder hosted a farewell party at his Hollywood home the night before he was to leave California for New York at which his distinguished guests, Chaplin, Fairbanks and Pickford were treated to a sneak screening of his new film. All were delighted and at that moment, being the founders of United Artists as they were, offered to bring Linder into the fold, as the first client for their new Allied Corporation.[91]

MAX LINDER IN "THE THREE MUST-GET-THERES"

The Three Must-Get-Theres (1922), courtesy Museum of Modern Art

The film was by now renamed the *Three Must-Get-Theres*."[92] So, in essence, Linder tried three different distributors for his three American films and was not happy with at least the first two. On the eve of his departure, he got the deal he wanted—and his new film would now be premiered at the best of venues, the Strand in New York. Even though he would take this deal home with him to France, it proved to be too little, too late.

MAX LINDER IN "THE THREE MUST-GET-THERES"

Three Must-Get-Theres (1922) on the Fairbanks set, courtesy Museum of Modern Art

Soon thereafter, Linder's bio appeared in *The Film Daily*'s "Biographies of Important Film Directors," described as having "36 years, born in Bordeaux, France. Started film work 17 years ago with Pathé Co. Previous to this was on the stage in France. He has written, played and directed over 300 pictures. Mr. Linder's hobby is all kinds of outdoor sports. Permanent address: Allied Corp., New York City."[93] This makes it seem like Linder was still open to offers, even though he most likely had plans to return to France by or well before this point. In fact, by the time his third American film was released, he had left the country, arriving in New York about June 27[94] and on a boat by July 5.[95] George Parent accompanied him. There are several photos labeled "last photo of Max in America," making it difficult to identify which is truly the last. Unlike his former departure, however, Chaplin was not at the station to see him off. The two men would never meet again.

The film premiered at the Strand in New York on August 27, 1922. Reviews ran the gamut. *The New York Times* reported that the film was "good-natured and a lot of fun. If it lacks subtlety and pointed satire, it abounds in broad and wholehearted mockery. Its method is that of absurdification."[96] The *Exhibitor's Trade Review* deemed it

> a clean, clever burlesque, served up in forty minutes of merry whirligig action....
>
> The introduction of such modern stuff as motor cycles, telephones, breech-loading rifles, etc. into a seventeenth-century plot contrasts oddly with the Dumas atmosphere and heightens the ridiculous effect for which Linder successfully strives. Also, there is a wealth of fun in the slangy, up-to-date subtitles, and what with galloping steeds, desperate combats and the madcap clowning in which the star and his aids indulge there isn't a dull moment to clog the action.[97]

Three Must-Get-Theres (1922), courtesy Museum of Modern Art

Perhaps *The Film Daily's* own analysis of the film's possible problems best sums up the reasons why Linder was already home in France: "Max Linder's name may be remembered because of some of his earlier comedies. But unless they went over big in your territory don't stress his name too much... Be careful to make plain that this is an American-made comedy, up to the minute, and well-produced, for Linder's name may give the impression that it was made abroad, and this might prove detrimental."[98] Linder's attempt to rejuvenate his career in America was over.

Linder had felt at liberty to critique the American film industry all the way back in March 1921, an interview so interesting that veteran film magazine writer Herbert Howe had excerpts of the original interview from Diamant-Berger's *The Film* translated into English for his article on European filmmaking. While American filmmaking had become intelligently divided among workers specially trained for their assigned tasks, the weakness in it lay, according to Linder, in the scenarios. Discerning filmgoers were growing weary of seeing "always the same stories." "That is why," sayeth Linder, "they seek the aide of the novelists and dramatists of old Europe." In other words, American filmmakers know how to make wine, so to speak, but prefer the less voluptuous taste of champagne only due to its higher price. American palates were not educated enough to appreciate the standard of taste provided by European filmmakers.[99]

Linder's "last" photo in America, by Robert Florey, Haven collection

Notes for Chapter 5

[1] Letter (TS) Linder to Henri Diamant-Berger, May 12, 1918 from Ouchy-Lausanne, "I have received, only five days ago, a letter from Charlie Chaplin in which he tells me that he has constructed a magnificent studio costing $300,000 in association with his brother Sydney Chaplin and his old secretary Tom Harrington. He finished the letter telling me to return quickly, that he waits for me impatiently." **FRA-CF-Par.**

[2] Letter Max Linder to Charlie Chaplin, May 15, 1918, from the **UK-BL-Lon**, Archives and Manuscripts, Max Reinhardt collection. Linder notes that two previous letters had gone to "the little fishes," i.e., had not made it across the Atlantic Ocean.

[3] English translation of *The Film* essay by Linder entitled "L'homme qui fait rire du monde," November 1, 1919, p. 38-39, from *Chaplin: The Mirror of Opinion* and used with permission from David Robinson.

[4] "Courrier des Spectacles" *La Presse*, December 16, 1914, p. 2.

[5] The September 28, 1916 issue of *La Rampe* reported that renovations had started, a full month and a half before Linder ever arrived in America the first time ("La Rampe du Cinema: On dit que," n.p.)

[6] Letter (TS) Linder to Henri Diamant-Berger, May 12, 1918 from Ouchy-Lausanne, "I have sold my cinématographe to l'Omnia, keeping a 25% interest in it." **FRA-CF-Par.**

[7] "Max Linder Recovers from Illness," *Motion Picture News*, Feb. 9, 1918, p. 852.

[8] *Les Tréteaux: Revue bimensuelle des théâtres*, May 16, 1916, p. 15.

[9] Letter (TS) Linder to Henri Diamant-Berger, May 12, 1918 from Ouchy-Lausanne, **FRA-CF-Par.**

[10] Letter (TS) Linder to Henri Diamant-Berger, May 12, 1918 from Ouchy-Lausanne, **FRA-CF-Par.**

[11] Letter (TS) Linder to Henri Diamant-Berger, July 12, 1918, **FRA-CF-Par.**

[12] G. de LaPlane, "Le Petit café" review, *La Rampe*, November 19, 1919, p. 16-17.

[13] "Pathé will publish Max Linder's Production as Special Attraction," May 1, 1920, p. 68.

[14] "Pathé will publish Max Linder's Production as Special Attraction," May 1, 1920, p. 68.

[15] "'Little Café' Good Summer Show, *The Moving Picture World*, May 29, 1920, p. 1230.

[16] "Ceux qui tournent ... Max Linder," Dec. 21, 1919 and Dec. 22, 1919 respectively.

[17] Henri DeBain, "Les Opinions de Vincent Gédéon," *Le Journal amusant*, April 7, 1923, p.12.

[18] "Max Linder Recovered Coming to America," February 9, 1918, p. 16.

[19] "Max Linder Coming Back," February 9, 1918, p. 798 and "Max Linder Coming Back to Us," March 21, 1918, p. 1640.

[20] "Max Linder Here Again," *Motion Picture News*, Dec. 27, 1919, p. 242. Also, "Green Room Jottings," *Motion Picture* magazine, March 1920, p. 84. There is no record that Linder ever received the medal, however.

[21] S. S. *France* ship manifest for the voyage leaving Le Havre, France for New York November 11, 1919.

[22] "Max Linder is Coming to U.S.," *Cleveland Plain Dealer*, November 19, 1919, n.p.

[23] A report in *Motion Picture News* entitled "Florida Beckoning to Max Linder" (April 6, 1918, p. 203), suggested that Linder had been receiving overtures from cities, if not particular studios, in Florida, which he obviously rejected.

[24] Edwin Schallert, "Max and the Wild-Reeler," *Los Angeles Sunday Times*, Aug. 22, 1920, p. III: 1.

[25] "Max Linder Pays High for Making Films Here," *Exhibitors Herald*, Aug. 21, 1920, p. 81.

[26] A. H. Giebler, "Max Linder Back," *Moving Picture World*, Jan. 17, 1920, p. 397 and "Max Linder Looking Around," *Camera!*, Jan. 3, 1920, p. 6 respectively. Obviously, Linder had not lost his attractiveness to women.

[27] "Linder Producing at Tourneur Studio," *Camera!*, July 3, 1920, p. 13.

28 A. H. Giebler, "Tourneur Moves to Universal City," *Moving Picture World*, Jan. 17, 1920, p. 397.
29 "R-C Signs Linder," *Camera!*, November 20, 1920, p. 6.
30 "Coast Picture News," *Variety*, Feb. 11, 1921, p. 43.
31 "Max Linder Comedy Offered," *Motion Picture News*, February 5, 1921, p. 1173. Interestingly, the *Detroit Free Press* noted that Linder himself was superstitious, in that he supposedly hired someone else to break the mirror on the *Seven Years* set (March 6, 1921).
32 "Heraldgrams," *Exhibitors Herald*, Aug. 28, 1920, p. 36.
33 "Clip and Paste," *The Moving Picture World*, July 17, 1920, p. 304.
34 "Max Linder Finishes Work on New Comedy," *Exhibitors Herald*, Aug. 7, 1920, p. 40.
35 Sam Spedon, "Keeping in Personal Touch," *Moving Picture World*, October 30, 1920, p. 1224.
36 p. 87.
37 Review of *Seven Years Bad Luck*, *Motion Picture News*, May 7, 1921, p. 2981.
38 "Max Fit and Almost Died but Now He's Back Again, *Chicago Daily Tribune*, Feb. 21, 1921, p. 14. Also, quoted in "Max Linder Scores a Hit," *Motion Picture News,* March 12, 1921, p. 1952.
39 Jessie Robb, Review of *Seven Years Bad Luck*, *Moving Picture World*, May 7, 1921, p. 87.
40 "Has Many Exploitation Angles," *Motion Picture News*, Feb. 19, 1921, p. 1486. Joseph M. Shverha, the theater owner, collected 214.
41 "Max Linder Entertains," *Los Angeles Sunday Times*, Jan. 16, 1921, p. III: 37.
42 "Linder Returns in Glory," *Motion Picture News*, May 7, 1921, p. 2944. Also, "Irvine Signs with Max Linder," *Camera!*, April 2, 1921, p. 6 and "Irvine with Linder," *Moving Picture World*, April 23, 1921, p. 859.
43 "World Film French Farce," *Los Angeles Sunday Times*, August 1, 1920, p. III: 16.
44 "Linder Negotiates for French Comedy Which He Will Produce Soon," *Exhibitors Herald*, August 14, 1920, p. 50.
45 I believe this author to be Vincent Bryan, announced in the *Los Angeles Times,* January 21, 1921, p. III:4, as an assistant collaborator on Linder's current project, which would have been the play in question. The writer notes that Linder felt the collaboration was necessary to "insure a correct angle on American humor." Bryan is listed as having been a writer for Chaplin, Mack Sennett, Harold Lloyd and Roscoe Arbuckle. He would also be hired in the same capacity on the *Three Must-Get-Theres.*
46 Letter Max Linder to Albin Valabrégue, typescript dated 18 Sept. 1920, **BNF-A**.
47 Letter Max Linder to Albin Valabrégue, typescript dated 20 Oct. 1920, **BNF-A**.
48 "Comedy Not Risqué," *Los Angeles Sunday Times*, Jan. 23, 1921, p. III: 16.
49 AlbinValabrégue and Maurice Hennequin, *Coralie & Cie.,* Paris: P. V. Stock, 1901. Act I, Scene VIII.
50 Quoted in "Viora Daniel: The Untold Story of a Film Comedienne, World Traveler, and 'Bank sitter'" by Michael G. Ankerich, Mar. 24, 2014, available at https://michaelgankerich.wordpress.com/2014/03/24/viora-daniel-the-untold-story-of-a-film-comedienne-world-traveler-and-bank-sitter/. Originally published in *Shadowland* in 1920 by Maude Cheatham. Daniel left show business for good in 1921.
51 Grace Kingsley, "Flashes: Max Linder Busy," *Los Angeles Daily News*, Dec. 4, 1920, p. II: 7.
52 Grace Kingsley, "Irma Interviews Viora," *Los Angeles Sunday Times*, Dec. 12, 1920, p. II: 1, 37.
53 Charles McHugh was injured in mid-February 1921 when he fell from a tree on the set. His injuries were not serious. "McHugh Injured," *Camera!*, Feb. 19, 1921, p. 7.
54 Grace Wilcox, "Fashions of the Screen," *It*, April 23, 1921, p. 12.
55 Willis Goldbeck, "Je Suis Content," *Motion Picture*, August 1921, p. 32.
56 Jack Spears noted elsewhere that this car was chosen to provide an interesting contrast to Charlie Chaplin's all-black Locomobile, *Hollywood, the Golden Era,* London: Thomas Yoseloff, Ltd., 1971, p. 98.

[57] There is no indication as to whether this pantomime was instigated by a reading of Robert Louis Stevenson's story of the same name, although it is known that Chaplin had read and enjoyed the story very much.
[58] Guillermo J. Reilly, "El hombre que sabe comer Macarrones," *Cine-Mundial*, July 1921, n. p.
[59] "Film Industry Boosts San Francisco: Roth Arranging Moving Picture Ball," *Moving Picture World*, March 12, 1921, p. 133.
[60] "Ingram Special Opens in West," *Motion Picture News*, April 9, 1921, p. 2469.
[61] H. C. Witwer, "Making Hay-akawa while the Sun Shines," *Picture-Play*, March 1921, p. 32, 95.
[62] "Linder to Entertain Prince Albert," *Camera!*, April 23, 1921, p. 7.
[63] " 'Federated Screen Snapshots No. 1'", *Moving Picture World*, June 25, 1921, p. 844.
[64] "New 'Snapshot' Completed," *Motion Picture News*, May 28, 1921, p. 3319.
[65] Grace Kingsley, "Flashes: Max Linder Comedy," *Los Angeles Daily Times*, April 28, 1921, p. III: 4.
[66] Fred Schader, "Coast Film Notes," *Variety*, May 20, 1921, p. 42.
[67] "[Max Linder has sent]," *Motion Picture News*, June 11, 1921, p. 3575.
[68] Interestingly, the title *Be My Wife* was not copyrighted by Linder until November 23, 1921 (*Catalog of Copyright Entries*, 1921)
[69] "Linder Leaves Robertson-Cole," *Motion Picture News*, May 28, 1921, p. 3309.
[70] "Pick-ups by the Staff: Linder Visits Georges Carpentier," *Camera!*, June 4, 1921, p. 7.
[71] "Max Linder Guest of Honor at A.M.P.A. Luncheon," *Motion Picture News*, June 4, 1921, p. 3412.
[72] "[The future of French motion pictures]", *Motion Picture News*, June 4, 1921, p. 3454.
[73] "Max Linder Arrives from Coast with Print of New Production, 'My Wife,' *Moving Picture World*, May 28, 1921, p. 392.
[74] Linder had filmed two other parodies, *Romeo se fait bandit* (1909), a parody of *Romeo and Juliet* and the aforementioned *Max victime de la main qui étreint* (1916).
[75] "[Max Linder waited]", *Moving Picture World*, October 15, 1921, p. 787.
[76] "[Max Linder has engaged]", *Moving Picture World*, November 19, 1921, p. 320.
[77] "Coast Brevities," *The Film Daily*, Jan. 20, 1922, p. 2.
[78] Robert Florey, *Filmland: Los Angeles et Hollywood les capitales du cinema*, Paris: Éditions de Cinémagazine, 1923, p. 239.
[79] "Linder on Benefit Program," *Camera!*, Dec. 31, 1921, p. 6.
[80] "Chaplin Not Now Engaged," *Moving Picture World*, Dec. 31, 1921, p. 1119.
[81] Jack Spears, *Hollywood, the Golden Era*, London: Thomas Yoseloff, Ltd., 1971, p. 98.
[82] Robert Florey, *Deux ans dans les studios Américains*, Paris: Publications Jean-Pascal, 1924, p. 229.
[83] " 'Foolish Wives' a Hit in Los Angeles," *Exhibitor's Trade Review*, March 11, 1922, p. 1029.
[84] Robert Florey, *Hollywood d'hier et d'aujourdhui*, Paris: Éditions Prisma, 1948, p. 64.
[85] Jack Spears noted that Jomier had lived in Hollywood 35 years, was a brilliant linguist and famous for his "poulet (chicken) à la Jomier" and other dishes from Bourgogne, *Hollywood, the Golden Era*, London: Thomas Yoseloff, Ltd., 1971, p. 98.
[86] "Forgery Is Charged," *Los Angeles Daily Times,* Dec. 30, 1921, p. II: 2.
[87] Clarke Irvine, "Views by Wire: Max Linder," *Philadelphia Inquirer*, March 5, 1922, p. 30.
[88] "Max Didn't Realize," *Los Angeles Daily Times*, Sept. 16, 1922, p. II: 11.
[89] Fritz Tidden, "Keeping in Personal Touch," *Moving Picture World*, May 6, 1922, p. 59.
[90] "French Comedian with Allied," *Camera!*, June 3, 1922, p. 4.
[91] "Linder's New Comedy Delights the Stars," *Los Angeles Daily Times*, June 2, 1922, p. II: 11.
[92] "First Linder Comedy Ready," *The Film Daily*, June 9, 1922, p. 2.
[93] June 11, 1922, p. 53.
[94] "Linder Here; Sails July 5," *The Film Daily*, June 27, 1922, p. 1.

[95] The *New York Times* reported that Linder nearly missed the boat, the S. S. *Paris*, because he had left his passport back at the Ritz-Carlton. His race back to the hotel, then back to the pier mirrors an earlier film, *Max et le sac* (1917) pretty well. "Liner Paris Taking a Thousand Abroad," *NYT*, n. d., n. p.
[96] *New York Times* review of the *Three Must-Get-Theres*, printed in *The Film Daily*, " 'The Three Must-Get-Theres'—Allied Prod. and Dist. Strand," August 29, 1922, p. 4.
[97] Review of the *Three Must-Get-Theres*, *Exhibitor's Trade Review*, September 9, 1922, p. 1025.
[98] "Tell Them It Is Unusual, a Burlesque and a Scream," *The Film Daily*, Sept. 10, 1922, 4.
[99] Qtd. in Herbert Howe, "A Trip through Europe's Filmland," *Picture-play*, March 1921, p. 18-19.

Chapter 6: Decline and Departure (1923 – 1925)

Linder's homecoming was marked by yet another scathing interview he gave to the press about filmmaking in America, this time for *La Cinématographie française*. Linder claimed that French films continued to be boycotted in America, due to the fact that 90% of American cinemas were owned by two companies, who employed "Americans of recent naturalization"—from Germany, a natural enemy of all things French. Also, Linder noted that if American and French films were compared, the defects of the American film could easily be seen and that the American audience, therefore, had become bored, causing the industry to decline a full 33%.[1] A writer from *Variety* countered that Linder, complaining about the cutting against his will of *Seven Years Bad Luck* before it hit the cinemas in this interview was indicating "simply a round-about way of declaring that the sympathies of America are pro-German."[2] Linder was to again uphold this "German-blaming" after his experience filming in Vienna, Austria in 1924.

Meanwhile, Linder had been broadcasting the idea that he might construct a new studio in Nice, France upon his return. Some thought he would go back to working for Pathé, even though he still had that deal with Allied Corp. for distribution. Others reported that he planned to make three films yearly for Allied, with the first year's production to be completed in Paris, followed by a return to the States to make others.[3] He didn't take that world tour, he didn't move his mother to America (in fact, he never went there again), but surely he wanted to make more films. Was getting married really a firm goal?

By July 22, it was being reported that Linder had completed construction of that studio in Nice, France,[4] although city records show no evidence of this. If he did plan to film in Nice, he might have gained permission to use La Victorine,[5] later used by Rex Ingram. In any event, Linder dove right into a nine-reel production,[6] one that never materialized. By September 23, he had abandoned this project and was talking of a return to America,[7] the trip being planned for no later than January 20, 1923.[8] As he was wont to do, Linder went to Switzerland to relax and unwind, returning to Paris in mid-November.[9] But January 20 was a more portentous day than it was meant to be. It was not a day of departure to the States, but a day of recuperation, for, back in Switzerland, Linder suffered severe injuries in an accident. He was swept into a deep crevasse by an avalanche, and supposedly saved by the loyalty of his dog, who alerted mountaineers in the area to his master's whereabouts. Luckily, the star did not break either his back or his neck but both arms. He also suffered some internal injuries. Traveling to America was put on hold,[10] while Linder tried to recover at the Clinique d'Ouchy in Lausanne. By January 27, he was reported out of danger and still planning to make the trip to Hollywood very soon,[11] but by the first of March, reports suggested his departure would take place in yet another month. This is where the chronology breaks down. One source reported that Linder would be bringing a wife with him to California,[12] another that he had suffered another accident, in a car this time, but back in Nice.[13] By May 3, the secret was out. Max was smitten with Hélène Jeanne "Ninette" Peters, the 17-year-old daughter of Linder's former acquaintance Mathilde Peters. Unsubstantiated rumor has it that 1) Linder and Mathilde Peters had once had a relationship and/or 2) Linder had known the mother and daughter for many years, meeting them in Chamonix often when he was there for relaxation. Why now? Had Ninette just come into her compelling beauty at the age of 17 and seeing her allowed his old ambition of having a loving marriage and family flame up once again? In fact, the problems with the chronology of events in Linder's life at this time had everything to do with Ninette. Linder was again in Nice, but not to rejuvenate his old project. He had "kidnapped" under-age Ninette and driven her there to elope.[14] The automobile accident amounted to, in one report, Linder losing control of his car due to a fly, driving up on the sidewalk beside the Promenade des Anglais accidently and thereby being ejected from the car. Ninette was not with him. One report even suggested this to be a suicide attempt.

The fact is that up until this time, Linder had virtually never been linked romantically in the press to a particular woman. As his daughter Maud later reported in her book, he had many lovers, but that aspect of his life was somehow off limits to the press. Two interviewers back in 1913 had ventured to ask Linder if he was married and he had the same answer for both: "No, single, but no desire to marry, just because I'm tired of living alone. Now it is very difficult for me to find a woman to my taste. For the kind of life that I am living, I cannot visit lounges where I could find the woman I seek; if I was not an artist in the scene living among theater people..."[15]

What had happened this time? Could Linder have been in such a frenzy about Ninette that he lost all sense and thereby forgot to take the usual precautions regarding the publicity surrounding such a romance? Perhaps a person must see the thing from Linder's perspective—a man in his late 30s hopelessly infatuated with a 17-year-old beauty. He was so enthralled with her that he went missing (she did, too) and the two were found *in flagrante delicto* in Nice, where mother Mathilde Peters threatened to press charges regarding Linder's kidnapping of her under-aged daughter. A Paris newspaper, *Le Populaire*, made light of the episode, but offered the story to its readers in detail:

> The prince of cinema and his sweet companion had, in fact, taken refuge in a large hotel in Nice, where they thought they had, quite at ease. "perfect film happiness."

But someone disturbed the party
They did not think of the policewoman's flair. The brigadier in charge of the investigation interrogated, at the Gare de Lyon, employees and controllers and finally learned that a couple, whose young man responded to Max's report, had taken the first steps for Antibes. Accompanied by the girl's mother, the policeman flew to the Côte d'Azur.

Palm trees, big blue sky, pier-promenade, hotels. One, two, three hotels. The door of an apartment. Knock! Knock! Ouff! They are the ones! After the beautiful love poem, the bourgeois vaudeville turn. Reproaches, fits of tears and a tirade on good morals.

In short, the lost sheep was brought back to Paris by the afflicted mother. Max Linder, remaining in Nice, dreams of paradise lost.

Another episode - that of marriage - will he find it?[16]

Mathilde Peters was a courtesan born of a courtesan and had raised her only child, born July 7, 1905, to be the same. For many years, Mathilde was the mistress of Jean Dupuy, owner of *Le Petit Parisien* and secretary of agriculture for France. Mathilde met Dupuy when he was 60 and she 22. Even though she had witnessed the suffering of her mother Hélène at the hands of her family when she had born Mathilde out of wedlock in Brussels, she decided to live the same sort of life. Even when his wife died in 1913, Dupuy refused to marry Mathilde, but continued to keep her in luxury, even buying her a two-floor flat at 9 rue Lota.[17] Ninette was Dupuy's daughter, born late in his life, and she and her mother never wanted for anything due to this relationship. After two generations of Peters women rejecting the sacrament of marriage, it's more than a little ironic that Ninette's marriage would end in tragedy.

Georg Renken states that shooting on Linder's next project directed by Abel Gance, began on June 21, but the papers were suggesting that the two would begin their version of *Cyrano de Bergerac* a month later.[18] In late July, the film was still being labeled a Cyrano de Bergerac film,[19] but perhaps this is due to the fact that the two friends were attempting something quite different and wanted to keep the story a secret.

Linder and Gance had known each other since the early days for both at Pathé, with Gance even taking several small roles in Linder's films at that time. By 1923, however, Gance had, by all accounts, long surpassed his old friend in artistic mastery, choosing to create behind the camera instead of in front of it. His second masterpiece, *La Roue* (1923), was filmed in many of the locations Linder had occasioned at the time—Chamonix, Mont Blanc and the Victorine studios in Nice. It is likely that Linder approached Gance at one of these locations with a bet: that the two collaborate on a film to be shot in only three days. In fact, a letter to Gance exists in which Linder expresses his appreciation for Gance's recent triumph (*La Roue*): "Dear Abel, bravo for your triumph!!! I am happy to send you my sincere felicitations because I have had for you in a certain film (a long time ago) a feeling of shared understanding that has transformed since into a profound friendship. Again one time—bravo!! To you, Max."[20] That 18-minute film was actually filmed in either 10 days or three weeks,[21] depending on the account,[22] and would eventually be titled *Au Secours!*, previewed in Paris on June 24 at the Gaumont Palace and premiered on March 21, 1924 at the Sans Souci theatre in Prague. Linder and Gance received a contract June 19, 1923 from an Italian distributor, Barattolo, who paid 180,000 francs for the world rights minus America and attached two checks of 10,000 francs each on the letter (the source of the money Linder mentioned in a letter written August 6).[23] As the premiere date suggests, although the filming took very little time, the processing of the print, the distribution and other factors delayed its release. A letter from the Unione Cinematografica Italiana to Gance dated October 10, 1923 stated that the negative was at their printing house and would be available to ship in a few days. Gance had outsourced this portion of the process to Rome,[24] but, as a cable to the Italian company asserts, was upset about how long it was taking, fearing a delay in having it in hand to sell to America.²⁵ Another cable Gance sent November 18 stated that still the delivery had not arrived back in Paris and "Max was furious," for their hopes of selling it in America were dashed.²⁶

Linder and Abel Gance on the set of *Au Secours!* (1924)

The plot of the film begins with Linder's character visiting his men's club the night of his honeymoon and taking a bet given him there that he could not remain in a certain haunted house for exactly one hour: 11:00PM to midnight. While he is greeted with various ghouls, phantoms and scary animals, Linder's character is only a minute or two away from success, when he receives a panicked telephone call from his new wife Sylvette, played by Gina Palerme, that she is being attacked by some monster. In an emotionally packed scene, Max succumbs easily to tears in his fear for his wife, ends the bet in failure and runs home to find his wife in no danger. The owner of the haunted house and a club member has developed this ruse in order to help him pay expenses, because he had yet to lose such a bet.

Au Secours! (1924) cover for *Cinéa-Ciné*, March 1925, Haven collection

The reviewer of the film for the Belgian *Mon Ciné* got it right in his assessment of the film: "We have already said a few words about this new work by Abel Gance and Max Linder who made it - at least it is they who tell us this - to have fun. It is therefore completely unpretentious and there is no need to look for the beauties of *La Roue* (1923), nor the remarkable finds of Max in *Be My Wife* or in *Seven Years Bad Luck*. *Au Secours!* is much more modest."[27] Most others, including the French, were not so kind. A critic named "Euréka" suggested that it wasn't all bad, but that the director had done a poor job. This person's only positive remark was for Linder. "Le Montrougien" suggested that the film had been made by a novice and that it resembled the antics of "Le Grand Guignol," as much as anything. "Ponocrates" asserted that the film simply wasn't French![28]

While the film was a popular failure—in fact correspondence exists as to the lengths Gance went in his attempts to get it distributed in America at all—it does contain some rudimentary Gance-isms, most notably his use of high-speed montage, negative image, slow motion and reverse image in certain scenes. For instance, in a scene in which Max is hanging from a chandelier, Gance distorted the image such that a sense of vertigo is effectively created.

Writer Oscar M. Sheridan with *Pictures and Picturegoer* out of the UK had interviewed Linder at his new apartment on 11 bis avenue Émile Deschanel, just a couple of blocks from the Eiffel Tower and presents an intimate picture of the star, right amidst his romantic turmoil and during the period of shooting *Au Secours!* (1924). After all these years, Linder had kept the same elderly housekeeper Marie—a perfect foil for anyone suspecting any shenanigans going on in the Linder household. Interviewers being greeted by Marie surely brought each of them back to reality quickly. Sheridan was led into a cheerful and comfortably furnished salon. Linder was seated at the dining room table and dressed in a large overcoat with a heavy traveling rug flung over his lap. It was 90 degrees outside, but he always complained of catching cold. The interview went well enough, until Sheridan mentioned Linder's impending marriage. The actor then rose from the table and freed a revolver from a nearby drawer. Sheridan thought it was a joke until the actor, "his eyes still clouded, still looking out of the window into vacancy, turned the weapon over in his hand and, one, two, three bullets dropped into his palm; as gently and as quickly as he had removed them, he replaced them."[29] Sheridan took his leave.

By the time Linder had chosen Ninette Peters as his wife to be, sometime in early summer 1923, he had given up all ideas of returning to America to film. The couple married in a private ceremony (photos were allowed only on the couple's exit from the church after the ceremony) on 2 August 1923 in l'Église de Saint Honoré d'Eylau in Paris. Gance received an announcement of the marriage from both the bride and groom's families, but was not permitted to attend, like everyone else. The press wondered at such secrecy now when it seemed so unimportant. More than one suggested that Linder had been forced into the marriage, a point proven, they suggested, by his glum expression on the doorstep of the church. Their daughter was not conceived until a month later, so this could have been no American type of shotgun wedding as Chaplin had faced more than once. And, as a Roman Catholic, Linder would have understood that such a move was final. Certainly, the atmosphere surrounding the marriage was a harbinger of things to come. The couple spent their honeymoon in Ouchy-Lausanne at the Palace, receiving a beautiful bouquet of congratulatory flowers from Gance upon arrival. Linder's letter to Gance August 6 from that location told Gance that he had found himself to be happy (in marriage?), but that the 10, 000 francs he had received from him for their film (*Au Secours!*) was already spent and that he hoped Gance would like to begin the next film as soon as possible.[30] This film project never materialized.

11 bis avenue Émile Deschanel, photo by Lisa Haven

Linder and Ninette Peters on their wedding day, August 2, 1923

After the Gance collaboration, Linder must have spent much time finagling around for a way to make another film in Europe. He continued to complain about the lack of good filming venues (studios) in France—filming in America with its (at the time) hard workers, large studio systems and endless land for location shooting might have spoiled him—so he ended up choosing the new Vita-Film studios just outside Vienna, Austria for his next effort. The Vita-Film studios began construction in 1919 at 121 to 123 Speisinger Straße south of Vienna. It was completed in 1923, just months before Linder's impending occupancy. The area, known as Rosenhügel (the studio would later be known by that name) was surrounded by hospitals and sanitoriums of one kind and another, an ironic situation if there ever was one. The studios were to offer the most innovative technology for the making of film known.[31]

Vita-Film Studios, Vienna, courtesy of Österreichische
Nationalbibliothek, Vienna

In early October 1923, it had been announced that Linder had been booked for a project directed by René Hervil, entitled "Clown by Love," but the studio and distribution company were not identified.[32] By early June, *Variety* announced that Hervil and Linder had signed with Vita-Film studios, studios A-G, to film what would be a circus film. Filming was supposed to commence in mid-September, but by November 22, the press noted it was "about to begin,"[33] but that was dependent on the Linders arriving in Vienna November 26 as planned. In fact, they did not leave on the train until November 29, arriving in Vienna the next day. Still the crowds waited on them, for the Linders were greeted by a large and enthusiastic group of admirers.

Work at Rosenhügel began in early December. Writer Felix Fischer of the *Neues Wiener Journal* may have over-exaggerated the problems, but his account is interesting in light of others' who told a different story. According to Fischer, by the date of his article, January 19, not a meter of film had yet been shot. Linder's contract included a furnished apartment, but not liking the one provided, he demanded a private one—a villa at XIII, Kupelwiesergaße 10, Vienna—very close to the studio. He had a thing about the temperature in the studio, too. He had ordered that the temperature be 18 degrees Celsius (64.4 degrees F), but upon arrival, found it to be 17 degrees:

> "Cold," said the master, raised his collar, and, unaware of the fact that the work day had been lost, had to be paid his giant salary. When this game had been played several times, the directors of the film company decided to build a new heating system. While working on this, the star stayed in his villa reading French newspapers and magazines.

Vita-Film Studios interior, Vienna, courtesy of Österreichische Nationalbibliothek, Vienna

So it went. "Once a scene was almost shot," reported Fischer. "In it, his partner [Vilma Banky] has to stretch out her hands against him. She did it for hours, but when he was satisfied with her posture, she had developed a spasm in her arms and the filming had to stop." Finally, Linder seems to have had a clause in his contract that the director must protect him[34] against attacks due to his nationality (something he had seemed to harp upon since serving in World War I).

Linder's residence at Kupelwiesergaße 10, Vienna, photo by Lisa Haven

Five days later, Fischer had to amend some of what he had written, first making the comment that Linder insisted he wasn't a drama queen (wasn't suffering from *Staralllüren*) and that progress was indeed being made on the film, with 10,000 meters already shot. The temperature in the studio had to do with Linder still being a convalescent (after his major fall about a year earlier). And there was really no need to protect him from the Viennese and any possible bias they might have against him, for he was much beloved there.

Fischer also reported that Édouard-Émile Violet had arrived about January 14 to replace Hervil, who had a coronary event that demanded his return to Paris. Whether or not Linder was the cause is up for debate.³⁵

Linder in *Max, der Zirkuskönig* (1924), courtesy Cinémathèque français

It seems this semi-retraction wasn't enough for a writer at *Der Filmbote* who came out fighting: "Here we shall discuss the rather transparent ground this daily newspaper, whose hostile attitude towards film is generally known, had given its 'facts,' which had no basis whatever, and, broadly stated, contained not a true word." He argued that Linder had been too long in the film business to postpone filming by "chicanery" (lächerliche Schikanen). And then he resorted to *ad hominem* by suggesting this same writer "demonstrates a child-like naïveté and a complete ignorance of the actual circumstances, even for a moment, that an entrepreneur of the importance of 'Vita' is willing to make regarding destructive star-whims, as they are to be acknowledged, this article with fictitious feuilletonistic skill, without contradiction—yes, seems helpless to accept it."³⁶ *Kino-Journal* seconded this writer's assertions, noting that "the hysteria described in the article [Fischer's] is not to be found in Max Linder, but in the author, who was in the unusual position of writing an original report for his readers, which made him nervous as a result of the rarity of such activity made."[37]

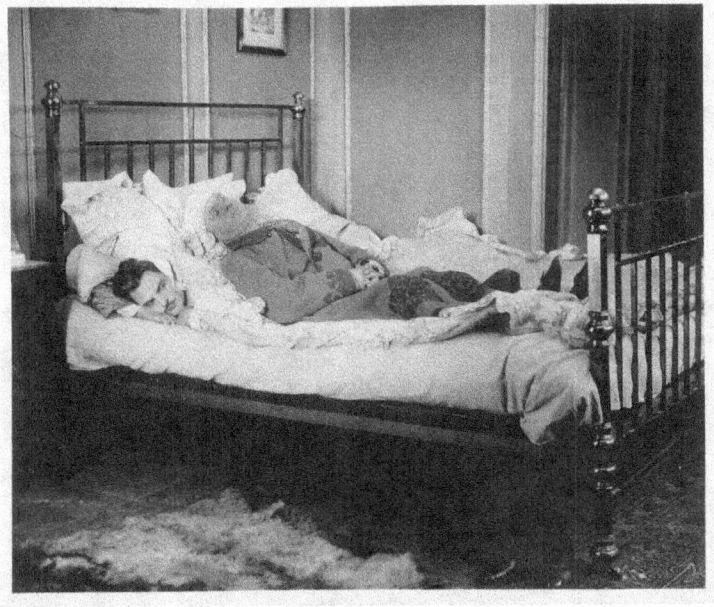

Linder in *Max, der Zirkuskönig* (1924), courtesy Cinémathèque français

The press was quiet on the subject of Linder and his Vita-Film adventures in February, until February 23, when Linder and his wife were reported to have attempted suicide by taking too many veronal pills. They had consumed the pills on the night of Friday, February 22 and so were found in a bad state about 2 o'clock in the morning. Some accounts suggest that Ninette purposely took fewer pills (five to Linder's 14) in order to call her mother in the morning and get some help out of the situation (also, she was pregnant). However, the papers told a different story. *Die Kleine Volks-Zeitung* reported that a maid in the adjoining room to the Linders was awakened by the couple's moaning, which, once she had a look, required her to call the Hietzinger rescue squad and transport the pair to the Offer Sanatorium. Upon arrival, doctors noted that the pair had slurred speech (it was recognized that they spoke only French) and seemed very restless. Antidotes for the veronal worked well, with Linder himself feeling well enough to be back filming at Vita on the next Tuesday, February 27—a miracle since he had consumed enough to kill the average human.³⁸

Linder in *Max, der Zirkuskönig* (1924), courtesy Filmarchiv Austria

Ironically, there is no police report of the incident (although the police were called initially), so somehow Linder managed to convince the authorities that it had all been a mistake, that he had not been sleeping well for some time and had probably become immune to the effects of the veronal such that he found himself taking more and more just to get some relief. Even Mrs. Linder's comments to her mother in Paris by cable (and printed in the newspaper) asserted that the whole thing was cooked up by Vita-Film studio for publicity's sake.³⁹ To counteract whatever bad press this incident might evoke, Linder called in both the public and the press to kibbutz on his lion-taming scene in the film March 21 and for the next few days. The fact that several long articles on the spectacle hit the press that week suggests that

Linder was successful in diverting attention away from his own personal problems and back to the film in progress, at least temporarily.

Linder with Vilma Banky and Julius Szöreghi, courtesy Filmarchiv Austria

Linder had had an entire full-sized circus tent constructed for the film, complete with wild animal cages. The animals, props and performers were provided by the Viennese branch of the Hagenbeck Circus, an American company. In the scene described by most writers, Linder, totally inexperienced in the fine art of lion-taming, was to somehow get the lead animal, named Prince, from his position in the cage up onto the back of a circus horse circling around the ring at a gallop. To add even more suspense, the Hagenbeck's lion tamer had witnessed his own first wife mauled to death by four lions. His reasoning for the animals still being alive was simply, "It was clear that she was beyond saving and the animals were just doing what was natural for them." The show went on.

Linder had invited the public, some as paid extras and others unpaid observers, to fill the seats in the circus tent. The *Reichspost* provided the most brilliantly written account of the authenticity a truly appreciative audience gave the scene: "The spectators were the most genuine. The joy on the faces, the expectant expressions, the diversity of the physiognomies made such an excellent circus audience. So many original types were among the crowd occupying the two thousand seats that the directors happily rubbed their hands together."[40] They were making people happy and increasing their chances of making more money besides! The commencement of the big "lion shot" began with a kingly entrance by Linder in his gold-bedecked lion tamer's costume. But before he could begin shooting, he had to master the fine art of whip-popping, "because lions have good ears and can tell right away whether or not someone knows what they're doing. The artist soon learned and was whip-popping like an old pro in less than half an hour."[41] Hagenbeck's tamer gave this advice: "Just do not lose sight of the animal. And show yourself quite fearless."[42] The lion, however, was not eager to obey

Linder with Vilma Banky and Julius Szöreghi, courtesy Filmarchiv Austria

the commands of a stranger, seeming not to listen to Linder's commands at all after a while. The Hagenbeck's tamer made a move to intervene, because Linder was now in some danger, when the star locked gazes with the predator, shouted his commands and finally succeeded in achieving the results for his film that he had wanted. The white stallion, L'Aiglon, behaved as he was supposed to, and the shot was completed. The crowd cheered, Linder bowed, and the moment became part of filmmaking history.

In many ways, this film hearkens back to a formula Linder used in many of his shorts for Pathé: the ne're-do-well son of a prominent aristocratic family is given an ultimatum to, in this case, marry or be disowned, finds a girl, but not the right one, but must impress her father with some talent he doesn't have by either learning it or pretending to have done so—convincingly. In *Max, der Zirkuskönig*, Linder's character, Max, Count de Pompadour, is down to choosing a bride with the eeny-meeny-miney-mo method (he had been given three choices, represented by photos), when he meets Ketty, an acrobat from the Cirque Buffalo, and the daughter of the owner. Even though Max's family does not approve of Ketty, he forges ahead, except that he finds a roadblock from her end as well. Her father tells Max that he must be an artist, not just a count. And like many past films, Max and his valet set about trying to learn how to do a circus act, but in his apartment, rather than in a more acrobatic-friendly place. Of course, he fails at it and returns to the circus defeated. The twist here is that he sees an ad for a flea circus at this point, buys it and will try to put it over as his "act." But the fleas escape in the circus tent, causing a bunch of itchy chaos (this scene just *had* to somehow emanate from Chaplin and his penchant for flea gags). During this mess, Max is able to knock out Ketty's acrobat partner, who is also in league for her affections, without much success. Ketty's father feels a bit sorry for Max by this time and offers him a job as a lion-tamer, with the very dangerous lion, Sultan. Max gets around this danger, or thinks he does, by swapping the real lion for the clown Antoine in a lion suit. But, having a vendetta towards Max now, the acrobat rival becomes wise to this subterfuge and swaps in Sultan. Much like Chaplin on the tightrope in his version, *The Circus* (1928), Max does well in the ring with the real lion until he finds out it's the real lion. And, unlike in some of his Pathé shorts with similar plots, Max de Pompadour ends up with the girl, whose poppa is happy, too. Besides Linder, the film featured Vilma Banky (Ketty), Julius Szöreghi (Circus owner), Eugen Burg (the elder Count), Ernst Günther (Emilio), Viktor Franz (Pompadour's valet), Kurt Labatt, Hans Lackner and Ilona Karolewna.

Linder and Vilma Banky, *Max, der Zirkuskönig* (1924), courtesy Filmarchiv Austria

With the film completed about April 10, it was soon screened for the press in three different locations this time: in Vienna at the Haydn Kino on May 23, in London at the Scala on June 12 and in Paris at the L'Empire on July 9. Its official premier took place the night of September 12 at the Cinema Royale in Rotterdam. *Variety* reported on the London preview screening that the film was "genuinely funny" and that Linder, in his comeback role as Count Pompadour (comeback role?) was great: "He never clowns and much of his business is delightfully original."[43] The *Film-Kurier* provided a fair and unvarnished account of the film and its star:

This Max Linder, who can be seen as a historical phenomenon today, is still amusing. . . . What captivates Linder time and again is the virtuosity with which he can turn his body into an instrument of strange effects. Linder is the direct descendant of the French Pierrot actor, a débureau and comrade, whose methods he transferred to the film. His comic, like any comic in general, is a critique of the form he has to embody, but without ever going so far as to deny the type he represents. His art of representation is not rooted like that of a Chaplin in a deep human pity for the pariahs of this earth, nor in a hatred of the figure to be embodied, . . .but he enjoys the ridiculousness of the figure, which at most sometimes increases to a mild irony.[44]

Austria's *Die Filmwelt* immediately took its fellow Austrian reporters to task for concentrating their efforts seemingly only on Linder's personal life and tribulations, claiming instead that Vienna was lucky to have an actor of such caliber in its midst.[45]

Linder in *Max, der Zirkuskönig* (1924), café scene, courtesy Filmarchiv Austria

As is often the case with the home folks, the French were less kind, with one critic remarking that "there is invention in this great comic film where Max Linder appears to us as brilliant as it has always been, but this very invention is sometimes exercised to the detriment of the subject. There are too many scenes that have nothing to do with the action.... Max Linder is always above his films. It's very good and yet it's a shame."[46] With such mixed reviews, Linder must have been disheartened. There would be no second film for Vita-Film, but not necessarily due to Linder's first effort there (although it was the last film before the declaration). *Variety* announced in September 1924 that Vita-Film was bankrupt,[47] only a year after opening its doors with the most advanced and modern equipment in the film business.

Linder far left and his wife Ninette far right on the *Max, der Zirkuskönig* (1924) set, courtesy Österreichisches Filmmuseum, Vienna

As was Linder's habit, he and Ninette recovered from the turmoil of Vienna in Switzerland. Back in Paris early in 1924, Linder purchased a four-story house at 29 avenue du Parc St. James, Neuilly-sur-Seine and began having it remodeled to his taste, while the couple continued to live in his apartment of many years at 11 bis avenue Émile Deschanel near the Eiffel

Tower. Linder's daughter, Maud, described the downturn of the Linder marriage in her memoir *Max Linder était mon père* (1992). The pregnancy must have been a relief for Ninette, because until it was evident, Linder started up a continuing tirade against her that displayed his extreme jealousy and irrational behavior. Perhaps this last frontier for him—marriage and family life—was not at all what he expected. Perhaps he could see that this situation was yet another "failure" of sorts in a several-year-long string of failures. Despite the fact that the press and the public seemed to continue to hold Linder in high esteem, Linder took his frustrations out on his young wife, slowing down only after the child's birth and then only temporarily. On June 27, Maud Lydie Marcelle Leuvielle Linder was born, to be called Josette in childhood and Maud as an adult.

By December 4, Ninette had her will drawn up, for she was in fear of her life. Linder became a part of his next film endeavor about the day before.[48] By February 3, 1925, it was announced that the story was to be collaboratively written by 50 writers and entitled *Le Chevalier Barkas*.[49] Another source reported the same day that the scenario had been completed with only six writers and the title was "Barkas le fou." Sets were ready and the interiors were to be shot at Joinville, the old Pathé studios near Vincennes.[50] In mid-June, the press claimed that young Josette (Maud), just about a year old, would be featured in the film.[51] The press claimed that Linder would be filming at all or near all of the various chateaux around France, but footage only remains of one location, the Chateaux de Tourbillon in Sion. A piece in *Les Spectacles* on September 9 suggested that he had also done some filming at the Chateau Chambord,[52] but stopped due to the cost of filming there, almost the same day as the *Exhibitor's Trade Review* announced a new film deal between Carl Laemmle and Linder for a series of films[53] (of course, this never materialized). Maud Linder includes several images of pages of a typescript and manuscript of the scenario in her book *Les Dieux du cinéma muet: Max Linder* (1992).[54] The first scene in these pages takes place in the Bois de Bologne.

Chateaux de Tourbillon in Sion, Switzerland, one of the exteriors for Linder's unfinished *Le Chevalier Barkas*, Haven collection

Back in February, Max participated in a Radio Paris 75-minute broadcast at about 8:45PM on the 13, titled "Festival of the cinema" (Festival du cinéma). The broadcast was a celebration of thirty years of the invention of filmmaking and featured an address by Mr. Léon Gaumont with presentation of the film star guests by Pierre Desclaux. These included Linder, Jean Angelo, Suzanne Bianchetti, Jacques Catelain, Germaine Dulac, Geneviève Félix, Marcel L'Herbier, Abel Gance, Sandra Milowanof, Gina Relly, Charles de Rochefort and Philippe Heriat. This event continued in a banquet at the Champs-

Elysées pavilion the next day, where Louis Lumière was present. At both events, it was noted that Linder, who regaled the audiences with stories of his twenty years in the business, had "a nice voice for a screen star."[55]

In March 1925, Linder's doctor convinced him to spend some time at Mon Repos, a medical facility in Vevey, Switzerland, which he did for six weeks, along with his wife, from April 9 to May 26. The psychologist in residence saw signs in Linder of "morbid jealousy," making the actor incapable of making rational decisions. After they returned to Paris, any good effects the rest had had on Linder disappeared. Ninette was forced to add a codicil to her will on June 18, stipulating that if she died at her husband's hand, her child should be brought up by her mother, Mathilde Peters.

Later, on the night of July 22, Linder was given the post of President of the Cinema Writers Association (Société des auteurs des films) at an evening event.[56] His colleagues heaped nothing but praise upon him that night—obviously unaware of Linder's true state of mind. Just three months later, on October 24, he resigned from that position, presenting the group with a gift of 10 million francs upon his retirement.

In August, Linder gave notice on his avenue Émile Deschanel apartment, work having been nearly completed on the new house in Neuilly and suggested that the child be taken to Cavernes to visit his mother. Ninette balked but kept her peace until the next evening when she took refuge with Maud in her mother's house at 15 rue Jeanne d'Arc. As had become his habit, Linder hired detectives to find and keep an eye on her, but she was able to file for divorce without his knowledge. She checked into a hotel, but Linder found her there, too, and talked his fearful wife into leaving with him. She also withdrew her request for a divorce shortly thereafter. Linder agreed to let his wife return to Mon Repos to regain her composure on August 15, but he stayed about 15 miles away in Montreux on Lac Léman, returning to fetch Ninette only two weeks later. He spent that two weeks shooting exteriors for *Barkas* in Sion, Switzerland, where he also practiced riding up and down the hilly terrain on a horse, as the film would require.[57] The only hint at the plot occurred in the *Paris-Soir* for August 22:

In *Barkas*, the film Max Linder is working on, there is a part set in the Middle Ages and one in modern times. In the modern part, we will see Americans visiting the castles of the Loire. Max did not incur the costs of hiring artists to play the roles of Yankees because the true ones have exaggerated pretensions and French people having an American physique are not numerous. Max Linder has tried tortoiseshell glasses, but, despite this, there is little resemblance to the inhabitants of free America.[58]

By August 31, however, Linder had taken a break from the film and was attempting dangerous climbs in the mountains around him.[59] Before they left Switzerland, Ninette arranged for Maud to remain in Switzerland with her nanny (not Nell Malone as yet). The Linders returned to Paris. It is probable that Ninette was now resigned to her fate.

Still, Linder publicized yet another film project in the press. On September 28, it was announced that he would be filming a version of the well-known *Le Chasseur de Chez Maxim's*. Production was to begin October 15, with the exteriors being shot either around Paris or on the Côte d'Azur and the interiors at Studio d'Epinay. Max Dearly was to play the lead with Linder casting himself as the marquis.[60]

The Linders' doctor, Dr. de Montet, provided some damning evidence against Linder that didn't see the light of day until Mathilde Peters brought the families back into the courtroom in 1931. His testimony was stricken from the proceedings at the time, because by giving it, he had violated Linder's doctor-patient confidentiality agreement. In it, he evaluates Ninette, not Max, but clearly Max Linder is both mentally unsound and a consummate abuser of, if not all women, at least his young wife:

> "[Ninette] had an intense desire to be delivered from this nightmare, but she was dominated by terror. She realized that she lived with a madman, but with an influential, powerful madman, with a strong reputation as an artist. She saw how he managed to

Hôtel Baltimore, 88 bis Avenue Kleber, Paris,
photo by Lisa Haven

conceal his delusional ideas from others and how he knew how to be lucid in his affairs. Consequently, she was convinced that she would neither succeed in divorcing nor in interning him, that on the contrary he was likely to make prevalent his point of view. She knew he was a constant threat. This was not an invention. Mr. Linder told me repeatedly, 'I have often thought of killing her.' So she signed what he asked her to sign and, the day before her husband left, she begged me to tell Mr. Linder that she had recognized before me the merits of the charges he had laid against her: he had threatened her with a revolver if she did not consent. The letter she wrote to me from Glion confirms my findings in an absolutely convincing way. I enclose it with this declaration. Since Mr. Linder certainly slandered his wife and dragged her through the mud in front of many of his acquaintances, I regard it as a moral obligation to declare that Mrs. Linder's observation revealed absolutely nothing incorrect or suspect in his conduct. I repeat that she was not mentally ill and that her nervousness came exclusively from the terror that her husband, a real persecutor, inspired in her. She was right to fear the decisions he could make, either with regard to him or with regard to the child, because they had to be dictated, necessarily by his desire."[61]

Linder had arranged for Ninette and himself to spend their last night before moving to Neuilly at a hotel, October 31. He chose the Hôtel Baltimore, 88 bis avenue Kleber, Paris. The two dined at the popular restaurant, Poccardi, then ventured back to the hotel, asking not to be disturbed. Linder began the double-suicide or murder-suicide, more correctly, by dosing each of them with veronal once again. When they were groggy, he slit the wrists of Ninette, so that she would bleed out. Next, he did the same to himself. Ninette's mother, Mathilde, arrived on the scene before the police, about 10AM, because she had not been able to reach her daughter by phone that morning. She had to have the hotel personnel force the door open and upon so doing, found both alive, but near death. The couple was transported to the Clinique Piccini on the street of that name. Ninette was to die first, a fact which caused her daughter Maud infinite problems in the years to come. Linder himself didn't die until about two in the morning November 1, 1925. His misery, such as it was, was now over. It would be nice to think that Ninette and her husband Max loved each other so much that they had both agreed to end their lives and go off into the ether, together forever. But this is not the end of a love story. It is the ending Linder had played with, dreamed about and finally enacted, simply because he couldn't stand his life anymore.[62] Left behind was 16-month-old Maud. It was a selfish act.

The Leuvielle family tomb, St-Pierre church, Saint-Loubès, France, photo by Lisa Haven

The Peters family tomb, Père-Lachaise Cimitière, Paris, photo by Lisa Haven

Even if Linder's act had not been murder but double suicide, it would have been against Roman Catholic doctrine and the press wondered how the Church would respond. Surprisingly, he was buried in sacred ground outside the St. Pierre's cathedral in Saint-Loubès in the Leuvielle family tomb on November 5. His cortege included his father, mother, brothers Gérard and Maurice, sister Marcelle (now Mrs. Crabit) and their children. One news source notes that Mathilde Peters and Maud Linder were invited but didn't attend. The funeral's exterior elements were recorded in a short newsreel entitled *L'Enterrement de Max Linder* (1925). Ninette was buried in the Peters family tomb in Père-Lachaise Cemetery in Paris on November 6. Only her mother and grandmother attended. Maud was retrieved from Switzerland by Mathilde, but it would be 10 years before the courts finally decided her fate. Charlie Chaplin's valet, Kono, wrote in his memoirs that a bouquet of flowers Linder had sent Chaplin would remain in his sparsely furnished bungalow for several years following the death of his French friend.[63] The rest of the world, however, would feast on the scandal and the horror of Linder's demise and then, slowly forget him, finally coming to a belief in his mental instability, as described by Dr. de Montet, and his culpability for an event that has done its best to sully his name and work from that day to this. While it is difficult to make allowances for Linder given this ending, it is possible that the demons that finally defeated him were the same ones that provided his many artistic gifts.

Max Linder as ever was, courtesy Museum of Modern Art

Notes for Chapter 6

[1] Cited in "Crónica de Paris," *Cine Mundial*, October 1922, p. 530.
[2] "London Film News," *Variety*, September 1, 1922, p. 43.
[3] "Linder Plans Three Yearly," *The Film Daily*, July 3, 1922, p. 1.
[4] "People," *Camera!*, July 22, 1922, p. 18.
[5] Studios de la Victorine in Nice, France were constructed in 1921, but Ingram didn't occupy them until 1923, so perhaps Linder preceded Ingram in their use. The studios still exist and are in the process of being conserved.
[6] "Film Capital Production Notes," *Camera!*, August 5, 1922, p. 4.
[7] Roger Ferri, "In the Independent Field: Trade Notes," *Motion Picture World*, September 23, 1922, p. 7.
[8] "Within Filmland's Interesting Inner Portals," *Camera!*, January 6, 1923, p. 7.
[9] "Cuts and Flashes," *The Film Daily*, November 16, 1922, p. 2.
[10] "Max Linder Falls 1000 Feet in Alps Crevasse and Hovers near Death," *Camera!*, January 20, 1923, p. 1.
[11] "French Comedian Is Out of Danger Now," *Camera!*, January 27, 1923, p. 1. Also, Grace Kingsley, "Max Linder Convalescing," *Los Angeles Daily Times*, Feb. 23, 1923, p. II: 11.
[12] "Food for Thought and Appetite," *Camera!*, February 10, 1923, p. 1.
[13] "Linder is Hurt Again," *Camera!*, April 7, 1923, p. 16.
[14] "News of the Dailies," *Variety*, May 3, 1923, p. 9.
[15] Javier Bueno, "Una Entrevista con Max Linder, *Caras y Caretas*, April 12, 1913, n. p.
[16] "On Retrouve Max Linder," *Le Populaire*, April 30-May 1, 1923, p. 1.
[17] Ross Davies, *Three Brilliant Careers: Nell Malone, Miles Franklin, Kath Ussher*, Salisbury, Australia: Boolanrong Press (2015), n. p.
[18] Roger Ferri, "In the Independent Field," *Motion Picture World*, June 30, 1923, n.p.
[19] "Pictures," *Variety*, July 19, 1923, p. 22.
[20] MS note Max Linder to Abel Gance, n. d., Fonds Gance, **BNF**.
[21] Article in *Le Petit Journal*, July 1, 1923, n. p. and in *Paris-Soir*, October 10, 1923, n. p. respectively.
[22] A scribbled note written by Gance and in the **BNF** notes that the film was finished in 15 days. Fonds Gance.
[23] TS Letter Barattolo to Max Linder and Abel Gance, June 19, 1923, Fonds Gance, **BNF**.
[24] TS Letter Unione Cinematografica Italiana to Abel Gance, October 10, 1923, Fonds Gance, **BNF**.
[25] M. S. telegram text, Abel Gance to Ambrosio of Unione Cinematografica Italiana, n. d., Fonds Gance, **BNF**.
[26] M. S. telegram text, Abel Gance to unknown recipient, November 18, 1923, Fonds Gance, **BNF**.
[27] "Les Nouveaux Films," *Mon Ciné*, n.d., p. 8.
[28] Sylvio Pelliculo, "Vous Avez La Parole," *Mon Ciné*, n.d., p. 2.
[29] Oscar M. Sheridan, "Charlie Chaplin's Professor," *Pictures and Picturegoer*, July 1923, n. p.
[30] Letter Max Linder to Abel Gance, Ouchy-Lausanne, n. d., but probably August 6, 1923, Fonds Gance, **BNF**.
[31] After a rough and rocky few years, Vita-Film studios came into the possession of Joseph Goebbels and the rising Nazi party in 1933, thereby tainting its legacy for years to come.
[32] "Pictures," *Variety*, Oct. 11, 1923, p. 23.
[33] "Linder's Austrian Picture," *Variety*, November 22, 1923, p. 2.
[34] Felix Fischer, "Der Große Filmstar in Wien," *Neues Wiener Journal*, January 19, 1924, n.p.
[35] Felix Fischer, "Wie Linder in Wien Filmt," *Neues Wiener Journal*, January 24, 1924, n. p.
[36] "Max Linder bei der 'Vita,'" *Der Filmbote*, January 26, 1924, n.p.
[37] "The Firm of Quittner, Zuckerberg & Co.," *Kino-Journal*, January 26, 1924, n. p.

[38] "Max Linder im Sanatorium," *Kleine Volks-Zeitung*, February 23, 1924, n. p. Also, "Veronalvergiftung des Filmschauspielers Linder," *Arbeiter-Zeitung*, February 24, 1924, n. p. and "The Linders Poisoned," *Variety*, February 28, 1924, p. 2.

[39] "Illness Story False Asserts Linder's Wife," *Los Angeles Daily Times,* February 27, 1924, p. I: 6.

[40] "Max Linder, Zirkuspferde und der neue Film der 'Vita,'" *Reichspost*, March 9, 1924, n. p.

[41] "Max Linder im – Löwenkäfig," *Neues Wiener Journal*, March 22, 1924, n. p.

[42] Friedrich Porges, "Filmzirkus," *Film-Kurier Nr. 73*, March 25, 1924, n. p.

[43] "Circusmania," *Variety*, June 25, 1924, p. 6.

[44] Review of *Max, der Zirkuskönig, Film-Kurier*, September 17, 1924, n.p.

[45] "*Clown aus Liebe*", *Die Filmwelt*, Yearbook 1924, p. 3-5.

[46] Review of *Roi du cirque*, *L'intransigeant*, February 28, 1925, n. p.

[47] "Viennese Film Company in Bankruptcy," *Variety*, September 3, 1924, p. 19.

[48] "French Film Notes," *Variety*, December 3, 1924, p. 23.

[49] "Informations," *La Rampe*, May 3, 1925, p. 19.

[50] "Max Linder Travaille," *Comoedia*, February 3, 1925, p. 4.

[51] "Informations," *La Rampe*, June 14, 1925, p. 19.

[52] "Max Linder et le Fisc," *Les Spectacles*, September 9, 1925, p. 20.

[53] "News at a Glance," *Exhibitors Trade Review*, September 20, 1924, p. 17.

[54] These documents are mostly likely in the Institut Max Linder, part of the Cinêmathèque de Lyon, France, unavailable during the researching of this book.

[55] *Comoedia*, February 16, 1925, n. p.

[56] "Chez les auteurs de film," *Comoedia*, July 24, 1925, p. 3.

[57] "[Max Linder est reparti en Suisse]," *Paris-Soir*, August 8, 1925.

[58] "[Dans Barkas]", *Paris-Soir*, August 22, 1925, n. p.

[59] "Nos Artists," *Paris-Soir*, August 31, 1925, n. p.

[60] "Max, Max et Maxim's," *Comoedia*, September 29, 1925, p. 4. Also, "Nos Artistes," *Paris-Soir*, September 28, 1925, n. p.

[61] J. P. Liausu and Maurice Leroy, "La rapport du Docteur de Montet, *Paris-Soir Dimanche*, 1938, n. p.

[62] As is known, many of Linder's early films featured scenes of suicide (by hanging) or death by duel, using a revolver to deal with a fly, or using it willy nilly for some other reason or another. Only *Max et Jane veulent faire du théâtre* (1911) came close to the scenario that Linder actually enacted when the time came. Some believe that he got the idea from a recent film he had seen, a production of *Quo Vadis* (1924), with Emil Jannings as Nero. In it, Petronius played by Andrea Habay, makes a pact with his wife that he will end both their lives if there is no alternative. Of course, this occurs late in the film and Petronius is shown slitting the wrists of his wife and she of him. It is a mutual suicide. Another example in history is the suicide of Seneca and his wife, which played out similarly, but Seneca had to also take hemlock and suffocate.

[63] Kiyohiko Ushihara, *Eiga Mangekyo (Movie Kaleidoscope)*, Chuo-Bijutsu-sha Publishing (1927), p. 172-174.

Epilogue: Court Cases, 1927, 1931, 1935

In a nutshell, what occurred after the Linders' deaths effected their daughter, Maud, first and Linder's legacy second. There's absolutely no way to completely understand what it's like to be pulled to and fro by two different sides of your family, to be raised as a boy when you are very small (and biologically a girl) and to have to refer to your maternal Grandmother as "Maman," the French word for "mother." Maud's tumultuous childhood is best understood by reading her memoir *Max Linder était mon père* (1992).

Mathilde Peters aggressively sought to be Maud's guardian and took off with the child after the funerals, without really accomplishing anything legally. What followed, until 1927, when Maurice Leuvielle decided to take her to court, was basically hiding the child out in England and presenting her with the person who became one of the most important people in her life, Nell Malone, her nanny. Nell and Maud would remain close until her death in 1963. She spent her last days in the Neuilly-sur-Seine mansion and would be buried in the Peters' tomb in Père-Lachaise cemetery in Paris, along with Maud's mother, grandmother and great-grandmother. Maud would join them on October 25, 2017.

There were exactly three trials concerning the custody of Maud, from 1927 and ending in 1935, when she was already 10 years old. In the first trial, which Linder's older brother, Maurice Leuvielle started in 1927, Mathilde Peters was determined to prove that Linder was insane at the time of the suicides, using testimony from Maud's nanny at the time, who supported this accusation. For his part, Maurice tried to do the same, asserting that instead it was Ninette who was a moral degenerate, constantly demanding that her husband engage in perverted sexual acts and drug abuse. Maurice Leuvielle won this round and Maud was carted out to Cavernes to live with her grandparents, even though Uncle Maurice was her legal guardian.

The second trial (an appeal) was brought in 1931 by Mathilde Peters in an effort to have her granddaughter restored to her. She attempted again to prove that Linder was insane, this time bolstered by the testimony of Linder's Swiss doctor, Dr. de Montet. However, it was unclear as to whether or not this testimony could even be admissible legally, due to the patient-doctor confidentiality agreement. It was finally rejected, and Madame Peters stymied once again. Maud went home to Cavernes.

By 1935, however, the tide had turned regarding Linder's reputation and general behavior. Madame Peters again appealed and had this time collected testimony from employees of the Hotel Baltimore, who confirmed the fact that Linder behaved abysmally towards his wife. This time, Peters was still not allowed to use Linder's doctor de Montet's testimony. The arguments were the same: the husband was mad and the wife morally repugnant. This time, however, Leuvielle's lawyer had to agree that, if not insane, Linder was at the very least a frustrated and jealous spouse. Peters won this time, at last, taking young Maud to her new home in Versailles, just outside Paris. This is where she would become a young adult.

The thing is, ten years had passed and by this time, the public had lost its fondness and support for Max Linder. In fact, his work had been forgotten by all except his closest compatriots (a Max Linder Reunion started about this time in Paris that brought those folks together). By 1938, a reader might find in the *Paris-Soir* of August 27, a headline such as "Max Linder ... Who

Committed Suicide After Having Killed His Wife." Such an article usually reported that Linder was indeed insane at the time, a verdict they would never have dared to print before. By the time daughter Maud first discovered her father's work in the mid-40s—the film *Seven Years Bad Luck* (1921)--few knew or cared about Linder and his work. Despite her hard feelings for what her father had done, Maud soon became his most ardent supporter, collecting memorabilia and films—more and more films. When Oscar M. Sheridan came to interview Linder at his avenue Émile Deschanel apartment in 1923, he saw a safe in the dining room that the star told him held 400 films. Maud found, to her horror, that Uncle Maurice had burned or buried all of those (and spent her inheritance, too) and so she spent the rest of her life trying to find them again, with some luck. Many thanks are due to Maud then for resurrecting the incredible career of the first cinema celebrity, Max Linder.

Maud Linder in 1976, Haven collection

Bibliography

Books

Abel, Richard. *The Ciné Goes to Town: French Cinema 1896-1914.* Berkeley, CA: U of California P, 1994.

Bardout, Pierre. *Saint-Loubès en Entre-Deux-Mers: Éléments de son histoire des origins à 1914.* Bordeaux: Centre de Recherche et de Documentation Pédagogiques, 1975.

Bernard, Tristan. *Le Petit café.* Paris: Librarie Théatrale, 1912.

Cerra, Julie Lugo and Marc Wanamaker. *Images of America: Movie Studios of Culver City.* Charleston, SC: Arcadia Publishing, 2011.

Chaplin, Charles. *My Autobiography.* London: The Bodley Head, 1964.

Coissac, G.-Michel. *Histoire du cinématographe: De ses origines à nos jours.* Paris: Éditions du "Cinéopse," 1925.

Corcoran, Michael and Arnie Bernstein. *Hollywood on Lake Michigan.* Second edition. Chicago: Chicago Review Press, 2013.

Davies, Ross. *Three Brilliant Careers: Nell Malone, Miles Franklin, Kath Ussher.* Salisbury, Australia: Boolanrong Press, 2015.

de Rochefort, Charles. *Secrets de vedettes.* Paris: Éditions Kergema, 1947.

Duca, Lo. *Histoire du cinéma.* Vendôme, France: Presses Universitaires de France, 1951.

Duvillars, Pierre. *Le Septième art: Cinéma mythologie du XXe siècle.* Paris: Éditions de L'Ermite, 1950.

Florey, Robert. *Deux ans dans les studios Américains.* Paris: Publications Jean-Pascal, 1924.

---. *Filmland: Los Angeles et Hollywood les capitals du cinema*, Paris: Éditions de Cinémagazine, 1923.

---. *Hollywood d'hier et d'aujourdhui.* Paris: Éditions Prisma, 1948.

Ford, Charles. *Max Linder,* Cinéma d'aujourd'hi 38. Paris: Éditions Seghers, 1966.

Golden, Eve. *Golden Images: 41 Essays on Silent Film Stars.* Jefferson, NC: McFarland & Co., Inc, 2001.

Kuchenbuch, Thomas, ed. *Maske und Kothurn: Internationale Beiträge zur Theater, Film und Medienwissenschaft.* 54, Heft 1-2. Wien: Böhlau Verlag, 2008.

Linder, Maud. *Le Dieux du cinéma muet: Max Linder.* Paris: Éditions Atlas, 1992.

---. *Max Linder était mon père.* Paris: Flammarion, 1992.

Marie, Michel and Laurent Le Forestier, eds. *La Firme Pathé Frères, 1896-1914.* Paris: Association française de recherche sur l'histoire du cinéma, 2004.

Massa, Steve. *Lame Brains and Lunatics: The Good, the Bad and the Forgotten of Silent Comedy.* Albany, GA: BearManorMedia, 2013.

---. *Slapstick Divas: The Women of Silent Comedy.* Albany, GA, BearManor Media, 2017.

Mathiesen, Snorre Smári. *Max Linder: Father of Film Comedy.* Albany, GA: BearManorMedia, 2018.

Mitry, Jean. *Max Linder.* Anthology du Cinema #16. Supplément à l'Avant-Scène du Cinéma, No. 60, June 1966.

Pathé: Premier empire du cinéma. Paris: Centre Georges Pompidou, 1994.

Robinson, David. *Chaplin: The Mirror of Opinion*. London: Secker & Warburg, 1983.

Salmon, Stéphanie. *Pathé: À la conquête du cinéma, 1896-1929*. Paris: Éditions Tallendier, 2014.

Smith, Michael Glover and Adam Selzer. *Flickering Empire: How Chicago Invented the U. S. Film Industry*. London: Wallflower Press, 2015.

Spears, Jack. *Hollywood: The Golden Era*. NY: A. S. Barnes and Co., 1971.

Steiner, Gertraud. *Film Book Austria: The History of the Austrian Film from Its Beginnings to the Present Day*. Vienna: Medium Owner, 1997.

Stoullig, Edmond. *Les Annales du théâtre et de la musique*. Paris: Librairie Paul Ollendorff, 1905. 326-328.

Ushihara, Kiyohiko. *Eiga Mangekyo (Movie Kaleidoscope)*. Chuo-Bijutsu-sha Publishing, 1927.

Vardac, A. Nicholas. *Stage to Screen: Theatrical Method from Garrick to Griffith*. NY: Benjamin Blom, 1968.

Von Dassanowsky, Robert. *Austrian Cinema: A History*. Jefferson, NC: McFarland & Co., Inc., 2005.

Vincendeau, Ginette. *Stars and Stardom in French Cinema*. London: Continuum, 2000.

Periodicals: Trade Publications

The Bioscope
Camera!
Caras y Caretas (Buenos Aires)
El Cine
Ciné Journal
Cine-Mundial
Cinémagazine
Comoedia
Dramatic Mirror
Erste Internationale Film-Zeitung
Essanay News

Exhibitors Herald
Le Figaro
Film Daily
The Film Index
Film-Kurier
Der Filmbote
Die Filmwelt
The Exhibitors Trade Review
L'Intransigeant
Kinematograph and Lantern weekly
Kinematographische Rundschau
Kino-Journal
Lichtbild-Bühne
Mon Ciné
Motion Picture Magazine
Motion Picture News
Motography
Moving Picture World
Photoplay
Picture-Play
Le Rappel
Les Spectacles
Variety

Periodicals: Newspapers and Magazines
A Capital
Arbeiter-Zeitung
Budapesti Hírlap
Chicago Tribune
Cleveland Plain Dealer
La Correspondencia de España

Délmagyarország
Diario de Tarragona
Le Gaulois
Gil Blas
El Globo
The Guardian
Hanford Kings County Sentinel
L'Humanité
El Imparcial
It
Le Journal
Le Journal Amusant
Le Journal du Dimanche
Kleine Volks-Zeitung
Kurier Warszawsk
Latwija
La Liberté
Los Angeles Daily News
Los Angeles Daily Times or *Los Angeles Times*
Il Messaggero
Neues Wiener Journal
New York Telegraph
New York Times
Nieuws van den dag voor Nederlandsch-Indië
Paris-Soir
La Petite Gironde
Le Petit-Journal
Philadelphia Inquirer
Le Populaire
La Presse
La Rampe
Ranneye Utro

Reichspost
Russkoye Slovo
Segdonia
Stol. Molva
Sunday Times
Vossische Zeitung
Washington Post
Wellington [Kansas] Daily News

Periodicals: Journal Articles

Bren, Frank. "Ripple Effect: The Theatrical Life of Max Linder," *National Theatre Quarterly*, 25:3 (August 2009). 241-254.

"Le Dossier du mois: Max Linder," *Cinema 64*, No. 82 (January 1964): 34-67.

Goudet, Stéphane. "Le jeux de miroir de Max Linder," *Positif*, 624 (February 2013): 78-80.

Grisham, William. "Those Marvelous Men and Their Movie Machines: Chicago's Film Pioneers Delighted Audiences with One-Reelers More Than 50 Years Ago and Turned Our Town into the Country's Movie Capital," *Chicago Tribune Magazine*, (December 7, 1969): 42-49.

Jeanne, René, "Max Linder et le théâtre," *Revue d'histoire du théâtre*, 2 (April-June 1965). 164-177.

Kessler, Frank "Pathé vs. Pathé, Exhibit A: Reading an Archival Document," *Film History*, 25: 1-2 (2013). 118-129.

Seguin Vergara, Jean-Claude, "Max Linder," *grimh.org* (1999-2020). Available at https://www.grimh.org/index.php?option=com_content&view=article&layout=edit&id=2716&lang=fr#2.

Shail, Andrew. "Max Linder and the Emergence of Film Stardom." *Early Popular Visual Culture* 14.1 (Spring 2016): 55-86.

Spears, Jack. "Max Linder Was the Motion Picture's First Truly International Star," *Films in Review*, XIV: 5 (1965), 272-291.

Tsvian, Yuri. "Russia, 1913: Cinema in the Cultural Landscape," *Griffithiana*, XXVII, No. 50 (May 1994). 124-147.

Websites

Lack, Roland-François. "Où est Max?" the cinetourist.net (n. d.). Available at https://www.thecinetourist.net/wheres-max.html.

Renken, Georg. maxlinder.de (October 2019). Available at https://web.archive.org/web/20190613213123/http://www.maxlinder.de/startdeutsch.htm.

Index

Numbers in **bold** indicate photographs

A

À Qui mon coeur? (1909) 270
Aghion, Max 75
Ah! Quel malheur d'avoir un gendre (1907) 232
Aimé par sa bonne (1909) **41**, 265
Allen, Alta 141, 142, 145, 147
Allied Corporation (European division of United Artists) 158, 159, 160, 169, 170
Ambigu-Comique theater 18, 19
Amour et fromage (1910) 282
Amour tenace (1912) 314
Amoureux de la femme à barbe (1909) 267
Amoureux de la teinturière (1912) 303
Anderson, G. M. 94-96
Âne jaloux, L' (1912) 307
Anglais tel que Max le parle, L' (1913) 334
Arbuckle, Roscoe 147, 149, 150, 165 (n.45)
Arcachon, France 46, 47, 50
Armoire, L' (1907) 242
Au music-hall (1907) 231
Au Secours! (1924) 173-176, 177, 357
Avant et après (1909) **42**, 273

B

Balieff, Nikita 72
Bandit par amour (1912) 305
Banky, Vilma 180, **185, 186, 188**

Barcelona, Spain 50, 51, 52, **53**, 54, 57, 326
Barelly, Andrée 135, **136**, **137**
Bargy, Le 19
Baromètre de la fidelité, Le (1915) 345
Baron, Gabriel (maternal grandfather) 9
Baron, Jeanne Carteyron (maternal grandmother) 9
Be My Wife (1921) **145**, 146-147, 151, 166 (n. 68), 175, 355
Bébe encombrant, Un (1908) 256
Berlin, Germany 58, 59, 60, 75, 78, 335
Bernard, Armand **137**
Bernard, Charles 124 (n. 7; n. 13)
Bernard, Raymond 133, 136, 137, 138
Bernard, Tristan 133, 134
Billet doux, Le (1913) 328
Bobo mal place, Un (1909) 265
Bonne pour monsieur, un domestique pour madame, Une (1910) **45**, 275
Bordeaux, France 15-18, 39-40, 78, 97, 99
Bordoni, Irene 76
Boxeur par amour (1912) 55, 315
Bryan, Vincent 153, 165 (n.5)
Budapest, Hungary 63, 67
Buffon (hospital) 81

C

Caillard, Adrien 15, 18, 19
Carpentier, Georges 63, 151
Carteyron, Jeanne Bertrand (maternal great-grandmother) 9
Carteyron, Matthieu (maternal great-grandfather) 9
Caught in a Cabaret (1914) 136
Cavalieri, Lina 105, 150
Cavernes, France 9, **10**, **11**, 12, 46, 193, 204
C'est Papa qui a pris la purge (1906) 231
C'est pour les Orphelins: Á l'improviste (1916) 349
C'est le tango qui est la cause de ça (sketch) 65, 67, 75
Chamonix, Switzerland 48, **78**, **79**, 89, 170, 173, 342, 348
Champion de Boxe (1910) 288
Chapeau de Max, Le (1913) 329
Chaplin, Charles (Charlie) 24, 32, 34, 69, 76, 83, 93, 94-96, 101, 109, 115-**117**, 120-123, 126 (n. 81 & 86), 127 (n. 94; n. 106), 129, **130**, 136-137, 139-140, 142, 143, 149, 151, **154**, 155, 158, 161, 164 (n. 1), 165 (n. 45; n. 56), 166 (n. 57), 177, 187, 189, 198
Chaplin, Sydney 96, 140, 164 (n. 1)
Chasseur de Chez Maxim's, Le (unfinished project) 194
Chaussure trop étroite (1907) 235

Chevalier Barkas, Le (unfinished project) 191, 192, 193, 194
Ciné Max Linder 124 (n. 13), **131**, 132, 133
cinema-theater 20, 21, 30, 36, 84 See also *film-sketch, film joué, film raccordé*
Coiffeur par amour (1914) 344
Collins, Mae 149, 154
Comédie française 18
Comment Max Linder fait le tour de monde (1910) 291
Conquête, Une (1909) 267
Conservatoire municipal de Bordeaux 16
Consultation improvisée (1908) 263
Contrexéville (hospital) 81, 97
Coralie et Cie 144-146
Coup de foudre, Le (1908) 260
Crabit, Jean Marie Pierre (brother-in-law) 9
Crabit, Marcelle Leuvielle (sister) 10, 13, 18, 46, 89, 198
Création de la serpentine (1908) 261
Cross-country original, Un (1910) 289
Cuisinier par amour (1914) 343

D

Daniel, Viora 147
Davis, Al 142
DeBain, Henri 134, 139
Débuts de Max Linder au cinématographe, Les (1910) 290
Débuts d'un aéronaute, Les (1907) 238
Débuts d'un patineur, Les (1907) 33, 235
Débuts d'un yachtman, Les (1913) 322
Deed, André 33, 36
de Limur, Jean 158
Delluc, Louis 138
DeMille, Cecil B. 150
Député (sketch) 76, 84
de Rochefort, Charles 65, 192
Deslys, Gaby 77
Deux août 1914 (1916) 83, 124 (n. 1), 347
Deux grandes douleurs (1908) **40**, 254
Diamant-Berger, Henri 133, 137, 162, 164 (n.1), 354
Dick est un chien savant (1914) 344
Dione, Rose 147
Domestique hypnotiseur, Le (1907) 239
Dorian, Charles 142
Drame à Séville, Un (1907) **36, 37**, 240
Duel de Max, Le (1913) 44, 65, 141, 327

Duel de monsieur Myope, Le (1910) 44, 283
Dupuy, Jean 172

E

Éffets des pilules, Les (1910) 43, **44**, 286
Elle est de . . . [sketch] (1914) 75
Empoisonneuse, L' (1907) 232
En Bombe (1909) 271
Enlèvement en hydroaéroplane, L' (1912) 318
Entente cordiale (1912) 55, 316
Épreuve difficile, Une (1910) 282
Essanay studios 88, 89, 93-94, **95**, 96-97, **98**, 99-101, **102**, 104-106, 108, 110-113, 115-118, 120-121, 124 (n. 12; n. 13), 131, 350, 351, 352
Étudiants de Paris, Les (1906) 228
Exploits d'un fou, Les (1907) 241
Exploits du jeune Tartarin, Les (1909) 274

F

Fairbanks, Douglas 132, **153**, 157, 159, 160, 316
Femme sandwich, La (1908) 248
Fiancé trop occupé, Un (1908) 258
film-joué 36
films raccordés 61 (n. 17), 219
film sketch 36, 48, 49, 52, 65 *See also cinema-theater; film joué; film raccordé*
Florey, Robert 13, 143, 154, **155**, 163
Flûte merveilleuse, La (1910) 289
Fuite de Gaz, La (1912) 312

G

Gance, Abel 151, **152**, 172, 173, **174**, 175, 176, 177, 178, 192, 200 (n. 22), 357
Gasnier, Louis 28, 43, 86
Gaumont, Léon 192

H

Hasard et l'amour, Le (1914) 65, 347
Hayakawa, Sessue 150
Hennequin, Maurice 144-145
Hervil, René 179, 182

I

Idée d'Apache (1907) 236
Idylle à la Ferme (1912) 310
Ingénieux attentat, L' (1910) **47**, 280
Irvine, Clarke 144, 151, 156

J

Jalousie (1912) 319
Je voudrais un enfant (1910) 277
Jeanne, René 18, 20-21
Jeffries, James 45
Jeffries contre Johnson by Tom Pender (sketch) 45
Jeune fille romanesque (1910) 275
Jeune homme timide, Un (1908) 255
Joffre, Jean 134
Johnson, Jack 45
Joinville-le-Pont 22, 23, **24**, 28, 35, 42, **43**, 191
Jomier, Georges **154**, 156, 166 (n. 85)
Joy, Leatrice 149, **154**, 156
Julot va dans le monde (1906) 229

K

K-E-S-E (Kleine-Edison-Selig-Essanay) 96, 105, 107, **111**, 120
Keystone studios 93, 94, 124 (n. 13)
Kiev, Ukraine 74
Kyrelor, bandit par amour (1910) **56**, 281

L

Lasky, Jesse 142, 150
Lausanne (Ouchy/Lausanne), Switzerland 83, 86, 87, 88, 89, 129, 133, 144, 170, 177
Légende de Polichinelle, Le (1907) 28, **35**, 237
Légion d'Honneur 139, 336
Leloir, Louis 18
Lender, Marcelle 18
Leuvielle, Gabriel (see Linder, Max)
Leuvielle, Gérard Laurent (brother) 9, 10, 12, 25 (n. 2), 198
Leuvielle, Marcel (Jean) (father) 9, 12, 13, 39, 46, 139
Leuvielle, Maurice (brother) 198, 203, 204, 205
Leuvielle, Suzanne Baron (mother) 9-10, 12, 46

Lèvres collées (1906) 229
Linder, Maud Lydie Marcelle Leuvielle (daughter) 3-5, 9, 10, 11, 12, 15, 18, 23, 37, 171,
    191, 193, 194, 196, 198, 203-204, **205**, 222, 224, 235, 287, 291, 296, 320, 326, 327,
    346, 348, 350, 356
Linder, Max (Leuvielle, Gabriel)
    Childhood in Cavernes and St. Loubès 9-14
    Education in Bordeaux 15-18
    Name change to Linder 18
    On stage in Paris (plays and playwrights in chronological order)
        Romanesques (Edmond Rostand) 17
        Par droit de conquête (Legouge) 17
        Les Ouvriers (L. Manuel) 17
        Les Fourberies de Scapin 18
        Le Crime d'Aix (Albert Pujol) 18
        Le Barbier de Séville 18
        Les Précieuses ridicules 18
        Le Tour du monde d'un enfant de Paris (Ernest Morel) 18
        La Conquête de l'air (Camille Audigier and Paul Géry) 20
        Les Deux orphelines (Adolphe d'Ennery and Eugène Cormon) 20
        Paillasse (Adolphe d'Ennery et Marc Fournier) 20
        La Belle Marsellaise (Pierre Berton) 20
        Les Aventures de Thomas Plumepatte (Gaston Maro) 20
        La Fleuriste des halles, (Henry Demesse) 20
        La Bande à Fifi (Gardel-Hervé and Maurice Varret) 20
        Crime d'un fils, (Maurice Lefèvre) 20
        Le Régiment, (Jules Mary and Georges Grisier) 20
        La Grande Famille, (Arquillière) 20
        L'Auvergnate (M. Meynet and Marie Geffrey) 21
        Pour sa patrie, (Marquis de Castellane) 21
        La Tourmente (Maurice Landay) 21
        La Goualeuse (Gaston Marot and Alevy) 21
        La Main droite (André Barde) 22
        La Revue de centenaire (Paul Gavault, P. L. Flers, and Eugène Héros) 28
        Les Deux écoles (Alfred Capus) 30
        Passez muscade! (Georges Lignereaux and Maxime Bertrand) 30
        Le Roi, (Gaston-Arman de Caillavet, Robert de Flers and Emmanual
            Arène) 30, 39-40
        La Chance du mari (Gaston Arman de Caillavet and Robert de Flers) 41
        Et aïe donc!,(Rip and Paul Ardot) 41
        Vive Paris! (Maurice Millot) 44
    Dandy persona 31-33
    Appendicitis 45-46
    Military Service (WWI) 78-82
    Notice of death in Aisnes 80-81
    Stage accidents 55, 65
    Fall in the Alps 170
    Kidnapping of Ninette Peters 171-172

Marriage 176-177
  Attempted suicide 183-184
  Death 196
Lisbon, Portugal 55, 57
Love, Bessie **154**, 155
Lycée de Talence **15**, **16**
Lyon, Wanda 134, **135**

M

Ma Montre retarde (1908) 245
Madame a ses vapeurs (1907) 236
Madieu, Léon 83, 87, 88
Madrid, Spain 52, 54, 57
Maitresse de piano, La (1908) 253
Mal de mer, Le (1912) 308
Malle au mariage, La (1912) 308
Malo, Georges 39
Malone, Nell 194, 203
Mansfield, Martha 104, 111, **112**, **114**, 118, 125 (n. 31 & 32), 126 (n. 74)
Mari de la doctoresse, Le (1907) 243
Mari jaloux (1914) 337
Mari peu veinard, Un (1908) 261
Mariage Américain, Un (1909) 268
Mariage au puzzle, Un (1910) 287
Mariage au téléphone (1912) 52, 315
Mariage forcé (1914) 340
Mariages imprévus (1913) 323
Massard, Armand 28, 42, 45, 52, 82, 144
Massard, Émile 82
Maupain, Ernest 103, 106, 350-351
Mauvaise vue (1910) 278
Max à Monaco (1914) 65, 78, 341
Max a trouvé une fiancée (1911) 296
Max a un duel (1911) 44, 299
Max and the Russian girl student (1913) MAKS I KURSISTKA 72, 74, 335
Max asthmatique (1914) 78, 341
Max au couvent (1914) 78, **85**, 343
Max cherche une fiancée (1910) 47, 294
Max cocher de fiacre (1912) 309
Max collectionne les chaussures (1913) 332
Max Comes Across (1917) 100, **103**, **106**, 107, 108, 131, 350
Max décoré (1914) 336
Max, der Zirkuskönig (1924) See *Der Zirkuskönig* (1924)
Max devrait porter des bretelles (1917) 89, 124 (n. 9), 219, 354
Max émule de Tartarin (1912) 314

Max entre deux feux (1917) 83, 89, 124 (n. 9), 131, 353
Max est charitable (1913) 323
Max est distrait (1910) 43, 285
Max et Jane veulent faire du théâtre (1911) See *Max veut faire du théâtre* (1911)
Max et la doctoresse (1914) 338
Max et le sac (1917) 89, 124 (n. 9), 167 (n. 95), 350
Max et les crêpes (1913) 325
Max et l'espion (1917) 89, 124 (n. 9), 131, 349
Max et l'inauguration de la statue (1913) **66**, 320
Max et sa belle-mère (1911) 65, 297
Max et sa belle-mère (1914) 78, **79**, 342
Max et son chien Dick (1912) 303
Max fait de la photographie (1913) 329
Max fait des conquêtes (1913) 331
Max fait du ski (1910) 284
Max hypnotisé (1910) 240, 294
Max illusioniste (1913) 332
Max in a Taxi (1917) 117-118, **119**, 120, 126 (n.87), 131, 352
Max joue le drame (1914) 339
Max lance la mode (1911) 302
Max Linder and Mrs. Prokhorov (1913) (MAKS LINDER I G-ZHA PROKHOROVA) 72, 75, 334
Max Linder contre Nick Winter (1912) **57**, 304
Max Linder en convalescence (1911) **47**, 299
Max Linder Productions 140, 144, 147, 355, 356,
Max Linder pratique tous les sports (1913) 64, 65, 324
Max, maître d'hôtel (1914) 337
Max manque un riche mariage (1910) 295
Max, médecin malgré lui (1917) 86, 89, 124 (n.9), 353
Max n'aime pas les chats (1913) 327
Max ne se mariera pas (1910) 295
Max pédicure (1914) **83**, 253, 336
Max prend un bain (1910) 292
Max professeur de tango (1914) 75, 335
Max reprend sa liberté (1912) 302
Max se marie (1911) 65, 297
Max se trompe d'étage (1910) 286
Max toréador (1912) 52, 64, 326
Max veut faire du théâtre (1911) 44, 211 (n. 62), 301
Max veut grandir (1912) 317
Max victime de la main qui étreint (1915) 86, 166 (n. 74), 348
Max virtuose (1913) 330
Max Wants a Divorce (1917) 111, **112, 113, 114**, 131, 351
Mayakovsky, Vladimir 69, 70
Médaille de sauvetage, La (1913) 331
Merindol, Flavienne 134, **137**
Mes voisins me font danser (1908) 257

Mon chien rapporte (1910) 290
Mon pantalon est décousu (1908) 244, 295
Monaco, Prince Albert of 150
Montana, Bull 157
Monte Carlo, Monaco 49, 65, 89
Moscow, Russia 70-72, 74, 334, 335
Muratore, Lucien 105, 125 (n. 38), 150

N

Napierkowska, Stacia 50, 52, **53**, 58, 313, 349
N'embrassez pas votre bonne (1913) 333
Nice, France 89, 169, 170-172, 173, 200 (n. 5)
Nonguet, Lucien 28, 43
Nourrice par nécessité (1907) 233
Nuit agitée, Une (1912) 306

O

Obsession de la belle mère, L' (1908) 251
Obsession de l'équilibre, L' (1908) 246
Odessa, Ukraine 74
Oh! Les femmes (1912) 309
Olympia theater 44, 45, 48, 63-64
On demande un gendre à l'essai (1908) 259
Oncle à héritage, L' (1908) 258

P

Pacte, Le (1910) 276
Palais-Galien 16, **17**
Palerme, Gina 174
Pari original, Un (1912) **60**, 311
Paris Conservatoire 18
Pathé, Charles 22, 23, 24, 27, 46, 86-87, 88, 93, 124 (n. 1; n. 7), 133
Pathé, Émile 22, 27, 28
Pathé, Suzanne 22, 23
Pathé, Théophile 22, 23, 24
Pathé-Frères **27**, 28, 33, 35, 40, 41, 42, 43, 44, 49, 50, 58, 60, 61 (n. 13), **64**, 66, 74, 77, 78, 80, 81, 86, 89, 90 (n. 25), 97, 121, 124 (n. 13), 131, 169, 187, 188, 191, 218, 219-220, 227
Pédicure par amour (1908) 252
Pédicure par amour [sketch] 52, 55, 59, 65, 67, 69, 72
Peintre par amour (1912) 311

Pendu, Le (1906) 33, **34**, 43, 230
Pendu, Le (1914) **84**, 339
Percy, Thelma 142
Pérégrinations d'une puce, Les (1908) 250
Péripéties d'une amant, Les (1907) 238
Peters, Hélène Jeanne "Ninette" 170, 171, 172, 176, **178**, 183, **190**, 191, 193, 194, 196, **197**, 198, 204
Peters, Mathilde 170, 171, 172, 193, **197**, 198, 202, 204
Petit café, Le (1919) 133, **134, 135, 136, 137, 138**, 139, 354
Petit café, Le (play) 133, 134
Petit jeune homme, Le (1909) 37, 42, 266
Petit roman (1912) 318
Petite rosse (1909) 247, 269
Petitmaître, Albert 81, 99, 156
Peur de l'eau, La (1912) 319
Pickford, Mary 83, 159
Pitou, bonne d'enfants (1907) 240
Plaisirs du soldat, Les (1907) **39**, 243
Pour un collier (1907) 28, **30**, 233
Premier cigare d'un collégien, Le (1908) 227, 246
Premier rendez-vous, Le (1909) 273
Première sortie (1905) 24, 227, 246, 274

Q

Que peut-il avoir? (1912) 306
Quel est l'assassin? (1910) 292

R

Radio Paris "Festival du cinema" broadcast 192
Ralston, Jobyna **157**
Rankin, Caroline 147, 157-158
Rastrelli, Amédée 97, 124 (n. 10)
Regamy, Frédéric 35
Réjane, Gabrielle 21
Rencontre imprévue (1905) 28, 228
Rendez-vous, Le (1912) 321
Représentation au cinéma, Une (1910) 279
Retour inattendu (1908) **41**, 250
Revolver arrange tout, Le (1910) 284
Rivalité (1913) 325
Robertson-Cole Productions 140, 147, 151
Rochester, New York 12
Rome, Italy 84-85, 173

Roméo se fait bandit (1909) 166 (n.74), 270
Ruse de Mari (1907) 234
Ruse de Mari (1910) 279

S

Saint-Loubès, France 9, 12, 15, 39, 139, **197**, 198
St. Petersburg, Russia 32, 67, **69**, 70
Saison de Max 63
Sam Goldwyn Productions 151, 153
Sechan, André 76, **77**
Sennett, Mack 33, 134, 165 (n. 45)
Serment d'un prince, Le (1910) 278
Seven Years' Bad Luck (1921) 66, **141**, 142, **143**, 144, 147, 165 (n. 31), 169, 175, 205, 355
Smith, Norwood 156
Société de Sainte-Cécile 16, **17**
Soldat par amour (1910) 277
Sosie, Le (1915) 346
Soulier trop petit, Le (1910) 236, 293
Spoor, George K. 93, **94**, 95-6, 97, 99, 101, 105, 121
Spoor, H. A. 97
Stedman, Lincoln 147
Succés de la prestidigitation, Le (1912) 307
Surprises de l'amour, Les (1909) 269
Suspension, La (1908) 247
Szöreghi, Julius **185**, **186**, 188

T

Théâtre des Arts de Bordeaux 16
Théâtre des Variétés 19, 22, 28, 30, 41, 77
Theakston, Jack 125 (n. 27)
Three Must-Get-Theres, The (1922) 153, **157**, 158, **159**, **160**, **161**, 165 (n. 45), 356
Tic nerveux contagieux, Un (1908) 255
Tillie's Punctured Romance (1914) 136
Timidité guérie par le sérum, La (1910) 274
Tiomkin, Dmitri 32, 61 (n. 8), 69
Tourneur, Maurice 140, 142, 143, 144
Tout est bien qui finit bien (1910) 280
Trés moutarde (1914) 132, 345
Tribulations d'un neveu, Les (1908) 264
Trop aimée (1910) 287
Tulipe merveilleuse, La (1915) 124 (n. 1), 346

Turin (Torino), Italy 81, 84
Turpin, Ben 150

U

Unione Cinematografica Italiana 173
Universal studios 140, 147

V

V-S-L-E (Vitagraph, Lubin, Selig, Essanay) 96
Vacances de Max, Les (1913) 64, 76, 326
Valabrégue, Alain 144, 145, 146
Valentino, Rudolph 149
Varenne-St. Hilaire, France 76
Veine de bossu, Une (1908) 252
Vengeance du bottier, La (1909) 272
La vengeance du domestique (1912) 312
Vertueux jeune homme, Le (1908) 262
Vevey, Switzerland 193
Victime du quinquina (1911) 300
Victorine studios, La 170, 200 (n. 5)
Vienna, Austria 58, 169, 179, 180, **181**, 188, 189
Vincennes, France 22, 28, 35, **38**, 39, 80, 191
Violet, Édouard Émile 124 (n. 10), 182
Vita-Film Studios (Rosenhügel) 178, **179**, **180**, 182, 183, 184, 190, 200 (n. 31), 357
Vive la vie de garçon (1908) 249
Voisin, voisine (1911) 47, **67**, 298
Voleur mondain, Le (1909) 40, 271
Voyage de noces (1912) 313

W

"Wah" **110**, 111, 112, 115, 126 (n. 63)
Warsaw, Poland 74
Welch, Wilton 142
White, Leo 101, **102**
Woman of Paris (1923) 137

Z

Zecca, Ferdinand 28, 35, 87, 88, 91 (n. 40)
Zirkuskönig, Der (1924) **182**, **183**, **184**, 187, **188**, **189**, **190**, 357

Part II: Filmography by Catherine Cormon

Preface

Establishing a list of films in which Max Linder appears as an actor is not an easy task. Many researchers have already attempted it, with varying success. The pioneers had to rely on fewer sources than available nowadays, and their attempts at being exhaustive sometimes introduced errors. The followers have occasionally reproduced the pioneers' mistakes, thereby giving them the status of facts, and increasing the confusion. Most written and online sources available today are, by and large, a big mess.

Max Linder's first appearances on the screen happened in a time when film production companies functioned a bit like theater troupes, with parts distributed among a group of actors who would get a leading role one week and a bit part the next week. Occasionally, even several actors would play the same character in different scenes of a film. Characters existed only in a generic form ("the student", "the lover", etc.) and actors were not named on the publicity material, let alone on the screen. Furthermore, a lot of films from this period have been lost. This makes the first years of his career particularly difficult to document.

At the same time that the film industry began to stabilize with established distribution circuits, sedentary screening venues, character series and international releases, Max Linder built a screen persona which made him extraordinarily famous, and therefore more systematically referenced. This, however, does not make the task simpler. Some of the films were re-made several times by the same or a different production company, with the same or an altered storyline. Max Linder's employer Pathé Frères also re-released their own films on different formats (28mm and 9,5mm), often under new titles. Other distributors made pirate copies under different titles. Look-alikes appeared in films with similar plots. And to make everything even more complicated, film archivists of the early years did not always have equipment to watch the fragile original films when documenting them and tended to attribute to Max Linder any film with a French comic wearing a mustache.

While this filmography is based on many sources, it is mostly indebted to the extraordinary research conducted by Georg Renken and published on his website www.maxlinder.de – the author would like to refer the readers to this source for a much more in-depth picture of Max Linder's career, both for theater and cinema activities, as well as for their critical and public reception. The research possibilities laying in the information Georg Renken has gathered are endless and absolutely fascinating. Sadly, Georg's death in October 2019 has caused the demise of his website, but it is still possible to consult it on www.archive.org.

The information listed here has been limited to a very simple template. The goal is threefold: first to minimize the chances for inaccuracies (in particular, many sources give mistaken information on the question of who directed the films, or who acted in them), secondly to leave space for detailed contents description in order to facilitate identification of film prints, and thirdly to emphasize the chronology of releases. Films have been numbered with a series number starting anew every year, to accommodate future new discoveries without invalidating more than one year of numbering. The numbering is based on the first published trace of each film, be it in the press or in a trade catalog.

Another choice was to reproduce here the most detailed content description made at or around the time of the first release, instead of providing new ones. A lot of the films are either difficult to access, incomplete, altogether lost, or have been modified since the first release, which would have made it difficult to write new accurate contents descriptions. Using period sources as much as possible also ensures a relative homogeneity of style.

The period 1905-1914 saw great changes in film making. Scrambles of chronology may interfere with the interpretation and evaluation of narrative, acting and shooting styles. It is therefore important to put the films in a precise context before undertaking their analysis. Some films have obviously been shot many months before their release (see the winter sport films released in August); others even appear to have been first held back --possibly as unworthy-- and later released when the production flow had dried-up (see *Max devrait porter des bretelles* in 1917, which a critic of the time qualified as "pieces of old films put together haphazardly"). Furthermore, considering that Max Linder's career before WWI contains two long breaks (late 1908-early 1909 and late 1910-early 1911), it is also possible that some of the films released during or near the end of his absence were older productions.

Paying special attention to the chronology of the releases can also give an interesting picture of the distribution practices of the time: many films appear to have been released on foreign markets ahead of the French domestic market, and Max's fame was established abroad before he became a celebrity in his own country.

Thanks to Georg Renken's research, we also know that Max Linder's theater shows were often containing "films raccordés" ("connected films"), often showing his difficulties in reaching the theater before he made his appearance live on the stage. These films were by their very nature more fragile than others, being probably unique copies modified to fit every city the show would be played in and are not known to survive. Due to their fluctuating nature and their lack of documentation, they have not been included here. In the same way, no newsreels featuring Max, or films with imitators of Max have been added in the present list, because these are still largely undocumented and would be more suitable as a separate research subject.

The list of dates attached to each film is limited and based on the following priorities: publication in the French Pathé catalogue, first known screening in

France, first known screening abroad, and eventually first known mention in foreign (trade) press or French press (if prior to the Pathé catalogue). It is not an exhaustive list, nor does it pretend to any exactness, being by nature changeable as research progresses. It aims at giving a first impression of possible release strategies by Pathé on their domestic and foreign markets.

I have also chosen to include a list of archives holding film material on the different titles. To quote the FIAF Treasures of the Film Archives database: **"Inclusion of a title in this list does not guarantee its availability nor completeness. Users should contact individual archives for more information."** This type of information is by nature ephemeral (hopefully, more films will be found as the years go by), and certainly contains many a mis-identified entry. Nevertheless, my position as an employee of a national film archive grants me access to sources of information like historical or unpublished documents, which are not easily available to outside researchers, and therefore worth publishing. Furthermore, the contributions of archivists around the world who have been willing to provide information on the holdings in their collections have been invaluable.

It is my hope that this filmography will enable fellow archivists and collectors to review their holdings, correct mistaken identifications, share information about available copies, however incomplete, and generally render this research obsolete by refining and enriching it.

Acknowledgments

To Lisa Haven for making this publication happen. To Dominique Dugros for his translations. To Gregor Schaefer for his support and understanding.

The saying goes: "We stand on the shoulders of giants", and it is certainly true. I would like to add that we are able to stand because we hold each other's hands. Thank you to my colleagues for sharing their information, and to all who care:

Annette Groschke, Arianna Turci, Brigitte Paulowitz, Caroline Yaeger, Clément Lafite, David Robinson, Deborah Stoiber, Dominique Michalak, Eric Lange, Irene Rivero, Janette Kronegger-Desagnat, Jared Case, Josh Yumibé, Ladislac Cubr, Laurent Guido, Laurent Le Forestier, Livio Jacob, Mariann Lewinsky Sträuli, Markus Wessolowski, Nikolaus Wostry, Prune Berge, Serge Bromberg, Stéphanie Salmon, Uli Ruedel, Vanessa Scharrer.

Thank you to the following institutions for sharing their information: Cineteca del Friuli, Cinémathèque Royale de Belgique, Deutsche Kinemathek, EYE Filmmuseum, Film Archiv Austria, Fédération Internationale des Archives de Films, FIAF Treasures of the Film Archives editors and contributors, Fondation Jérome Seydoux-Pathé, George Eastman Museum, Lobster Films, Österreichisches Film Museum.

There are three persons who cannot receive thanks anymore, but whose memory I would like to honour. First Henri Bousquet, whose transcription and edition of the complete Pathé catalogues have given film archivists and researchers a source that is truly invaluable. Thirty years after the first volume was published, it remains the most important reference on Pathé films. Merci, Monsieur Bousquet. Secondly, Maud Linder, whose tireless efforts to rescue Max Linder's work from oblivion have been both a source of immense joy and a lifelong burden, as her autobiography showed. Chapeau, Maud, and may you rest in peace (though I suspect that wherever you are, you must be chasing Max around to kick his behind). And thirdly to Georg Renken whose extraordinary website on Max Linder has been of the utmost importance to all scholars working on the subject over the last fifteen years. It was the richest source on a silent comedian and director I have ever seen, and a large part of the information gathered here stems directly from it. His research talent was truly exceptional, as well as his generosity in sharing the results. His untimely death is a great loss for the community of silent film lovers. Vielen Dank, Georg.

Sources and abbreviations

[ ]: indicates uncertainty, or additional information
00:04:05 durations are noted in HH:MM:SS
AFI: American Film Institute
ARG-FCA-Bue: Argentina - Fundación Cinemateca Argentina - Buenos Aires
AUS: Australia
AUS-NFSA-Can: Australia - National Film and Sound Archive - Canberra
AUT: Austria
AUT-FAA-Wie: Austria - Film Archiv Austria - Wien
AUT-ÖFM-Wie: Austria - Österreichisches Filmmuseum - Wien
b&w: black & white
BEL-CRB-Bru: Belgium - Cinémathèque Royale de Belgique (Cinematek) - Bruxelles
BGR-BNF-Sof: Bulgaria - Bulgarska Nacionalna Filmoteka - Sofia
BNF: Bibliothèque Nationale de France, Paris
Bousquet: Bousquet, Henri: Catalogue Pathé des années 1896 à 1914 (France: Edition Henri Bousquet, 1993-1996)
BRA: Brazil
BRA-CMAM-Rio: Brazil - Cinemateca do Museu de Arte Moderna - Rio de Janeiro
CAN-CQ-Mon: Canada - Cinémathèque Québécoise - Montréal
CAN-LAC-Ott: Canada - Library and Archives Canada - Ottawa / Gatineau
Catalogue Pathé-KOK: Catalogue Pathé-Kok at BNF (undated)
CC: Catherine Cormon
CHE: Switzerland
CHE-CS-Lau: Switzerland - Cinémathèque Suisse - Lausanne
Chirat: Chirat, Raymond: Catalogue des films français de long métrage - Film de fiction 1919-1929 (Toulouse: Cinémathèque de Toulouse, 1984)
Chirat et LeRoy: Chirat, Raymond and Le Roy, Eric: Catalogue des films français de fiction de 1908 à 1918 (Paris: Cinémathèque Française, 1995)
CR: Copyright / Legal deposit
CS: Censorship
CUB-CdC-LaH: Cuba - Cinemateca de Cuba - La Habana

CZE-NFA-Pra: Czechia - Národný Filmový Archiv - Praha
DD: Dominique Dugros
DEU: Germany
DEU-B/F-Ber: Germany - Bundesarchiv/Filmarchiv - Berlin
DEU-DK-Ber: Germany - Deutsche Kinemathek - Berlin
DEU-DFF-Fra: Germany - Deutsches Filminstitut & Filmmuseum - Frankfurt / Wiesbaden
DNK-DFI-Køb: Denmark - Danish Film Institute - København
ESP-FdC-Bar: Spain - Filmoteca de Catalunya - Barcelona
ESP-FdV-Val: Spain - Filmoteca de Valencià - Valencià
ESP-FE-Mad: Spain - Filmoteca Española - Madrid
FIAF TFA db: Fédération Internationale des Archives de Film - Treasures of the Film Archives database
FIN: Finland
Ford: Ford, Charles and Jeanne, René: Dictionnaire Universel du Cinéma (Paris: Robert Laffont, 1970)
fps: frames per second
ft: feet
FRA: France
FRA-CF-Par: France - Cinémathèque Française - Paris
FRA-CdN-Nic: France - Cinémathèque de Nice - Nice
FRA-CdT-Tou: France - Cinémathèque de Toulouse - Toulouse
FRA-CNC-Par: France - Centre National de la Cinématographie - Paris / Bois d'Arcy
FRA-FJSP-Par: France - Fondation Jérôme Seydoux-Pathé - Paris
FRA-GPA-Par: France - Gaumont-Pathé Archives - Paris
FRA-IJV-Per: France - Institut Jean Vigo - Perpignan
FRA-CML: France - Collection Maud Linder
FRA-Lob-Par: France - Lobster Films - Paris
Gaudreault et all: Pathé 1900 - fragments d'une filmographie analytique du cinéma des premiers temps (Québec: Presses de l'Université de Laval, 1993)
GBR: Great Britain
GBR-BFI-Lon: Great Britain - British Film Institute - London
HUN-MNF-Bud: Magyar Nemzeti Filmarchívum - Budapest
ITA: Italy
ITA-CdB-Bol: Italy - Cineteca di Bologna - Bologna
ITA-CdF-Gem: Italy - Cineteca del Friuli - Gemona
ITA-CN-Rom: Italy - Cineteca Nazionale - Roma
ITA-FCI-Mil: Italy - Fondazione Cineteca Italiana - Milano
ITA-MNC-Tor: Italy - Museo Nazionale del Cinema - Torino
JPN-NFAJ-Tōk: Japan - National Film Archive of Japan - Tōkyō
m: meters
mm: milimeters
Magliozzi: Magliozzi, Ronald S.: Treasures from the Film Archives: a catalog of short silent fiction films held by FIAF archives (London: Scarecrow Press, 1988)
Maud Linder: Linder, Maud: Les Dieux du cinéma muet: Max Linder (Paris: Atlas, 1992) / Linder, Maud: Patrimoine Max Linder - Collection de Maud Linder (Paris: unpublished, 2005)
MEX-FUNAM-Mex: Mexico - Filmoteca de la UNAM - México
Mitry: Mitry, Jean: Max Linder (Paris: Anthologie du cinéma, 1966) / Mitry, Jean: Filmographie universelle (Paris: IDHEC, 1964)
NLD: The Netherlands

NLD-EFM-Ams: The Netherlands - EYE Filmmuseum - Amsterdam
NZL-NTSV-Wel: New Zealand - Ngā Taonga Sound & Vision - Wellington
Ö-UM: Österreichisch-Ungarische Monarchie
Pathé dépôt légal: Legal deposit files at BNF
Poisson: Poisson, François: Catalogue général des éditions de films de format 9,5mm en langue française de 1922 à 1986 (Brest: Éditions Cinémathèque de Bretagne, 1997)
PR: Press
Renken: website of Georg Renken www.maxlinder.de - capture by the author in April 2019. As of 2020 this website has disappeared but can still be found on www.archive.org
ROU-ANF-Buc: Romania - Arhiva Nationala de Filme - București
RUS-GFF-Mos: Russia - Gosfilmofond - Moskva
TR-PR: Trade Press
Turconi : 35mm nitrate film frame clippings collected by Italian film historian Davide Turconi (1911-2005). See http://www.cinetecadelfriuli.org/progettoturconi/database.html. Frame clips from the Turconi collection are not mentioned in the list of archives holdings.
SWE-SFI-Sto: Sweden - Svenska Filminstitutet - Stockholm
URY-ANIP-Mon: Uruguay - Archivo Nacional de la Imagen y la Palabra, Sodre - Montevideo
USA: United States of America
USA-AFA-Los: United States of America - Academy Film Archive - Los Angeles (CA)
USA-BkHk: United States of America - Blackhawk Collection (in several archives)
USA-GEM-Roc: United States of America - George Eastman Museum - Rochester (NY)
USA-HFA-Cam: United States of America - Harvard Film Archive - Cambridge (MA)
USA-LoC-Was: United States of America - Library of Congress - Washington (DC)
USA-MoMA-New: United States of America - Museum of Modern Art - New York (NY)
USA-UCLA-Los: United States of America - University of California Los Angeles Film & Television Archive - Los Angeles (CA)

Filmography

General note: all films were produced by Pathé Frères in France, unless otherwise noted.

1905-01
PREMIÈRE SORTIE
110 m = 361 ft = 0:05:20 if at 18 fps
b&w

Première sortie - French release title (original - FRA) - Bousquet
Nächtliche Bummelei - German release title (DEU) - Renken
His First Night Out - English release title (GBR+USA) - Renken
Primera Salida - Spanish listing title [attribution] - FIAF TFA db
Première sortie d'un collégien, La - French listing title (attribution) - Mitry
Erste Rendez-vous, Das - German listing title (attribution) - FIAF TFA db
First Night Out - English listing title [attribution] - FIAF TFA db

In search of some happy time, a young student asks Daddy for some money and is given a 20 franc coin. Considering the offering too small, the young man turns to his more compassionate Mommy, who discretely gives him a bank note. Satisfied, he goes out and meets one of his friends waiting outside a café with two young ladies. We find them in a restaurant, sitting in a private room. Unfortunately, too many libations have led both of them to fall asleep. Faced with such ill-disposed friends, the ladies have left them alone with the bill. The waiter brings the latter, then, being paid, he gives a hand to the more able-bodied man to come down the stairs with the young student, who is pulled up with great effort into a cab that drives him back to his father's house. In the dark, he gropes his way to the dining-room, shoves the still laid table, and makes so much noise that his awakened parents rush in towards their child, who is unable -at least right now- to give any explanation. *(Translation DD from Bousquet nr 1254)*

1905.07 - FRA - TR-PR: Catalogue Pathé - Bousquet
1905.09.03 - USA - Niagara Falls (NY): Lyceum Theater - Renken
1905.10.07 - FRA - Bourges: Cinématographe Texas - Renken

Archives: DEU-DK-Ber; ESP-FdC-Bar; ESP-FE-Mad; FRA-CF-Par; FRA-CML; FRA-CNC-Par; USA-LoC-Was

Note: some sources have mixed PREMIÈRE SORTIE and LE PREMIER CIGARE D'UN COLLÉGIEN (1908-03). This confusion is reflected in the list of archive holdings commonly available.

1905-02
RENCONTRE IMPRÉVUE
85 m = 279 ft = 0:04:07 if at 18 fps
b&w

Rencontre imprévue - French release title (original - FRA) - Bousquet
Unvorhergesehene Begegnung - German release title (DEU) - Renken
Unforeseen Meeting, An - English release title (GBR+USA) - Renken

Father and son are in their study. Both have a love date and would like to go out without the other knowing it. The son finally decides to leave, and then arrives at his mistress' home, who is getting impatient. As soon as he lies in bed, the maid rushes in, introducing Madame's official date. The young woman finds no better solution than to run away and leave the two men to cope with the situation. However, the old man, being sure that what he can see in the bed is the object of his love, hurriedly undresses, then gets into bed while his son jumps out of it and runs away, taking with him the first clothes he can get his hands on. Bewildered, and ignorant of his rival's face, the old man puts on the remaining clothes and runs after the young man who unsuccessfully tries to fit into garments too loose for him. When he recognizes his son attired that way, his anger vanishes and gives way to the sincerest roar of laughter. Both men go away arm in arm.
(Translation DD from Bousquet nr 1271)

1905.08 - FRA - TR-PR: Catalogue Pathé - Bousquet
1906.06.17 - FRA - Dijon: Grand Café de Paris - Renken

Archives: CZE-NFA-Pra

1906-01
LES ÉTUDIANTS DE PARIS
175 m = 574 ft = 0:08:30 if at 18 fps
b&w

Étudiants de Paris, Les - French release title (original - FRA) - Bousquet
Pariser Studenten - German release title (DEU) - Renken
Paris Students - English release title (USA) - Renken
Studenti di Parigi, Gli - Italian [release] title - FIAF TFA db

A good-natured notary who lives in a very remote part of France sends his son to Paris to attend law school. He has given him a letter of recommendation for a young painter who lives in the French capital and enjoys partying. Immediately after arrival, the student is quickly informed by this mentor about the pleasures of the Latin Quarter. Because he doesn't lack funds he doesn't lack friends either. Every day brings a new pleasure: fine dinners at restaurants, heckling at school, student celebrations, and so on, i.e. the Latin Quarter's usual amusements for young men. However, all good things must come to an end: the parents arrive unexpectedly and find their son at the Bullier ballroom in an eccentric realistic quadrille.
1- A father's letter to his son, the student. 2- Parents bid farewell. 3- Departure. 4- Arrival in Paris. 5- The students' hotel. 6- Hotel rooms. 7- A joyful party. 8- The students' restaurant. 9- A romantic affair in the Latin Quarter. 10- The Faculty of Law entrance. 11- Inside the Faculty of Law (heckling). 12- Students' celebration in the Latin Quarter. 13- Students' celebration on Saint Michel boulevard. 14- The student at home. 15- The Harcourt Café. 16- Parents arrive. 17- The Bullier ballroom entrance. 18- Bullier ballroom (eccentric quadrille). *(Translation DD from Bousquet nr 1416)*

1906.05.27 - FRA - Paris: Salle du Trocadéro, Fête de Photo-Ciné-Gazette - Bousquet
1906.06 - FRA - TR-PR: Catalogue Pathé - Bousquet
1906.12.01 - DEU - München: Welt-Kinematograph - Renken

Archives: FRA-CNC-Par; ITA-FCI-Mil

Note: identification as a Max Linder film by Georg Renken, confirmed by Lisa Haven.

1906-02
JULOT VA DANS LE MONDE
75 m = 246 ft = 0:03:38 if at 18 fps
b&w

Julot va dans le monde - French release title (original - FRA) - Bousquet
August geht zum Ball - German release title (DEU) - Renken
Bill Goes to a Party - English release title (GBR+USA) - Renken

In this we see Bill preparing himself for his evening out, and his facial contortions in knotting and adjusting his necktie cause screams of laughter. Immediately on his arrival at the house where the party is held Bill has an argument with the footman and manages to send a bust that is standing on a pedestal in the hall crashing to the floor. When entering the drawing room, he trips over a mat and spreads himself on the floor to the amusement of the remaining guests. Later on, he takes possession of a young lady, and leads her to a secluded spot, where he produces his old pipe and commences to smoke. Then her lover or husband arrives and takes her off, after he has extinguished a table cloth which Bill has set on fire. Bill now returns to the drawing room, where he collides with a waiter carrying a tray, and there is an awful mix-up. Bill extricates himself, and in his hurried retreat backward strikes an old gentleman in the stomach and topples him over. The company show resentment at Bill's behavior, and he decides to withdraw, but not before he smashes all the furniture and ornaments he can find in the hallway. *(Zeehan and Dundas Herald, 1908.10.03, in Renken)*

1906.05.27 - FRA - Paris: Salle du Trocadéro - Bousquet
1906.06 - FRA - TR-PR: Catalogue Pathé - Bousquet
1906.10.20 - DEU - Hamburg [Altona]: Belle-Alliance Theater - Renken

Archives: no film print known to this date

Note: identification as a Max Linder film by Georg Renken based on German press.

1906-03
LÈVRES COLLÉES
50 m = 164 ft = 0:02:25 if at 18 fps
b&w

Lèvres collées - French release title (original - FRA) - Bousquet
Verbundene Lippen - German release title (DEU) - AUT-FAA
Joined Lips - English release title (USA) - Renken

Madame comes in the post office with Victoire, the maid, and begins to put stamps on a huge bundle of letters. Madame fears germs, so she uses poor tired Victoire's tongue as a stamp pad.

Behind them, a man, interested by the scene, looks at the young maid with excitement. This well-intentioned man realizes that this big fresh mouth could be used differently, and when the action is over, he kisses it passionately. However, the glue was strong on her lips and all the spectators' efforts were needed to free them. Everybody will tell you: at the end of her trial, Victoire had a moustache! *(Translation DD from adaptation CC from Catalogue Pathé 1907 at BNF 8-RK-1210)*

1906.11 - FRA - TR-PR: Catalogue Pathé - Bousquet
1906.11.23 - MEX - México: Salón Rojo, Coliseo Nuevo y San Francisco - Renken
1906.12.01 - FRA - Marseille: Imperator Cinéma - Renken

Archives: AUT-FAA-Wie; FRA-CNC-Par; GBR-BFI-Lon

Note: bit part (a client in the post office) - see also 1906 Gaumont: LA FEMME COLLANTE with a similar plot.

1906-04
LE PENDU [1906]
155 m = 508 ft = 0:07:32 if at 18 fps
partially toned

Pendu, Le - French release title (original - FRA) - Bousquet
Moderne Schaukelpartie - German release title (DEU+Ö-UM) - Renken
Jongmensch heeft zich ophangen, Een - Dutch release title (NLD) - NLD-EYE
Attempted Suicide - English release title (USA) - Renken
Man Who Hanged Himself, The - English re-release title (28mm) - DVD publisher (Cinerdistan)
Ahoreado, El - Spanish listing title [attribution] - FIAF TFA db

A young man has decided to hang himself, because his sweetheart's hand is withheld. He chooses a very solid branch, and with shaking hands ties a slipknot: he is guided by some sort of fever. Farewell Sidonie, farewell unfulfilled expectations, farewell! Passing by a few seconds later, a boy suddenly saw two feet, two human feet hanging at eye level. Looking up, he saw a body swaying among the leaves at the end of a rope with frantic and wriggling movements, its swinging arms and hands searching for a place on which to lean. Frightened, he ran away to alert the local authority. The latter arrived rapidly and evaluated the situation. Then he called upon the policemen. Respectful of their chain of command, the policemen referred to their brigadier, who referred to the Police Commissioner, who rapidly arrived on the scene. When he was duly informed of the situation, and all the analyses were done, recorded and commented, the hanged man was untied. He was already cold and he stuck his tongue out horribly in a pain-contorted face. A cyclist offers his pump and the poor self-murdered man's lungs are soon filled with life-saving air; he wriggles and he comes back to life. His ears hear and his eyes see Sidonie. For this is her indeed, and she falls into his arms. The forest's big oak trees then witnessed a very pathetic scene: tears, kisses, joy, and finally the cutting of the rope. *(Translation DD from Bousquet nr 1592)*

1906.11 - FRA - TR-PR: Catalogue Pathé - Bousquet
1906.12.14 - FRA - Paris: Omnia Pathé (soirée d'inauguration) - Bousquet
1907.02.10 - Ö-UM - Graz: Grazer Bioskop - Renken

Archives: BEL-CRB-Bru; FRA-CML; FRA-Lob-Par; ITA-CdB-Bol; ITA-CdF-Gem; NLD-EFM-Ams

Note: See also LE PENDU [1914] (1914-07). Premiered in Paris for the opening of the Omnia-Pathé

theater, accompanied by the homonymous song by Mac-Nab. There exist several other versions of this film, with the same title and different actors. The holdings of the Cineteca del Friuli are unconfirmed (could be the 1914 version).

1906-05
C'EST PAPA QUI A PRIS LA PURGE
[90.5 m = 296 ft = 00:04:24 if at 18 fps]
b&w

C'est Papa qui a pris la purge - French release title (original - FRA) - Bousquet
Kleine Schlaumeier, Der - German release title (DEU+Ö-UM) - GBR-BFI
Daarlig Mave - Danish listing title [attribution] - DNK-DFI

A mother obtains from the chemist some castor oil for her young son. The latter switches cups at breakfast, so that his father unwittingly drinks the medicine. The father becomes distressed while detained by a friend in the street, then manages to find a lavatory. He next relieves himself in some bushes, to the consternation of a courting couple on a park bench; in a news vendor's stall; and finally, in a mortar at the chemist's, where the mother has returned with the son. *(Shotlist GBR-BFI 358672)*

1906 - FRA - TR-PR: Catalogue Pathé - Bousquet
1907.01.23 - FRA - Le Havre: Théâtre Cirque - Bousquet
1908.03 - DEU - Straubing: Neumayers Konzerthalle - Renken

Archives: DNK-DFI-Køb; GBR-BFI-Lon

Note: bit part (the lover on the park bench).

1907-01
AU MUSIC-HALL
100 m = 328 ft = 0:04:51 if at 18 fps
b&w

Au Music-hall - French release title (original - FRA) - Bousquet
Im Musik-Hall - German release title (DEU+Ö-UM) - Renken
At the Music Hall - English release title (GBR) - Renken
En el café concerto - Spanish [release or archive] title (MEX) - print at FRA-CNC
Max au Music-Hall - French [re-release] title - FIAF TFA db

A young man, dressed in evening clothes and top hat, gets out of a cab in front of a music hall entrance. Inebriated, he gives his cigarette as a tip, and then, once seated in a front row box on the front stage right, he drinks and engages in bad behavior. He spits at the usherette, throws the programs away, spoils the magician's trick, sprays water on the female singer, hits a valet, attacks a dummy. The strong Hercules and finally the entire staff succeeds in kicking him out by force. *(Translation DD from CC in film projection, Bologna 2007)*

1907.01 - FRA - TR-PR: Catalogue Pathé - Bousquet
1907.01.26 - FRA - Paris: Omnia Pathé - Renken
1907.10.06 - Ö-UM - Graz: Grazer Bioskop - Renken

Archives: FRA-CNC-Par; ITA-CdF-Gem; MEX-FUNAM-Méx

1907-02
L'EMPOISONNEUSE
70 m = 230 ft = 0:03:24 if at 18 fps
b&w

Empoisonneuse, L' - French release title (original - FRA) - Bousquet
Giftmischerin - German release title (DEU+Ö-UM) - Renken
Phial of Poison, The - English release title (GBR+USA) - Renken
Poison, Le - French listing title (attribution) - Mitry

Their adventurous meetings, their risky relationship, all the emotions of a crime novel, their dreams filled with visions of trial, policemen and jail: everything constituted the basis of their love, enhanced by the threat of losing everything they had. The husband, whose weird illness left the doctors puzzled, was languishing in an adjacent room. One day, he caught the two lovers. She was walking towards him with open arms, she was kissing him lovingly; he was giving her a small bottle that she was at first unwilling to accept. That was like a flash! The slow accumulation of apparently insignificant facts suddenly becomes particularly relevant. He feels as if he has just received a fatal blow. However, he doesn't want his death to benefit the miserable lovers. So, when his duplicitous wife offers him the glass filled with poison, he blows her head off, and then swallows the lethal beverage in a one-shot drink. *(Translation DD from Bousquet nr 1596)*

1907.01 - FRA - TR-PR: Catalogue Pathé - Bousquet
1907.02.10 - Ö-UM - Wien: L. Genis Grand-Bioscop - Renken
1907.03.01 - FRA - Lyon: Le Scala - Bousquet

Archives: no film print known to this date

1907-03
AH! QUEL MALHEUR D'AVOIR UN GENDRE
125 m = 410 ft = 0:06:04 if at 18 fps
b&w

Ah! Quel malheur d'avoir un gendre - French release title (original - FRA) - Bousquet
Nur keinen Schwiegersohn - German release title (DEU+Ö-UM) - Renken
Mother-in-Law's Visit - English release title (GBR+USA) - Renken
Max Linder gaat uit rijden - Dutch listing title (attribution) - NLD-EFM

Well, a letter! Madame, very happy, gives it to her husband who reads it cursorily "My dear daughter, here's a good piece of news! I'm on my way, I'll be very pleased to kiss my son-in-law...". However, "my son-in-law" hated his mother-in-law as deeply as most of sons-in-law hate their mothers-in-law in every civilized country. Whereas his wife rejoices, he tries with melancholy to find out how to rapidly get rid of his difficult mother-in-law. And that should be done in a smooth, polite and gentle way. An idea comes to his mind: he rings the servants and gets their immediate complicity thanks to a 5 Franc coin and expressive mimicry. How good these servants are! He could have convinced them for nothing. The mother-in-law comes in... clownish attire... a she-monkey dressed in lady's clothes... in a touching scene, she shows us how tender she is... before a series of various domestic scenes ensues: the gardener waters her, the maid dusts her, Azor's fleas bite her, she is sprayed in the face by a hose. Eventually, disheveled, puzzled, stunned, she inadvertently falls out of her seat during a car ride. "My son-in-law" enjoys his mother-in-law's mishaps with a malicious innocence and a Machiavellian naivety. The final scene shows the infuriated lady leaving the inhospitable house with all her luggage. *(Translation DD from Bousquet nr 1658)*

1907.02-03 - FRA - TR-PR: Catalogue Pathé - Bousquet
1907.02.23 - FRA - Paris: Omnia Pathé - Renken
1907.05.18 - Ö-UM - Wien: Floridsdorfer Biograph-Theater - Renken

Archives: NLD-EFM-Ams

1907-04
POUR UN COLLIER
110 m = 361 ft = 0:05:20 if at 18 fps
b&w

Pour un collier - French release title (original - FRA) - Bousquet
Um ein Halsband - German release title (DEU) - Renken
All for a Necklace - English release title (GBR+USA) - Renken

A husband desires to buy a necklace for his wife, but the price is too stiff, and the jewels are sent back, leaving the lady in a rather bad temper as a consequence. At a friend's house, the pair notice the necklace on the throat of their hostess. The latter presently sends her maid to put it in her room, and overcome with the desire for possession, the man follows, and is abstracting the necklace when the owner enters. He murders her and goes off with the jewels, and when his wife enters, presents them to her. However, his intense remorse so affects him that he imagines his wife to be his victim, and in terror flings himself from the window. The film ends dramatically as the dying man turns to attract his wife's attention, but she is occupied in inspecting herself and the necklace in the glass and takes no notice of him. *(The Optical Lantern and Kinematograph Journal, 1907.04, in Renken)*

1907.02 - FRA - TR-PR: Catalogue Pathé - Bousquet
1907.04.26 - FRA - Lyon: Le Scala - Bousquet

Archives: FRA-CNC-Par; USA-GEM-Roc

Note: bit part (the jeweller).

1907-05
NOURRICE PAR NÉCESSITÉ
125 m = 410 ft = 0:06:04 if at 18 fps
b&w

Nourrice par nécessité - French release title (original - FRA) - Bousquet
Amme aus Not - German release title (DEU) - Renken
Ama secca por necessidade - Portuguese release title (BRA) - Renken

The interior of a bachelor's apartment, on a binge drinking day. A meeting of boisterous young people, fascinated by wine and women. The host's father barges in among the joyful group and his announcement of cutting funds resonates like setting a cat among the pigeons. No more

money, no more friends, and above all no more women... Suddenly sober, the young man was considering his sad situation when he had an epiphany, thanks to a newspaper article: "Baby-sitters wanted. Please apply...". Given the extreme difficulty for young people to find attractive employment, the young man can be considered very lucky. Thanks to various paddings, and to Victoria, the cook, who willy-nilly gave her blonde wig and her working clothes, the young man transformed himself into a very attractive young baby-sitter. An employment agency, where Parisian babies can select their nannies. Immediately hired, our opportunist nanny begins to work. Various scenes: the newborn's bath time. The nanny catches and ties the small parcel in an obviously unusual way, which provokes loud cries from the poor child. The nanny suddenly freezes, bewildered by the young maid's entrance. The nanny grabs the maid's waist who rapidly runs away. At the same time, Monsieur comes in. He is attracted by the nanny and begins to flirt with her. Chastely looking down, the baby-sitter minces. Madame appears; arguments, protests and various actions ensue. Finally, thanks to Toto's astuteness, the cat is truly out of the bag.
(Translation DD from Bousquet nr 1657)

1907.02 - FRA - TR-PR: Catalogue Pathé - Bousquet
1907.05.01 - FRA - Lyon: Grand Théatre - Renken
1907.07.27 - Ö-UM - Wien: Floridsdorfer Biograph-Theater - Renken

Archives: CHE-CS-Lau; FRA-CNC-Par

Note: identification as a Max Linder film by Georg Renken based on Brazilian press.

1907-06
RUSE DE MARI [1907]
85 m = 279 ft = 0:04:07 if at 18 fps
partially toned

Ruse de mari - French release title (original - FRA) - Bousquet
Pfiffige Gate, Der - German release title (DEU+Ö-UM) - Renken
Artful Husband - English release title (USA) - Renken
Tricking his Wife - English listing title (attribution) - Gaudreault et all: Pathé 1900
Husband's Trickery - English listing title (attribution) - FRA-FJSP

A man leaves home to go for a drink under instructions from his wife not to return late. The wife dozes off and on waking notices that he is late. She sets off for the bar to fetch him. Forewarned of her arrival the man slips out the back way and returns home. Finding he is not in the bar the woman returns to her husband, who pretends he has been in bed all along, then laughs behind her back. *(GBR-BFI nr 304940)*

1907.02 - FRA - TR-PR: Catalogue Pathé - Bousquet
1907.05.03 - FRA - Lyon: Le Scala - Bousquet
1907.05.18 - Ö-UM - Wien: Floridsdorfer Biograph-Theater - Renken

Archives: DNK-DFI-Køb; GBR-BFI-Lon; RUS-GFF-Mos; USA-LoC-Was

Note: bit part (husband's mate at the café)- See also UNE RUSE DE MARI [1910](1910-09).

1907-07
DÉBUTS D'UN PATINEUR
125 m = 410 ft = 0:06:04 if at 18 fps
b&w

Débuts d'un patineur - French release title (original - FRA) - Bousquet
Erster Versuch eines Schlittschuhläufers - German release title (DEU+Ö-UM) - Renken
Unskillful Skater, The - English release title (GBR+USA) - Renken
Max veut patiner - French re-release title (28mm) - Catalogue Pathé-Kok
Max Goes Skating - English listing title (attribution) - FIAF TFA db
Max Learns to Skate - English listing title (attribution) - Magliozzi
Max veut apprendre à patiner - French listing title (attribution) - Maud Linder
Max fait du patinage - French re-release title - Chirat et LeRoy

In the snowy park, an elegantly dressed young man rents ice skates that an employee fits on his feet. He refuses the instructor's help, tries to walk on the ice, falls and falls again, flattening his top hat. He asks for the instructor's assistance and gets a turn on the ice with him. Left alone, he is knocked down by a child, who gets a slap in return. The child's comrades take their revenge by throwing snowballs at the young man, a pursuit ensues that ends in a collision with a lady who falls out of her chair. The young man is carried off the ice where he has his skates removed. He is in tears. *(Translation DD from CC in film projection, Bologna 2007)*

1907.03.23 - FRA - Paris: Omnia Pathé - Renken
1907.04 - FRA - TR-PR: Catalogue Pathé - Bousquet
1907.04.27 - Ö-UM - Wien: Welt-Biograph Theater - Renken

Archives: CZE-NFA-Pra; FRA-CF-Par; FRA-CML; FRA-CNC-Par; FRA-Lob-Par; GBR-BFI-Lon; ITA-CdF-Gem; ITA-MNC-Tor; MEX-FUNAM-Méx; NLD-EFM-Ams; USA-HFA-Cam; USA-AFA-Los; USA-BkHk; USA-GEM-Roc; USA-MoMA-New

Note: re-released 28mm Pathé-Kok nr 21b MAX VEUT PATINER on reel with LES MÉDUSES, total lenght 123 m (= 190 m in 35mm).

1907-08
CHAUSSURE TROP ÉTROITE
130 m = 427 ft = 0:06:19 if at 18 fps
b&w

Chaussure trop étroite - French release title (original - FRA) - Bousquet
Joys of Tight Boots, The - English release title (GBR+USA) - Renken
Zu enge Schuhe - German release title (DEU+Ö-UM) - Renken
Escarpins de Max, Les - French [re-release] title - Chirat et LeRoy

Invited at the Lenglumé's to discuss advantageous marriage projects, Gontran leaves his home in a very excited state. He stops at his shoemaker's, where he unsuccessfully tries on various shoes before finding an elegant pair of evening boots… that rapidly proves less comfortable than he thought. Over dinner, unable to take it any longer, Gontran frees his foot from its vise, and while his toes wriggle like an animal enjoying its recovered freedom, the guests' sense of smell is unpleasantly affected by an unidentifiable odor. Fortunately, cheese has been served. His foot now free, Gontran can concentrate on Miss Lenglumé's dowry. However, Azor, "enticed by the smell", triumphantly brings the fragrant boot to the living room where the guests are reunited for coffee. Chaos and confusion! *(Translation DD from Bousquet nr 1705)*

1907.04 - FRA - TR-PR: Catalogue Pathé - Bousquet
1907.04.12 - FRA - Paris: Omnia Pathé - Bousquet
1907.09.15 - DEU - München: Welt-Kinematograph - Renken

Archives: AUT-ÖFM-Wie; FRA-CF-Par; FRA-CML; FRA-CNC-Par; USA-GEM-Roc

Note: this film has long been mixed-up with LE SOULIER TROP PETIT (1910-32), and this is reflected in the confusion surrounding archives' holdings. Re-released 28mm Pathé-Kok nr 327b CHAUSSURE TROP ÉTROITE, on reel with BIGORNO GARDE MALADE, total length 119 m (= 151 m in 35mm).

1907-09
IDÉE D'APACHE
110 m = 361 ft = 0:05:20 if at 18 fps
b&w

Idée d'apache - French release title (original - FRA) - Bousquet
Hooligan Idea, A - English release title (GBR+USA) - Renken
Verbrecher-Idee - German release title (DEU+Ö-UM) - Renken

In a junk store, "Bibi" and "the Ternes' bully" have just found a little-used policeman uniform, which gives them a brilliant idea. Bibi plays the role of the enemy, whose attractive attitude flatters his ego, while the bully contemplates him with a stupid and vicious look on his face. The two silent and invisible shapes move into the night... While Bibi is on the watch, the bully enters a building whose exits had been examined beforehand... Awakened by the noise, the scared and armed "bourgeois" partially open the door with trembling hands. Heartened by this impressive demonstration of courage, the bully finds a comfortable position and faces them, nonchalantly smoking. The maid runs outside to get the police and meets Bibi, blessing God who placed a policeman on her way when she needed one. Without any hesitation, Bibi enters the building to properly and discreetly complete the robbery and leaves with a reward and his victims' gratitude. *(Translation DD from Bousquet nr 1708)*

1907.04.20 - FRA - Paris: Omnia Pathé - Bousquet
1907.05 - FRA - TR-PR: Catalogue Pathé - Bousquet
1907.08.18 - DEU - München: Welt-Kinematograph - Renken

Archives: FRA-CNC-Par; USA-GEM-Roc

1907-10
MADAME A SES VAPEURS
75 m = 246 ft = 0:03:38 if at 18 fps
b&w

Madame a ses vapeurs - French release title (original - FRA) - Bousquet
Gnädige Frau bei schlechter Laune, Die - German release title (DEU+Ö-UM) - Renken
Madam's Tantrums - English release title (GBR+USA) - Renken

Madame gets up, rather unnerved. Her maid brings a letter, but she is dismissed and the letter is dropped on the floor. A moment later, Madame, seated at her dressing table, gets her hair done by the maid, who is suddenly slapped in the face because she has pulled Madame's hair a little bit too strongly! Madame's lover comes in, kneels and presents her with a bunch of flowers. She pushes him away, throws the flowers in his face, and violently throws him out of the door, knocking over the table and chair, pursues him on the stairs, and even attacks the concierge. The servants, who had already begun to tidy the place, are also dismissed with such violence that the table and chairs are once more knocked over. Madame goes downstairs to the kitchen where she finds the cook asleep, which infuriates her. Then she sits down and has a drink of wine. Now appeased, she returns to the living room, calls her servants, and then moves towards her maid who instinctively steps back, protected by a valet. Madame bursts out laughing, and so does everybody. The storm has passed. *(Translation DD from Bousquet nr 1749)*

1907.06 - FRA - TR-PR: Catalogue Pathé - Bousquet
1907.06.01 - FRA - Paris: Théatre Montparnasse - Renken
1907.07.06 - Ö-UM - Wien: Floridsdorfer Biograph-Theater - Renken

Archives: FRA-CF-Par; FRA-Lob-Par

Note: bit part (the lover).

1907-11
LA LÉGENDE DE POLICHINELLE
410 m = 1345 ft = 0:19:55 if at 18 fps
Pathécolor - 40 m in colors

Légende de Polichinelle, La - French release title (original - FRA) - Bousquet
Kasperles Erlebnisse - German release title (DEU) - Renken
Geschichten über Hanswurst - German release title (Ö-UM) - Renken
Harlequin's Story, A - English release title (GBR+USA) - Renken
Leggenda di Pulcinella, La - Italian [release] title - FIAF TFA db
Vie de Polichinelle, La - French listing title (attribution) - Ford
Legend of Ponchinella - English re-release title (USA) - DVD publisher (Grapevine Video)

The harlequin is an automatic doll in love with a lady figure which resides in the same shop. The lady is bought and carried away, and with the aid of a good fairy "Harlequin" follows, and after various wonderful adventures arrives at the house of the purchaser in time to save her from a death by fire - this circumstance giving a chance for a realistic fire scene which is well utilised. There is also a good scene in which the Harlequin turns the tables on two men who follow him to take him back to the shop. The latter enter a hotel, the doll being hidden in the clock. As the men sit down to the table, a wave of the doll's wand suffices to make the table whisk away and the chairs to go from underneath them. *(Kinematograph and Lantern Weekly, 1907.06.27, in Renken)*

1907.06 - FRA - TR-PR: Catalogue Pathé - Bousquet
1907.06.14 - FRA - Paris: Omnia Pathé - Renken
1907.07.28 - DEU - Stuttgart: Kinematograph-International - Renken

Archives: FRA-CNC-Par; GBR-BFI-Lon; ITA-CdF-Gem; ITA-CN-Rom; JPN-NFAJ-Tōk; USA-BkHk; USA-GEM-Roc; USA-LoC-Was; USA-MoMA-New

Note: film directed by Albert Capellani.

1907-12
LES PÉRIPÉTIES D'UN AMANT
90 m = 295 ft = 0:04:22 if at 18 fps
b&w

Péripéties d'un amant, Les - French release title (original - FRA) - Bousquet
Erlebnisse eines Verliebten - German release title (DEU+Ö-UM) - Renken
Lover's Ill Luck - English release title (USA) - Renken
Gestörtes Rendez-vous, Ein - German listing title (attribution) - FIAF TFA db
Surprise inattendue, Une - French listing title (attribution) - FIAF TFA db
Péripéties d'un amoureux, Les - French listing title (attribution) - Bousquet

A dashing young woman who is bored to death by her old husband sends a note to her young admirer, inviting him to call, and when he receives the love letter, he leaves for her home post haste. The lady in question feigns illness and insists upon being left in solitude to quiet her nerves. The husband, thinking she is very ill, goes out. As soon as he has left, she is as bright and gay as a soubrette and makes hasty preparations to receive her lover. Soon the bashful young man is on the scene and is very cordially received by the hostess. He does not forget, on entering, to tip the maid, who promises to inform him when the old man returns. The amorous young Romeo is soon making desperate love to the queen of his heart, when in rushes the maid, warning them of the husband's return. The woman quickly hides her companion in a wardrobe and turns just in time to welcome her husband. He, however, heard the excitement and accuses her of having some one secreted in the closet. She proclaims her innocence, and just as the old man is about to investigate, out walks her friend disguised as a woman and giving the old fellow a coquettish nudge, departs for the street and liberty. The old man falls on his knees and begs forgiveness from his loved one for daring to suspect her. We next see the young man hastening down the street in a very ladylike manner and followed by a string of old sports who mistake him for a woman. The chase continues for some time and finally, to rid himself of his admirers, he jumps into a baker's cart and pulls the lid down, thereby giving the old men the slip. Finally, we see the baker start off with the cart, and as they near the masquerader's home, he jumps out and rushes in, glad to be back after such a strenuous experience. *(Moving Picture World, 1908.06.27, in Renken)*

1907.07 - FRA - TR-PR: Catalogue Pathé - Bousquet
1907.07.05 - FRA - Paris: Omnia Pathé - Bousquet
1907.10.26 - Ö-UM - Wien: Floridsdorfer Biograph-Theater - Renken

Archives: BEL-CRB-Bru; CZE-NFA-Pra; DEU-DK-Ber; FRA-CNC-Par

1907-13
LES DÉBUTS D'UN AÉRONAUTE
165 m = 541 ft = 0:08:01 if at 18 fps
b&w

Débuts d'un aéronaute, Les - French release title (original - FRA) - Bousquet
Lehrzeit eines Luftschiffers - German release title (DEU+Ö-UM) - Renken
Aeronaut's First Appearance, The - English release title (GBR) - Renken
Glorious Start, A - English release title (USA) - Renken
Max dans les airs - French re-release title (1916) - Bousquet
Débuts d'un aéronaute, Les - French re-release title (28mm) - Catalogue Pathé-Kok
Max in den Lüften - German re-release title (CHE) - Renken
Max aéronaute - French listing title (attribution) - Mitry

Max aviateur - French listing title (attribution) - Mitry
His First Air Trip - English listing title (attribution) - USA-LoC
Prima ascensione di un aeronauta, La - Italian [release] title - ITA-MNC

An amateur aeronaut makes a successful ascension and is soon seen far up in the clouds. He is throwing out ballast and the sand boxes cause discomfiture for the pedestrians below. When the balloon has attained its maximum height, it begins to descend; and the anchor, which hangs from the long cable beneath the basket of the balloon begins to cause trouble. First it picks up a gendarme and taking him on an involuntary trip through the air, drops him in the river. Then it picks up a newspaper booth which falls to the street. A lady sewing is the next victim. The anchor then picks up a kennel to which a dog is fastened, dropping both on a pile of hay. All of the victims go in pursuit of the balloonist. He sails close to a roof top, grazing and throwing over chimneys and smokestacks until the anchor catches in a window. The balloonist begins to ascend and the entire side of the house comes off. Still sailing low, the balloon becomes entangled in a tree and the basket comes to the ground. The aeronaut tries to escape but the crowd is upon him and gives him a severe pummelling. *(Pathé films [Supplement 1], 1908, in Renken)*

1907.07 - FRA - TR-PR: Catalogue Pathé - Bousquet
1907.07.06 - FRA - Paris: Théatre Montparnasse - Renken
1907.08.18 - Ö-UM - Graz: Grazer Bioskop - Renken

Archives: CZE-NFA-Pra; FRA-CML; FRA-CNC-Par; FRA-Lob-Par; GBR-BFI-Lon; ITA-CdF-Gem; ITA-MNC-Tor; MEX-FUNAM-Méx; ROU-ANF-Buc; USA-GEM-Roc; USA-LoC-Was

Note: re-released 28mm Pathé-Kok nr 57b LES DÉBUTS D'UN AÉRONAUTE, on reel with BELLE-MÈRE EMBALLÉE, total lenght 117 m (= 150 m in 35mm) - MAX DANS LES AIRS is the title of the 35mm re-release 1916 and has a new Pathé catalog number (7569).

1907-14
LE DOMESTIQUE HYPNOTISEUR
140 m = 459 ft = 0:06:48 if at 18 fps
b&w

Domestique hypnotiseur, Le - French release title (original - FRA) - Bousquet
Diener als Hypnotiseur, Der - German release title (DEU+Ö-UM) - Renken
Servant Hypnotist, The - English release title (GBR+USA) - Renken
Max Linder ipnotizzato dal domestica - Italian listing title (attribution) - Turconi
Servant's Good Joke, The - English listing title (attribution) - FIAF TFA db

This is the story of a butler who has a hypnotic influence over his master. This master is a young man who receives a note from his prospective father-in-law inviting him to call and sign the marriage contract. The butler comes into possession of the note and decides to have some fun. While he is cleaning the room, the young man is seated in a chair reading and smoking. The butler hypnotizes him and they change places, with the result that the young man does all the work around the room, and before he comes out of the hypnotic state he is back in the chair reading again, not knowing that he has done some strenuous labour. At dinner the butler manages to eat his master's meal, while the latter, in a hypnotic trance, waits on him. The final scene shows the young man, attired in his finest, at the home of his prospective father-in-law. The guests and notaries are gathered, and in their presence the bride-to-be signs the contract. The young man takes up his pen and is just about to put his signature to it when the butler appears and throws him into a spell, with the result that instead of signing the paper he begins to rage around the room, smashing furniture, jumping on the piano with his feet, pulling down pictures and routing all the guests, until the butler places his finger in front of his master's nose and the young man follows it out of the room. *(Pathé films [Supplement 1], 1908, in Renken)*

1907.07 - FRA - TR-PR: Catalogue Pathé - Bousquet
1907.07.06 - FRA - Paris: Théatre Montparnasse - Renken
1907.10.06 - DEU - München: Welt-Kinematograph - Renken

Archives: GBR-BFI-Lon; ITA-CN-Rom

Note: *A few frames are visible in the Turconi collection: nr 7387, 7388 and 7389. This film is often confused with MAX HYPNOTISÉ (1910-34).*

1907-15
PITOU, BONNE D'ENFANTS
105 m = 345 ft = 0:05:06 if at 18 fps
b&w

Pitou, bonne d'enfants - French release title (original - FRA) - Bousquet
Johann als Kindermädchen - German release title (DEU) - Renken
Private Atkins Minds a Baby - English release title (GBR+USA) - Renken
Tommy Atkins Minds a Baby - English listing title (attribution) - Renken
Soldier and the Baby, The - English listing title (attribution) - GBR-BFI

The hero [...] is left in charge of a baby on a seat in the park by his sweetheart, its nurse, and walks up and down with it trying to keep it in a good temper. He shortly spies an officer approaching him, and hastily places the baby in a wheelbarrow, while he stands to attention and salutes. While he is engaged in talk with his officer the park cleaner comes up and wheels off his barrow, without noticing its occupant. Several following scenes show him shoveling dirt on to the infant until it is quite covered, and at last it is thrown on the rubbish heap with the rest of the refuse he has collected. There it is discovered by a policeman. Meanwhile, Atkins has discovered his loss, and he takes another baby from its pram and makes his way back to the seat. Here, however, he meets the policeman with the lost infant, and the consequence is that he has two babies in his arms when his lady love comes back. The nurse whose baby he had appropriated also turns up and between the two ladies he is roughly used. *(Kinematograph and Lantern Weekly, 1907.08.15, in Renken)*

1907.07.26 - FRA - Paris: Omnia Pathé - Renken
1907.08 - FRA - TR-PR: Catalogue Pathé - Bousquet
1907.08.31 - DEU - Worms: Internationale Kinematographen Gesellschaft - Renken

Archives: FRA-CNC-Par; GBR-BFI-Lon

1907-16
UN DRAME À SÉVILLE
155 m = 508 ft = 0:07:32 if at 18 fps
b&w

Drame à Séville, Un - French release title (original - FRA) - Bousquet

Drama in Sevilla, Ein - German release title (DEU+Ö-UM) - Renken
Drama in Seville, A - English release title (GBR+USA) - Renken
Mort d'un toréador, La - French listing title (attribution) - Mitry
Amour de toréador, Un - French archive title (attribution) - print at BEL-CRB

The story tells of a matador - the leading figure in the Spanish bull ring - whose lady love proves fickle. He finds her in a restaurant with another man, quarrels with the latter, and the two adjourn to the courtyard, where a duel in the Spanish fashion, with daggers and a cloak wound round the arm, ends in the matador wounding his rival. The lady goes off with the wounded man, and the matador despondently makes his way to the ring, and from his dressing room sends a reproachful note to the lady, in which he expresses a fear that his impending appearance in the ring will be his last. This communication the girl tears up, and with her lover makes her way to the ring to see the sport. The following scene gives us glimpses alternately of the girl and her companions watching the bull baiting and of the actual scenes in the ring, which have been obviously taken from a real bull fight and are a most realistic record of the Spanish national sport. Men with red cloaks madden the bull, lead it round the arena at a furious charge, and then avoid its rush with a quick turn. These events take place in many cases so close to the camera that one can distinguish the features of the men. Following this the picadors, mounted on worn-out horses and armed with lances, take their turn. [...] After the picadors the bandoleros take a turn, plant their spears in the bulls' shoulders, and make way for the matador, the hero of the story, whose place it is to give the coup-de-grace. This hero takes his place before the bull, and has raised his sword to give the blow, when the animal rushes at him, with head down, and hurls him into the air. The battered man is then carried to a room outside the ring, and expires in the presence of his repentant sweetheart, who afterwards indignantly dismisses the rival. *(Kinematograph and Lantern Weekly, 1907.10.03, in Renken)*

1907.08 - FRA - TR-PR: Catalogue Pathé - Bousquet
1907.08.16 - FRA - Paris: Théatre Montparnasse - Renken
1907.10.05 - Ö-UM - Wien: Sofiensaal, "The Royal Bio Co." - Renken

Archives: BEL-CRB-Bru; FRA-CF-Par; FRA-CNC-Par; FRA-Lob-Par; GBR-BFI-Lon; ITA-CdB-Bol; NLD-EFM-Ams; USA-GEM-Roc; USA-LoC-Was

Note: the print at BEL-CRB-Bru is longer due to an addition of bull fight footage.

1907-17
LES EXPLOITS D'UN FOU
130 m = 427 ft = 0:06:19 if at 18 fps
b&w

Exploits d'un fou, Les - French release title (original - FRA) - Bousquet
Erlebnisse eines Narren - German release title (DEU+Ö-UM) - Renken
Doings of a Maniac - English release title (GBR+USA) - Renken
Adventures of a Madman - English listing title (attribution) - GBR-BFI

Some maniacs are seen at exercise under their keepers. They are being marched to their cells, when the last one, who is a comical fellow, hurdles the wall and dashes to freedom. Amuck in the streets, he begins a series of pranks, the first of which is when he kisses two women on the street. He follows this by drinking the gasoline belonging to a chauffeur and going to a riverbank, he eats the soap with which a woman is washing, at the same time throwing her into the water. He next mounts a street cleaner's cart, creates damage with this, after which he calmly enters the house of a citizen through the window. A couple are engaged at dinner, and they flee, leaving the lunatic to the feast. They summon the police, but while they are gone the lunatic finds an officer's uniform and dons it with the result that when he walks out of the house the policemen stand at attention. His last is an effort to make a speech at the river front, where a number of longshoremen place a rope around his waist and give him several duckings. The last picture shows how many funny faces a crazy man can make. *(Pathé films [Supplement 1], 1908, in Renken)*

1907.10 - FRA - TR-PR: Catalogue Pathé - Bousquet
1907.11.06 - FRA - Le Havre: Omnia Pathé, Théâtre Cirque - Bousquet
1907.11.24 - Ö-UM - Graz: Grazer Bioskop - Renken

Archives: GBR-BFI-Lon

Note: bit part (the man with the straw hat by the canal).

1907-18
L'ARMOIRE
140 m = 459 ft = 0:06:48 if at 18 fps
b&w

Armoire, L' - French release title (original - FRA) - Bousquet
Schrank, Der - German release title (DEU+Ö-UM) - Renken
Cupboard, The - English release title (GBR+USA) - Renken
Max dans l'armoire - French listing title (attribution) - ITA-CdF
Max in a Wardrobe - English listing title (attribution) - AUT-ÖFM

A young husband and his pretty wife are seen in their home, the former explaining that he has an important engagement. As soon as he is out of the door the wife finds a note from a damsel named "Ethel", who invites him for a "cold bottle and a hot bird." She knows what this means and sets off on their track. The husband is now seen with "Ethel", he seated at a table and she lovingly waiting on him. He hears a familiar knock at the door and a more familiar voice. He ducks under the table just as his wife comes storming in. She demands the surrender of hubby and goes in another room to find him. While there "Hubby" comes out of his corner under the table and makes for the stairway, but is followed by his wife, who sees him, and a merry chase through the house ensues. He dashes into a room and shuts himself in a cupboard. This ruse is successful so far that his wife does not find him, but it means the beginning of his troubles. The cupboard is about to be moved, with the rest of the furniture and two expressmen now enter for it. They turn the cupboard upside down and yank it through the window. It is piled on a wagon and as the vehicle starts off the frantic attempts of the man inside to retain his equilibrium cause the cupboard to take on an aspect of animation. The truck is lifted by a derrick on board a train and the train starts. At the end of the journey it is again transferred to wheels, and the handlers do not seem to be particular in the transfer of that cupboard. Reaching the new home, it is to grace the dining-room. The expressmen throw it off the wagon and take it there. The owner arrives in her new home, drinks her health with the two movers, when suddenly the cupboard behind them begins to rock. This alarms them and the men, tossing off the liquor, depart. The lady begins to place things in order, the cupboard suddenly rears on end and then bangs down upon her head. The door smashes and "Ethel's Affinity" marches forth, bumped and dilapidated. He makes a hasty exit and, catching a train, goes home. His wife is seen at home, partially reconciled to her lot, when the door opens and "Hubby" slides in, but stands by meekly waiting for her to lift her eyes, which she finally does and recognizing that the visitor is her own, dear, little, etc., etc., she hugs him and soothes the pain of his bumps, etc. *(Pathé Films [Supplement 1], 1908, in Renken)*

1907.10 - FRA - TR-PR: Catalogue Pathé - Bousquet
1907.11.09 - Ö-UM - Wien: Floridsdorfer Biograph-Theater - Renken
1907.12.21 - FRA - Paris: Le Cirque d'hiver - Bousquet

Archives: AUT-FAA-Wie; AUT-ÖFM-Wie; CZE-NFA-Pra; ITA-CdF-Gem

1907-19
LE MARI DE LA DOCTORESSE
185 m = 607 ft = 0:08:59 if at 18 fps
b&w

Mari de la doctoresse, Le - French release title (original - FRA) - Bousquet
Gatte der Frau Doctor, Der - German release title (Ö-UM) - Renken
Lady Doctor's Husband - English release title (GBR+USA) - Renken

A gentleman stops on the street to pet a parrot and is bitten on the finger. A female doctor administers to the injured digit. She is so pretty and captivating that the man submits willingly to the treatment and finds himself in love with her. When she is finished ,she accepts his thanks in a businesslike way and walks ahead, but he follows her and discovers where she lives. Later, with his bandaged finger, he is ringing her doorbell and he is ushered into the torture chamber. Here the pretty doctor again administers to him, but while she does so he persists in telling her about another ailment troubling him. Before she can realize it he has proposed, and he is so handsome and dashing that she accepts him. The next scene breaches the courtship and she is seen in a bride's veil, he the groom. As he is alone with her, her maid enters and tells her of waiting patients. She leaves him abruptly and goes to attend to her business. He does not exactly like the idea but must submit. Now is shown how his young wife has not time enough to love him. Whenever he begins to bother her for attention, she turns upon him severely and he can say naught. He sees her occupied with sick people, dabbling with wounds, etc., as if he does not exist. At dinner she eats quickly, denies him his wine and leaves him without any kiss. He sees a man enter her office and he suspects. Watching through the keyhole, he witnesses how she places her hands on his person but does not understand that it is only in a professional capacity, and in a fit of jealous rage he bursts into the room. She promptly ejects him, however, and proceeds with her patient. In the last scene she is at study and he is bothering her for some evidence of attention. Again and again she puts him off, and finally seats him in a chair and places in his lap a basket full of socks for darning. She puts a needle in his hand and orders him to darn and then resumes her studies. A close-range view shows him diligently at work plying the needle. *(Pathé films [Supplement 1], 1908, in Renken)*

1907.11.01 - FRA - Saint Quentin: Omnia Cinématographe Pathé - Renken
1907.12 - FRA - TR-PR: Catalogue Pathé - Bousquet
1908.01.19 - Ö-UM - Wien: Floridsdorfer Biograph-Theater - Renken

Archives: no film print known to this date

1907-20
LES PLAISIRS DU SOLDAT
205 m = 672 ft = 00:09:57 if at 18 fps
b&w

Plaisirs du soldat, Les - French release title (original - FRA) - Bousquet

Soldatenvergnügen - German release title (DEU+Ö-UM) - Renken
Pleasant Side of a Soldier's Life, The - English release title (GBR+USA) - Renken

The young candidate for military training is brought to the colonel's home by his fond mother, where his extremely courteous air finds him favor. Left alone he is seen being given in charge to the sergeant, who takes him out to fit him with a uniform. His monocle and Chesterfieldian air are greatly out of place among the troopers and soon he loses his dream of prancing behind a brass band in bright gilt and laces. The troopers ridicule him and make sport of him, and he find his first uniform an awkward one. He does not realize what discipline means, and when he is lined up with the other men at drill, he seems to consider it his privilege to step out of line to shake hand with the colonel. The latter looks at him sternly, becomes angry and orders him taken to the repair shop, where his monocle is done away with and his beautiful locks detached from his scalp. Reconciled to his altered appearance, he is still something of a Chesterfield however, and seizes every opportunity to bow and smile. He goes to a music hall with some of his comrades, and as they sit there, he confides to one of the troopers near him that he thinks the girl on the stage is "very nice". As it happens, the man he spoke to is interested himself in the actress, and the result is that the "rookie" receives a good beating. Still clinging to his drawing room etiquette, the would-be soldier is seen performing various duties, and in the performance of which he meets nothing but trouble. When he complains of illness the doctor finds him perfectly sound and prescribes for him the task of carrying garbage cans. He performs this duty with gloved hands, holding a dainty handkerchief to his nose. Now one of the petty officers orders the young man to blacken his boots, but the latter has backbone enough to refuse him and deliberately blackens his own instead. While thus engaged the colonel touches him on the shoulder, and, thinking it is the petty officer still wishing to annoy him, quickly turns and polishes the colonel's face. For this offense the rookie is marched off and placed in a cell with two drunken soldiers, and what he suffers there is a caution. After a few more adventures in the barracks, our hero is seen waiting on the table at the colonel's house, where a dinner party is in progress. Here he smashes dishes right and left, and all at once, his attention being attracted by a fly in the air, he makes frantic efforts to capture it. Of course, his antics naturally disturb the guests, but the worst is to come, for in making one final dash for the fly he succeeds in pulling down the portieres, upsets a buffet and wrecks the room generally. *(The Auburn Citizen, 1908.01.31 in Renken)*

1907.12.28 - FRA - Marseille: Eden Cinema Pathé - Renken
1908.01 - FRA - TR-PR: Catalogue Pathé - Bousquet
1908.02.16 - Ö-UM - Graz: Grazer Bioskop - Renken

Archives: [ARG-Private collection]

Note: identification as a Max Linder film by Georg Renken based on Brazilian press.

1908-01
MON PANTALON EST DÉCOUSU
100 m = 328 ft = 0:04:51 if at 18 fps
b&w

Mon pantalon est décousu - French release title (original - FRA) - Bousquet
Meine Hose ist geplatzt - German release title (DEU+Ö-UM) - Renken
In a Difficult Position - English release title (USA) - Renken
Torn Trousers, The - English listing title (attribution) - FIAF TFA db
Mon pantalon est déchiré - French listing title (attribution) - FIAF TFA db

It is just a few moments before the ball, and the beau, by his strenuousness in dressing, has torn a huge rent in the seat of his only pair of trousers. Hastily seizing a needle and thread, he tries to sew them while on his person, and just manages to get a few stitches in; thus depending only on his own ingenuity, he decides to go to the function. He does well by summoning a cab. He reaches his destination all right, and is next seen in the reception room, where he uses a cushion to shield the faulty spot, bowing to right and left, but holding fast to the cushion. Going to the buffet with a lady, he keeps a chair close to the rent, and when an obliging waiter takes this from him, he frantically grabs a platter and manages to cover up. But in the ballroom, he dances with a handkerchief trailing gracefully behind him, finding this protection meagre, however, he appropriates his partner's fan for the purpose. His downfall comes only when the lady asks him to tie her shoelace. He is stunned by the request but pulls himself together and makes a daring attempt to oblige one-handed; but this feat being impossible he gives up, and the guests discover the tear. The beau sits on the floor in despair, but too late, for all are already gathered round him, and amid much laughter and ridicule he succeeds in dashing out of the room without turning his back toward the company. *(Moving Picture World, 1908.03.14, in Renken)*

1908.01.04 - FRA - Cherbourg: Salle des Enfants de Cherbourg - Renken
1908.02 - FRA - TR-PR: Catalogue Pathé - Bousquet
1908.03.28 - DEU - Lübeck: Metropol-Theater - Renken

Archives: FRA-CML; FRA-CNC-Par; FRA-Lob-Par; GBR-BFI-Lon; ITA-CdF-Gem; NLD-EFM-Ams

Note: re-released 28mm Pathé-Kok nr72b MON PANTALON EST DÉCOUSU, on reel with LE CROCODILE, total lenght 119 m (= 151 m in 35mm).

1908-02
MA MONTRE RETARDE
90 m = 295 ft = 0:04:22 if at 18 fps
b&w

Ma montre retarde - French release title (original - FRA) - Bousquet
Meine Uhr geht zu spät - German release title (Ö-UM) - Renken
My Watch is Slow - English release title (GBR+USA) - Renken

A young clerk buys a new watch which happens to be a bad timekeeper. In blissful ignorance of this fact, he carries it off and it begins to make trouble for him. He departs for his desk at the office in ample time, according to the watch, but when he arrives there, he finds himself several hours late, and his only plea being a new watch, the employer decides that something is wrong. He is next seen as he keeps an appointment with his sweetheart, taking his deficient time piece as a guide. When he reaches the rendezvous he waits patiently but the lady does not appear. When he makes inquiry, however, a waiter hands him a note from her, in which she states that she waited for him for an hour after he was due, and being fully convinced that he is not sincere, earnest, etc., etc., does never again want to hear from him. The poor fellow almost collapses when he compares his time piece with another; but his troubles are not yet over, for on reaching home he finds a letter from his employer telling him that his presence need no more cast its brilliancy over the establishment - fired. *(Moving Picture World, 1908.03.14, in Renken)*

1908.01.04 - FRA - Cherbourg: Salle des Enfants de Cherbourg - Renken
1908.03 - FRA - TR-PR: Catalogue Pathé - Bousquet

Archives: no film print known to this day

Note: identification as a Max Linder film by Georg Renken based on French press.

1908-03
LE PREMIER CIGARE D'UN COLLÉGIEN
140 m = 459 ft = 0:06:48 if at 18 fps
b&w

Premier cigare d'un collégien, Le - French release title (original - FRA) - Bousquet
Erste Zigarre des Primaners, Die - German release title (DEU+Ö-UM) - Renken
His First Cigar - English release title (USA) - Renken
Premier cigare de Max - French re-release title (28mm) - Catalogue Pathé-Kok
Premier cigare, Le - French release title (alternative) - Bousquet
First Cigar - English listing title (attribution) - AFI

A well-grown boy sees a box of his father's cigars, and pockets one. He goes downstairs, and no sooner is he out of the building when he joyously sticks the cheroot into his mouth. Feeling like a man, he goes to a nearby café, orders a drink, and then lights the weed. A close-range view of his face is now given. He is flirting with a girl sitting near him. In a little while the cigar begins to act, and between the smiles towards the damsel there is interspersed a sickly expression. The sick feeling gains, but the young man keeps on smoking until he feels very ill; still unwilling to admit defeat. He loosens his collar and coat in an endeavor to be comfortable, but the waiter finally sees him and starts him home. Very ill and groggy, he finds the keyhole after much groping, and enters the wrong room. Here an indignant lodger seizes him and fires him downstairs. This seems to revive him somewhat, and the poor, sick boy makes his way to his own home where his fond mother is seen administering to the would-be man. *(Pathé films [Supplement 1], 1908, in Renken)*

1908.01.11 - FRA - Cherbourg: Salle des Enfants de Cherbourg - Renken
1908.01.18 - USA - TR-PR: Trade listing - AFI
1908.03 - FRA - TR-PR: Catalogue Pathé - Bousquet
1908.03.30 - Ö-UM - Budapest: Franz Fisch's Elektro Bioscop - Renken

Archives: AUS-NFSA-Can; BRA-CMAM-Rio; DEU-DK-Ber; ESP-FE-Mad; FRA-CNC-Par; FRA-Lob-Par; ITA-CdF-Gem; NLD-EFM-Ams; USA-BkHk; USA-LoC-Was

Note: some sources have mixed PREMIÈRE SORTIE (1905-01) and LE PREMIER CIGARE D'UN COLLÉGIEN. This confusion is reflected in the list of archive holdings commonly available. Re-released 28mm Pathé-Kok nr 7a LE PREMIER CIGARE / LE PREMIER CIGARE DE MAX, 56 m (= 71.1 m in 35mm), on reel with JIU-JITSU, total length 124 m (= 157.5 m in 35mm). See also: LE PREMIER CIGARE DU COLLÉGIEN, Pathé 1902, actor: Albens, 30 m, Bousquet nr 623 and LE PREMIER CIGARE DU COLLÉGIEN, Pathé 1904, actor: Galipaux, 40 m, Bousquet nr 844.

1908-04
L'OBSESSION DE L'ÉQUILIBRE
165 m = 541 ft = 0:08:01 if at 18 fps
b&w

Obsession de l'équilibre, L' - French release title (original - FRA) - Bousquet

Ungeschikte Equilibrist, Der - German release title (DEU+Ö-UM) - Renken
Amateur Acrobat - English release title (GBR+USA) - Renken
Max équilibriste - French re-release title (28mm) - Catalogue Pathé-Kok
Max the Juggler - English re-release title (28mm) - DVD publisher (Cinerdistan)
Max jongleur - French listing title (attribution) - Chirat et LeRoy
Would-be Juggler, The - English listing title (attribution) - GBR-BFI
Jongleur im Restaurant - German listing title (attribution) - GBR-BFI
Maniac Juggler, The - English listing title (attribution) - GBR-BFI

Fascinated by the doings of a skillful acrobat, a young bean jumps from his box on to the stage just as the artist is performing a difficult stunt with a whole lot of chairs piled on top of one another. In his endeavors to do likewise, our young greenhorn pushes the juggler, thus causing the chairs to come raining down on his own head. Having been put out of the theater, but not discouraged by his first failure, our young acrobat, after having had a few strength restorers, goes on his way looking for opportunities to exercise his new-born talent. He tries to balance on his nose the tall hat of a stately old gentleman, who, however, resenting his familiarity, boxes his ears with remarkable vigor for his old age, and goes on. All these rebukes and failures, instead of sobering our ambitious artist, seem to make him all the more anxious to exercise his skill, and, after a few more comic attempts and failures, he comes to a restaurant and decides to rest and refresh himself. A glass cleaner perched at the top of his ladder being, however, too much of a temptation for his juggling mania, he seizes the ladder by the foot and in his attempt to balance it, sends glass cleaner and ladder through the glass plate amongst the terrified occupants of the inner salon. A last scene shows him in his own room playing havoc with tables, vases and costly knicknacks in his vain attempt to balance them on his nose. *(Moving Picture World, 1908.04.04, in Renken)*

1908.01.17 - FRA - Paris: Omnia Pathé - Renken
1908.03 - FRA - TR-PR: Catalogue Pathé - Bousquet
1908.04.05 - Ö-UM - Graz: Grazer Bioskop - Renken

Archives: AUS-NFSA-Can; FRA-CF-Par; FRA-CNC-Par; GBR-BFI-Lon; ITA-CN-Rom; NLD-EFM-Ams

Note: this film is occasionally mixed-up with PETITE ROSSE (1909-08). Re-released 28mm Pathé-Kok nr 26a MAX ÉQUILIBRISTE, on reel with DANSE SERPENTINE, total lenght 125 m (= 159 m in 35mm).

1908-05
LA SUSPENSION
90 m = 295 ft = 0:04:22 if at 18 fps
b&w

Suspension, La - French release title (original - FRA) - Bousquet
Hängelampe, Die - German release title (DEU+Ö-UM) - Renken
Hanging Lamp, The - English release title (GBR+USA) - Renken

The table lamp being upset by the maid while serving dinner, the head of the house decides to have a hanging lamp and is seen going forth to make his purchase. Having selected a stylish and heavy brass article, he returns, followed by a workman who is to hang it up immediately, for our friend has things done at once if he has to have them done at all. Arriving on the premises the workman starts to bore a hole in the ceiling with a tremendous wimble, and we will leave him at his work showering the whole family with plaster dust to go for a few minutes to the upper floor. There a fat old gentleman is endeavoring to put his boots on, and as he is too stout to bend from a chair he sits on the floor and has nearly succeeded in his attempt when he gives a terrible cry of pain and distress as he endeavors to rise. Alas! he is fastened to the floor by a fiendish demon who gnaws at his vitals like a hungry wolf and won't let go of his struggling prey. The cries of the old gentleman arouse the whole neighborhood, including the fire brigade, and they all come to the rescue. Upon pulling up the fainting man from his place of torture they find out that the lamp hanger has gone too deep in the ceiling with his wimble and the sharp tool has been trespassing on private property in the room above. They all rush back to the lower room and kick the clumsy workman out of the house, sending his tools tumbling down after him. *(Views and Films Index; Moving Picture World, 1908.05.02, in Renken)*

1908.02.07 - FRA - Paris: Artistic Cinéma - Bousquet
1908.04 - FRA - TR-PR: Catalogue Pathé - Bousquet
1908.04.26 - Ö-UM - Graz: Grazer Bioskop - Renken
Archives: GBR-BFI-Lon

Note: identification as a Max Linder film by Richard Abel, and by Georg Renken based on Brazilian press.

1908-06
LA FEMME SANDWICH
100 m = 328 ft = 0:04:51 if at 18 fps
b&w

Femme sandwich, La - French release title (original - FRA) - Bousquet
Reklamefrau, Die - German release title (DEU+Ö-UM) - Renken
Sandwich Woman - English release title (GBR+USA) - Renken

A shopkeeper finding his business slow hits upon a novel scheme. He is a boot and shoe merchant and employs a pretty cashier. He fits to her feet a pair of the finest shoes he keeps in stock and hangs a sandwich sign upon her, asking her to demonstrate his wares to whoever she may meet. She is a vivacious little miss and takes to the proposition at once. She goes forth into the street and coming upon a group of old gentlemen she lifts her skirt and shows them a dainty limb, and of course the shoe. They immediately follow her, and soon she is leading a veritable army, for all she needs to do is to exhibit her ankle and the spectator joins the ranks. Through streets and avenues they go, all following joyfully. Arriving at a police station, a number of officers endeavor to stop the throng, but the girl shows them what the others saw and they, too, are seen following her. When they reach the shop the girl's employer is waiting for them anxiously. Some fifty in number swarm into the store and soon the entire stock is spread out before them, and they are carrying bundles under their arms; even the policemen depart with new boots. When they all depart the shop looks as if a cyclone struck it, but the merchant and his cashier overlook this when they begin the count of their huge pile of money. *(Moving Picture World, 1908.02.08, in Renken)*

1908.02.08 - USA - TR-PR: Moving Picture World
1908.02.14 - USA - Batavaia, NY: Dreamland - Renken
1908.03.07 - FRA - Saint-Étienne: Omnia Pathé - Renken
1908.05 - FRA - TR-PR: Catalogue Pathé - Bousquet

Archives: FRA-FJSP-Par

Note: identification as a Max Linder film by Georg Renken based on Brazilian press.

1908-07
VIVE LA VIE DE GARÇON
195 m = 640 ft = 0:09:28 if at 18 fps
b&w

Vive la vie de garçon - French release title (original - FRA) - Bousquet
Es lebe das Junggesellenleben - German release title (DEU+Ö-UM) - Renken
Hurrah for Bachelorhood - English release title (GBR) - Renken
Troubles of a Grasswidower - English release title (USA) - Renken
Max célibataire - French listing title (attribution) - Mitry
Junggesellenleben Lebe Hoch! Das - German listing title (attribution) - GBR-BFI

Having had a quarrel with his wife, a young husband is left alone at home, his better half having "gone back to mother". He chides himself into the belief that he can manage the house himself, and the manner in which he begins to clear the dishes away from the table does not discourage him. He uses a pair of gloves to wash them, but it does not work quickly enough, and he turns the hose on the whole business. When he has finally cleaned everything, he drops the tray and all the dishes are smashed. He next attempts to prepare the dinner and goes out marketing. His difficulties in this accomplishment are many, but he finally reaches home. He finds plucking feathers undesirable work, so he cuts them off with a pair of shears; he places the whole chicken in a pan, throws in a sliced unpeeled potato, and spills some wine in for gravy. After a few more additions to his display of culinary ignorance he has the concoction smoking pretty well. Suddenly he finds himself about to sneeze and raising his hands to his face he explodes so violently that his arm strikes the pan and the entire contents fall upon the floor. But he goes to bed, and after a hard scuffle with the sheets manages to fall asleep. In the morning he is unable to find his tie and begins to upset things in a nervous search for his neckwear. After throwing out everything in that room he goes to another and pulls out and smashes all the drawers in a bureau. Frenzied, he turns to a wardrobe and is knocking things about in wild disorder, when the whole outfit falls on his head. As he is floundering in the wreckage his wife and her mother enter, and while the old lady faints he falls on his knees, begging for relief. *(Moving Picture World, 1908.02.29, in Renken)*

1908.02.22 - FRA - Cherbourg: Salle des Enfants de Cherbourg - Renken
1908.02.29 - USA - TR-PR: Moving Picture World - Bousquet
1908.04 - FRA - TR-PR: Catalogue Pathé - Bousquet
1908.04.18 - DEU - Mülhausen/Mulhouse: Kinematograph Wintergarten - Renken

Archives: CZE-NFA-Pra; FRA-Lob-Par; GBR-BFI-Lon; ITA-CdF-Gem; ITA-CN-Rom; NLD-EFM-Ams; USA-AFA-Los; USA-BkHk; USA-GEM-Roc; USA-MoMA-New; USA-UCLA-Los

Note: re-released 28mm Pathé-Kok nr 109 VIVE LA VIE DE GARÇON 114 m (= 145 m in 35mm). Many frames are visible in the Turconi collection: nr 6127 to 6140, nr 8519, nr 14970 to 15020 and nr 22833 to 22838.

1908-08
LES PÉRÉGRINATIONS D'UNE PUCE
130 m = 427 ft = 0:06:19 if at 18 fps
b&w

Pérégrinations d'une puce, Les - French release title (original - FRA) - Bousquet
Wanderung des Flohs, Die - German release title (DEU) - Renken
Wanderungen eines Floh's - German release title (Ö-UM) - Renken
Travels of a Flea, The - English release title (USA) - Renken
Peregrinação de uma pulga - Portuguese release title (BRA) - Renken

In a glass case a woman is exhibiting a few trained fleas for a livelihood, and the spectators get the benefit of the whole performance for two cents. After the fleas have performed their stunts the public depart, when all at once the last spectator starts to scratch himself frantically. He rushes out and stops to tell a policeman what his trouble is. He has scarcely finished his tale when the officer also gets the itch. At the same moment the flea trainer comes running out of her menagerie, screaming that one of her artists has been stolen. Seeing the policeman going his way, scratching, she pursues him. He, however, stops to talk to a nurse, the flea jumps on her; she goes her way, and stopping to have a drink, the troublesome animal jumps on the waiter. From waiter to officer, from officer to a row of soldiers, from soldiers to a college boy, does the flea jump and bite, until the trainer, who has followed all the peregrinations of her beloved pet, and has vainly endeavored to catch up with the last but always changing, flea-troubled citizen, catches hold of the young student, and after having secured her beloved scholar, goes home, taking the youth along with her. *(Moving Picture World, 1908.04.11, in Renken)*

1908.02.29 - FRA - Cherbourg: Salle des Enfants de Cherbourg - Renken
1908.04 - FRA - TR-PR: Catalogue Pathé - Bousquet

Archives: no film print known to this date

Note: identification as a Max Linder film by Georg Renken based on Brazilian press.

1908-09
RETOUR INATTENDU
105 m = 345 ft = 0:05:06 if at 18 fps
b&w

Retour inattendu - French release title (original - FRA) - Bousquet
Unerwartete Rückkehr - German release title (DEU+Ö-UM) - Renken

A man leaves his home for a trip, escorted to the railway station by a friend of his. The latter leaves him at the station before going back, in order to meet his friend's wife. But, realizing that he has forgotten his purse, the traveler also comes back home. Wearing nothing but his pants, the lover jumps out of the window. He sees a fat man, waits for him and threatens him with his hidden pipe as if it were a gun in order to obtain the fat man's clothes. Infuriated because he has vainly looked for the lover in the whole house, the husband goes out, sees the fat man dressed in pants only, and beats him out, confusing him for his wife's lover. *(Translation DD from Bousquet nr 2136)*

1908.03.18 - FRA - Le Havre: Omnia Pathé, Théâtre Cirque - FRA-FJSP
1908.05 - FRA - TR-PR: Catalogue Pathé - Bousquet
1908.05.23 - DEU - Mülhausen/Mulhouse: Kinematograph Wintergarten - Renken

Archives: no film print known to this date

Note: identification as a Max Linder film by Susan Buhrman based on production still, cited by Georg Renken.

**1908-10
L'OBSESSION DE LA BELLE-MÈRE
105 m = 345 ft = 0:05:06 if at 18 fps
b&w**

Obsession de la belle-mère, L' - French release title (original - FRA) - Bousquet
Ach diese Schwiegermütter - German release title (DEU+Ö-UM) - Renken
Tormented by His Mother-in-Law - English release title (GBR+USA) - Renken
Obsessão da Sogra - Portuguese release title (BRA) - Renken

Mr. and Mrs. Wellmarried would be the happiest couple on earth were it not for the terrible skeleton in the husband's cupboard, his mother-in-law.... That dragon in woman's clothes always appears at the wrong moment, always says the wrong things and is therefore thoroughly hated by the young spouse. In this film we see the happy couple having lunch in perfect harmony when in comes wifey's mother.... The husband glares at his enemy and, the intruder having made a remark concerning the quality of the food, the infuriated husband seizes the soup tureen and gives the guest a good ducking. Still furious the young man goes out and, passing a café, thinks he will quiet his nerves with a soda. He orders the beverage but, as he is about to mix his drink, the bottle takes the shape of his abhorred mother-in-law. Desperate he grabs for his enemy and shakes her violently. Water comes rushing out of the bottle, and customers having been doused by the apparent lunatic, he is compelled to leave. Arriving before a moving van our friend looks into a mirror leaning against the vehicle, and again he beholds the fiendish face of his wife's parent. Kicking viciously at it the glass is smashed to atoms. From there he goes on to where a pretty girl is sitting on a bench and, seeing an opportunity to forget his woes in a little flirtation, he bends over to talk to the girl — but horrors! again mother-in-law is glaring at him. The poor man, half crazy, rushes to his home once more and, seeing the picture of the accursed woman hanging on the wall, takes an old regiment sword from its scabbard, slashes viciously at the innocent portrait and has soon cut the fat grinning face to pieces. Exhausted he lies down and is soon in the land where mothers-in-law are not permitted to enter. *(Moving Picture World, 1908.06.06, in Renken)*

1908.03.21 - FRA - Saint Quentin: Omnia Cinématographe Pathé - Renken
1908.05 - FRA - TR-PR: Catalogue Pathé - Bousquet
1908.05.30 - DEU - Mülheim: Mülheimer Viktoria Theater - Renken

Archives: FRA-CF-Par; USA-GEM-Roc

Notes: the film print in the collection of the George Eastman Museum has a story line which differs from the contents summary in the trade press. After the café scene: the mother-in-law appears as the newspaper stand seller, as the park rental chairs collector and as a horse-cart driver. Stories converge again at the end with the return home and the destruction of the portrait. GEM's print finishes in a pillow-fight producing a snow-fall of feathers (print viewed CC 2006).

1908-11
UNE VEINE DE BOSSU
120 m = 394 ft = 0:05:49 if at 18 fps
b&w

Veine de bossu, Une - French release title (original - FRA) - Bousquet
Glück des Buckligen, Das - German release title (DEU) - Renken
Hunchback Brings Luck - English release title (GBR+USA) - Renken
Gobbo portafortuna, Il - Italian listing title [attribution] - FIAF TFA db
Max diventa alto - Italian listing title [attribution] - FIAF TFA db

Mr. Hardup not being able to pay his rent, his landlord goes to all the petty traders of the district and tells them of our friend's bankruptcy, and they are all seen crowding in the apartment of the distracted tenant. Not knowing what to do to soothe the angry crowd, our poor man makes a desperate attempt for the door, but not succeeding to break away, jumps out of the window. A poor hunchback, selling lottery tickets in the street, receives the whole human load on his crippled back, and after a severe tumble is rewarded for his bruises by the pursued man buying his last ticket with his last quarter. The next scene represents our pauper friend in a garret reading a paper. He suddenly sees the results of the lottery in one of the columns, and having found out that he is the winner of the big prize, has an ad put in all the papers promising a reward to the hunchback that has unconsciously saved his life and unwittingly replenished his purse. A hundred cripples answer the ad, but they all return empty handed, and Mr. Hardup is despairing of ever finding his benefactor when the original hunchback makes his appearance, and soon after he is seen departing, handsomely rewarded by our new wealthy citizen. *(Moving Picture World, 1908.04.18, in Renken)*

1908.03.27 - DEU - Lübeck: Metropol-Theater - Renken
1908.05 - FRA - TR-PR: Catalogue Pathé - Bousquet
1908.08.14 - FRA - Saint-Étienne: Géant Forézien - Renken

Archives: ITA-FCI-Mil; MEX-FUNAM-Méx

Note: identification as a Max Linder film by Elio Quiroga, cited by Georg Renken.

1908-12
PÉDICURE PAR AMOUR
170 m = 558 ft = 0:08:15 if at 18 fps
b&w

Pédicure par amour - French release title (original - FRA) - Bousquet
Hühneraugenoperateur aus Liebe - German release title (DEU+Ö-UM) - Renken
Pedicure for Love - English release title (GBR) - Renken
Unwilling Chiropodist - English release title (USA) - Renken
Pedicuro por amor - Spanish [release or archive] title - Magliozzi

Her husband being at his office, Madame bids the chiropodist come and attend to her aching feet, and the specialist is seen entering the room to fulfill his duty. Madame's lover, however, entering at that moment, Mr. "Pedicure" is sent to the kitchen, and our guilty lovers are enjoying each other's company when in comes her husband. Our young gallant is feeling very small and uncomfortable, not knowing what to do, when he sees the chiropodist's outfit and immediately assuming the specialist's ways, offers his services. Now, Mr. Husband may seem a fool, but he

is up to a great many tricks himself, and seeing through the whole game, soon avenges himself. He forces the young lover to cut his corns. Our young Romeo would not mind performing this operation for his love, but his face shows how deeply he resents his present situation. At last Monsieur's feet are at ease and our young lover is already retreating with his stolen goods when the postman enters, and he must operate on him. Then comes the man servant, the grocer, the coachman, they all require his skill and attention, and at last, unable to stand the strain any longer, our sham doctor rushes out into the street, much to the amusement of the revenged husband.
(Moving Picture World, 1908.04.25, in Renken)

1908.04.04 - FRA - Saint Quentin: Omnia Cinématographe Pathé - Renken
1908.05 - FRA - TR-PR: Catalogue Pathé - Bousquet
1908.05.30 - DEU - Mülhausen/Mulhouse: Kinematograph Wintergarten - Renken

Archives: ARG-private collection; FRA-BNF-Par; NLD-EFM-Ams; URY-ANIP-Mon

Note: this film is occasionally mixed-up with MAX PÉDICURE (1914-02).

1908-13
LA MAÎTRESSE DE PIANO
130 m = 427 ft = 0:06:19 if at 18 fps
b&w

Maîtresse de piano, La - French release title (original - FRA) - Bousquet
Klavierlehrerin, Die - German release title (Ö-UM) - Renken
Music Teacher, The - English release title (GBR+USA) - Renken
Bella professora de piano, A - Portuguese release title (BRA) - Renken
Max maîtresse de piano - French listing title (attribution) - Mitry

A young girl, falling in love with a youth, a friend of the house, begs her father for permission to marry the chosen one of her heart, but the head of the family, for reasons of his own, refuses, in a great rage and at the next call the unsuspecting suitor makes at the house he finds the butler changed into an immovable guardian and is forbidden to enter. Returning home and finding a letter from his love telling him that her father wants a female music teacher, our young beau decides on a plan, and we next see him dressing op in feminine clothes and bound for the kingdom of love. On entering, he is introduced to the lord and master of his destinies, and being accepted, at once starts his new career as music instructor. The pupil is very unwilling at first, but when she finds out who the female teacher really is, she takes a sudden renewed interest for Mozart and Schubert. The lesson is going on brilliantly for both parties when the door opens and the father bids his daughter leave the room and starts flirting desperately with the music teacher. Things get so uncomfortable for the disguised lover that he makes an attempt to escape, but his movements being too quick and abrupt, and his wig falling off, the whole plot is discovered. The father wants to expel the intruder, but the youth threatens him with exposure regarding his conduct of a few minutes before if he does not consent to his marrying his daughter. The father reluctantly calls the young bride and joins their hands, making a comical attempt to look happy.
(Views and Film Index; Moving Picture World, 1908.05.02, in Renken)

1908.04.04 - FRA - Saint Quentin: Omnia Cinématographe Pathé - Renken
1908.05.02 - USA - TR-PR: Moving Picture World - Bousquet
1908.06 - FRA - TR-PR: Catalogue Pathé - Bousquet
1908.06.06 - DEU - Mülhausen/Mulhouse: Kinematograph Wintergarten - Renken

Archives: JPN-NFAJ-Tōk

Note: identification as a Max Linder film by Georg Renken based on Brazilian press.

**1908-14
DEUX GRANDES DOULEURS
125 m = 410 ft = 0:06:04 if at 18 fps
b&w**

Deux grandes douleurs - French release title (original - FRA) - Bousquet
Zwei Untröstliche - German release title (DEU) - Renken
Two Great Griefs - English release title (GBR+USA) - Renken

A young man is seen entering a cemetery, and in sorrow placing some flowers on the grave of his lately deceased wife. While thus engaged, his attention is attracted to a beautiful young woman who kneels, weeping piteously, over a nearby tomb. These two sorrow-stricken people – both craving for sympathy – soon strike up an acquaintance and before very long it looks as if an interesting romance would be the outcome. The next scene shows the young widower on his return home, where everything reminds him of his dead wife. We see him as he takes the portrait of the latter from the wall and places it on the bed, decorating it meantime with fresh flowers. A view of the interior of the widow's apartment is also given, and a truly somber picture she presents as she reverently lights the candles in front of her husband's portrait while gazing, with tear dimmed eyes, on the well-loved features of her lost one. The following day the two mourners meet again at the cemetery gate and the widower presents his acquaintance of yesterday with a beautiful bouquet of flowers, which [...] was intended for his wife's grave. It is quite evident now that not withstanding their short acquaintance, these two are deeply in love, and we are not surprised, therefore, to see the man down on his knees proposing when the couple return to the widow's apartment. The next picture, which is after the marriage, shows the pair living like turtle doves, but from a sense of duty they kept the portraits of their former mates hanging on the wall; the latter, therefore, witness many interesting love scenes between the newly married pair. Soon, however, these dumb spectators are too much for the happy couple, who decide, rather than remove the pictures, to drape them over with black. This accomplished, they go back to their billing and cooing with easier consciences. The time comes, however, when the dear departed are forgotten and the pictures become an eyesore, so are sent up to the attic to be added to a lot of other articles, once so highly valued, but which have unfortunately outlived their usefulness. A landscape now fills the place on the wall where the portraits used to hang, and the couple, happy in each other's love, have quite forgotten their early sorrows. *(Moving Picture World, 1908.10.10, in Renken)*

1908.04.25 - FRA - Saint Quentin: Omnia Cinématographe Pathé - Renken
1908.06 - FRA - TR-PR: Catalogue Pathé - Bousquet

Archives: DEU-DK-Ber; FRA-CF-Par; FRA-CNC-Par; FRA-Lob-Par; ITA-CdF-Gem

Note: re-released 28mm Pathé-Kok nr 63b DEUX GRANDES DOULEURS, on reel with VOLEUR MYSTÉRIEUX, total lenght 124 m (= 157 m in 35mm).

1908-15
UN TIC NERVEUX CONTAGIEUX
125 m = 410 ft = 0:06:04 if at 18 fps
b&w

Tic nerveux contagieux, Un - French release title (original - FRA) - Bousquet
Ansteckendes Nervenzucken - German release title (DEU) - Renken
Nervous Twitching is Catching, A - English release title (GBR) - Renken
Contagious Nervous Twitching - English release title (USA) - Renken
Cacoete contagioso - Portuguese release title (BRA) - Renken

A young fellow, who is afflicted with a nervous disorder, gets fits of twitching, which is contagious to all within sight, for it passes from one to another. We see him take his medicine and start out, and as he goes down the stairs his knees give an awful twirl and immediately the old janitor does the same. Going down the street he gets it while passing a man on a wheel and the rider sprawls all over the street. He is going by a new building, where the architect is taking notes, and he is seized with another convulsion. Immediately the busy man gets it and it passes along to a hodcarrier going up the ladder who falls in a heap, upsetting the mortar all over the architect. He goes along still further and meets a wedding party, and is seized with the twitching which everyone in the party gets, and when he joins them at the breakfast they are all glad to see him leave, for he breaks up the fathering with his twitching. He is passing through the park when he gives it to a statue, and immediately it bends in the knees also. A man and woman are seated on the dock when he comes along, and when they are seized with the twitching the woman plunges headlong into the water. Finally, he meets a policeman, and when he sees the condition of the young man, he starts to take him home. A citizen lends a hand also, and as they are going along the street, they are all twitching like the invalid. Finally, they arrive at his home, and the doctor gives them all a good dose of medicine which settles their nerves. *(Moving Picture World, 1908.07.18, in Renken)*

1908.06 - FRA - TR-PR: Catalogue Pathé - Bousquet
1908.07.10 - BRA - Rio de Janeiro: Cinematographo Pathé - Renken
1908.11.24 - FRA - Troyes: Cinéma Pathé - Renken

Archives: AUS-NFSA-Can; FRA-BNF-Par; FRA-Lob-Par; NLD-EFM-Ams

Note: re-released 28mm Pathé-Kok nr 78b UN TIC NERVEUX CONTAGIEUX, on reel with L'ÉVENTAIL, total length 115 m (= 146 m in 35mm).

1908-16
UN JEUNE HOMME TIMIDE
135 m = 443 ft = 0:06:33 if at 18 fps
b&w

Jeune homme timide, Un - French release title (original - FRA) - Bousquet
Furchtsamer junger Mann, Ein - German release title (DEU+Ö-UM) - Renken
Shy Fellow, A - English release title (GBR) - Renken
Bashful Young Man, A - English release title (USA) - Renken
Moço timido, Um - Portuguese release title (BRA) - Renken

A young lady, walking down the street, is overtaken by an elongated piece of humanity, who seems to be terribly smitten by the young maiden's charms, but he is so bashful that he hasn't the courage to address her. He follows her as far as her home, however, where she enters, apparently unconscious of the impression she has made. He tries to pluck up courage to follow her, but fails, and dejectedly goes back to his room, where he writes her a note telling of his love. This accomplished, he decides to carry the note himself to his loved one, but just as he is about to pull the bell cord, he loses his nerve and beats a hasty retreat. Going down the street, he purchases a large bouquet, and hailing a cab, once more returns to the young lady's abode, but instead of going in himself he gives the note and flowers to the cab driver and directs him to deliver them to the girl. The innocent cabby goes up to the apartment and walks in on the family unannounced and presents the daughter with the young man's offering. When her father learns the nature of his errand, he unceremoniously kicks him downstairs. The poor driver comes out the worse for his experience, and after giving the masher a good beating, drives away. Finally, the fellow goes to a nearby café and drinks enough wine to give him courage to fight a bull. He staggers back to the home of the adored one and walks deliberately in on the quiet family gathering. Throwing himself at the feet of the girl, he tells her of his infatuation, while she stands dumbfounded at his effrontery. The enraged father grabs the would-be suitor and throws him bodily out of the house; he lands in a heap on the sidewalk, where he dejectedly sits nursing his many wounds. *(Moving Picture World, 1908.07.18, in Renken)*

1908.06 - FRA - TR-PR: Catalogue Pathé - Bousquet
1908.07.14 - BRA - Rio de Janeiro: Cinematographo Pathé - Renken
1908.07.18 - USA - TR-PR: Moving Picture World - Bousquet

Archives: no film print known to this date

Note: identification as a Max Linder film by Georg Renken based on Brazilian press.

1908-17
UN BÉBÉ ENCOMBRANT
185 m = 607 ft = 0:08:59 if at 18 fps
b&w

Bébé encombrant, Un - French release title (original - FRA) - Bousquet
Sonderbare Erlebnisse eines Babys - German release title (DEU+Ö-UM) - Renken
Lost Baby, The - English release title (GBR) - Renken
Cumbersome Baby - English release title (USA) - Renken

A young couple, whose baby is in the country, send a letter to its nurse telling her to bring it home. She starts out and arrives in the city safely, but being tired, lays the baby on a bench in a park, and while she turns her back, a mischievous boy takes the youngster and carries it down the street and leaves it with the grocer. The latter does not know what to do with it and hands it over to the first woman that comes along. She being very fond of children, takes it home, but her mother will not have it, so throws it out of the window into the basket of a refuse gatherer, who happens to be passing. He, unconscious of his burden, dumps it into an ash can. A janitor finds it and starts down the street to find the owner and, not being successful, throws it into a passing carriage. The occupant being a man, is not elated over the present, and he turns it over to a waiter in a café, who in turn takes it and places it in a railroad train beside an old soldier who is taking a nap. When he awakens and finds the unfortunate child he throws it out of the window of the fast-moving train. It lands, none the worse for its experience, beside the track and is picked up by the flagman, who hastens to get rid of it by throwing it in the sewer. A man is fishing at the outlet and is amazed to see the baby float down with the current. He takes it and puts it in the basket of a girl who is washing clothes on the bank of the stream. In the meantime, the nurse is looking all over for the child and beats everyone that she comes in contact with in her wild excitement. Finally she goes to the parents and when she tells them of her misfortune they are on the verge of desperation, when in walks the laundress with their clothes, and when she uncovers the basket they find the child snugged up and all are happy at the good fortune of having the little one returned after all worry caused by the nurse's carelessness. *(Views and Films Index; Moving Picture World, 1908.07.11, in Renken)*

1908.06 - FRA - TR-PR: Catalogue Pathé - Bousquet
1908.07.24 - USA - Glenn Falls, NY: Fairyland - Renken
1908.09.12 - FRA - Lille: Omnia Cinéma Pathé - Renken

Archives: FRA-CNC-Par

Note: identification as a Max Linder film by Georg Renken based on the reproduction of a production still.

1908-18
MES VOISINS ME FONT DANSER
70 m = 230 ft = 0:03:24 if at 18 fps
b&w

Mes voisins me font danser - French release title (original - FRA) - Bousquet
Tanzvergnügen bei den Nachbarn, Ein - German release title (DEU) - Renken
My Neighbours are Giving a Dance - English release title (GBR) - Renken
Noisy Neighbors - English release title (USA) - Renken
Meus visinhos dansam - Portuguese release title (BRA) - Renken
Repos impossible - French re-release title (28mm) - Catalogue Pathé-Kok
Impossible to Get Sleep - English listing title [attribution] - Richard Abel: The Ciné Goes to Town
Impossible Rest - English listing title [attribution] - FIAF TFA db

A young man is seen entering his room and from the many expressions on his worn face one could not doubt that he is just returning from one grand night with the boys and is in no condition to be annoyed or disturbed. After administering to his wants in the form of headache tablets, he goes to lie down for a while and sleep the effects of the previous night off. In a room directly over him are a number of people conducting a rehearsal. They sing and dance and make as much noise as possible for civilized people. The poor fellow is nearly frantic and tosses around in bed until at last, he seizes a chair and knocks on the ceiling. As soon as the neighbors realize that they are annoying someone, they take on new vim and move all the furniture out of the room and start to dance and jig over the man's head until he is wild with indignation. Finally, they get so strenuous in their efforts to annoy him that they break through the floor and come down into the fellow's room with a crash, and he has the satisfaction of giving them all a good drubbing as they lay in a heap on the floor. *(Moving Picture World, 1908.07.11, in Renken)*

1908.06.06 - FRA - Cherbourg: Salle des Enfants de Cherbourg - Renken
1908.07 - FRA - TR-PR: Catalogue Pathé - Bousquet
1908.08.01 - DEU - Leipzig: Colosseum - Renken

Archives: DEU-DK-Ber; FRA-CML; FRA-CNC-Par; FRA-Lob-Par; NLD-EFM-Ams; USA-AFA-Los; USA-GEM-Roc; USA-LoC-Was

Note: re-released 28mm Pathé-Kok nr 8a REPOS IMPOSSIBLE on reel with LES CHATS, total 109 m (= 138.5 m in 35mm).

1908-19
UN FIANCÉ TROP OCCUPÉ
165 m = 541 ft = 0:08:01 if at 18 fps
b&w

Fiancé trop occupé, Un - French release title (original - FRA) - Bousquet
Zu viel beschäftigte Bräutigam, Der - German release title (Ö-UM) - Renken
Vielbeschäftigter Bräutigam - German release title (DEU) - Renken
Busy Fiancé, The - English release title (USA) - Renken
Noivo occupadissimo - Portuguese release title (BRA) - Renken

A man who is so overwhelmed with business engagements that he cannot find time to pay the proper court to his fiancée, finds himself in a peculiar position, and at the mercy of his secretary, whom he sends in his place each time that he has an engagement with the young lady. We see the busy fellow write a note and give it to his secretary introducing the latter to the girl and stating that he will take his place and go driving with her. When the young man arrives at the girl's home, she is growing impatient, and when she reads the note she is indignant, but makes the most of the situation and away they go in a rig to a lonely part of the wood. They get out and gather wildflowers, and while the girl is climbing over a rock, she injures her foot and the young man is compelled to hurry her home before he has an opportunity to tell her of his infatuation for her. He comes again and things are beginning to take a serious turn for the young lady is conscious of his attentions. Her fiancée drops in for a moment and rushes away unheeding the entreaties of the girl and her parents to remain. This infuriates the father, and much to the satisfaction of the secretary, he writes a note to the busy lover telling him that as he is much too busy to think of marrying, his daughter has decided to wed the secretary. The young couple then receive the father's blessing and are happy ever after. *(Moving Picture World, 1908.07.04, in Renken)*

1908.06.13 - FRA - Cherbourg: Salle des Enfants de Cherbourg - Renken
1908.07.04 - USA - TR-PR: Moving Picture World - Bousquet
1908.08 - FRA - TR-PR: Catalogue Pathé - Bousquet
1908.08.25 - DEU - Lübeck: Tonhalle - Renken

Archives: no film print known to this date

Note: identification as a Max Linder film by Lobster Films based on production still.

1908-20
L'ONCLE À HÉRITAGE
160 m = 525 ft = 0:07:46 if at 18 fps
b&w

Oncle à héritage, L' - French release title (original - FRA) - Bousquet
Schlaue Erbonkel, Der - German release title (DEU) - Renken
Uncle's Will - English release title (GBR) - Renken
Prospective heirs - English release title (USA) - Renken

We see a young sport call on his rich uncle, who is delighted to see him, but the frigid youth receives the old man's embraces with utter indifference, which naturally infuriates the uncle. While they are conversing, another young man arrives and returns the uncle's affectionate embraces, and it is easily seen that he stands higher in the old man's good graces than the first comer. The uncle shows both young men his will and then places it in his safe in the study. He bequeaths to each of them a very comfortable fortune but is curious to know if they have any real affection for him and how his death would affect them now that they are his heirs, so decides upon a plan to find this out. After they leave, he and the maid go up into the garret and procure a dummy and dress it up in his clothes and hang it by the neck to a chandelier in the library. This done he sends the maid to inform the nephews of the terrible state of affairs and awaits developments to learn for himself their true love. When the first fellow hears the news, he is so delighted that he is overcome with glee, and after jumping around like a maniac he hastens to the home of his benefactor and makes a bee-line for the safe, hardly noticing the supposed suicide in the center of the room. As he is helping himself to the gold the uncle walks in and confronts him, and he is nearly overcome with surprise and disappointment, and can hardly believe his eyes. The second nephew comes in broken hearted at the sad news, and when the old man sees his grief, he speaks to him, and the young man is immediately changed into a happy being on seeing that his benefactor is really living. The uncle orders the mercenary fellow out of the house and gives everything to the one who has shown himself worthy of the old man's generosity. *(Moving Picture World, 1908.08.15, in Renken)*

1908.06.26 - DEU - München: Welt-Kinematograph - Renken
1908.07 - FRA - TR-PR: Catalogue Pathé - Bousquet

Archives: FRA-CF-Par

Note: identification as a Max Linder film by Georg Renken based on Brazilian press and the reproduction of a production still.

1908-21
ON DEMANDE UN GENDRE À L'ESSAI
175 m = 574 ft = 0:08:30 if at 18 fps
b&w

On demande un gendre à l'essai - French release title (original - FRA) - Bousquet
Schwiegersohn auf Probe verlangt - German release title (DEU+Ö-UM) - Renken
Wanted a Son-in-Law - English release title (GBR) - Renken
Wanted, a Son-in-Law on Trial - English release title (USA) - Renken
Precisa-se de um genro - Portuguese release title (BRA) - Renken

A young man reads an advertisement in a newspaper, stating that a wealthy woman desires to marry her daughter to a man who is willing to prove himself worthy of such a match by showing respect for the girl's mother and complying with her wishes in every particular. He sees visions of a large fortune, so starts out to win the fair maiden, undaunted by the thoughts of an exacting mother-in-law. Stopping at a flower stand, he purchases a beautiful bouquet, and saunters off to meet his fate. Arriving at the home of the girl, he is shown in and received very graciously by mother and daughter. He presents the young lady with his token of affection, and then the old woman proceeds at once to test his qualifications for the position of son-in-law. She gives him an apron and leads him into the kitchen, where he is made to scour the kettles and pans. Next they take him to the hall and compel him to take up the rug and shake it, which he does so vigorously that the old woman is nearly smothered with the dust. He is then shown into the parlor, and, to the accompaniment of the piano played by the girl, he is compelled to sweep and polish the floor

under the direction of the old woman. The latter, satisfied with the test, and finding the young man all that she desires, decides to give her consent to the marriage. The next scene shows the happy couple and their guests at the wedding breakfast, and the mother seems the happiest of the group, for she has at last found a son-in-law worthy of her daughter. When the honeymoon is over, however, and they are settled down to quiet married life, things take on a different aspect, for the young man, as head of the house, decides to assert himself. We see him lead the old woman very gently into the kitchen, where she is made to wash the dishes and clean up generally, while he struts around like a mighty monarch, and enjoys seeing her taking a dose of her own medicine.
(Moving Picture World, 1908.08.01, in Renken)

1908.07.04 - FRA - Saint Quentin: Omnia Cinématographe Pathé - Renken
1908.08 - FRA - TR-PR: Catalogue Pathé - Bousquet
1908.08.13 - Ö-UM - Graz: Grazer Bioskop - Renken

Archives: FRA-CNC-Par

Note: identification as a Max Linder film by Georg Renken based on Brazilian press and the reproduction of a production still.

1908-22
LE COUP DE FOUDRE
200 m = 656 ft = 0:09:43 if at 18 fps
b&w

Coup de foudre, Le - French release title (original - FRA) - Bousquet
Von Amors Pfeil getroffen - German release title (DEU+Ö-UM) - Renken
Lady-Killer Foiled - English release title (USA) - Renken
Raio, O - Portuguese release title (BRA) - Renken

In this extremely funny picture, we see a fellow who cannot resist the charms of the fair sex, and who gets himself into all kinds of trouble as a consequence. One day he meets a young woman by chance on the street and is so much attracted by her good looks that he follows her to her home, where she enters and slams the door in his impertinent face. This does not discourage him, however, for he goes in and sends up his card. The lady consents to see the stranger, but when she recognizes in him the fellow who has been annoying her, she immediately throws him out of the house. Undaunted by this treatment, he tries another scheme, and gets on good terms with the maid, and when madam sends for the hairdresser the girl sends word to the love smitten young man, who disguises himself as a coiffeur and once more enters the apartment of his adored one, who is seated passively in an easy chair, awaiting her hair treatment. The fellow fumbles around in an awkward manner and tries his best to comb her tresses, but gets so nervous that he tortures the woman, who resents such treatment. When she looks up, she is horrified upon recognizing her unwelcome admirer, and proceeds to give him a beating and kick him out. Next he meets a fellow entering the apartment to do some cleaning and give him some money to change clothes with him, which he does. We see our hero once more under the same roof with his enchantress, but this time her husband is a barrier and the fellow does everything to rid the place of the old fellow. He tortures him by incessantly pounding the stepladder down on his foot, till the head of the house seeks refuge in the street. When the coast is clear the ardent wooer again tries to make love to the woman, but he finds her as steadfast as ever, and this time she throws him bodily out of the window, where he falls on her unfortunate husband, who is seated underneath. Completely out of patience with the state of affairs, she discharges the maid for allowing the man to annoy her so much, and as the girl is leaving she meets the masher at the door, and gives him a case of female wearing apparel, which he dons and gets the position as new maid in the house. When he enters upon his duties it is not long before he is recognized, for he makes an attempt to kiss the madam, but is caught by her husband who gives him such a beating that he is glad to give up his wooing as a failure. *(Moving Picture World, 1908.08.15, in Renken)*

1908.07.17 - FRA - Paris: Le Cirque d'hiver - Bousquet
1908.08 - FRA - TR-PR: Catalogue Pathé - Bousquet
1908.09.12 - DEU - Lübeck: Metropol-Theater - Renken

Archives: no film print known to this day

Note: identification as a Max Linder film by Georg Renken based on French press.

1908-23
CRÉATION DE LA SERPENTINE
125 m = 410 ft = 0:06:04 if at 18 fps
Pathécolor - 122 m in colors

Création de la serpentine - French release title (original - FRA) - Bousquet
Schöpfung des Serpentintanzes - German release title (DEU+Ö-UM) - Renken
Beginning of the Serpentine Dance - English release title (GBR+USA) - Renken

In this beautifully colored picture we see a dancing master in his studio playing the violin and giving instructions to a number of beautiful maidens. They go through a minuet, and suddenly their costumes change before our very eyes, seemingly without the aid of human hands. A fellow enters, and is very much interested in the dancing lesson, but casts a spell over the group, and instantly we see them disappear into space. The visitor is then transformed into Mephistopheles and takes the dancing teacher into a large laboratory, where stands a large caldron and into which he pours some sort of fluid from a number of bottles. Stirring up the mixture, flames soon begin to shoot out, and with them a long piece of marvelously colored silk. When the cloth is shaken out a beautiful girl in flowing silk robe steps forth and dances the serpentine. As she trips around, other girls appear, and all group in a magnificent ensemble. The light effects are wonderful as they swing their draperies and gracefully go through many different figures. Finally, they all disappear into a burst of flame. *(Moving Picture World, 1909.01.16, in Renken)*

1908.07 - FRA - Paris: Le Cirque d'hiver - Bousquet
1908.09 - FRA - TR-PR: Catalogue Pathé - Bousquet
1908.10.10 - DEU - Lübeck: Metropol-Theater - Renken

Archives: FRA-CF-Par; FRA-CNC-Par; GBR-BFI-Lon; NLD-EFM-Ams; USA-LoC-Was

Note: film directed by Segundo de Chomón.

1908-24
UN MARI PEU VEINARD
170 m = 558 ft = 0:08:15 if at 18 fps
b&w

Mari peu veinard, Un - French release title (original - FRA) - Bousquet
Ehemann der Pech hat, Ein - German release title (DEU) - Renken

Pech des Gatten, Das - German release title (Ö-UM) - Renken
Hapless Hubby, The - English release title (USA) - Renken
Marido caipora - Portuguese release title (BRA) - Renken

An old man is making preparations to go on a journey, and his young and beautiful wife is assisting and hurrying him out of the way, for she is expecting a man. As the old fellow steps out of the room the young lover arrives, and the wife hides him under the table till the coast is clear. The old fellow leaves but from the look on his wife's face he sees that there is something on her mind, and he becomes suspicious. He gets outside of the room and makes a noise with his feet to mislead her and makes her think that he has gone downstairs, but instead he peers through the keyhole and, to his horror, sees his wife and the young man greet each other very affectionately. He acts upon a scheme whereby he will catch the two unawares and have revenge. He hastens down the street and spies a ladder belonging to a window cleaner, and going over, he takes it and brings it to his house and is about to climb in through his window when the owner of the ladder and a couple of policemen come along, and after a struggle, arrest the unfortunate husband as a burglar. In the meantime, the wife and her friend hear the commotion, and peering out of the window see the cause of all the trouble, and availing themselves of the opportunity, escape from the room and elope. When the husband is brought before the magistrate, he has a hard time explaining the situation but finally, after convincing the officer that he is telling the truth, he is allowed to go and he starts back home, vowing vengeance. Upon entering his apartment, he is set upon by two burglars and bound hand and foot and left to himself, while they escape with all the valuables. A messenger enters and releases him and hands him a note stating that he lost his position for neglecting his duty in not making the intended trip. *(Moving Picture World, 1908.08.29, in Renken)*

1908.07 - FRA - Paris: Omnia Pathé - Bousquet
1908.09 - FRA - TR-PR: Catalogue Pathé - Bousquet
1908.10.17 - DEU - Lübeck: Metropol-Theater - Renken

Archives: FRA-CF-Par

Note: *identification as a Max Linder film by Georg Renken based on Brazilian pres. Interestingly, Henri Bousquet notes his contents description as based on a viewing but does not mention Linder (Bousquet nr 2328).*

1908-25
LE VERTUEUX JEUNE HOMME
185 m = 607 ft = 0:08:59 if at 18 fps
b&w

Vertueux jeune homme, Le - French release title (original - FRA) - Bousquet
Tugendhafter junger Mann, Ein - German release title (DEU+Ö-UM) - Renken
Virtuous Young Man, A - English release title (GBR) - Renken
Country Lad, A - English release title (USA) - Renken
Moço virtuoso - Portuguese release title (BRA) - Renken

A young fellow from the country arrives in the city with a note from his father to an old friend, in which the parent states that the youth is about to be married, and as he is far from being up in the ways of the world, he is to have him remain in town for a while to learn something of city ways. When the young man, who is an awkward, supercilious identity, arrives at the home of the friend, he is received very cordially by the man and his loving wife. The young fellow shows at once that he has a very keen eye for beauty and is deeply impressed with his hostess. In the next picture we see the host taking the young fellow out to show him the sights. They sit at a café and are enjoying some refreshments when two pretty girls at the next table notice that our friend is a green one from the country. They carry on a flirtation, but the youth is too timid to make any advances, so finally the girls take sole possession of him and lead him away from his friend. He escapes, but they pursue him and overtake him sitting on a bench in the park, and after relieving him of his watch and money they let him trot along. He hurries back to the home of his friend and finds the wife alone, and she, being rather attracted by his demure and winning ways, makes him sit on the couch with her, and soon they are having a very pretty little love scene, when, to their horror, in walks the enraged husband. He immediately proceeds to give his guest a good beating. After kicking him all over the house, he sits down and writes a note to his father, telling him that he is returning his son after one day's stay in town, for he has graduated with honors and could even give him pointers now. He then starts the young man on his way home with a kick. *(Moving Picture World, 1908.08.29, in Renken)*

1908.08.29 - USA - Newport News: Bell Theatre - Renken
1908.09.12 - FRA - Lille: Omnia Cinéma Pathé - Renken
1908.09.15 - FRA - TR-PR: Phono-Ciné Gazette - Bousquet
1908.10 - FRA - TR-PR: Catalogue Pathé - Bousquet

Archives: no film print known to this day

Note: identification as a Max Linder film by Georg Renken based on German speaking and Brazilian press.

1908-26
CONSULTATION IMPROVISÉE
155 m = 508 ft = 0:07:32 if at 18 fps
b&w

Consultation improvisée - French release title (original - FRA) - Bousquet
Gelegenheitsarzt, Der - German release title (DEU+Ö-UM) - Renken
Improvised Consultation - English release title (GBR) - Renken
Fake Doctor, The - English release title (USA) - Renken
Consulta improvisada - Portuguese release title (BRA) - Renken

A well-known practitioner is sent for in a great hurry, and the case being a serious one, he is compelled to leave at once, although it is his office hours and a dozen or more patients are left waiting in the reception room. The doctor's servant, seeing the roomful of weary faces, decides to treat the people himself, so he disguises himself as the physician and invites each one into the office, where he attends to his complaints. The first is an unfortunate woman whom he gives an electric shock with a hand battery, not forgetting when all is over to collect his fee. Next is a soldier with a sore foot, and after nearly killing the poor fellow by burning the injured member with caustic, he takes his money and turns him out. A crazy man then enters, whom he soon soothes with a little spirits and allows to pass quietly out. Finally, a fellow with a very bad toothache comes in, and as soon as the fake doctor relieves him of his pain, the two start out to have a jolly time. They go to a café, where they imbibe freely of the luscious beverages. In the meantime, the doctor returns to his office and is horrified at the condition of the place, and hardly has he regained his composure before he is set upon by the crowd of angry patients treated by his servant, who all join in giving him an unmerciful beating. *(Moving Picture World, 1908.10.10, in Renken)*

1908.10.10 - USA - TR-PR: Moving Picture World - Renken
1908.10.11 - USA - Brooklyn, NY: Majestic - Renken
1908.12 - FRA - TR-PR: Catalogue Pathé - Bousquet
1908.12.19 - FRA - Bordeaux: Cinéma Pathé - Renken

Archives: no film print known to this day

Note: identification as a Max Linder film by Georg Renken based on Brazilian press.

1908-27
LES TRIBULATIONS D'UN NEVEU
155 m = 508 ft = 0:07:32 if at 18 fps
b&w

Tribulations d'un neveu, Les - French release title (original - FRA) - Bousquet
Erbneffe, Der - German release title (DEU+Ö-UM) - Renken
Tribulations of a Nephew, The - English re-release title (GBR) - Renken
Surprise Package - English release title (USA) - Renken

A young student from the country, who is attending college in the city, receives a letter from his aunt, telling him that she is lonely and wishes him to return and pay her a visit. He is anxious to comply with her wishes, but his little sweetheart, who is deeply in love with him, cannot bear the thought of being separated from him even for a day. He, however, manages to get away, and arriving at his aunt's home, is enjoying a quiet little chat with the old lady when the servant announces the arrival of his trunk. The young man gives orders to have it placed in his room, and upon opening it shortly afterwards, is dumbfounded to see his fiancée pop out. He is greatly excited, for he does not want the old lady to see the girl, and when they hear her footsteps on the stairs, he places her back in the trunk and assumes a careless air as his aunt enters, but manages to keep sitting on the trunk till she leaves. He then releases his prisoner and makes haste to get her out of the place, but as they are going down the stairs, the old lady puts in her appearance, and this time they seek refuge in a store room, and from there sneak into the aunt's room and hide under her bed. By this time the house is in an uproar and everybody helps to look for the young man, but their efforts being unsuccessful, the aunt prepares to retire. She gets into bed and is soon in the Land of Nod but is suddenly awakened when the couple try to make their escape. She gives the alarm and soon the whole household is on the trail of the pair, who rush down into the cellar, and try to get out through the window. The fellow manages it and is trying to drag the unfortunate girl after him when the searching party captures her. They carry her back to the room and leave her there while they summon the police, but the youth manages to get her into the trunk again and quickly locking it, throws it out the window. It lands on the sidewalk and breaks open, thus liberating the prisoner, who makes good her escape, while the people in the house are searching everywhere for her. *(The Billboard, 1908.12.12, in Renken)*

1908.11 - FRA - TR-PR: Catalogue Pathé - Bousquet
1908.11.13 - FRA - Paris: Omnia Pathé - Renken
1908.12.06 - Ö-UM - Graz: Grazer Bioskop - Renken

Archives: no film print known to this day

Note: identification as a Max Linder film by Georg Renken based on Brazilian press.

1909-01
UN BOBO MAL PLACÉ
100 m = 328 ft = 0:04:51 if at 18 fps
b&w

Bobo mal placé, Un - French release title (original - FRA) - Bousquet
Wunde an schlechter Stelle, Eine - German release title (DEU) - Renken
Case of Lumbago, A - English release title (USA) - Renken
Espinha mal collocada, Uma - Portuguese release title (BRA) - Renken

This very amusing picture shows a fellow who is suffering from a bad case of lumbago, and the excruciating pains which shoot through his system at every move cause him to wince and turn into all sorts of grotesque shapes. He has a very important social engagement and must keep it at any cost, never daring to let such a little thing as lumbago deter him. After going through all sorts of misery in dressing, he finally gets out on the street, where he hails a cab, and when he tries to enter, he is not physically capable of such a task, so the cabby is pressed into service and lifts him bodily into the rig, where now he is unable to sit down. At one jolt of the cab he falls into the seat, and is compelled to remain there until, reaching his destination, the driver lifts him out and starts him on his merry way. Entering the reception room where all the guests are assembled, he tries his best to look pleasant and he is succeeding nobly until they ask him to have a seat. Not satisfied to sit down, he refuses, whereupon one of the other guests gives him a push and with a terrible shriek he falls into the chair, nearly causing a panic among the fair ones. Finally his lady friend gets him into a cozy corner, and when he refuses to be seated she upbraids him and after giving him a rather cutting "call down", she leaves him and joins another man of a more charming disposition. *(Moving Picture World, 1909.07.17, in Renken)*

1909.05 - FRA - TR-PR: Catalogue Pathé - Bousquet
1909.06.22 - BRA - Rio de Janeiro: Cinematographo Pathé - Renken
1909.07.09 - FRA - Saint Quentin: Omnia Cinématographe Pathé - Renken

Archives: no film print known to this day

Note: identification as a Max Linder film by Georg Renken based on Brazilian press. The cause of the character's discomfort is a boil in the French and Brazilian releases, a lumbago in the American release, and an unspecified wound in the German release.

1909-02
AIMÉ PAR SA BONNE
165 m = 541 ft = 0:08:01 if at 18 fps
partially toned

Aimé par sa bonne - French release title (original - FRA) - Bousquet
Vom Dienstmädchen geliebt - German release title (DEU+Ö-UM) - Renken
Loved by his Servant - English release title (GBR) - Renken
Servant's Good Joke, The - English release title (USA) - Renken
Bonne bonne, Une - French listing title (attribution) - Pathé scénario at BNF

Max is to celebrate his engagement to a most charming young lady at her father's house. The sulky humour of the maid, Mary, passes unnoticed, for Max little guesses that Mary has fallen in love with him. Mary forms a plot to break off the engagement. She mixes an oil in the salad, which has the effect of causing Max to become unwell. For an hour or two after meeting his fiancée at her home all goes well; then a crisis of pain causes him to depart hurriedly. His intended father-in-law is so angry at what he considers an insult, that he breaks off the engagement. In the meantime, Mary has told her master the real cause of his suffering, and flattered by the feelings she expresses for him, he forgives her. *(The Bioscope, 1909.07.29 in Renken)*

1909.07.07 - DEU - CS: Zensurkarte Berlin - Renken
1909.07.24 - Ö-UM - Innsbruck: Theater-Kinematograph - Renken
1909.08 - FRA - TR-PR: Catalogue Pathé - Bousquet
1909.09.04 - FRA - Saint Quentin: Omnia Cinématographe Pathé - Renken

Archives: [FRA-FJSP-Pa or FRA-GPA-Par]

1909-03
LE PETIT JEUNE HOMME
145 m = 476 ft = 0:07:02 if at 18 fps
b&w

Petit jeune homme, Le - French release title (original - FRA) - Bousquet
Grünschnabel, Ein - German release title (DEU+Ö-UM) - Renken
Young Lady-Killer, A - English release title (GBR) - Renken
Willyboy Gets His - English release title (USA) - Renken

Willyboy, just home from college for a short holiday, starts out for a stroll. His clothes he knows are of the latest cut, and with his handsome face, killingly stylish way of walking and swinging his stick, he is not surprised at the glances of admiration directed at him by all the girls he meets. Just as he turns a corner, he collides with two queens of fashion and, bowing to the ground, begs them to excuse his awkwardness. They reply so sweetly and are altogether so charming that Willyboy decides to turn back and follow them. They are highly amused when they see the conquest they have made and throw smiling glances every now and then over their shoulders. They finally enter a bake shop and are hardly seated at one of the tables when in comes faithful Willyboy and takes a seat right next to them. He looks very demure, indeed, just as if he happened in there by the merest accident and ordering the first thing that comes into his head, finds himself compelled to eat a half dozen of the richest chocolate éclairs while he waits for the girls to finish their lunch. When they leave the store he follows right along, feeling anything but comfortable, however, after his heavy lunch. Their next stop is at the dentist's – but great indeed is his consternation as the young ladies beg the dentist to attend to him first as they are not in a hurry and can wait. Willyboy is game, however, and actually has two molars and one incisor extracted while the girls in the waiting room shriek with merriment at the trick they have played on him. When the operation is over he passes out with his handkerchief to his poor mouth and is astonished to hear the girls tell the doctor that they will put off their engagement until another day. He follows them to their home, where they invite him in and offer him some cigarettes. Now just at this particular moment smoking is the very last thing that Willyboy feels like doing. Anything but well when he left the bake shop, the teeth extracting completely finished him, and consequently after the first few puffs of the strong cigarettes provided by his chance acquaintances, our poor hero feels as if he were on the high seas and the vessel was doing a terrible lot of rolling. *(Film Index and Moving Picture World, 1909.12.11, in Renken)*

1909.08.13 - Ö-UM - Wien: Gisela-Theater - Renken
1909.09 - FRA - TR-PR: Catalogue Pathé - Bousquet
1909.09.24 - FRA - Paris: Omnia Pathé - Renken

Archives: CZE-NFA-Pra; DEU-DK-Ber; GBR-BFI-Lon

1909-04
AMOUREUX DE LA FEMME À BARBE
135 m = 443 ft = 0:06:33 if at 18 fps
b&w

Amoureux de la femme à barbe - French release title (original - FRA) - Bousquet
In eine bärtige Frau verliebt - German release title (DEU+Ö-UM) - Renken
In Love with the Bearded Woman - English release title (GBR) - Renken
Max als circus artist - Dutch re-release title [1929] - print at NLD-EFM

We have here yet another adventure of the sprightly Theodore, whose destiny seems much bound up with beards. This time it is he who succumbs to the fascinating hair, falling in love with a "bearded lady" at a fair. Her charms move him so greatly that he is induced to join the troupe with whom he is to play the part of "performing bear", doing antic gambles clad in a bearskin. Whilst he is caressing the beard, however, it comes off in his hand, and he perceives that it is an imposture. Disillusioned and filled with grief he rushes from the scene, still wearing the skin, and causes panic wherever he goes. Back into the bosom of his family the enraged showman follows him, but he is protected by maternal arms and the intruder routed. *(The Bioscope, 1909.08.26, in Renken)*

1909.08 - FRA - TR-PR: Catalogue Pathé - Bousquet
1909.08.14 - Ö-UM - Innsbruck: Apollo-Kinematograph - Renken
1909.09.24 - FRA - Lyon: Pathé Grolée - Bousquet

Archives: NLD-EFM-Ams

1909-05
UNE CONQUÊTE
130 m = 427 ft = 0:06:19 if at 18 fps
b&w

Conquête, Une - French release title (original - FRA) - Bousquet
Schlecht belohnter Verehrer, Ein - German release title (DEU+Ö-UM) - Renken
Conquest, A - English release title (GBR+USA) - Renken

George, passing a pretty woman in the street, has recourse to that old-time trick of dropping his own handkerchief and hurrying after her, making believe that he thinks it is hers. On examining the handkerchief, the beauty returns it, telling George that it does not belong to her. He then confesses that he knows very well that it is not her property, as it happens to be his own, and his offering it to her was only an excuse to make her acquaintance, so struck was he by her beauty. Upon this frank declaration the young woman draws herself up haughtily, but George is not to be discouraged, but follows closely behind her, ready to be of any assistance on the slightest pretext. We therefore see him arriving at the lady's house laden down with such articles as a lampshade, a statuette, a bunch of roses, a bundle of dress goods, and, in addition, leading an enormous dog on a leash, against whose attacks he is endeavoring to protect himself. Thinking, however, that the tête-a-tête which he expects to have with the beauty now that they have reached her home is well worth all the humiliation and inconvenience that he has suffered, George enters the house smiling like a basket of chips, only to be met by the woman's husband, who promptly kicks the officious stranger down the steps. *(The Film Index; Moving Picture World, 1910.03.26, in Renken)*

1909.09.05 - Ö-UM - Graz: Grazer Bioskop - Renken
1909.10 - FRA - TR-PR: Catalogue Pathé - Bousquet
1909.10.22 - FRA - Paris: Le Cirque d'hiver - Bousquet

Archives: FRA-CNC-Par; GBR-BFI-Lon

Note: USA release A CONQUEST on split-reel with FOXY ERNEST, 1910.03.26 b&w 350 ft of [total 384 ft] (= 106.7 m = 00:05:11 if at 18 fps).

1909-06
UN MARIAGE AMÉRICAIN
185 m = 607 ft = 0:08:59 if at 18 fps
b&w

Mariage américain, Un - French release title (original - FRA) - Bousquet
Amerikanische Hochzeit - German release title (DEU+Ö-UM) - Renken
American Marriage, An - English release title (GBR) - Renken
Miss Moneybags Wishes to Wed - English release title (USA) - Renken
Mariage à l'américaine, Un - French listing title (attribution) - Mitry

The heiress, Miss Moneybags, makes up her mind to marry, so, accompanied by her father and mother, she applies at a matrimonial agency where she is shown photographs of the different eligibles on their list, for he must possess good looks besides being a man of aristocratic birth. Several photographs are examined and cast aside until the proprietor of the agency shows them a picture of a handsome but impecunious nobleman who immediately attracts the young girl's fancy. In the next scene we see the handsome, impecunious one receiving the telephone message from the agent, saying he has an heiress for him and to come at once to the office. In his haste he wrecks the room, knocks down a fat woman on the stairs and collides with everything from an automobile to a baby carriage he meets on the way. Although spick-and-span enough when he started out, he arrives at the matrimonial agency looking like the only surviving member of a railroad wreck. When the girl sees him, she begins to cry with disappointment and the father storms around the room at the deception that has been practiced upon them. The aspirant pleads for mercy and taking the father aside explains the case to him and prevails upon him to change clothes with him. When he reappears wearing the old gentleman's frock coat he is quite presentable and the girl takes him to her heart. But the poor father who is waiting in another room decked out in the torn and tattered garments of the young man is soon set upon by a howling mob that bursts into the place looking for the man who in his hasty dash through the streets but a few moments before had aroused their indignation by colliding with and injuring each and every one of them in turn. *(The Film Index, 1910.01.15, in Renken)*

1909.09.22 - DEU - CS: Zensurkarte Berlin - Renken
1909.09.24 - Ö-UM - Wien: Welt-Biograph Theater - Renken
1909.10 - FRA - TR-PR: Catalogue Pathé - Bousquet
1909.11.05 - FRA - Paris: Omnia Pathé - Bousquet

Archives: CZE-NFA-Pra; DNK-DFI-Køb; FRA-CNC-Par; GBR-BFI-Lon; ROU-ANF-Buc

1909-07
LES SURPRISES DE L'AMOUR
140 m = 459 ft = 0:06:48 if at 18 fps
Pathécolor - 133 m in colours

Surprises de l'amour, Les - French release title (original - FRA) - Bousquet
Was Liebe zusammenbringt - German release title (DEU+Ö-UM) - Renken
Surprises of a Flirtation, The - English release title (GBR) - Renken
Love's Surprises - English listing title (attribution) - GBR-BFI

A man, his wife and their two sons are having a meal. One of the sons leaves the room pretending to be ill and collects a bunch of flowers form a cupboard and goes out. The other son takes a bunch of flowers from under his bed and he too leaves, followed by their father, also carrying flowers. The two sons and their father call on the same young women one after the other; as each arrives, the previous suitor is hidden in a piece of furniture: the father under a chair cover, one son in a cupboard and the other in a piano. A girlfriend of the young woman visits and the two play pranks on the hiding men by playing the piano and sitting on the chair cover. The three men emerge and the father chases his two sons outside until they remind him of his own folly; he gives his sons some money and urges them to keep silent. *(GBR-BFI nr 2398)*

1909.10 - FRA - TR-PR: Catalogue Pathé - Bousquet
1909.10.15 - Ö-UM - Wien: Welt-Biograph Theater - Renken
1909.12.04 - FRA - Saint Quentin: Omnia Cinématographe Pathé - Renken

Archives: DEU-DK-Ber; FRA-CNC-Par; FRA-Lob-Par; GBR-BFI-Lon; USA-AFA-Los

Note: re-released 28mm Pathé-Kok LES SURPRISES DE L'AMOUR nr 269 111 m (= 141 m in 35mm).

1909-08
PETITE ROSSE
165 m = 541 ft = 0:08:01 if at 18 fps
Pathécolor - 115 m in colours

Petite rosse - French release title (original - FRA) - Bousquet
Geprüfte Heiratskandidat, Der - German release title (DEU+Ö-UM) - Renken
Tantalising Young Lady, A - English release title (GBR) - Renken
Little Vixen, The - English release title (USA) - Renken
Max jongleur par amour - French listing title (attribution) - ITA-CdF

The daughter of the house is a domineering little miss, altogether too particular about the qualities which her sweetheart should have. He is too awkward to suit her and she recommends a course in juggling to overcome his defect. The scheme fails to work, although he tries hard enough in various foolish ways. At length he tries to win her by a ruse, inviting her and her father to visit his apartment to see him perform various feats of juggling skill. He goes through his act from behind a screen with only head and hands exposed, and the manner in which he juggles would do credit to a professional. But the miss is curious and pulls away the screen, exposing a professional who has been doing the performing. However, the trick wins the girl after all, as she is convinced that such persistence should be rewarded. *(The New York Dramatic Mirror, 1910.04.09, in Renken)*

1909.10.20 - DEU - CS: Zensurkarte Berlin - Renken
1909.10.22 - Ö-UM - Wien: Welt-Biograph Theater - Renken
1909.11 - FRA - TR-PR: Catalogue Pathé - Bousquet
1909.12.03 - FRA - Paris: Artistic Cinéma - Bousquet

Archives: CZE-NFA-Pra; ITA-CdF-Gem; USA-GEM-Roc; USA-LoC-Was

Notes: USA release THE LITTLE VIXEN on split-reel with POLAR BEAR HUNT IN THE ARCTIC SEAS 1910.03.28 b&w total 528 ft (161 m). This title is occasionally mixed-up with L'OBSESSION DE L'ÉQUILIBRE (1908-04).

1909-09
À QUI MON CŒUR?
95 m = 311.7 ft = 0:04:37 if at 18 fps
b&w

À qui mon cœur? - French release title (original - FRA) - Bousquet
Dem ersten das Herz, dem letzten die Hand - German release title (DEU+Ö-UM) - Renken
Who Will Win My Heart - English release title (GBR+USA) - Renken

A number of young men are suitors for the hand of a playful Miss, who tells them that the one that first joins her on top of the mountain shall have her heart. She starts on ahead to ascend the mountain, a series of petty scenes, and the young men follow in a wild scramble, at the end of which Max comes in last. The girl then gives the winner a paper on which she has drawn the outlines of a heart, and, turning to Max, she gives him her hand. *(The New York Dramatic Mirror, 1910.05.28, in Renken)*

1909.10.29 - Ö-UM - Wien: Welt-Biograph Theater - Renken
1909.11 - FRA - TR-PR: Catalogue Pathé - Bousquet
1909.12.06 - FRA - Paris: Omnia Pathé - Bousquet

Archives: no film print known to this day

1909-10
ROMÉO SE FAIT BANDIT
165 m = 541 ft = 0:08:01 if at 18 fps
Pathécolor - 140 m in colours

Roméo se fait bandit - French release title (original - FRA) - Bousquet
Romeo als Dieb - German release title (DEU+Ö-UM) - Renken
Romeo Turns Brigand - English release title (GBR) - Renken
Romeo Turns Bandit - English release title (USA) - Renken

Max Linder [...] appears again as an ardent suitor for a young lady's hand, the father being opposed to his pretensions. To convince him, the lover arranges with two of his friends to masquerade as bandits. They capture the father and leave him tied in a way that permits of his gaining his freedom in a short time. Then they pretend to kidnap the girl and send word that they are holding her for ransom. Max now presents himself before the father and offers to rescue her, accomplishing the feat with a droll show of bravery and prowess that wins the old gentleman's gratitude and the hand of his daughter. *(The New York Dramatic Mirror, 1910.06.04, in Renken)*

1909.11 - FRA - TR-PR: Catalogue Pathé - Bousquet
1909.11.19 - Ö-UM - Wien: Welt-Biograph Theater - Renken
1909.12.17 - FRA - Paris: Omnia Pathé - Bousquet

Archives: USA-LoC-Was; USA-MoMA-New

Note: USA release ROMEO TURNS BANDIT on split-reel with LITTLE MARY AND HER DOLLY 1910.05.23 b&w total 528 ft (161 m).

1909-11
LE VOLEUR MONDAIN
175 m = 574 ft = 0:08:30 if at 18 fps
b&w

Voleur mondain, Le - French release title (original - FRA) - Bousquet
Gentleman als Dieb, Der - German release title (DEU+Ö-UM) - Renken
Gentleman Thief, The - English release title (GBR) - Renken
Max Leads Them a Novel Chase - English release title (USA - 1910) - Renken

Arsène Lupin, as a member of the "black-dressed thieves club", has been ordered by the latter to steal Lady W's jewels in the Embassy of Pennsylvania. He accepts without any hesitation and uses every advantage conferred by his good-looking appearance to get a private meeting with Lady W, during which he succeeds in taking away the precious jewels, thanks to his prodigious ability. However, the theft is rapidly detected and a pursuit ensues. The thief uses every bit of the resources of his mind: a coat, stolen from a passerby by threatening him with a gun, a stand in a fair where he hides among the dummies, and so on. Arsène Lupin finally disappears into the crowd of the "Luna Park" fair. Nearly caught, he jumps onto a waterslide and reaches the velodrome, still chased. Finally, his pursuers hot on his trail, he arrives in front of the hot-air balloon just in time to hear the "Release!" order. So, he jumps into the basket, cuts the rope, and begins to rise into the air under the noses of his amazed and furious pursuers. *(Translation DD from Bousquet nr 3212)*

1909.11.12 - Ö-UM - Wien: Gisela-Theater - Renken
1909.12 - FRA - TR-PR: Catalogue Pathé - Bousquet
1910.01.07 - FRA - Saint Quentin: Omnia Cinématographe Pathé - Renken

Archives: DEU-DK-Ber

1909-12
EN BOMBE
185 m = 607 ft = 0:08:59 if at 18 fps
partially toned

En bombe - French release title (original - FRA) - Bousquet
Nach dem glücklich bestandenen Abiturienten Examen - German release title (DEU+Ö-UM) - Renken
Student on the Spree, A - English release title (GBR) - Renken
On a Racket - English release title (USA) - Renken
Student aan de Boemel, Een - Dutch release title (NLD) - NLD-EFM

A young man has just received his degree from college, and his delighted father gives him a pocketful of money and tells him to go out for a celebration. The youth sets out with three companions, a young man and two women, and they try to consume all the wine in Maxim's, with the result that the youth is taken home a helpless "drunk". In the dining room of his home he hangs his clothes out of the window, and goes to sleep on the dinner table, falling to the floor, where he is found by his astonished parents. *(The New York Dramatic Mirror, 1910.01.22, in Renken)*

1909.11.16 - DEU - CS: Zensurkarte Berlin - Renken
1909.11.21 - Ö-UM - Graz: Bioskop Theater Annenhof - Renken
1909.12 - FRA - TR-PR: Catalogue Pathé - Bousquet
1909.12.31 - FRA - Paris: Le Cirque d'hiver - Renken

Archives: FRA-CNC-Par; FRA-Lob-Par; NLD-EFM-Ams

1909-13
LA VENGEANCE DU BOTTIER
175 m = 574 ft = 0:08:30 if at 18 fps
partially toned

Vengeance du bottier, La - French release title (original - FRA) - Bousquet
Rache des Schuhhändlers, Die - German release title (DEU+Ö-UM) - Renken
Bootmaker's Revenge, The - English release title (GBR) - Renken
One on Max - English release title (USA - 1910) - Renken
Max fait du patinage à roulettes - French listing title (attribution) - Mitry

This time Max appears in the character of a newly engaged man, dressing with particular care to make his official entry, as it were, into the bride-elect's family. Unluckily his shoes are a wee bit tight. He resigns himself to a momentary inconvenience, and, putting on his slippers, sallies forth to purchase a new pair of shoes on his way to his fiancée's home. But, alas! for the constancy of man. Max is soon making love to the wife of the storekeeper, who, out of revenge, screws a pair of roller skates tightly on to the boots with which he is about to shoe his customer. Thus equipped, he pushes Max into the street, and his efforts to maintain his equilibrium, and to capture his silk hat, which has rolled off, makes a sight worth seeing. Failing to get the skates off, he takes a cab, into which he is assisted by the driver. Arriving at his destination he makes a precipitous entry. Once seated on a chair he refuses to move but is persuaded to take his place among the dancers, where his erratic movements cause considerable alarm. At last he relates his adventure, and amidst bursts of general laughter, someone suggests that the obvious remedy is to take the shoes off. *(The Nickelodeon, 1910.10.15, in Renken)*

1909.11.24 - DEU - CS: Zensurkarte Berlin - Renken
1909.11.25 - Ö-UM - Prag: Grand Kinematograf Orient - Renken
1909.12 - FRA - TR-PR: Catalogue Pathé - Bousquet
1910.01.28 - FRA - Paris: Le Cirque d'hiver - Bousquet

Archives: DEU-DK-Ber; GBR-BFI-Lon; ITA-FCI-Mil

Note: many frames are visible in the Turconi collection: nr 5814 to 5840.

1909-14
AVANT ET... APRÈS
140 m = 459 ft = 0:06:48 if at 18 fps
b&w

Avant et... après - French release title (original - FRA) - Bousquet
Vorher und Nachher - German release title (DEU+Ö-UM) - Renken
Before and After - English release title (GBR+USA) - Renken
Râtelier de la belle-mère, Le - French listing title (attribution) - Mitry

"Before", the suitor showers his mother-in-law-to-be with gifts and attentions, in hopes of marrying her daughter. However, "afterwards" is a different story. The very evening of the marriage, Mother-in-law insists that the young couple follow her recommendations, forcing the newlyweds to seek refuge in the kitchen. One year later, the situation has become so unbearable that Mother-in-law, in a fit of rage, grabs her son-in-law by the seat of his pants and leaves her dentures into the fleshiest part of his anatomy. *(Translation DD from Bousquet nr 3242)*

1909.12.02 - Ö-UM - Prag: Grand Kinematograf Orient - Renken
1909.12 - FRA - TR-PR: Catalogue Pathé - Bousquet
1910.01.21 - FRA - Saint Quentin: Cinéma Pathé Omnia - Renken

Archives: FRA-CdN-Nice; ITA-CdF-Gem; NLD-EFM-Ams

1909-15
LE PREMIER RENDEZ-VOUS
180 m = 591 ft = 0:08:44 if at 18 fps
partially toned

Premier rendez-vous, Le - French release title (original - FRA) - Pathé dépôt légal
Erste Rendez-vous, Das - German release title (DEU+Ö-UM) - Renken
Primeiro rendez-vous, O - Portuguese release title (BRA) - Renken
Ensimäinen kosintaretki - Finnish release title (FIN) - Renken

Young Max is enjoying his first love story. That very night, he has a date with a middle-aged woman he had met during the summer and who, while visiting Paris with her husband, had decided to succumb to his advances. Max has to walk through his parents' bedroom to go out. Quite confused, he topples some pieces of furniture and falls down on the floor making a deafening noise while his parents get out of bed and quickly send him back to his room... The desperate lover suddenly gets an idea and exits by the window thanks to a knotted rope. Immediately arrested, the mischievous young man shows the policemen the love letter. They let him go, and while laughing, they threaten him with their raised fingers. He finally reaches the "Modern Hotel", aim of his future happiness, where he asks for the room noted in the letter. Well! There's a huge pair of boots in front of the door. There is no doubt that's an error. And a pair of cute shoes in front of next door indicates where his beloved date is waiting for him. He comes in and hears a peaceful breathing: She's sleeping! He comes near the bed, grasps a hand, tenderly kisses it and begins to fully enjoy that moment of grace when he is suddenly kicked and punched so vigorously that he rolls on the floor, more dead than alive. He had pushed the wrong door and entered the husband's room. Bruised and miserable, the poor lover rapidly walks away. He goes home, where his elopement has been discovered. Already traumatized by the experience, he has now to undergo his parents' barrage of blame and criticism. *(Translation DD from scénario Pathé pour dépôt légal 1909 nr 9004)*

1909.12.03 - FIN - Helsinki: Maailman Kuvat - Renken
1910.01 - FRA - TR-PR: Catalogue Pathé - Bousquet
1910.04.10 - FRA - Dunkerque: Cinéma Pathé - Renken

Archives: DEU-DK-Ber

Note: the film strip accompanying the legal deposit file at the BNF shows a different actor. The German title DAS ERSTE RENDEZ-VOUS is also linked to the film PREMIÈRE SORTIE (1905-01) by German archives.

1909-16
LES EXPLOITS DU JEUNE TARTARIN
135 m = 443 ft = 0:06:33 if at 18 fps
partially toned

Exploits du jeune Tartarin, Les - French release title (original - FRA) - Bousquet
Prahlhansens Heldentaten - German release title (DEU+Ö-UM) - Renken
Adventures of Tartarin the Younger - English release title (GBR) - Renken

Back from Africa, Daniel Tartarin details his adventures to his bride and his in-laws: "I killed 25 lions, 19 elephants, 50 panthers… I saw death coming to me and I've never been afraid…" His audience, captivated, is hanging on every word. The clock strikes midnight when our hero goes home. There's nobody in the street. A man with a sinister look approaches. Tartarin runs away, the man quickens his pace. Trapped, his knees shaking, a gun in each trembling hand, young Tartarin turns to face his enemy. "Gimme a light, please." Back home, Tartarin dreams that, attacked by a huge rat, he loses that ridiculous fight, and that consequently his bride turns her back on him. Fortunately, it was just a dream and our hero, now fully awakened, regains his glory and his bride.
(Translation DD from Bousquet nr 3306)

1909.12.31 - Ö-UM - Wien: Welt-Biograph Theater - Renken
1910.01 - FRA - TR-PR: Catalogue Pathé - Bousquet
1910.02.11 - FRA - Paris: Omnia Pathé - Bousquet

Archives: no film print known to this day

1910-01
LA TIMIDITÉ GUÉRIE PAR LE SÉRUM
140 m = 459 ft = 0:06:48 if at 18 fps
b&w

Timidité guérie par le sérum, La - French release title (original - FRA) - Bousquet
Serum gegen Schüchternheit, Ein - German release title (DEU+Ö-UM) - Renken
Cure for Cowardice, A - English release title (GBR) - Renken
Cure for Timidity, A - English release title (USA) - Renken
Timidez curada pelo serum, La - Portuguese release title (BRA) - Renken
Timidité vaincue, La - French listing title (attribution) - Mitry
Timidez curada, La - Spanish listing title [attribution] - Magliozzi

We see [Max Linder as] a weak coward, who lives in constant terror of his wife and mother-in-law, and who is intimidated even by the servants. One day he notices an advertisement in the paper, announcing that a certain learned doctor has discovered a simple but infallible cure for cowardice. The timorous one immediately sets forth to be cured, and promptly proves his boldness by sternly refusing to pay the medical man more than half his fee. He encounters trams, which he pushes valiantly out of his way, sending them running backwards on their courses by the strength of his arm, and, having arrived home, he very shortly demonstrates to his household that his temperament has undergone a considerable change. A final picture of much humor shows him in the arms of his now devoted wife and mother-in-law, being waited upon by them hand and foot with the utmost servility. *(The Bioscope, 1910.01.27, in Renken)*

1910.01 - FRA - TR-PR: Catalogue Pathé - Bousquet
1910.01.14 - Ö-UM - Wien: Graben-Kino - Renken
1910.03.12 - FRA - Saint Quentin: Cinéma Pathé Omnia - Renken

Archives: GBR-BFI-Lon; URY-ANIP-Mon

Note: USA release A CURE FOR TIMIDITY on split -reel with A SEASIDE FLIRTATION 1910.03.11 b&w total 564 ft (172 m).

1910-02
UNE BONNE POUR MONSIEUR, UN DOMESTIQUE POUR MADAME
150 m = 492 ft = 0:07:17 if at 18 fps
partially toned

Bonne pour Monsieur, un domestique pour Madame, Une - French release title (original - FRA) - Bousquet
Dienstmädchen für den Herrn, einen Diener für die Frau, Ein - German release title (DEU+Ö-UM) - Renken
Servants and Masters - English release title (GBR) - Renken

Monsieur has great sympathy for his maid, Madame for her servant. Both rascals take advantage of the situation to have their work done by their employers, while they go out partying. They even dare to pay a visit to some of their masters' friends, where they create a great scandal under the names of Baron and Baroness of Copurchick. Monsieur and Madame, who see things more clearly now, fire the two associates. *(Translation DD from Bousquet nr 3361)*

1910.01.21 - DEN - København: Kosmorama - Renken
1910.02 - FRA - TR-PR: Catalogue Pathé - Bousquet
1910.03.11 - FRA - Paris: Omnia Pathé - Bousquet

Archives: CZE-NFA-Pra

1910-03
JEUNE FILLE ROMANESQUE
135 m = 443 ft = 0:06:33 if at 18 fps
partially toned

Jeune fille romanesque - French release title (original - FRA) - Bousquet
Schwärmerisches Mädchen, Ein - German release title (DEU+Ö-UM) - Renken
Romantic Young Lady, A - English release title (GBR) - Renken
Romantic Girl, A - English release title (USA) - Renken

Her head filled with the thrilling feats of Arsène Lupin, Dolly decides to marry only one who can perform some deed worthy of the great Arsène himself. The most ardent of her admirers is the ever-sprightly Max, who accepts the challenge with alacrity. After a few moments' thought Max announces that he will stand a supper to Dolly and the others present without paying for it. His invitation is accepted with glee, and with Dolly herself at the head, the party assembles at the restaurant named by Max. The supper is a huge success, but the time for reckoning soon comes. Max, however, is quite imperturbable, and calmly requests his guests each to make a feint of being eager to pay the bill when it is presented. The waiter is accordingly perplexed and it is therefore suggested that the waiter be blindfolded, and the one caught by him shall pay. The waiter agrees, allows himself to be blindfolded, and eventually succeeds in catching the proprietor of the restaurant long after Max and his guests have got away through the open window. *(The Film Index; Moving Picture World, 1910.05.07, in Renken)*

1910.01.28 - Ö-UM - Wien: Graben-Kino - Renken
1910.02 - FRA - TR-PR: Catalogue Pathé - Bousquet
1910.03.18 - FRA - Paris: Omnia Pathé - Bousquet

Archives: no film print known to this day

1910-04
LE PACTE
155 m = 508 ft = 0:07:32 if at 18 fps
partially toned

Pacte, Le - French release title (original - FRA) - Bousquet
Vertrag, Der - German release title (DEU+Ö-UM) - Renken
Pact, The - English release title (GBR) - Renken
Max in a Dilemma - English release title (USA) - Renken

In a condition of dire poverty [Max] nevertheless proposes for a fair maiden's hand; but, although she is willing to give her consent, her father, a gentleman of stern and forbidding appearance, makes strong and decided objections to the alliance, and turns the wretched Max summarily into the street. The poor youth goes home and attempts a horrid suicide, but his courage fails him and he employs a burglar -who puts in an opportune appearance- to undertake that he shall be dead by midnight in return for a consideration of money. Immediately the thief has departed; however, a solicitor enters to inform Max that he has become the heir to an enormous fortune. Overjoyed, he rushes back to the home of his beloved and announces his good fortune. He is now the honored guest and dear friend of his prospective father-in-law, and all goes merrily until the servant enters to say that someone has called to see Mr. Linder. He rises from the table and goes to the next room, where he is horrified to find the burglar who has promised to kill him. Immediately he turns and flies from the place, hotly followed by the thief, who pursues him, wildly brandishing a tremendous knife, previously given to him by Max for the execution of the bloody deed. The chase continues for a long time, and eventually the flying lover is caught, only to learn that the burglar has repented of his contract and wishes, with an honesty surely somewhat unnatural, to restore the knife and the money. *(The Bioscope, 1910.02.24, in Renken)*

1910.02 - FRA - TR-PR: Catalogue Pathé - Bousquet
1910.02.11 - Ö-UM - Wien: Welt-Biograph Theater - Renken
1910.04.16 - FRA - Saint Quentin: Cinéma Pathé Omnia - Renken

Archives: FRA-CF-Par; FRA-CNC-Par

Note: USA release MAX IN A DILEMMA on split-reel with THE MEXICAN TUMBLERS 1910.09.23 b&w 446 ft (136 m) or on split-reel with MICRO-CINEMATOGRAPHY: RECURRENT FEVER 1910.11.07.

1910-05
SOLDAT PAR AMOUR
135 m = 443 ft = 0:06:33 if at 18 fps
b&w

Soldat par amour - French release title (original - FRA) - Bousquet
Soldat aus Liebe - German release title (DEU+Ö-UM) - Renken
Max soldat de 2eme classe - French re-release title (28mm) - Catalogue Pathé-Kok
Max Serves as a Soldier - English re-release title (28mm) - print at USA-GEM
Max soldat - French listing title (attribution) - ITA-CdF
Max Soldier, 2nd Class - English listing title (attribution) - FIAF TFA db

Max, a dashing lover, flirts with his captain's daughter when the father comes home unexpectedly. Feeling very embarrassed, the young man decides to put the secretary's uniform on and to clean the furniture energetically. The captain sends him to the troop headquarters where the new draftee stumbles from one mistake to the other, infuriates his superiors, and is finally put in jail. Driven out of military career for a lifetime, Max gets rid of his uniform and puts on civilian clothes. Everything is clear now. Confused, the captain forgives him. *(Translation DD from Bousquet nr 3426)*

1910.02.17 - Ö-UM - TR-PR: Kinematographische Rundschau - Renken
1910.02.25 - Ö-UM - Wien: Graben-Kino - Renken
1910.03 - FRA - TR-PR: Catalogue Pathé - Bousquet
1910.04.15 - FRA - Paris: Omnia Pathé - Bousquet

Archives: ESP-FdC-Bar; FRA-Lob-Par; ITA-CdF-Gem; USA-GEM-Roc

Note: re-released 28mm Pathé-Kok nr 204b MAX SOLDAT DE 2E CLASSE, on reel with ROMÉO COLLECTIONNE LES PAPILLONS, total length 112 m (= 142 m in 35mm).

1910-06
JE VOUDRAIS UN ENFANT
160 m = 525 ft = 0:07:46 if at 18 fps
b&w

Je voudrais un enfant - French release title (original - FRA) - Bousquet
Sehnsucht nach einem Kind - German release title (DEU) - Renken
Max Linder's Big Family - English release title (GBR) - Renken
Ich möchte ein Kind - German re-release title (28mm) - AUT-FAA

The young couple Kalsourir is unable to have a baby. Out of desperation, they decide to test a new technique of spontaneous generation that proves so successful that they give birth to a dozen children, including a black one! *(Translation DD from Bousquet nr 3418)*

1910.02.18 - DEN - København: Kosmorama - Renken
1910.03 - FRA - TR-PR: Catalogue Pathé - Bousquet
1910.04.08 - FRA - Paris: Omnia Pathé - Bousquet

Archives: AUT-FAA-Wie; DEU-DK-Ber; FRA-CF-Par; FRA-CML; FRA-CNC-Par; FRA-Lob-Par

Note: re-released 28mm Pathé-Kok nr 85 JE VOUDRAIS UN ENFANT 120 m (= 152 m in 35mm).

1910-07
LE SERMENT D'UN PRINCE
175 m = 574 ft = 0:08:30 if at 18 fps
partially toned

Serment d'un prince, Le - French release title (original - FRA) - Bousquet
Schwur eines Fürsten, Der - German release title (DEU+Ö-UM) - Renken
Prince's Honour, A - English release title (GBR) - Renken
Prince of Worth, A - English release title (USA) - Renken

A young prince secretly married to a gypsy girl is forced to disclose the fact when his father desires him to marry a wealthy girl. Cast out by his parents he is forced to earn his own living and commencing in the streets as an acrobat he eventually becomes the star turn in a prominent vaudeville house. His father one night sees his son's performance and pleased with his success agrees to a reconciliation with him, his wife and little child. Max Linder plays the chief part in the film and his cleverness on the trapeze shows him in a new light. *(The Film Index; Moving Picture World, 1910.05.28, in Renken)*

1910.02.24 - Ö-UM - TR-PR: Kinematographische Rundschau - Renken
1910.03 - FRA - TR-PR: Catalogue Pathé - Bousquet
1910.03.08 - DEN - København: Royal-Biograf Theater - Renken
1910.04.22 - FRA - Paris: Omnia Pathé - Bousquet

Archives: SWE-SFI-Sto

1910-08
MAUVAISE VUE
135 m = 443 ft = 0:06:33 if at 18 fps
partially toned

Mauvaise vue - French release title (original - FRA) - Bousquet
Schlechte Augen - German release title (DEU+Ö-UM) - Renken
Double Sight, A - English release title (GBR) - Renken
One Can't Believe One's Eyes - English release title (USA) - Renken
Mauvaise vie, Une - French listing title (attribution) - Ford

The wife of a jealous Colonel is surprised by her husband talking with one of his officers, who immediately runs away, leaving her to assure her husband that he was surely the subject of hallucinations. Mrs. Colonel finds her maid in the hall making love to a private and sees a chance of deluding the Colonel into the belief that he was mistaken. So, she instructs him to make a noise under the Colonel's window so that he will see that he is not dressed according to the regulations, she having made him take off his sword. The Colonel on looking out notices this and calls him up and is about to reprimand him when he sees the sword is now on the soldier's belt, having meantime been replaced with the help of the Colonel's wife. This happens again and the Colonel begins to think his eyesight is really leaving him and he tells his wife that his eyes are not what they were and that he was mistaken in the first place. *(The Film Index; Moving Picture World, 1910.06.04, in Renken)*

1910.03 - FRA - TR-PR: Catalogue Pathé - Bousquet
1910.03.11 - Ö-UM - Wien: Welt-Biograph Theater - Renken
1910.04.29 - FRA - Paris: Le Cirque d'hiver - Renken

Achives: FRA-CF-Par

1910-09
UNE RUSE DE MARI [1910]
140 m = 459 ft = 0:06:48 if at 18 fps
b&w

Ruse de mari, Une - French release title (original - FRA) - Bousquet
List des Gatten - German release title (DEU+Ö-UM) - Renken
Hubby Cures His Wife of Flirting - English release title (GBR) - Renken

The spouses Follichon come to bitter words about a trifle. In a state of terrible excitement, Madame, determined to take her revenge, sends a letter to one of her suitors so that he can come and flirt with her. In the meantime, Mr Follichon comes back repentant and finds the message. A Machiavellian idea comes into his mind: he sends the same letter to another suitor. What ensues can easily been imagined. Reunited in the same place, the two young lovers fight while the astute husband regains his wife. *(Translation DD from Bousquet nr 3471)*

1910.03.10 - DEU - TR-PR: Kinematographische Rundschau - Renken
1910.03.21 - DEN - København: Kosmorama - Renken
1910.04 - FRA - TR-PR: Catalogue Pathé - Bousquet
1910.05.06 - FRA - Paris: Le Cirque d'hiver - Renken

Archives: no film print known to this day

Note: see also RUSE DE MARI [1907] (1907-06).

1910-10
UNE REPRÉSENTATION AU CINÉMA
150 m = 492 ft = 0:07:17 if at 18 fps
partially toned

Représentation au cinéma, Une - French release title (original - FRA) - Bousquet
Vorstellung im Kinematograph - German release title (DEU+Ö-UM) - Renken
At the Cinematograph Theatre - English release title (GBR) - Renken
Représentation au Cinématographe - French listing title (attribution) - Mitry
Scéance de cinématographie, Une - French listing title (attribution) - Ford

In the packed movie theater, an enthusiastic audience waits for the film to begin. The first act is a drama: a husband finds his wife embracing a man. He protests vigorously. Gunshots, bloodbath.

The spectators, terrified, dry their tears with handkerchiefs. Act nr 2, Gugusse enters. The audience roars with laughter at the clown's antics. Then news and various events ensue; we can see the gate of a house that hides a horrible drama... a desperate man has jumped out of a wide open window. Then a car that has broken down when its 40 horsepowers jumped out of the engine to follow a mare. Finally, the frightening vision of a stormy sea with small boats in danger provokes in the audience the same reactions as those experienced on ocean liners by passengers who are not veterans of the sea. The spectators go out silently in small groups, much too happy to put their feet back on the asphalted and solid Parisian ground. *(Translation DD from Bousquet nr 3493)*

1910.03.17 - Ö-UM - TR-PR: Kinematographische Rundschau - Renken
1910.03.25 - Ö-UM - Wien: Graben-Kino - Renken
1910.04 - FRA - TR-PR: Catalogue Pathé - Bousquet
1910.05.27 - FRA - Saint Quentin: Cinéma Pathé Omnia - Renken

Archives: no film print known to this day

1910-11
L'INGÉNIEUX ATTENTAT
130 m = 427 ft = 0:06:19 if at 18 fps
partially toned

Ingénieux attentat, L' - French release title (original - FRA) - Bousquet
Geldnot macht erfinderisch - German release title (DEU+Ö-UM) - Renken
Poor Pa Pays Again - English release title (GBR) - Renken
Max Makes a Touch - English release title (USA) - Renken

Max and Mick, two brothers, have prepared for a merry spree and are actually stepping into their cab when it occurs to them they are penniless. Lots are drawn to see who shall beard stern father and make the necessary touch. The choice falls on Max who is far from successful in his mission, and he communicates the bad news to his brother Mick, who after some thinking announces that he has an idea. One disguises as a thief and the other as a policeman. The thief holds up his parents as they leave the house, but the constable puts him to flight and receives a handsome reward. Their parents out of sight they discard their disguises, divide the reward and proceed out to enjoy themselves. *(The Film Index; Moving Picture World, 1910.06.18, in Renken)*

1910.03.24 - ÖST - TR-PR: Kinematographische Rundschau - Renken
1910.04 - FRA - TR-PR: Catalogue Pathé - Bousquet
1910.04.01 - Ö-UM - Wien: Graben-Kino - Renken
1910.05.20 - FRA - Paris: Omnia Pathé - Bousquet

Archives: FRA-CF-Par; FRA-CML; FRA-CNC-Par; NLD-EFM-Ams

Note: re-released 28mm Pathé-Kok nr 869 L'INGÉNIEUX ATTENTAT 100 m (= 127 m in 35mm).

1910-12
TOUT EST BIEN QUI FINIT BIEN
140 m = 459 ft = 0:06:48 if at 18 fps
b&w

Tout est bien qui finit bien - French release title (original - FRA) - Bousquet
Verliebte Max, Der - German release title (DEU+Ö-UM) - Renken

All's Well That Ends Well - English release title (GBR) - Renken
Perseverance Rewarded - English release title (USA) - Renken

For weeks Max has been vainly endeavoring to make the acquaintance of a young lady living in the opposite house; her charms have captured his fancy, but his love-lorn looks and the persistency with which he hovers in the vicinity when she takes walks abroad, have not the slightest effect upon her. He is therefore obliged to resort to stratagem He bribes a tramp to make an assumed assault upon the damsel, courageously rescues her at the proper moment, and is rewarded for his gallantry by permission to see her safely to her door. From that day forth Max makes rapid progress in his lovemaking, and kisses are often blown across the street from one window to the other. It happens, however, that the two young people are caught one afternoon in the exercise of this agreeable pastime, the one by her mother, the other by his father. They being desirous of discovering the object of such passionate demonstrations, look out of the window across the street. Their stupefaction is mutual at the view of a visage from which the beauty of youth has long since passed and finds vent on the exchange of notes the reverse of flattering. Their discussion is continued in the street and observing that it is likely to last some time, the young couple slip from their windows to the ground and walk hurriedly away arm in arm. Their disappearing backs are suddenly perceived by their elders, and a gasp of amazement announces the realization of their mistake, which is quickly followed by the conviction that it would be well to continue their own acquaintanceship so inauspiciously commenced. *(The Film Index; Moving Picture World, 1910.06.26, in Renken)*

1910.03.31 - Ö-UM - TR-PR: Kinematographische Rundschau - Renken
1910.04 - FRA - TR-PR: Catalogue Pathé - Bousquet
1910.04.08 - Ö-UM - Wien: Graben-Kino - Renken
1910.05.27 - FRA - Paris: Le Cirque d'hiver - Bousquet

Archives: BEL-CRB-Bru; FRA-Lob-Par; NLD-EFM-Am; USA-GEM-Roc

1910-13
KYRELOR, BANDIT PAR AMOUR
185 m = 607 ft = 0:08:59 if at 18 fps
partially toned

Kyrelor, bandit par amour - French release title (original - FRA) - Bousquet
Kyrelor, Bandit aus Liebe - German release title (DEU+Ö-UM) - Renken
Baffles, Bandit - English release title (GBR) - Renken
Max Foils the Police - English release title (USA) - Renken
Kirelor, bandit par amour - French listing title (attribution) - Bousquet

With the aid of two friends Max carries off a damsel whose parents wish to force her into a distasteful marriage. Thereafter he checkmates the police at every turn, and finally penetrates into the office of the chief of police. Here a struggle takes place between the two men. Max underneath his opponent is forced into a large chest, the struggle continues, the chief presently emerges, locks the box upon his captive, and gives instructions for the chest and the man inside to be incarcerated. The moment his subordinates have left the room to carry out his instructions, he removes his wig, and lo, and behold, it is Max, who calmly makes his way to the cell and turns the key upon the police and the real chief of the police inside the box. To inveigle his rival into stabbing a life size dummy of himself is Max's next act, and then having scared the guilty man pretty well out of his senses by his sudden apparition, this imperturbable outlaw finds time to turn his attention to the delights of lovemaking. *(The Nickelodeon, 1911.07.01, in Renken)*

1910.04.15 - Ö-UM - Wien: Graben-Kino - Renken
1910.05 - FRA - TR-PR: Catalogue Pathé - Bousquet
1910.07.03 - FRA - Lille: Omnia Cinéma Pathé - Renken

Archives: DEU-DK-Ber; FRA-CNC-Par

Note: USA release MAX FOILS THE POLICE on split-reel with RIDING FEATS BY COSSACKS 1910.07.02 b&w total 571 ft (174 m).

1910-14
AMOUR ET FROMAGE
180 m = 591 ft = 0:08:44 if at 18 fps
b&w

Amour et fromage - French release title (original - FRA) - Bousquet
Liebe und Käse - German release title (DEU+Ö-UM) - Renken
Cheese and Kisses - English release title (GBR) - Renken
Love and Cheese - English release title (USA) - Renken

Marie, the maid, loves Monsieur. However, Monsieur is engaged, and Marie is thus burning with love and jealousy. She concocts in her mind many sinister projects whose only aim is to prevent Monsieur from marrying Miss Binjouin. At last, the pungent fragrance of a cheese gives birth to a strategy. She superstitiously puts the odorous camembert cheese into her beloved master's pocket, when he is about to go out to his future in-laws'. He displays the talents and skills that usually turn him into the life of the party, but all the members of the Binjouin family turn away because of the specific smell that emanates from him. The lover, bewildered, checks his shoe soles. Nothing! He then scrutinizes his clothes and finally finds out about it, i.e. the camembert cheese that, to his great surprise, travels by itself towards the cheese cover. *(Translation DD from Bousquet nr 3562)*

1910.04.27 - DEU - CS: Zensurkarte Berlin - Renken
1910.04.29 - Ö-UM - Wien: Graben-Kino - Renken
1910.05 - FRA - TR-PR: Catalogue Pathé - Bousquet
1910.07.15 - FRA - Lille: Omnia Cinéma Pathé - Renken
Archives: AUT-ÖFM-Wie; FRA-Lob-Par; USA-AFA-Los; USA-UCLA-Los
Note: re-released 28mm Pathé-Kok nr 286 AMOUR ET FROMAGE 118 m (= 150 m in 35mm).

1910-15
UNE ÉPREUVE DIFFICILE
190 m = 623 ft = 0:09:14 if at 18 fps
b&w

Épreuve difficile, Une - French release title (original - FRA) - Bousquet
Max und das Edelweiss - German release title (DEU+Ö-UM) - Renken
Difficult Task, A - English release title (GBR) - Renken
Max in the Alps - English release title (USA) - Renken
Max et l'edelweiss - French listing title (attribution) - Magliozzi
Max dans les Alpes - French listing title (attribution) - Bousquet

Max has fallen in love with a pretty widow staying in the Alpine district. The widow is not at all certain that her light-hearted adorer will not soon turn to other loves. She proposes, therefore, as a test of his devotion, that he shall gather her a sprig of edelweiss, that rare flower that is only to be found on the tops of the mountains. Max starts out to execute his mission, and with his immaculate silk hat, light cane, and accurately creased trousers commences forthwith the ascent of an Alpine peak, evidently considering that the warmth of his passion will keep the cold out. He sights one of the blossoms through his telescope and heroically plunges through the snow, prodding his way with his stick and stumbling, slipping, and falling. Now he will disappear almost entirely beneath a mass of snow, with the top of his hat only to be seen, the next minute he has emerged and is struggling upwards, it is a hopeless task to attempt to describe the whole of the climb, which is rich in humor of the right sort. We will pass over the various incidents until the time when Max, having measurably decreased the distance between him and the longed-for flower, makes a false step and falls down the mountain. Luckily, he is unhurt, but his spirits and his silk hat are both crushed. He screws his eye to the glass, takes a peek at the far-away flower which seems to mock at his misery, and decides to relinquish the task. He accordingly picks himself up and makes his way towards his hotel. On the way he meets an edelweiss seller, and in an instant makes up his mind what to do. He purchases a blossom, and bearing it away with great care, lays it in triumph at the feet of his enchantress. *(The Film Index; Moving Picture World, 1910.10.29, in Renken)*

1910.05 - FRA - TR-PR: Catalogue Pathé - Bousquet
1910.05.06 - Ö-UM - Wien: Welt-Biograph Theater - Renken
1910.07.09 - FRA - Saint Quentin: Cinéma Pathé Omnia - Renken

Archives: BEL-CRB-Bru; CZE-NFA-Pra; USA-MoMA-New

Note: USA release MAX IN THE ALPS on split-reel with BUFFALO FIGHT 1910.10.28 b&w 610 ft (186 m).

1910-16
LE DUEL DE MR MYOPE
130 m = 427 ft = 0:06:19 if at 18 fps
b&w

Duel de Mr Myope, Le - French release title (original - FRA) - Bousquet
Maxens Duell - German release title (DEU+Ö-UM) - Renken
Short-Sighted Duelist, A - English release title (GBR) - Renken
Max Has Trouble With His Eyes - English release title (USA) - Renken
Kurzsichtige Max, Der - German listing title (attribution) - DEU-B/F
Duel du monsieur myope, Le - French listing title (attribution) - Mitry
Duel d'un Monsieur Myope, Le - French listing title (attribution) - FRA-CF

Max Linder [...] has had the misfortune to become exceedingly short-sighted; so much so that we see him stumbling into various inanimate objects, and profusely apologizing to them. Having received a note from his inamorata making an appointment with him at a café, Max sets off, and arrives there first. Here he mistakes another lady for his sweetheart, and fondly embraces her, to the extreme annoyance of her male companion. Max apologizes, but that does not satisfy the angry man and his friend, and a duel is arranged. The two meet, accompanied by their respective seconds, and Max's opponent fires first and then climbs up the nearest tree. Max has been peering in all directions, and then, advancing close to the afore-mentioned with the result that he inflicts a wound after all upon his tree-climbing adversary. *(The Bioscope, 1910.05.26, in Renken)*

1910.05 - FRA - TR-PR: Catalogue Pathé - Bousquet
1910.05.13 - Ö-UM - Wien: Welt-Biograph Theater - Renken

1910.07.01 - FRA - Paris: Omnia Pathé - Bousquet

Archives: CAN-CQ-Mon; FRA-CF-Par; FRA-CML; JPN-NFAJ-Tōk; USA-MoMA-New

Note: USA release MAX HAS TROUBLE WITH HIS EYES on split-reel with DARJILING and NEW STYLE INKWELL 1910.10.31 b&w [total] 394 ft (120 m).

1910-17
LE REVOLVER ARRANGE TOUT
170 m = 558 ft = 0:08:15 if at 18 fps
b&w

Revolver arrange tout, Le - French release title (original - FRA) - Bousquet
Macht des Revolvers, Die - German release title (DEU+Ö-UM) - Renken
Persuasive Powers of a Revolver, The - English release title (GBR) - Renken
Max Has to Change - English release title (USA) - Renken

Max, having made the acquaintance of a millionaire, is invited to a social evening to help entertain the guests. The host's daughter falls violently in love with him and announces to her father that she means to marry him. Her ideas do not coincide with those of her father, who declares to that young man of genius that if he does not find some means of breaking it off, he will blow his (Max's) brains out. Max politely refuses, but the barrel of a revolver brings him to a more amenable frame of mind, and we find him next day doing his best to destroy the good impression that the young heiress has of him. For some time the girl tries hard to believe that to dust boots with a serviette and to use fingers instead of a fork are but the vagaries of a genius. She, however, gets thoroughly disgusted when Max, feigning to be intoxicated, does some most outrageous things. She rushes out of the room, leaving her father convulsed at Max's antics. So thoroughly diverted is he and so excellent a fellow does he now find Max that he abruptly changes his mind and insists that Max must marry his daughter. Again, Max refuses, but the ever-ready gun is whipped out, and at the point of the revolver he makes his peace with the girl and confesses that he was compelled by her father to behave as he did. *(The Nickelodeon, 1910.08.15, in Renken)*

1910.05.20 - Ö-UM - Wien: Welt-Biograph Theater - Renken
1910.06 - FRA - TR-PR: Catalogue Pathé - Bousquet
1910.07.08 - FRA - Paris: Omnia Pathé - Bousquet

Archives: no film print known to this day

Note: USA release MAX HAS TO CHANGE on split-reel with BACK TO LIFE AFTER 2,000 YEARS 1910.08.15 b&w total 476 ft (145 m).

1910-18
MAX FAIT DU SKI
135 m = 443 ft = 0:06:33 if at 18 fps
b&w

Max fait du ski - French release title (original - FRA) - Bousquet
Max lernt Skilaufen - German release title (DEU+Ö-UM) - Renken
Max Tries Ski-ing - English release title (GBR) - Renken
Max Goes Ski-ing - English release title (USA) - Renken

Max la schi - Romanian title - ROU-ANF

In a snowy Alpine district Max takes his first lessons in the art of ski-ing. He leaves his hotel with his skis fixed to his shoes, and his efforts and contortions to get through the door of his room are absurdly ludicrous. Finally, he manages to get out and we see him making frantic efforts to maintain his equilibrium on a fairly gentle slope. Max is plucky, and in spite of numerous falls, sticks to his purpose, although his attitudes and the knots in which he ties himself are excruciatingly funny. Finally, we find him making his first leap; it is not exactly successful, and in the last scene the unhappy novice appears to be endeavoring to escape from the snowballs that the children of the village are pelting him with. *(The Nickelodeon, 1910.12.15, in Renken)*

1910.05.27 - Ö-UM - Wien: Welt-Biograph Theater - Renken
1910.06 - FRA - TR-PR: Catalogue Pathé - Bousquet
1910.07.15 - FRA - Paris: Omnia Pathé - Bousquet

Archives: FRA-CF-Par; FRA-CML; FRA-CNC-Par; FRA-Lob-Par; ROU-ANF-Buc

Note: USA release MAX GOES SKI-ING on split-reel with THE RUNAWAY MOTOR CAR 1910.12.21 b&w total 430 ft (131 m) – re-released 28mm Pathé-Kok nr 699 MAX FAIT DU SKI 105 m (= 133 m in 35mm).

1910-19
MAX EST DISTRAIT
190 m = 623 ft = 0:09:14 if at 24 fps
b&w

Max est distrait - French release title (original - FRA) - Bousquet
Zerstreute Max, Der - German release title (DEU+Ö-UM) - Renken
Absent-Minded Max - English release title (GBR) - Renken
Max is Absent Minded - English release title (USA) - Renken
Max distrait - French listing title (attribution) - FRA-CNC

Max appears to have grown absent-minded, and we see him pouring coffee into his hat, deserting fair companions in the street, and borrowing lights without returning the cigarettes to their rightful owners. Max is about to be married, and he is also negotiating for the purchase of a mare. However, he finds the animal unsuitable, and writes a note to the dealer to the effect that he is not inclined to buy. He has hardly signed the letter, when he receives another from his future father-in-law, with an invitation to dine and to fix the date of the wedding. Max replies, but slips his notes into the wrong envelopes, so that the old gentleman receives the following: "It is useless your reckoning upon me. I do not want her for several reasons: first, because she is too old; secondly, she is knock-kneed; and, lastly, she bites." It now appears that the engagement has been broken off! *(The Bioscope, 1910.06.30, in Renken)*

1910.06.17 - Ö-UM - Wien: Welt-Biograph Theater - Renken
1910.06.26 - Ö-UM - TR-PR: Oesterreichischer Komet - Renken
1910.07 - FRA - TR-PR: Catalogue Pathé - Bousquet
1910.08.20 - FRA - Saint Quentin: Cinéma Pathé Omnia - Renken

Archives: BEL-CRB-Bru; FRA-CF-Par; FRA-CNC-Par; FRA-CML
Note: USA release MAX IS ABSENT-MINDED on split-reel with COLOMBO AND ITS ENVIRONS 1910.09.26 b&w 551 ft (168 m).

1910-20
LES EFFETS DES PILULES
180 m = 591 ft = 0:08:44 if at 18 fps
b&w

Effets des pilules, Les - French release title (original - FRA) - Bousquet
Wirkung der Pillen - German release title (DEU+Ö-UM) - Renken
Love and Goodfellowship Pills - English release title (GBR) - Renken
Maxens Pillen - German listing title (attribution) - Zensurkarte Berlin
Effets des pilules de Max, Les - French listing title (attribution) - Ford

Max Linder is out of sorts and bad-tempered. He is rude to his wife, who tells him she will leave him, and Max replies that he doesn't care if she does. Mrs. Max flounces out of the room, and Max turns to his newspaper. The first thing his eye lights upon is an advertisement relating to some wonderful pills, which promote universal love and good fellowship. Max goes off to buy a box, and the result leads to his embracing all the pretty girls. Unfortunately, he leaves the box on the table, and his wife helps herself, with the consequence that she feels impelled to kiss all the men she meets. Max feels it his duty to punch the heads of all the recipients of her favors and finds himself with three duels on hand. But luckily Mrs. Max succeeds in making each of her hubby's opponents partake of the pills just before the duel, with the result that seconds and adversaries fall into each other's arms, and all is peace. *(The Bioscope, 1910.07.07, in Renken)*

1910.06.22 - DEU - CS: Zensurkarte Berlin - Renken
1910.07 - FRA - TR-PR: Catalogue Pathé - Bousquet
1910.07.10 - Ö-UM - Graz: Bioskop Theater Annenhof - Renken
1910.08.27 - FRA - Saint Quentin: Cinéma Pathé Omnia - Renken

Archives: FRA-GPA-Par

1910-21
MAX SE TROMPE D'ÉTAGE
150 m = 492 ft = 0:07:17 if at 18 fps
partially toned

Max se trompe d'étage - French release title (original - FRA) - Bousquet
Max hat sich in der Etage geirrt - German release title (DEU+Ö-UM) - Renken
Wrong Floor, The - English release title (GBR) - Renken
Max Comes Home - English release title (USA) - Renken
Coup d'œil à chaque étage - French listing title (attribution) - Ford

Max, who is living in a flat, comes home very drunk. He stumbles past his own door up to the flat on the second floor. Here he disturbs an amatory couple and is promptly ejected. Upon the third floor he enters a flat where a family broil is occurring. Things have got to the missile stage, and Max is in time to receive a dish on his head. On the fourth floor Max's feet carry him into a nursery. A dish of cream is on the table, and one of the youngsters hurls it at the intruder's head. Max is not discouraged, and he climbs on his hands and knees into a miser's attic. A bullet from a pistol is his welcome, and he falls down the stairs from the top of the house to his own floor. Here he is picked up by his parents, and soothing treatment administered to him. *(The Bioscope, 1910.08.18, in Renken)*

1910.08 - FRA - TR-PR: Catalogue Pathé - Bousquet
1910.08.28 - Ö-UM - Graz: Bioskop Theater Annenhof - Renken
1910.09.30 - FRA - Paris: Omnia Pathé - Renken

Archives: CAN-CQ-Mon; DEU-DK-Ber; FRA-CF-Par; FRA-CNC-Par; FRA-IJV-Per; FRA-CML; FRA-GPA-Par

Note: re-released 28mm Pathé-Kok nr 328 MAX SE TROMPE D'ÉTAGE 115 m (= 146 m in 35mm).

1910-22
TROP AIMÉE
180 m = 591 ft = 0:08:44 if at 18 fps
partially toned

Trop aimée - French release title (original - FRA) - Bousquet
Verliebte Max und seine Hunde, Der - German release title (DEU+Ö-UM) - Renken
Affectionate Pets - English release title (GBR) - Renken
Max is Almost Married - English release title (USA) - Renken
Max a peur des chiens - French re-release title (FRA) - Maud Linder
Max Fears the Dogs - English re-release title (USA) - DVD publisher (Grapevine Video)

Max is in an embarrassed financial condition and reads with delight the following: "A young American millionairess desires to marry a man of good family". Max calls upon the lady and is pleased to find she is both young and charming. The lady's pets, seeing in Max a rival in their mistress's affections, growl at him. Everything goes well, and the day is fixed. The lady is persuaded to have her pets locked up, and Max breathes a sigh of relief. But the faithful animals scamper into the room where the guests have assembled. Seeing Max, they spring at him, and he rushes out. Finally, Max is brought to bay on a roof, and he scribbles a note: "I fear I would much sooner give you up than be devoured by your canine friends". This he proffers to the foremost dog, and they all run off to their mistress. *(The Bioscope, 1910.09.08, in Renken)*

1910.09 - FRA - TR-PR: Catalogue Pathé - Bousquet
1910.09.02 - Ö-UM - Wien: Graben-Kino - Renken
1910.10.27 - FRA - Paris: Cinématographe du Petit Journal - Renken

Archives: CAN-CQ-Mon; FRA-CML; FRA-CNC-Par; FRA-Lob-Par; GBR-BFI-Lon

Note: re-released 28mm Pathé-Kok nr 172b TROP AIMÉE, on reel with LA CONCIERGE DE BÉBÉ AIME LA MUSIQUE, total lenght 123 m (= 156 m in 35mm) - re-release year unknown MAX A PEUR DES CHIENS, shortened at head with changed title at end: "Ne mords pas - j'ai la rage - Max" ("Don't bite - I have rabbies - Max").

1910-23
UN MARIAGE AU PUZZLE
200 m = 656 ft = 0:09:43 if at 18 fps
partially toned

Mariage au puzzle, Un - French release title (original - FRA) - Bousquet

Max und der spiellustige Schwiegervater - German release title (DEU+Ö-UM) - Renken
Puzzle, The - English release title (GBR) - Renken

Max Linder and his fiancée, Madge, scheme to get a few minutes' lovemaking, for Max's prospective Pa-in-law is inclined to monopolise Max over a game of draughts or whist. First, they play a game of blind man's buff and, while Papa is blindfolded, Max and his fiancée repair to the next room, and a blissful interval follows. Poor Papa is quite unable to catch anyone! At last the recreant pair steal back, and when Papa angrily removes his bandage the lovers are sitting demurely in different parts of the room. Papa is a little suspicious at first, but a new puzzle game which Max has brought diverts his attention. Seated around the table, they each set to work to unfold the puzzle. Papa soon becomes so preoccupied that Max and his lady-love are able so steal away. In a short time they return, and slip back into their seats, but Papa has not noticed their absence. He is overjoyed because he alone has succeeded in solving the puzzle and has won the game! *(The Bioscope, 1910.09.15, in Renken)*

1910.09 - FRA - TR-PR: Catalogue Pathé - Bousquet
1910.09.24 - Ö-UM - Graz: Bioskop Theater Annenhof - Renken
1910.10.28 - FRA - Paris: Omnia Pathé - Bousquet

Archives: FRA-CNC-Par; FRA-Lob-Par

Note: re-released 28mm Pathé-Kok nr 855 MARIAGE AU PUZZLE 119 m (= 151 m in 35mm).

1910-24
CHAMPION DE BOXE
210 m = 689 ft = 0:10:12 if at 18 fps
partially toned

Champion de boxe - French release title (original - FRA) - Bousquet
Max als Boxer - German release title (DEU+Ö-UM) - Renken
Champion Boxer, A - English release title (GBR) - Renken
Max Has the Boxing Fever - English release title (USA) - Renken
Max champion de boxe - French listing title (attribution) - Mitry
Match de boxe entre patineurs à roulettes - French listing title (attribution) - Mitry

Max goes to see a boxing match and becomes an enthusiast forthwith. He buys a punching ball and fixes it to the chandelier. Unluckily, the house in which he lives is only a jerry-built one, and the second blow brings the chandelier to the ground. Max zealously practices, and in the end, he becomes a first-class boxer. After having too freely drunk of the champagne cup, he issues a challenge to his friend Grehan to settle a difference of opinion with the gloves. The challenge is accepted, and the two friends, mounted on roller skates, pummel and punch each other with comic solemnity. Finally, Grehan gets a knock-out blow, and is declared the loser, whilst Max is vigorously applauded. *(The Bioscope, 1910.09.29, in Renken)*

1910.09.17 - Ö-UM - TR-PR: Trade listing - Renken
1910.09.23 - Ö-UM - Wien: Welt-Biograph Theater - Renken
1910.10 - FRA - TR-PR: Catalogue Pathé - Bousquet
1910.11.11 - FRA - Paris: Omnia Pathé - Renken

Archives: FRA-CNC-Par

1910-25
LA FLÛTE MERVEILLEUSE
155 m = 508 ft = 0:07:32 if at 18 fps
partially toned

Flûte merveilleuse, La - French release title (original - FRA) - Bousquet
Wunderbare Flöte, Die - German release title (DEU+Ö-UM) - Renken
Magic Flute, The - English release title (GBR) - Renken
Max Makes Music - English release title (USA) - Renken
Zauberflöte, Die - German listing title (attribution) - ITA-CdF

Max buys a flute, which is guaranteed to make all who hear its music dance until further orders, and he tries its powers upon a squad of recruits. The results are perfect, and Max experiments in a cake-walk within the hearing of a wedding group posing for a deaf photographer. When the latter turns, he is dismayed at the demoralization of his artistically posed group. Max then happens upon a man who has been stabbed by hooligans. Over his dead body Max blows his flute, the dead man arises, and is soon dancing. The noise attracts the police, who arrest Max. He escapes and returns home where a little dog is sitting on the step. The flute is again brought into action, and doggie performs a grave little dance. At length Max retires to rest, and in his room plays another tune which causes the portraits, chairs, tables, bed, and even Max himself, to dance. *(The Bioscope, 1910.09.22, in Renken)*

1910.09.22 - UK - TR-PR: The Bisoscope - Bousquet
1910.09.23 - Ö-UM - Prag: Grand Kinematograf Orient - Renken
1910.10 - FRA - TR-PR: Catalogue Pathé - Bousquet
1910.11.04 - FRA - Paris: Omnia Pathé - Bousquet

Archives: ITA-CdF-Gem

1910-26
UN CROSS-COUNTRY ORIGINAL
105 m = 345 ft = 0:05:06 if at 18 fps
b&w

Cross-country original, Un - French release title (original - FRA) - Bousquet
Originelles Wettlaufen, Ein - German release title (DEU+Ö-UM) - Renken
Original Cross-Country Running, An - English release title (GBR) - Renken
Cross-country - French listing title (attribution) - Ford

The entering conditions of a race ran thus: "Each competitor must be attired in a dress suit and a top hat; he must carry an umbrella in one hand, a lighted pipe in his mouth, lead a dog on a leash, and must be mounted on roller skates." Dogs of all sizes, shapes and breeds yelp, bark and dance on their leashes; perspiring and unhappy-looking men struggle to make headway or surmount high obstacles, whilst open umbrellas wave wildly in the air, or curvet and gambol merrily along the ground. However, all things must come to an end, and in due course the race is finished. In the last picture we see Max Linder bestowing a crown of paper laurels on the winner. *(The Bioscope, 1910.09.22, in Renken)*

1910.09.22 - UK - TR-PR: The Bisoscope - Bousquet
1910.10 - FRA - TR-PR: Catalogue Pathé - Bousquet
1910.10.01 - Ö-UM - Graz: Grazer Bioskop - Renken

1910.11.04 - FRA - Paris: Omnia Pathé - Renken

Archives: FRA-CNC-Par

1910-27
MON CHIEN RAPPORTE
140 m = 459 ft = 0:06:48 if at 18 fps
b&w

Mon chien rapporte - French release title (original - FRA) - Bousquet
Mein Hund ist ein Genie - German release title (DEU+Ö-UM) - Renken
Clever Dog, A - English release title (GBR) - Renken
Chien qui rapporte, Un - French listing title (attribution) - Mitry

Max takes the part of a broken-down specimen of humanity, who dispatches his dog, Snap, in search of provisions. Snap brings back bread, a lobster, and a cold roast chicken. All these and other good things he purloins from sundry shopkeepers, but the sufferers call in the aid of the police and make a raid upon his master's lair. A general scrimmage is the outcome, but the dog is equal to driving out all intruders. As a novel termination to the film, Max reappears in the last picture - his usual self, and with his usual well-known smile. *(The Bioscope, 1910.10.06, in Renken)*

1910.09.24 - Ö-UM - TR-PR: Trade listing - Renken
1910.10 - FRA - TR-PR: Catalogue Pathé - Bousquet
1910.10.07 - Ö-UM - Prag: Grand Kinematograf Orient - Renken
1910.11.18 - FRA - Paris: Omnia Pathé - Renken

Archives: FRA-CF-Par; HUN-MNF-Bud; ROU-ANF-Buc

1910-28
LES DÉBUTS DE MAX LINDER AU CINÉMATOGRAPHE
185 m = 607 ft = 0:08:59 if at 18 fps
b&w

Débuts de Max Linder au cinématographe, Les - French release title (original - FRA) - Pathé dépôt légal
Débuts de Max au cinématographe, Les - French listing title (attribution) - Bousquet
Max als Anfänger in der Kinematographie - German release title (DEU+Ö-UM) - Renken
Max Linder's Debut as a Cinematograph Artist - English release title (GBR) - Renken
Max's First Job - English release title (USA) - Renken
Débuts de Max au cinéma - French re-release title (28mm) - Catalogue Pathé-Kok
Max fait du cinéma - French listing title (attribution) - ITA-CdF
Max Makes a Movie - English listing title (attribution) - USA-UCLA
Max's First Efforts - English listing title (attribution) - FIAF TFA db
Max's Debut as a Cinematograph Artist - English listing title (attribution) - FIAF TFA db
Débuts au Cinématographe - French listing title (attribution) - Ford

Max pays a visit to Mr Charles Pathé with an introductory letter. He passes from one office to another until he is received by a stage director who asks him to make some tests: singing, dancing, performing antics, being slapped in the face. A few days later, he receives an invitation to make a screen-test. One can see him fighting with his wife and above all with his mother-in-law who both succeed in ejecting him through the window. While the camera is still cranking, they throw a table at him, a cupboard, a mattress, and so on. Finally, the director asks him to make a face in front of the camera. At last, Max rebels against his tormentors. *(Translation DD from Bousquet nr 3895)*

1910.10 - FRA - TR-PR: Catalogue Pathé - Bousquet
1910.10.07 - Ö-UM - Wien: Welt-Biograph Theater - Renken
1910.11.25 - FRA - Paris: Omnia Pathé - Renken

Archives: ARG-FCA-Bue; FRA-CF-Par; FRA-CML; FRA-CNC-Par; FRA-Lob-Par; GBR-BFI-Lon; ITA-CdF-Gem; USA-GEM-Roc; USA-UCLA-Los

Note: re-released 28mm Pathé-Kok nr 117 DÉBUTS DE MAX AU CINEMA 97 m (= 123 m in 35mm).

1910-29
COMMENT MAX LINDER FAIT LE TOUR DU MONDE
225 m = 738 ft = 0:10:56 if at 18 fps
b&w

Comment Max Linder fait le tour du monde - French release title (original - FRA) - Bousquet
Wie Max eine Weltreise macht - German release title (DEU+Ö-UM) - Renken
How Max Linder Traveled Round the World - English release title (GBR) - Renken
How Max Went Around the World - English release title (USA) - Renken
Max on Tour - English re-release title (GBR) - Renken
Comment Max fait le tour du monde - French re-release title (28mm) - Catalogue Pathé-Kok
Max fait le tour du monde - French listing title (attribution) - Ford
Comment on fait le tour du monde - French listing title (attribution) - Maud Linder

Max has announced to his wife his intention of taking a trip round the world, and he bids her a fond adieu. The arch deceiver's intention, however, is to have a good time in town for three months. But the good time comes to an end that night, for Max drinks too much champagne, and is taken home by a waiter. Next morning, Mrs. Max finds her husband deposited on a sofa, and he declares that the train ran off the rails, and he has come back to tell her he is safe. A few weeks elapse when a host of telegrams begin to arrive for Mrs. Max from different countries. Max has arranged for them to be sent and has forgotten to cancel his instructions. Mrs. Max forms her own conclusions, and for several weeks the fun waxes fast and furious. Then one day Max meets the telegraph boy himself, and he tears the missive open to read: "Sahara. - You brute. It's snowing, and I am frozen. - Your wife". Max falls on his knees and sobs bitterly at Mrs. Max's desertion, until the light touch of his forgiving wife brings him to his senses. *(The Bioscope, 1910.10.20, in Renken)*

1910.10 - FRA - TR-PR: Catalogue Pathé - Bousquet
1910.10.21 - Ö-UM - Prag: Grand Kinematograf Orient - Renken
1910.12.08 - FRA - Paris: Cinématographe du Petit Journal - Renken

Archives: DEU-DK-Ber; FRA-CNC-Par; FRA-CML

Note: re-released 28mm Pathé-Kok nr 155 COMMENT MAX FAIT LE TOUR DU MONDE 115 m (= 146 m in 35mm).

1910-30
QUEL EST L'ASSASSIN?
215 m = 705 ft = 0:10:26 if at 18 fps
b&w

Quel est l'assassin? - French release title (original - FRA) - Bousquet
Wer ist der Täter - German release title (DEU+Ö-UM) - Renken
Who Did the Deed - English release title (GBR) - Renken
Who Killed Max? - English release title (USA) - Renken
Qui est l'assassin? - French listing title (attribution) - Ford
Qui a tué Max? - French listing title (attribution) - Mitry
Max assassin - French listing title (attribution) - Ford
Max assassiné - French listing title (attribution) - Mitry

A wild carouse has ended in Max returning unsteadily home. Instead of retiring to bed he practices revolver shooting, breaking various little statuettes with delighted self-appreciation. At length he tumbles into a huddled heap on the floor, and his parents rush in. They find their son apparently without sign of life and enlist the services of Shamluck Holmes to discover the perpetrator of the deed. Max awakens beneath a mass of wreaths and epitaphs. After pinching himself for a few moments the true situation dawns upon him. Then he resumes his position on the bed. The detective enters, makes an examination of the room, and departs. Max jumps up and makes his way to his café. The detective returns, observes a footmark, and is soon on the track of Max. He arrests him at the café, carries him off to the police-station, and then phones to the parents. Needless to say both hurry off to the station, and on Max being produced as the murderer, fall overjoyed into his arms. *(The Bioscope, 1910.10.27, in Renken)*

1910.10.12 - DEU - CS: Zensurkarte Berlin - Renken
1910.10.23 - Ö-UM - Wien: Welt-Biograph Theater - Renken
1910.11 - FRA - TR-PR: Catalogue Pathé - Bousquet
1910.12.09 - FRA - Paris: Omnia Pathé - Renken

Archives: FRA-Lob-Par; GBR-BFI-Lon

Note: re-released 28mm Pathé-Kok nr 875 QUEL EST L'ASSASSIN? 121 m (= 154 m in 35mm).

1910-31
MAX PREND UN BAIN
210 m = 689 ft = 0:10:12 if at 18 fps
b&w

Max prend un bain - French release title (original - FRA) - Bousquet
Maxens Bad - German release title (DEU+Ö-UM) - Renken
By the Doctor's Orders - English release title (GBR) - Renken
Max Takes a Bath - English listing title (attribution) - FIAF TFA db

Max is suffering from a twitch of the shoulders, and consults a doctor, who prescribes a bath of one hour's duration every day. Max buys an enormous bath, and, arrived at his rooms, his next care is to fill the bath. The tap is on the landing, so he takes his water pitcher, which he speedily breaks. He then drags the bath on to the landing to fill it, but when he comes to drag it back it is too heavy. Max resolves to have his bath on the landing and is just tickling his toes when a lady ascends the stairs. Max subsides beneath the water until all danger is past. The next person to mount the stairs is a tramp, who decides to take a foot bath, with the result that he discovers he is trespassing. There is an altercation, the house porter hears it and fetches the police, who call upon the wrongdoer "to come out". Max refuses, but the police carry the culprit to the police station in the bath. On the way Max is condoled by two charming female acquaintances and goes through it all again at the police station before a stolid inspector, who orders Max again to come out. He refuses, and so the police turn the bath upside down. Max escapes through the streets with the bath on top of him. He reaches his house, arrives at the top attic, gets through the skylight, and heaves the bath down upon the top of the police. *(The Bioscope, 1910.11.03, in Renken)*

1910.10.22 - Ö-UM - TR-PR: Trade listing - Renken
1910.11 - FRA - TR-PR: Catalogue Pathé - Bousquet
1910.11.04 - Ö-UM - Prag: Grand Kinematograf Orient - Renken
1910.12.30 - FRA - Paris: Omnia Pathé - Renken

Archives: CAN-CQ-Mon; FRA-CF-Par; FRA-CNC-Par; FRA-IJV-Per; FRA-CML; FRA-Lob-Par; ITA-FCI-Mil: NLD-EFM-Ams; USA-AFA-Los; USA-GEM-Roc

Note: re-released 28mm Pathé-Kok nr 98 MAX PREND UN BAIN 120 m (= 152 m in 35mm).

1910-32
LE SOULIER TROP PETIT
155 m = 508 ft = 0:07:32 if at 18 fps
b&w

Soulier trop petit, Le - French release title (original - FRA) - Bousquet
Max hat neue Stiefel an - German release title (DEU+Ö-UM) - Renken
When the Shoe Pinches - English release title (GBR) - Renken
Max's Feet are Pinched - English release title (USA) - Renken
Max ha le scarpe strette - Italian [release] title - Turconi Collection

Max is invited to the home of his sweetheart for dinner, and as he dresses, he finds that his shoes are scarcely all that they should be, so he decides to invest in a new pair. Slipping out of the house in a pair of carpet slippers, he makes his way to the nearest shoe store, and after considerable time, gets a pair of shoes which the shoemaker assures him are a perfect fit. Although they are a trifle tight, Max decides to accept them and proceeds on his way. Every step brings its quota of pain, and finally in desperation Max takes off the shoe that hurts the worst and ambles along in his stocking feet. Arriving at his sweetheart's house, he slips his shoe on, but suffers so much that it is necessary to take it off again. While at the dinner table, his sweetheart's pet dog runs off with it and Max is in a dilemma. Finally, he fits a wine basket on his foot and gets along very favorably until the guests commence to dance. [Max's shoeless condition is observed by his companions,

and he is obliged to admit his vanity, which ends in his fiancée giving him his dismissal.] *(The Film Index, Moving Picture World, 1911.03.18, in Renken)*

1910.10.29 - Ö-UM - TR-PR: Trade listing - Renken
1910.11 - FRA - TR-PR: Catalogue Pathé - Bousquet
1910.11.19 - Ö-UM - Graz: Bioskop Theater Annenhof - Renken
1910.12.23 - FRA - Paris: Omnia Pathé - Renken

Archives: AUS-NFSA-Can; CAN-CQ-Mon; FRA-Lob-Par; ITA-CdF-Gem; ITA-CN-Rom; USA-MoMA-New

Note: this film appears to be a remake of CHAUSSURE TROP ÉTROITE (1908-07) and has long been mixed-up with it. This is reflected in the confusion surrounding archives holdings.

1910-33
MAX CHERCHE UNE FIANCÉE
200 m = 656 ft = 0:09:43 if at 18 fps
b&w

Max cherche une fiancée - French release title (original - FRA) - Bousquet
Max sucht eine Braut - German release title (DEU+Ö-UM) - Renken
Max in Search of a Sweetheart - English release title (GBR) - Renken
Max Embarrassed - English release title (USA) - Renken
Max a la richerca di una fidanzata - Italian title - FIAF TFA db

Max makes a great hit with two sisters but is undecided as to which one he likes the best, and when he attempts to ascertain what the feelings are of the two young ladies, his embarrassment is so great that he gives up in despair. Finally, he prepares a little verse and drops two copies where the girls can find them, little thinking that they would show them to each other. This they do, however, and decide to be avenged. They write him to meet them at the mountain top and hide in a big barrel until they arrive. Max obeys and when they do finally come, they quickly clamp the barrel top in place, and turning the barrel on its side, give it a shove and away it goes, landing finally in a swift stream. Here it floats rapidly along, over rapids and falls, and at last out to sea, and here Max breaks the top off and looks about him. In the barrel he finds a carrier pigeon placed there by the girls before they put the top on; so, scribbling a note he fastens it on the bird, which flies away to its home. Here the girls read the letter, which thanks them for their courtesy, and says that he's glad to be rid of both of them. *(The Film Index, Moving Picture World, The Billboard, 1911.03.11, in Renken)*

1910.11.09 - DEU - CS: Zensurkarte Berlin - Renken
1910.11.25 - Ö-UM - Prag: Grand Kinematograf Orient - Renken
1910.12 - FRA - TR-PR: Catalogue Pathé - Bousquet
1911.01.19 - FRA - Paris: Cinématographe du Petit Journal - Renken

Archives: CAN-CQ-Mon; FRA-CNC-Par; FRA-IJV-Per; FRA-CML; FRA-Lob-Par; ITA-MNC-Tor; NZL-NTSV-Wel; USA-MoMA-New

Note: re-released 28mm Pathé-Kok nr 323 MAX CHERCHE UNE FIANCÉE 124 m (= 157 m in 35mm).

1910-34
MAX HYPNOTISÉ
160 m = 525 ft = 0:07:46 if at 18 fps
b&w

Max hypnotisé - French release title (original - FRA) - Bousquet
Max ist hypnotisiert - German release title (DEU+Ö-UM) - Renken
Max Hypnotized - English release title (GBR) - Renken
Max Linder ipnotizzato - Italian listing title (attribution) - FIAF TFA db

Max Linder's two servants practice their proficiency in hypnotizing others upon him. Max proves to be a good subject and is forced to do his work thoroughly. After an excellent dinner, James insists that Max must be funny to amuse them. Max tries his best, and Mary and James express their approval. James declares that Max must commit a crime and gives him a knife with which to do the deed. His master searches for a victim, and finally stabs a Camembert cheese, with the result that he awakes and puts his house in order again. *(The Bioscope, 1910.12.01, in Renken)*

1910.11.19 - Ö-UM - TR-PR: Trade listing - Renken
1910.12 - FRA - TR-PR: Catalogue Pathé - Bousquet
1910.12.02 - Ö-UM - Prag: Grand Kinematograf Orient - Renken
1911.01.26 - FRA - Paris: Cinématographe du Petit Journal - Renken

Archives: FRA-CF-Par; FRA-CML; FRA-CNC-Par; ITA-CdF-Gem; ITA-FCI-Mil; USA-MoMA-New

1910-35
MAX MANQUE UN RICHE MARIAGE
140 m = 459 ft = 0:06:48 if at 18 fps
b&w

Max manque un riche mariage - French release title (original - FRA) - Bousquet
Max verfehlt eine reiche Heirat - German release title (DEU+Ö-UM) - Renken
Good Chance Lost, A - English release title (GBR) - Renken
Shame on Max - English release title (USA) - Renken

Max gets an introduction to a family of Americans and makes a careful toilet preparatory to responding to an invitation to an evening gathering. He makes the horrible discovery that a lacuna exists in a seam of his lower garment. Max does what he can to repair the damage with the aid of a needle and thread, but he feels very dubious of his handiwork. So much so, that in a cab he takes extreme care not to sit down. Amongst the ladies Max finds his fears vanish, but a sudden movement causes disaster. He conceals the catastrophe as well as he can - at first with a chair, and then his partner's fan. But his eccentric behavior arouses the curiosity of his hostess, and her skirmishing brings discovery and shame upon her guest. *(The Bioscope, 1910.12.15, in Renken)*

1910.12 - FRA - TR-PR: Catalogue Pathé - Bousquet
1910.12.10 - Ö-UM - Wien: Rotenturm Kino - Renken
1911.02.03 - FRA - Paris: Omnia Pathé - Renken

Archives: CAN-CQ-Mon; FRA-CNC-Par; FRA-CML

Note: this is film appears to be either a remake or a re-issue of MON PANTALON EST DÉCOUSU (1908-01).

1910-36
MAX NE SE MARIERA PAS
155 m = 508 ft = 0:07:32 if at 18 fps
b&w

Max ne se mariera pas - French release title (original - FRA) - Bousquet
Max bleibt ledig - German release title (DEU+Ö-UM) - Renken

Max Misses Another Good Chance - English release title (GBR) - Renken
Max is Stuck Up - English release title (USA) - Renken
Max et le papier tue-mouche - French listing title (attribution) - FIAF TFA db

[Max is invited to a dinner party. He] puts on his best and smartest suit, and proceeds to a candy store to purchase a box of the best. It being summer, the confectioner deems it wise to place flypaper on all the chairs, counters and even on the door. Max, of course, didn't see these little novelties, and before he is aware of it, he has a nice fresh piece plastered on his shoe. The confectioner helps him out of the first difficulty, but neither notice the piece that is stuck on his sleeve when he goes out. Max arrives at the home of his sweetheart, where he is introduced to her father. Here is where real complications arrive, for no sooner does he attempt to shake hands with papa than he finds out there is something sticky holding him back. Papa looks strangely at Max, and Max tries to look pleasant at papa, but it's a hard job. After the old man leaves the lovers together, Max still tries to conceal his predicament; but when she asks him to hook her collar, he finds his fingers more than thumbs and that they won't work on such a delicate job. Finding it utterly useless his sweetheart does it herself and tells Max to follow her to the dining-room, as dinner is ready. Before Max really gets out of the room, he tries to get the flypaper off his fingers by putting his foot on it. He starts to follow his sweetheart, but takes part of the rug along, and by the time he reaches the table, he has nearly all the furniture tagging after him. Getting rid of these, he soon has the plates, platters, glasses, knives and forks stuck to his fingers. This causes not only his sweetheart and mamma much embarrassment, but father, too, loses his temper, and before Max can really tell his troubles, he finds himself thrown out of the house. *(The Film Index, 1911.03.18, in Renken)*

1910.12.31 - Ö-UM - TR-PR: Trade listing - Renken
1911.01 - FRA - TR-PR: Catalogue Pathé - Bousquet
1911.01.06 - Ö-UM - Wien: Rotenturm Kino - Renken
1911.03.03 - FRA - Paris: Omnia Pathé - Bousquet

Archives: DEU-DK-Ber; FRA-CML; FRA-CNC-Par; FRA-Lob-Par; USA-AFA-Los

1911-01
MAX A TROUVÉ UNE FIANCÉE
215 m = 705 ft = 0:10:26 if at 18 fps
b&w

Max a trouvé une fiancée - French release title (original - FRA) - Bousquet
Max hat eine Braut gefunden - German release title (DEU+Ö-UM) - Renken
Max Engaged - English release title (GBR) - Renken
Max is Forced to Work - English release title (USA) - Renken
Max heeft een bruid gevonden - Dutch release title (NLD) - NLD-EFM
Max a trovato una fidanzata - Italian title - ITA-CNR
Max cherche un emploi - French listing title (attribution) - CAN-CQ
Max trouve une fiancée - French listing title (attribution) - Maud Linder
Max fiancé - French listing title (attribution) - Ford

Max is refused admittance one night to the family nest. He wanders about for two days in evening attire, when he picks up a dance invitation. Max decides to attend the dance. He does so, and not only satisfies his hunger, but captures the heart of the daughter of the house. He has a troublesome problem - how to earn sufficient for his daily needs? - and solves it at last by turning waiter. Unluckily his sweetheart and her parents stumble upon him one day, and the engagement is broken off. Max is in a desperate plight, but he adopts the manly course of deciding to confide all to his sweetheart and begs her to come to the café. She does so, and Max whispers the whole story to her during the intervals between the bawling of an American customer, who receives but scant attention. The sudden appearance on the scene of Max's father also smooths matters. *(The Bioscope, 1911.02.16, in Renken)*

1911.02.03 - Ö-UM - TR-PR: Trade listing - Renken
1911.02.17 - Ö-UM - Prag: Grand Kinematograf Orient - Renken
1911.03 - FRA - TR-PR: Catalogue Pathé - Bousquet
1911.04.07 - FRA - Paris: Omnia Pathé - Bousquet

Archives: CAN-CQ-Mon; FRA-CML; FRA-CNC-Par; GBR-BFI-Lon; ITA-CN-Rom; NLD-EFM-Ams

1911-02
MAX SE MARIE
155 m = 508 ft = 0:07:32 if at 18 fps
partially toned

Max se marie - French release title (original - FRA) - Bousquet
Max heiratet - German release title (DEU+Ö-UM) - Renken
Max Gets Married - English release title (GBR) - Renken
Max's Divorce - English release title (USA) - Renken
Mariage de Max, Le - French listing title (attribution) - Mitry

Having endured many well-known predicaments, at last Max gets married. After lunch, a party is organized. Suddenly, while dancing with his bride, the groom begins to gesticulate due to an irrepressible itching. When he cannot take it any longer, he discreetly goes out onto the balcony, pulls off his trousers and looks for the flea that has hidden there insidiously. In his misfortune, the trousers fall on the sidewalk. In underpants, poor Max seizes a curtain that he wraps himself in and enters the living-room triumphantly. However, Mr Ziccarini, the father-in-law, is so upset by his son-in-law's eccentricities that he obliges his daughter to apply for a divorce. Deeply sorry, Max thinks about a subterfuge that could help his lawyer. He buys a bushel of fleas and frees them inside the court room during the trial. The result cannot be contested: the judges, the lawyer, the audience, everybody behaves as Max did when his father-in-law thought he was going insane. And the young man wins his case, to everyone's satisfaction. *(Translation DD from Bousquet nr 4236)*

1911.03.17 - Ö-UM - TR-PR: Trade listing - Renken
1911.03.31 - Ö-UM - Prag: Grand Kinematograf Orient - Bousquet
1911.04 - FRA - TR-PR: Catalogue Pathé - Bousquet
1911.05.25 - FRA - Paris: Cinématographe du Petit Journal - Renken

Archives: FRA-CF-Par

1911-03
MAX ET SA BELLE-MÈRE [1911]
150 m = 492 ft = 0:07:17 if at 18 fps
partially toned

Max et sa belle-mère - French release title (original - FRA) - Bousquet
Max und seine Schwiegermutter - German release title (DEU+Ö-UM) - Renken
Max and His Mother-in-Law - English release title (GBR) - Renken
Max et sa belle négresse - French listing title (attribution) - Ford

Like every son-in-law in every civilized country, Max dislikes his mother-in-law very much. The mother-in-law has announced that she is on her way. Furious, Max ensures that the servants will work hand in hand with him to make her stay as unbearable as possible. The latter support him beyond his expectations. Thanks to their untiring zeal, Mother-in-law falls again and again, she is doused by the gardener's hose, she is dusted by the beaten rugs, she is scalded by a soup tureen poured over her head; during her sleep, her bed collapses. Finally, after a series of ineffable predicaments, Mother-in-law is embraced by Max's best friend, a real bear. Distraught, wounded, she jumps onto the first departing train, swearing that this would never happen again. *(Translation DD from Bousquet nr 4297)*

1911.04.26 - DEU - CS: Zensurkarte Berlin - Renken
1911.04.28 - Ö-UM - Wien: Graben-Kino - Renken
1911.05 - FRA - TR-PR: Catalogue Pathé - Bousquet
1911.06.23 - FRA - Paris: Omnia Pathé - Renken

Archives: CAN-CQ-Mon; ESP-FE-Mad; FRA-GPA-Par; FRA-CML; FRA-Lob-Par; GBR-BFI-Lon; ITA-CdF-Gem; MEX-FUNAM-Méx; USA-AFA-Los; USA-BkHk

Note: re-relased 28mm Pathé-Kok nr 392 *MAX ET SA BELLE-MÈRE* 117 m (= 149 m in 35mm). The title *MAX ET SA BELLE NÉGRESSE* is based on the Pathé telegraphic code "Négresse".

1911-04
VOISIN, VOISINE
200 m = 656 ft = 0:09:43 if at 18 fps
b&w

Voisin, voisine - French release title (original - FRA) - Bousquet
Nachbar und Nachbarin - German release title (DEU+Ö-UM) - Renken
Neighbours - English release title (GBR) - Renken
Max et sa voisine - French listing title (attribution) - GBR-BFI

Max and Nettgi, two lovers who are neighbors with adjacent windows, use a bird cage as a P.O. box. That very day, Max is about to ask Nettgi's father for the hand of his daughter. Unfortunately, the careless young man loses a letter that clearly states that he's cheating on his sweetheart with a Miss Lulu. Infuriated, Nettgi unleashes all her wrath on the culprit and insidiously tortures him during the dinner he was invited to. Finally, despite his efforts to put on a brave face, Max can't stand it anymore. With painstaking care, the father of the infuriated Nettgi succeeds in reconciling her with her fiancé, the latter swearing out unbreakable oaths that he will ignore every Miss Lulu forever. *(Translation DD from Bousquet nr 4499)*

1911.07.26 - DEU - CS: Zensurkarte Berlin - Renken
1911.08 - FRA - TR-PR: Catalogue Pathé - Bousquet
1911.08.12 - Ö-UM - Graz: Bioskop Theater Annenhof - Renken
1911.09.22 - FRA - Paris: Omnia Pathé - Bousquet / Lyon: Pathé Grolée - Renken

Archives: GBR-BFI-Lon

1911-05
MAX EN CONVALESCENCE
245 m = 804 ft = 0:11:54 if at 18 fps
b&w

Max en convalescence - French release title (original - FRA) - Bousquet
Max auf dem Wege zur Genesung - German release title (DEU+Ö-UM) - Renken
Max is Convalescent - English release title (GBR+USA) - Renken
Max dans sa famille - French listing title (attribution) - Mitry

Max's own convalescence is the subject, and we find him light heartedly coming to his parents' home in a little country place to recruit health and new vigor. He accompanies his sister round the little estate to renew acquaintance with old friends. Castor, the dog, gives him a royal welcome, but Kiss, his own pony, exhibits no pleasure at seeing him again. On the contrary, Kiss passes the next few days in inventing tricks to play upon Max, who receives a shower bath in the stables through the horse giving a tug at the releasing chain. Max is indignant and endeavors to imprison the horse in the paddock, but Kiss retaliates by boxing him soundly. However, Max triumphs in the end, and feeling safe goes off to fish by the stream. Subsequently, Kiss breaks down the paddock fence, and finding his master tips him into the river. Luckily Castor rescues the poor convalescent, who by this time feels that he were better back in town. *(The Bioscope, 1911.08.31, in Renken)*

1911.08.25 - DEU - CS: Zensurkarte Berlin - Renken
1911.08.25 - Ö-UM - Wien: Lichtspiel-Theater - Renken
1911.09 - FRA - TR-PR: Catalogue Pathé - Bousquet
1911.10.13 - FRA - Lyon: Pathé Grolée - Renken

Archives: CAN-CQ-Mon; FRA-CNC-Par; FRA-GPA-Par; JPN-NFAJ-Tōk

1911-06
MAX A UN DUEL
235 m = 771 ft = 0:11:25 if at 18 fps
b&w

Max a un duel - French release title (original - FRA) - Bousquet
Max duelliert sich - German release title (DEU+Ö-UM) - Renken
Max and His Duel - English release title (GBR) - Renken

Max Fights a Duel - English release title (USA) - Renken
Duelista por amor - Spanish listing title (attribution) - Magliozzi

Max Linder is forced by the stern fiancée into an embarrassing situation. She insists upon Max fighting a duel. Max goes home and practices theatrical attitudes in front of a picture. It seems simple enough there, and Max sets forth in search of a likely foe. He thinks he espies one in a man sitting in the park, and Max places himself at his side and tries to screw up his courage to the point of insulting the unconscious individual. A closer inspection of his burly figure gives Max the impression that he is not exactly the person he is seeking, and he moves quickly away. He comes down heavily on a man's toes, spoils another man's drink for him, but though he proffers his card, none of these are anxious to fight a duel with him. Later, he informs his fiancée and her father that he has found an adversary and that a duel has been arranged. The fiancée's father offers himself as one of the seconds. The eventful day arrives and the duel is fought. Max, after spoiling his opponent's hat, succeeds in disabling him and is declared the victor. His fiancée regards him with loving pride and her father congratulates him warmly. Suddenly his adversary comes up and puts a paper into his hand. His fiancée and her father read it curiously! It is the bill from the fencing master with whom he has just fought a duel! His fiancée and her father turn upon him with scorn and indignation, and poor Max seems likely to loose his fiancée after all. *(The Bioscope, 1911.09.28, in Renken)*

1911.09.20 - DEU - CS: Zensurkarte Berlin - Renken
1911.10 - FRA - TR-PR: Catalogue Pathé - Bousquet
1911.10.07 - Ö-UM - Graz: Bioskop Theater Annenhof - Renken
1911.11.17 - FRA - Lyon: Pathé Grolée - Renken

Archives: AUT-ÖFM-Wie; BEL-CRB-Bru; CAN-CQ-Mon; FRA-CML; FRA-CNC-Par; SWE-SFI-Sto; URY-ANIP-Mon

Note: re-released 9.5 mm Film Office MAX A UN DUEL full-lenght titles, 100 m (1 reel).

1911-07
VICTIME DU QUINQUINA
375 m = 1230 ft = 0:18:13 if at 18 fps
partially toned

Victime du quinquina - French release title (original - FRA) - Bousquet
Max als Opfer des Bordeaux-Weines - German release title (DEU+Ö-UM) - Renken
Max and His Prescription - English release title (GBR) - Renken
Max Takes Tonics - English release title (USA) - Renken
Max slachtoffer van de Bordeaux-wijn - Dutch release title (NLD) - NLD-EFM
Max et le quinquina - French re-release title (9.5mm) - Poisson
Max victime du quinquina - French listing title (attribution) - Mitry
Max e l'aperitivo - Italian listing title (attribution) - FIAF TFA db

The play opens with a picture of Max consulting his physician. The doctor gives him a tonic wine and tells him to take a wine-glassful every day. On his return home Max quickly empties the bottle. After that he feels much happier. He changes rapidly into his evening clothes and marches off to take a taxi. But a gentleman opens the opposite door of the taxi at the same moment. Who is to give way? Max, with drunken obstinacy, refuses, and an exchange of cards takes place. On the one Max receives is inscribed "John Andy-Cuff, Commissioner of Police". The taxi having departed, Max makes for a gay restaurant, where he encounters a young beauty. His insinuating manners lead up to other challenges, one from General Snobsky, of the War Office, and the other from the Marquis de Salvador, of the Elbanian Embassy. Max stuffs the cards into his pocket and departs homewards. But home is not easily found, and we find Max leaning against a lamp post, when a policeman orders him to move on. Max requests him to dive into his pockets for a card. The man finds the Police Commissioner's, and his gruff attitude disappearing he lovingly carries Max to the address given. Here he leaves him, Max being ultimately thrown out by the Commissioner. A second time an agent of the law comes to Max's assistance. He receives the Ambassador's card, and full of solicitude, gently conveys Max to his address. Once more Max finds himself in the street. Again, he is picked up by a constable, who gets the General's card. A third time is Max gently lifted into a policeman's arms and left in safety. He is thrown out of the window, to fall at the feet of the three constables, who have met. Each claims him as his special charge, and the cards being produced, and found to be all different, Max feels the full strength of the arm of the law. *(The Bioscope, 1912.01.04, in Renken)*

1911.12.15 - FRA - Paris: Le Cirque d'hiver - Renken
1911.12.20 - DEU - CS: Zensurkarte Berlin - Renken
1911.12.29 - Ö-UM - Wien: Kino Theater - Renken
1912.01 - FRA - TR-PR: Catalogue Pathé - Bousquet

Archives: AUT-ÖFM-Wie; BEL-CRB-Bru; BRA-CMAM-Rio; CAN-CQ-Mon; CUB-CdC-LaH; FRA-CF-Par; FRA-CML; FRA-CNC-Par; FRA-Lob-Par; ITA-CdF-Gem; ITA-CN-Rom; NLD-EFM-Ams; USA-AFA-Los; USA-BkHk; USA-MoMA-New; USA-UCLA-Los

Note: re-released 9,5mm Film Office MAX ET LE QUINQUINA full-lenght titles 200 m (2 reels).

1911-08
MAX VEUT FAIRE DU THÉÂTRE
295 m = 968 ft = 0:14:20 if at 18 fps
b&w

Max veut faire du théâtre - French release title (original - FRA) - Bousquet
Max und Jane wollen Schauspieler werden - German release title (DEU+Ö-UM) - Renken
Their Common Destiny - English release title (GBR) - Renken
Max's Tragedy - English release title (USA) - Renken
Verrassing, Een - Dutch release title (NLD) - www.cinemacontext.nl
Feu sacré, Le - French re-release title (1920) - Renken
Max et Jane veulent faire du théâtre - French listing title (attribution) - FRA-CF
Max a le feu sacré - French listing title (attribution) - Chirat et LeRoy
Max ne veut pas se marier - French listing title (attribution) - Ford

Max is stage struck, and is highly indignant when his father suggests that it is time he thought about marrying: "A man with a career must be free." His father, losing patience, marches him off to make acquaintance with the young lady whom he has selected as his son's future wife. Now this young lady is also stage struck, and she rebels at the thought that her career is to be blighted by a husband. The only escape is to disgust her would-be helpmate, and she drags her hair back and with a scowl upon her charming face welcomes Max, who, struck by a similar idea, has made himself unrecognizable. The young people are not polite to each other, and at the end of the afternoon are clawing each other's hair. The disappointed parents separate them, and Max is dragged away by his crest-fallen parent. In the hurry, Max forgets his stick, and returns for it. To his astonishment he finds Jenny with her hair well dressed, and altogether charming. On her part, Jenny is surprised to see that Max is a good-looking young man. Each is smitten and both confide their reasons for their deception. They kiss and make it up, preparatory to treading the road of their common destiny. They get married. But what's that shabby interior where the young lady, while rocking her child in her arms, is waiting for her husband, late once more? He finally arrives, drunk and violent. They engage in an argument and the man, in a heavy drunken state, knocks the poor woman out. Applause and "bravos" suddenly ring out, the audience is roaring. Max and Jenny are now two great artists. *(Partly The Bioscope, 1911.12.28, in Renken; partly translation DD from Bousquet nr 4911)*

1911.12.22 - Ö-UM - Wien: Kino Theater des "Invalidendank" - Renken
1911.12.28 - UK - TR-PR: The Bisoscope - Renken
1912.01 - FRA - TR-PR: Catalogue Pathé - Bousquet
1912.02.23 - FRA - Paris: Omnia Pathé - Bousquet

Archives: FRA-CF-Par; FRA-CML; FRA-Lob-Par; NLD-EFM-Ams

1911-09
MAX LANCE LA MODE
180 m = 591 ft = 0:08:44 if at 18 fps
b&w

Max lance la mode - French release title (original - FRA) - Bousquet
Max als Modekönig - German release title (DEU+Ö-UM) - Renken
Max Sets the Fashion - English release title (GBR+USA) - Renken
Max lance la mode - French re-release title (28mm) - Catalogue Pathé-Kok
Max Sets the Style - English [re-release title] (USA) - USA-UCLA
Max Starts the Fashion - English listing title (attribution) - GBR-BFI

Max, awakening on his wedding morning, discovers that it is close on the hour when he should be at the church. He dresses hastily, and in struggling with a refractory collar, allows his boots to be burnt by the fire. There is no time to change them, and he hastens off to the bride's house. On the way his soles part company with their uppers, and poor Max enters into negotiations with a passing laborer for the purchase of his footgear. The wretched bridegroom draws the boots on his cold feet and stamps up the stairs to greet his waiting bride. She catches sight of his footwear, and in a flood of tears points them out to her father. This gentleman, furiously angry, stops the proceedings and orders Max off the premises, in spite of the latter's protestation that his boots are the latest fashion. Finding that his protestations are pooh-poohed, Max treacherously makes an ally of one of the lady guests, renowned for setting fashions, by poking his boots underneath her skirt. His father-in-law, unable to doubt any longer, recalls him, and the wedding duly takes place. *(The Bioscope, 1912.01.11, in Renken)*

1911.12.27 - DEU - CS: Zensurkarte Berlin Nr.15347 - Renken
1912.01 - FRA - TR-PR: Catalogue Pathé - Bousquet
1912.01.05 - Ö-UM - Wien: Kino Theater Mizzi Schäffer - Renken
1912.03.01 - FRA - Lyon: Pathé Grolée - Renken

Archives: ARG-FCA-Bue; BEL-CRB-Bru; FRA-CNC-Par; FRA-GPA-Par; FRA-IJV-Per; FRA-CML; FRA-Lob-Par; GBR-BFI-Lon; ITA-CdF-Gem; USA-UCLA-Los

Note: re-released 28mm Pathé-Kok nr 748 MAX LANCE LA MODE 122 m (= 155 m in 35mm).

1912-01
MAX REPREND SA LIBERTÉ
190 m = 623 ft = 0:09:14 if at 18 fps
b&w

Max reprend sa liberté - French release title (original - FRA) - Bousquet
Max liebt seine Freiheit - German release title (DEU+Ö-UM) - Renken
Max and the Fowl - English release title (GBR) - Renken

Max quarrels so with his wife that the lady leaves him. Our hero then attempts to do his own cooking, etc. He buys a fowl, but it proves to be still alive, and after he has chased it with a revolver, partly plucked it, shaved and finally half-roasted it, the bird is still alive and wings its way off. Max next turns his attention to blacking his boots, upsets the liquid blacking, spoons it up, and a minute later is using the same spoon to stir the broth. He writes for his wife to return home, but soon after sending the letter hears he is heir to a large fortune, and lives in the seventh heaven of delight - until his wife returns. *(The Bioscope, 1912.02.15, in Renken)*

1912.01.17 - DEU - CS: Zensurkarte Berlin - Renken
1912.01.26 - Ö-UM - Wien: Kino Theater des "Invalidendank" - Renken
1912.02 - FRA - TR-PR: Catalogue Pathé - Bousquet
1912.03.29 - FRA - Paris: Omnia Pathé - Bousquet

Archives FRA-CML; FRA-CNC-Par; FRA-Lob-Par; ITA-MNC-Tor

1912-02
MAX ET SON CHIEN DICK
195 m = 640 ft = 0:09:28 if at 18 fps
b&w

Max et son chien Dick - French release title (original - FRA) - Bousquet
Max und sein Hund - German release title (DEU+Ö-UM) - Renken
Max and Dog Dick - English release title (GBR) - Renken
Max et son bon chien Dick - French re-release title (28mm) - Catalogue Pathé-Kok

Jenny is a young lady with two strings to her bow, but she fails to determine which most meets with her approval. Finally, she begs Max and Bertie to draw two strips of paper. Max draws the longer one and marries Jenny. After marriage, Jenny wishes he had not. Max discovers her writing a loving note to somebody and has strong suspicions that it is Bertie. He instructs Dick, his dog, to keep a watch over his wife, and on the first approach of a masculine visitor, to telephone him over the private wire to his office. The dog obeys his instructions literally. The coming of Bertie is the signal for Dick to unhook the receiver and to bark loudly into the telephone. Max hastens home and finds Mrs. Max in Bertie's arms. He says nothing, but tells Dick to bring their hats, and coldly points to the door. The culprits depart like whipped children, and from this day onwards Max settles down to a happy bachelor life, with Dog Dick to keep him company. *(The Bioscope, 1912.02.22, in Renken)*

1912.02.09 - Ö-UM - Wien: Kino Theater des "Invalidendank" - Renken
1912.03 - FRA - TR-PR: Catalogue Pathé - Bousquet
1912.03.09 - DEU - Berlin: Lichtspiele "Mozartsaal" - Renken
1912.04.12 - FRA - Paris: Omnia Pathé - Bousquet

Archives: BEL-CRB-Bru; CZE-NFA-Pra; FRA-CNC-Par; FRA-GPA-Par; FRA-CML; ITA-CdF-Gem; JPN-NFAJ-Tōk; NLD-EFM-Ams; USA-AFA-Los; USA-BkHk; USA-MoMA-New

Note: re-released 28mm Pathé-Kok nr 375 MAX ET SON BON CHIEN DICK 124 m (= 157 m in 35mm).

1912-03
AMOUREUX DE LA TEINTURIÈRE
260 m = 853 ft = 0:12:38 if at 18 fps
partially toned

Amoureux de la teinturière - French release title (original - FRA) - Bousquet
Verliebte Max, Der - German release title (DEU+Ö-UM) - Renken
Of the Deepest Dye - English release title (GBR) - Renken
Op des ververs dochter verliefd - Dutch release title (NLD) - www.cinemacontext.nl
Max amoureux de la teinturière - French re-release title (9.5mm) - Catalogue Pathé-Baby 1926
Max et la teinturière - French listing title (attribution) - Ford
Max negro - Spanish archive title [attribution] - ARG-FCA

Max is in love with a pretty girl, and one evening pays a stolen visit to his sweetheart's, whose father, a successful dyer, has to leave by a late train for the provinces. Arrayed in a pale grey frock coat, Max meets his sweetheart's father on the threshold of his front door. The meeting is not to Max's liking, although he is unknown to the dyer. He makes a dash for it, but the dyer sees his grey form disappearing up the staircase and returns to his flat. Max hears his footsteps just as he is about to kiss his sweetheart, and the girl pushes him into one of the dyeing rooms. Here there is no place of concealment except a huge receptacle full of black dye. In this Max plunges as the dyer enters. When the latter has again departed, Max emerges dyed black. He escapes by the window, returns home, and tumbles into bed without removing his clothes. Next morning the maid is horrified to find a negro in bed. She hurriedly goes out to call for her mistress and the police. Before they return Max awakes, and escapes by the window to return to the dyer's to be dry-cleaned. When the police enter, nothing but a black impression of Max's form is to be seen on the bed, and his mother is arrested for daring to play practical jokes upon the authorities. In the meantime, Max has returned to the dyer's, and some amusing scenes, in which he mystifies the proprietor and remains undiscovered, terminate the film. *(The Bioscope, 1912.03.07, in Renken)*

1912.02.23 - Ö-UM - Wien: Rotenturm Kino - Renken
1912.03 - FRA - TR-PR: Catalogue Pathé - Bousquet
1912.03.23 - DEU - Berlin: U.T.-Unter den Linden - Renken
1912.04.26 - FRA - Paris: Omnia Pathé - Bousquet

Archives: ARG-FCA-Bue; AUT-ÖFM-Wie; BEL-CRB-Bru; CZE-NFA-Pra; DEU-DK-Ber; FRA-CNC-Par; ITA-CdF-Gem; NLD-EFM-Ams;

Note: re-released 28mm Pathé-Kok nr 344 AMOUREUX DE LA TEINTURIÈRE 120 m (= 152 m in 35m). Re-released 9,5mm Pathé-Baby nr 671 MAX AMOUREUX DE LA TEINTURIÈRE, notches, 20 m (2 cassettes).

1912-04
MAX LINDER CONTRE NICK WINTER
420 m = 1378 ft = 0:20:24 if at 18 fps
partially toned

Max Linder contre Nick Winter - French release title (original - FRA) - Bousquet
Max Linder gegen Nick Winter - German release title (DEU+Ö-UM) - Renken
Max Linder v. Nick Winter - English release title (GBR) - Renken
Max Gets the Reward - English release title (USA) - Renken
Robo de la Giaconda, El - Spanish listing title [misattribution] - GBR-BFI

For diversion Max undertakes the study of the principles of magnetism and soon learns how to extract pocketbooks and other rather personal belongings from passers-by. He considers it a great joke, but the victims think otherwise, and, accordingly, notify the police. A detective is assigned to the case and a reward is offered for the apprehension of the mysterious burglar. Then begins the battle of wits. The detective becomes suspicious of Max and sets a trap for him. The trap is a logical one, for by it, Max is invited to call upon a young lady admirer and give an exhibition of his powers. Max, flattered, accepts the invitation, but one glance at the sleuth in the guise of a young girl is enough to tip Max off to the situation. Feigning that he is unaware of the detective's real identity, Max watches him grow careless trough over-confidence and with a dexterous movement has him at his mercy. Max places the now helpless official in a canvas sack and then, disguising himself as the detective, he turns the bundle over to the chief of police and is quickly paid the reward. *(Moving Picture World, 1912.11.16, in Renken)*

1912.03.16 - DEU - CS: Zensurkarte Berlin - Renken
1912.03.29 - Ö-UM - Wien: Kino Theater des "Invalidendank" - Renken
1912.04 - FRA - TR-PR: Catalogue Pathé - Bousquet
1912.05.31 - FRA - Paris: Omnia Pathé - Bousquet

Archives: FRA-CML; FRA-CNC-Par; GBR-BFI-Lon

**1912-05
BANDIT PAR AMOUR
210 m = 689 ft = 0:10:12 if at 18 fps
b&w**

Bandit par amour - French release title (original - FRA) - Bousquet
Triumph der Liebe, Der - German release title (DEU+Ö-UM) - Renken
For Love of a Maid - English release title (GBR) - Renken
Max bandit par amour - French listing title (attribution) - Mitry

There are rumors of many deeds of violence committed by a society of criminals, known as the "Black Band". Max and his family experience thrills of apprehension in reading warnings couched in the fervid jargon of journalists. The thrills do not keep Max from going love-making, and he is happy until he discovers that his brother is courting his girl. There is a brotherly square up, and Max, victor and jubilant, hurries away to pay a call upon the lady. He is mounting the stairs of her house when a note is thrust into his hand. The note warns him that the father of the lady he is about to visit is a member of the "Black Band". Max continues on his way unperturbedly and sends in his card. The girl's father makes himself pleasant to Max, and at lunch time often unconsciously emphasizes his conversation by pointing his dinner knife at his young guest. Suddenly the door opens, and a servant, bringing in a gun, whispers to his master that one of his cronies is waiting for him to start out for an afternoon's sport. Max sees only the gun, and with a yell jumps from his chair. Into the drawing-room he rushes, only to come face to face with another man holding a gun! There can be no more doubt. He is in love with the daughter of a member of the "Black Band", all murderers and thieves. Poor Max, for very love of the maid, resolves to become an assassin and robber, too. Clad in rough tweeds, with a belt adorned with many weapons, he goes back to his lady love's father and declares that he is one of the band. How matters are cleared up, and how Max discovers that he has been fooled by his brother are things which end a lively bit of comedy in the best of farcical styles. *(The Bioscope, 1912.04.12, in Renken)*

1912.03.25 - DEU - CS: Zensurkarte Berlin - Renken
1912.04 - FRA - TR-PR: Catalogue Pathé - Bousquet
1912.04.05 - Ö-UM - Wien: Kino Theater des "Invalidendank" - Renken
1912.06.07 - FRA - Paris: Omnia Pathé - Bousquet

Archives: no film print known to this date

1912-06
QUE PEUT-IL AVOIR?
145 m = 476 ft = 0:07:02 if at 18 fps
b&w

Que peut-il avoir? - French release title (original - FRA) - Bousquet
Max beim Diner - German release title (DEU+Ö-UM) - Renken
Sad Dilemma, A - English release title (GBR) - Renken
Que peut-il arriver? - French listing title (attribution) - Chirat et LeRoy

Bob, Max's valet, has drunk his master's bottle of whisky. In order to hide his mischief, he fills the bottle with a laxative. Confidently, Max drinks that mixture before going out to have lunch at his future in-law's. The results begin to be felt rapidly. Max rushes out of the room several times without any explanation, all the guests wonder: "What's wrong with him?" Finally, the furious in-law dismisses poor Max! The poor man then confesses his unfortunate experience and everyone bursts with laughter. *(Translation DD from Bousquet nr 5091)*

1912.04.03 - DEU - CS: Zensurkarte Berlin - Renken
1912.04.12 - Ö-UM - Wien: Rotenturm Kino - Renken
1912.05 - FRA - TR-PR: Catalogue Pathé - Bousquet
1912.06.14 - FRA - Paris: Omnia Pathé - Bousquet

Archives: no film print known to this date

1912-07
UNE NUIT AGITÉE
160 m = 525 ft = 0:07:46 if at 18 fps
b&w

Nuit agitée, Une - French release title (original - FRA) - Bousquet
Kleine Störenfried, Der - German release title (DEU) - Renken

Alone, at last! The wedding ceremony over, Max takes his wife to the sweet home he has prepared, and after having enjoyed the first hours of their intimate relationship they fall asleep. Max is suddenly awakened by a violent insect bite. He unsuccessfully tries to get rid of the intruder. The flea bites him again as he is going back to sleep. Max decides to bring out the heavy artillery: he fires a shot at the flea, which awakes his wife with a start. She finds her husband a little bit mad and goes back to sleep. Her shoulders are then doused by some water, poured from a pitcher, aimed at the insect. She decides to retire on a deck chair to get a more peaceful sleep. In the morning, Max succeeds at last to capture the insect. He confines it in a bag, then brings it... on the railroad tracks! *(Translation DD from Bousquet nr 5125)*

1912.05 - FRA - TR-PR: Catalogue Pathé - Bousquet
1912.05.08 - ESP - Barcelona: Iris Park - Renken
1912.06.28 - FRA - Paris: Omnia Pathé - Bousquet

Archives: BEL-CRB-Bru; DEU-DFF-Fra; DEU-DK-Ber; FRA-CF-Par; FRA-CNC-Par; FRA-CML

1912-08
LE SUCCÈS DE LA PRESTIDIGITATION
240 m = 787 ft = 0:11:39 if at 18 fps
b&w

Succès de la prestidigitation, Le - French release title (original - FRA) - Bousquet
Erfolg des Gaukelspiels, Der - German release title (DEU+Ö-UM) - Renken
Conjurer's Triumph, The - English release title (GBR) - Renken
Max, the Magician - English release title (USA) - Renken
Max escamoteur - French listing title (attribution) - Ford

Max is angry because a rival outshines him at a social evening, through the production of a spout of water from his host's head by forcing air into that gentleman's mouth with a pair of bellows. Max tries to copy the trick on reaching home. The results are worse than negative. His rival decides to rid himself once and for all of Max. He orders his own valet to write to Max as if he were a conjuror, and to promise to teach him a good trick. Max parts with a liberal sum in exchange for a bottle of water, supposed, if previously applied to the cheek, to deaden the pain of any blow. Max brags about his new trick and dabs a little of the water on the cheek of his hostess. Needless to say, the terrific blow he gives her almost stuns her, and in social circles Max's star has now disappeared. *(The Bioscope, 1912.05.02, in Renken)*

1912.04.19 - Ö-UM - Wien: Kino Theater des "Invalidendank" - Renken
1912.05 - FRA - TR-PR: Catalogue Pathé - Bousquet
1912.06.21 - FRA - Paris: Omnia Pathé - Bousquet

Archives: ITA-CdF-Gem

Note: re-released 28mm Pathé-Kok nr 371 LE SUCCÈS DE LA PRESTIDIGITATION 127 m (= 161 m in 35mm).

1912-09
L'ÂNE JALOUX
170 m = 558 ft = 0:08:15 if at 18 fps
b&w

Âne jaloux, L - French release title (original - FRA) - Bousquet
Eifersüchtige Esel, Der - German release title (DEU+Ö-UM) - Renken
Max and the Donkey - English release title (GBR) - Renken
Max et son âne - French listing title (attribution) - Mitry
Joe Teaches Max a Lesson - English archive title (attribution) - GBR-BFI

Miss Lili has many suitors. She has chosen Joe Dawson. Every morning, pretty Lili takes a ride on her donkey. Max, one of her admirers, never misses a ride. One day, he decides to declare his love. The fiancé, jealous, decides to dress up as a donkey. So attired, he spies the two young persons' conversation and shows his feelings with violent kicks on poor Max's feet. He expresses his hostility even more clearly by chasing his enemy, pursuing him in his house, climbing the stairs all the way to the roof. Pushed to the wall, Max asks for mercy: he solemnly swears in writing that he won't court Miss Lili anymore. Satisfied, Master Aliboron leaves, bowing with great distinction, leaving poor Max bewildered and bruised. *(Translation DD from Bousquet nr 5136)*

1912.04.27 - DEU - CS: Zensurkarte Berlin - Renken
1912.05 - FRA - TR-PR: Catalogue Pathé - Bousquet
1912.05.03 - Ö-UM - Wien: Rotenturm Kino - Renken
1912.07.05 - FRA - Paris: Omnia Pathé - Renken

Archives: FRA-CF-Par; FRA-CML; FRA-CNC-Par; GBR-BFI-Lon

Note: re-released 28mm Pathé-Kok nr 845 L'ÂNE JALOUX 120 m (= 152 m in 35mm).

1912-10
LA MALLE AU MARIAGE
210 m = 689 ft = 0:10:12 if at 18 fps
b&w

Malle au mariage, La - French release title (original - FRA) - Bousquet
Rivale im Koffer, Der - German release title (DEU+Ö-UM) - Renken
Max and the Maid - English release title (GBR) - Renken

The guardian of Mamie, with whom Max is in love, wishes to make the girl his wife. Mamie, holding her guardian in mortal terror, insists upon Max concealing himself one day when the former obtrudes his presence upon them. Max obeys and finding behind the hanging wardrobe a lady's long plush coat and hat, he dons both articles to make his escape. The disguise leads the guardian, who observes him depart, into supposing that a pretty woman is the owner of the coat. He follows "her", and Max inveigles him into his own rooms, shams a scare on account of a supposed husband, and manages to get him locked up in a big trunk, from which he is released only on his giving his consent to Max's engagement to Mamie. *(The Bioscope, 1912.05.30, in Renken)*

1912.05.08 - DEU - CS: Zensurkarte Berlin - Renken
1912.05.17 - Ö-UM - Wien: Rotenturm Kino - Renken
1912.06 - FRA - TR-PR: Catalogue Pathé - Bousquet
1912.07.19 - FRA - Paris: Omnia Pathé - Bousquet

Archives: FRA-CF-Par; FRA-CML; FRA-CNC-Par; NLD-EFM-Ams

1912-13
LE MAL DE MER
150 m = 492 ft = 0:07:17 if at 18 fps
b&w

Mal de mer, Le - French release title (original - FRA) - Bousquet
Seekrankheit, Die - German release title (DEU+Ö-UM) - Renken
Motor Boat Trip, A - English release title (GBR) - Renken

Max, who has been paying rather more attention to a friend's wife than pleases the latter gentleman, is persuaded by him to accompany him on a motorboat trip. The friend devoutly hopes that Max will suffer from mal de mer, and cut a ridiculous figure before his wife, whom he trusts will be cured of her admiration for Max. He chooses a particularly windy day for the trip, and with his wife and Max, well prepared for rough weather, he sets off. Max sternly refuses to acknowledge any qualmish feelings, and it is the husband who first collapses. Max is not long in following suit, and the wife is heartily amused at the weakness of her escorts, until suddenly she, too, falls in a heap in the bottom of the boat. *(The Bioscope, 1912.08.01, in Renken)*

1912.05.08 - DEU - CS: Zensurkarte Berlin - Renken
1912.07.31 - ESP - Barcelona: Ciné Diana - Renken
1912.08 - FRA - TR-PR: Catalogue Pathé - Bousquet
1912.09.20 - FRA - Paris: Omnia Pathé - Bousquet

Archives: FRA-CF-Par; FRA-CNC-Par; NLD-EFM-Ams

1912-14
MAX COCHER DE FIACRE
285 m = 935 ft = 0:13:51 if at 18 fps
b&w

Max cocher de fiacre - French release title (original - FRA) - Bousquet
Max wird Droschkenkutscher - German release title (DEU+Ö-UM) - Renken
Max as Cab Driver - English release title (GBR) - Renken

Max, head over ears in debt, sees his goods seized one morning. He is left with a mattress, one suit of clothes, and his top hat. Next morning, he goes out into the streets in the hope that Providence will look after him. Max drifts aimlessly about, until he is suddenly pulled up short by a notice reading, "Taxi Strike - Cab Drivers Wanted". Max goes into the cab yard to ask for a job. He gets it, and, declining the offer of a cabby's hat and top coat, drives through the crowded fashionable streets for a fare. Eventually he picks up a fare, who requests him to drive quickly to the station with a heavy trunk. On the route he passes a car containing four of his best friends. They hail him delightedly, and carry him off to luncheon, regardless of his actual occupation. Max goes, forgetting fare and cab. A small urchin comes along and unbuckles the girths of the horse. When Max, on returning, mounts the box and applies the whip, the horse moves off, leaving the cab at a standstill. Max is rescued from his dilemma by his friends, who utilize their motor to drag his fare to the station, where he claims and receives, after much expostulation, the sum of nineteen and ten, and Max has no regrets about leaving the horseless cab to its fate outside the station. *(The Bioscope, 1912.06.13, in Renken)*

1912.05.16 - DEU - CS: Zensurkarte Berlin - Renken
1912.05.31 - Ö-UM - Wien: Maxims-Bio - Renken
1912.06 - FRA - TR-PR: Catalogue Pathé - Bousquet
1912.08.02 - FRA - Paris: Omnia Pathé - Bousquet

Archives: no film print known to this date

Note: re-released 28mm Pathé-Kok nr 348 MAX COCHER DE FIACRE 123 m (= 156 m in 35mm).

1912-15
OH! LES FEMMES
150 m = 492 ft = 0:07:17 if at 18 fps
b&w

Oh! les femmes - French release title (original - FRA) - Bousquet
O' diese Frauen - German release title (DEU+Ö-UM) - Renken

Eternal Woman - English release title (GBR) - Renken
Max et les femmes - French listing title (attribution) - Mitry
Ah les femmes! - French listing title (attribution) - Jeanne et Ford

Like the debonair dandy he is, Max hastens off just before one o'clock to keep his engagements. Louisa he greets with affection; in fact, he kisses her, and Louisa is annoyed. She slaps his face and walks away. Max's second engagement being so close upon the first, it is not surprising that his face should still be puckered into a rueful grimace, as the result of this slap, when he meets Emily. Now, Emily wants to be kissed, and she tells him to kiss her. Max refuses, on account of his recent lesson, and receives a second slap. Joan appears in view. Seeing him with a lady, Joan immediately vents her indignation in a third slap. Max takes to his heels, meets Alice, and fairly bolts down a long road, as he asks himself, "Whatever is a man to do to please a woman?" *(The Bioscope, 1912.06.20, in Renken)*

1912.06 - FRA - TR-PR: Catalogue Pathé - Bousquet
1912.06.07 - Ö-UM - Wien: Wiener Lichtspiel-Theater - Renken
1912.08.09 - FRA - Paris: Omnia Pathé - Bousquet

Archives: FRA-CF-Par; FRA-CNC-Par

Note: re-released 28mm Pathé-Kok nr 863 OH! LES FEMMES 121 m (= 154 m in 35mm).

1912-16
IDYLLE À LA FERME
240 m = 787 ft = 0:11:39 if at 18 fps
b&w

Idylle à la ferme - French release title (original - FRA) - Bousquet
Idyll im Gutshofe, Ein - German release title (DEU+Ö-UM) - Renken

Farm-House Romance, A - English release title (GBR+USA) - Renken
Idyll on a Farm, An - English re-release title (28mm) - print at USA-GEM

Max, who has sponged upon a wealthy uncle, is told by that worthy to marry one of the daughters of an old friend of his. Max goes down to the farm. At a family council, it is hastily decided that Max must be induced to marry the elder daughter. The daughter shrewdly foresees that Max is more likely to want to marry her younger sister, and she accordingly insists on the sister being disguised as a servant during his stay. Max does not find farm life very congenial. The appearance of a pretty maid introduces some element of pleasure, and he has an exciting time for a few hours in maneuvering to obtain glimpses of her. His indignation at finding her in his host's arms is expressed rather vehemently, and the father is forced to disclose the real facts of the case. Max promptly begs for the pretty maid for a wife and gets her. *(The Bioscope, 27.6.1912.06.27, in Renken)*

1912.06.14 - Ö-UM - TR-PR: Trade listing - Renken
1912.06.21 - Ö-UM - Wien: Weltbild - Renken
1912.07 - FRA - TR-PR: Catalogue Pathé - Bousquet
1912.08.16 - FRA - Paris: Omnia Pathé - Bousquet

Archives: ESP-FdV-Val; FRA-CF-Par; FRA-CML; FRA-CNC-Par; FRA-Lob-Par; JPN-NFAJ-Tôk; USA-GEM-Roc

Note: re-relased 28mm Pathé-Kok nr 380-381a IDYLLE À LA FERME, on reel with ROSALIE EST JALOUSE, total lenght 255 m (= 324 m in 35mm).

1912-17
UN PARI ORIGINAL
125 m = 410 ft = 0:06:04 if at 18 fps
b&w

Pari original, Un - French release title (original - FRA) - Bousquet
Originelle Wette, Eine - German release title (DEU+Ö-UM) - Renken
Bet, The - English release title (GBR) - Renken
Strange Bet, A - English [re-release title] (28mm) - DVD publisher (Cinerdistan)

Max and his wife each blame the other for a nagging tongue. Max offers to bet his wife fifty pounds, even money both ways, that she will be the first to speak or make a sign after the acceptance of the bet. His wife accepts the wager, and the two young people allow their flat to be burgled rather than move or murmur. Max sits out the ordeal in agony, up to the time the burglar attempts to kiss his wife. Then, with a yell, he rises to punch the burglar's head. There is joy in the punch, but less in the drawing of the cheque. *(The Bioscope, 1912.07.04, in Renken)*

1912.06.21 - Ö-UM - TR-PR: Trade listing - Renken
1912.06.28 - Ö-UM - Prag: Grand Kinematograf Orient - Renken
1912.07 - FRA - TR-PR: Catalogue Pathé - Bousquet
1912.08.23 - FRA - Paris: Omnia Pathé - Bousquet

Archives: BEL-CRB-Bru; GBR-Private collection

Note: re-released 28mm Pathé-Kok nr 408a UN PARI ORIGNAL, on reel with UNE CHEMINÉE BIEN RAMONÉE, total length 128 m (= 163 m in 35mm).

1912-18
PEINTRE PAR AMOUR
210 m = 689 ft = 0:10:12 if at 18 fps
b&w

Peintre par amour - French release title (original - FRA) - Bousquet
Maler aus Liebe - German release title (Ö-UM) - Renken
Artist Max - English release title (GBR) - Renken
Max peintre par amour - French listing title (attribution) - Mitry

Max is in love with the daughter of a lady who is not very approving of his suit. He ascertains that she wishes to have her portrait painted, and he undertakes to execute a fine picture of her. The lady immediately accepts the offer. Max has overlooked the fact that he has not the slightest notion of drawing or painting. He makes a brave effort to fulfil his part, and the portrait he turns out is as absurd a caricature as could be imagined. It arouses the sitter's ire, and its perpetrator is shown the front door. Max rouses from his despair. A happy inspiration flies through his brain. Quickly he sets to work to develop it, and, under an assumed name, he writes to the lady that he has been struck by her resemblance to Mona Lisa, the subject of the stolen picture from the Louvre. He wishes to make a copy of the missing masterpiece and begs for the favor of a sitting. The bait is swallowed, and Max, disguised by a short brown beard, hurries off the next day with a large canvas under his arm. The surface is of a pristine whiteness, but, once his sitter is settled, he tears off a paper covering unseen, and reveals a ready-made copy of the Mona Lisa picture. A few awkward touches are added, and then Max, asked by his pleased sitter to state his price for the portrait, begs for the hand of her daughter. *(The Bioscope, 1912.07.18, in Renken)*

1912.07 - FRA - TR-PR: Catalogue Pathé - Bousquet
1912.07.13 - Ö-UM - Graz: Bioskop Theater Annenhof - Renken
1912.09.06 - FRA - Paris: Omnia Pathé - Bousquet

Archives: FRA-CF-Par; FRA-CNC-Par; GBR-BFI-Lon; ITA-CdF-Gem

Note: re-released 28mm Pathé-Kok nr 428 PEINTRE PAR AMOUR 125 m (= 159 m in 35mm).

1912-19
LA VENGEANCE DU DOMESTIQUE
225 m = 738 ft = 0:10:56 if at 18 fps
b&w

Vengeance du domestique, La - French release title (original - FRA) - Bousquet
Streich des Dieners, Der - German release title (DEU+Ö-UM) - Renken

François, a servant in Max's parents' home, asks for a certificate from the father and a tip from the son, as a reward for his acts of complicity. Both men fire him quite vigorously. François has an oversensitive temperament and he is resentful. As a revenge, he rents a nice furnished flat and sends to father and son the same letter that reads: "To see you is to love you. I've seen you, and I love you. I'll be waiting for you tonight in my apartment. Nini, 122 Breda street." Max and his father, both delighted to be so lucky, don't miss the appointment. François, perfect in his part of a servant, tells them with great detail how beautiful the woman whose heart they have won is. He is so convincing that father and son, both over-excited, finally realize with surprise and disgust that they are about to fall into each other's arms instead of embracing their sweetheart. *(Translation DD from Bousquet nr 5310)*

1912.07.06 - Ö-UM - TR-PR: Oesterreichischer Komet - Renken
1912.08 - FRA - TR-PR: Catalogue Pathé - Bousquet
1912.08.07 - ESP - Barcelona: Teatro Condal - Renken
1912.10.03 - FRA - Paris: Cinématographe du Petit Journal - Renken

Archives: NLD-EFM-Ams

Note: re-released 28mm Pathé-Kok nr 370 LA VENGEANCE DU DOMESTIQUE 123 m (= 156 m in 35mm).

1912-20
LA FUITE DE GAZ
210 m = 689 ft = 0:10:12 if at 18 fps
b&w

Fuite de gaz, La - French release title (original - FRA) - Bousquet
Defekte Gasleitung, Die - German release title (DEU+Ö-UM) - Renken
Escape of Gas, An - English release title (GBR+USA) - Renken
Max et la fuite de gaz - French listing title (attribution) - Mitry
Smitten - English listing title (attribution) - GBR-BFI

Beatrice is walking home when she is met by Max. He hurries after her till she reaches her home, and gets his fingers jammed in the gate. Beatrice detects the smell of gas; she informs her husband, and the maid is dispatched for the gas-fitter. The latter is accosted by Max, who sees an opportunity of gaining an entrance to the house. He changes clothes with the gas-fitter. Max diligently searches for the escape, and plants his steps on the toe of Beatrice's husband. Many comical situations take place, and Beatrice and her husband eventually retire to a safer retreat. Max continues to bang away with a hammer at the wall; in the end he bursts a water pipe and the room is flooded. After several vain attempts to stem the leakage with cushions and chairs, he puts his fist into the hole. In the midst of all this confusion Beatrice and her husband reappear, and the latter places his fist over the hole. This leaves the way free for Max to make love to Beatrice. In his endeavors to keep Max from Beatrice, the husband has to leave the hole in the water pipe, and consequently the three get a thorough drenching. *(The Bioscope, 1912.07.25, in Renken)*

1912.07.11 - UK - TR-PR: The Bisoscope - Renken
1912.07.27 - ESP - Barcelona: Iris Park - Renken
1912.08 - FRA - TR-PR: Catalogue Pathé - Bousquet
1912.09.13 - FRA - Paris: Omnia Pathé - Bousquet

Archives: GBR-BFI-Lon; NLD-EFM-Ams

**1912-21
VOYAGE DE NOCES
135 m = 443 ft = 0:06:33 if at 18 fps
b&w**

Voyage de noces - French release title (original - FRA) - Bousquet
Auf der Hochzeitsreise - German release title (DEU+Ö-UM) - Renken
On the Honeymoon - English release title (GBR) - Renken
Max et Jane en voyage de noces - French listing title (attribution) - Mitry

Max en voyage de noces - French listing title (attribution) - Ford
Voyage de noces (en Espagne) - French listing title (attribution) - Chirat et LeRoy

Max has married the woman he is in love with. So, he decides to take a honeymoon trip with her and to leave immediately. Max and his young wife enjoy the funniest situations they could have dreamt of. In the end, Max, his outfit tattered, his hat spoiled, black-eyed but still deeply in love, catches up with his wife who regrets to have left her home the very day of her marriage.
(Translation DD from Le cinéma et l'écho du cinéma réunis, 1912.10.12, in Renken)

1912.07.26 - CS: Zensurkarte Berlin - Renken
1912.08.23 - Ö-UM - Prag: Grand Kinematograf Orient - Renken
1912.09 - FRA - TR-PR: Catalogue Pathé - Bousquet
1912.12.18 - FRA - Paris: Omnia Pathé - Renken

Archives: no film print known to this date

Note: re-released 28mm Pathé-Kok nr 101 VOYAGE DE NOCES 115 m (= 146 m in 35mm). References to this film are somewhat confused: Chirat-LeRoy list two VOYAGE DE NOCES: one with Jane Renouardt (1911) and one with Stacia Napierkowska (1912). Similarly, the 28mm Pathé-Kok catalog length of 115 m has an equivalent of 146 m in 35mm, which is longer than the catalog length of the original release (135 m).

1912-22
AMOUR TENACE
410 m = 1345 ft = 0:19:55 if at 18 fps
b&w

Amour tenace - French release title (original - FRA) - Bousquet
Hartnäckige Liebe - German release title (DEU+Ö-UM) - Renken
Love Unconquerable - English release title (GBR+USA) - Renken

The story is of Max's pertinacity in following everywhere the girl with whom he happens to be in love, much to the disgust of her father. The elder man takes the girl off to the Swiss mountains. Max follows in the same train, so the father engages a special. Max follows on a donkey, hitched to the rear of the train. At the destination of father and daughter, he finds that they engage a carriage to convey them and their luggage to the hotel. He follows in a sleigh fastened to the back. The following week he appears constantly on the ice in a delightful rig-out and falls foul of a pugnacious instructor engaged for the benefit of the girl. Then the father adopts the plan of taking his daughter for trips into the mountains. Max still follows and is able to rescue his enemy from a ravine into which he has fallen. Failing, then, to extract a consent to his suit, he pushes him back again, and refuses to assist him until he has given the required promise. Even then the old gentleman breaks his word, and Max has to make a blatant announcement of his coming marriage in the newspaper, and then to feign unwillingness, before the capricious parent realizes how desirable he will be as a son-in-law. *(The Bioscope, 1912.08.15, in Renken)*

1912.08 - FRA - TR-PR: Catalogue Pathé - Bousquet
1912.08.10 - Ö-UM - Graz: Bioskop Theater Annenhof - Renken
1912.10.04 - FRA - Paris: Omnia Pathé - Bousquet

Archives: FRA-CNC-Par; FRA-CML

1912-23
MAX ÉMULE DE TARTARIN
225 m = 738 ft = 0:10:56 if at 18 fps
b&w

Max émule de Tartarin - French release title (original - FRA) - Bousquet
Max ist ein Aufschneider - German release title (DEU+Ö-UM) - Renken
Wanted: a Bearskin - English release title (GBR) - Renken

Max, vacationing with his bride in a remote snowy village, enjoys exploring the mountains. He fears, however, facing some chamois or lost cow, who knows? Maybe a bear! After all, there are some in France, in the Pyrénées mountains. Max's fertile imagination, similar to Tartarin de Tarascon's, persuades him to write a letter to his bride about a hunting trip: "Dear Diane, I've just killed a huge bear in the mountains. I wanted to give you its skin as a present, unfortunately my dogs ate it." Diane answers his unwise letter: "Dear Max, as your dogs have prevented me from enjoying that lovely present, I'm sure your love for me can guide you at once towards another bear you'll kill for me." Max hasn't much choice, so he goes hunting. Unfortunately, he only faces an animal crowned with horns that pushes him down the mountain. Max doesn't want to go back empty-handed, so he buys a splendid skin, which he triumphantly presents to his bride. However, the devil is always in the details: Max has forgotten to remove a sewn label that reads "goat skin 10,75 French Francs". He is caught red-handed. *(Translation DD from Bousquet nr 5387)*

1912.08.09 - DEU - CS: Zensurkarte Berlin - Renken
1912.09 - FRA - TR-PR: Catalogue Pathé - Bousquet
1912.09.06 - Ö-UM - Prag: Grand Kinematograf Orient - Renken
1912.11.01 - FRA - Paris: Omnia Pathé - Bousquet

Archives: BEL-CRB-Bru; ESP-FdV-Val; FRA-CF-Par; FRA-CML; FRA-CNC-Par; ITA-CdF-Gem; NLD-EFM-Ams

Note: re-released 28mm Pathé-Kok nr 361 MAX ÉMULE DE TARTARIN 124 m (= 157 m in 35mm). Pathé-Baby UN ÉMULE DE TARTARIN is a Harold Lloyd film.

1912-24
BOXEUR PAR AMOUR
235 m = 771 ft = 0:11:25 if at 18 fps
b&w

Boxeur par amour - French release title (original - FRA) - Bousquet
Boxer aus Liebe - German release title (DEU+Ö-UM) - Renken
Love and Boxing - English release title (GBR) - Renken
Max boxeur par amour - French listing title (attribution) - Mitry
Max boxeur - French re-release title (9.5mm) - Catalogue Pathé-Baby 1926
Max Boxer - English archive title [attribution] - FIAF TFA db

Max falls in love with Miss Diana Jeffroies, daughter of Jack Jeffroies, a boxer. Diana does not lack in suitors and declares that the man to win her will be the one who can beat her in a boxing match. Max goes into training at once, and boxes vigorously with his valet, who, not daring to retaliate, causes his master to feel considerably elated. On the day of the match, Diana "knocks out" her opponents one after the other until it is the turn of Max. That gentleman soon finds he has little hope of being the winner, and resorts to clinches, during which he gives Diana some resounding kisses. Diana, surprised by this novel method of attack, "throws up the sponge", and Max wins the day. *(The Bioscope, 1912.09.05, in Renken)*

1912.08.23 - Ö-UM - TR-PR: Trade listing - Renken
1912.08.31 - Ö-UM - Graz: Bioskop Theater Annenhof - Renken
1912.09 - FRA - TR-PR: Catalogue Pathé - Bousquet
1912.10.25 - FRA - Paris: Omnia Pathé - Renken

Archives: BEL-CRB-Bru; CZE-NFA-Pra; DEU-DFF-Fra; DNK-DFI-Køb; FRA-CML; FRA-CNC-Par; FRA-Lob-Par; ROU-ANF-Buc; USA-AFA-Los

Note: re-released 9,5mm Pathé-Baby nr 746 MAX BOXEUR, notches 10 m (1 cassette).

1912-25
MARIAGE AU TÉLÉPHONE
245 m = 804 ft = 0:11:54 if at 18 fps
b&w

Mariage au téléphone - French release title (original - FRA) - Bousquet
Telephonische Verbindung - German release title (DEU+Ö-UM) - Renken
Over the 'Phone - English release title (GBR+USA) - Renken

Max et le téléphone - French re-release title (9.5mm) - Catalogue Pathé-Baby 1926
Max and the telephone - English re-release title (9.5mm) - Newnham www.pathefilm.uk
Mariage par téléphone, Un - French listing title (attribution) - JPN-NFAJ

Max wishes to ring up Mr. Charles Pathé, but cannot get an answering call, and he departs in high dudgeon for Pathé's. Meantime the fair operator at Pathé's, absorbed in a thrilling love romance, is not to be aroused there from by telephone bells. She hardly looks up when Max enters and pours out a flood of angry remonstrances. When his eyes fall on the pretty face of the telephone maid, Max's tirade ends with an apologetic smile. He looks down the page she is reading and is almost impelled to follow the example of the hero, and to kiss the cheek so near to him. The next morning Max moons around his room, longing, yet fearing, to ring up his lady-love on the telephone. She, on her part, listens eagerly for the telephone bell. Presently Max rings her up, and the lovers find some outlet for the love fever consuming them. A few days later, Max, over the 'phone, asks the fair operator to dine with him. Unfortunately, his lady-love has been replaced temporarily by an elderly spinster, and she accepts the invitation. Max is early at the rendezvous and awaits his guest. When at last the lady enters, attired in fearful finery, Max is rendered almost hysterical. He tries to explain, but the lady will listen to nothing, neither will she let him go. With difficulty he throws her off and makes his escape. The next morning Max sends a decisive message over the 'phone - "I would rather die than marry an ugly-faced girl like you!" This message is received by his legitimate sweetheart, and she seeks Max. Explanations disperse the cloud of misunderstanding, and the lovers are happy again. *(The Bioscope, 1912.11.21, in Renken)*

1912.09.20 - ESP - Barcelona: Teatre Novetats - Renken
1912.11 - FRA - TR-PR: Catalogue Pathé - Bousquet
1913.01.10 - FRA - Paris: Omnia Pathé - Bousquet

Archives: FRA-Lob-Par; ITA-CN-Rom; JPN-NFAJ-Tōk; NLD-EFM-Ams

Note: re-released 28mm Pathé-Kok nr 357 MARIAGE AU TÉLÉPHONE 126 m (= 160 m in 35mm). Re-released 9,5mm Pathé-Baby nr 754 MAX ET LE TÉLÉPHONE / MAX AND THE TELEPHONE, notches 10 m (1 cassette). Pathé-Baby nr 10025 MARIAGE AU TÉLÉPHONE / A TELEPHONE MARRIAGE is a film with Douglas Fairbanks.

**1912-26
ENTENTE CORDIALE
380 m = 1247 ft = 0:18:28 if at 18 fps
b&w**

Entente cordiale - French release title (original - FRA) - Bousquet
Max und sein Rivale - German release title (DEU+Ö-UM) - Renken
Entente Cordiale - English release title (GBR) - Renken
Deux coqs vivaient en paix - French re-release title (9.5mm) - Poisson
Max et l'entente cordiale - French listing title (attribution) - Mitry

Fragson, famous humorist, crosses the Channel to spend a month in Paris. He has been invited by his French counterpart Max Linder, the King of Comedy. Max hires a maid, a pretty blonde maid, who enchants the two men's hearts. Naturally, the roles are reversed. Both men become the too cute maid's knights-servants. She is at leisure to dream of her Prince Charming, who appears to be Max. But Fragson is jealous. Consequently, when he meets his rival in front of his sweetheart's door, the two men engage in a merciless duel: six gunshots are fired at a distance of six feet, each man aiming at the one coming towards him. Fortunately, the maid had ordered that the guns not be loaded. That favorable outcome allows Max to give the beloved young woman his heart and his name. The maid proves to be an immensely rich heiress, daughter of the American billionaire Rock-fell-hair. She had elaborated that scheme because she was afraid to be married for her fortune. *(Translation DD from Bousquet nr 5402)*

1912.09.20 - Ö-UM - TR-PR: Trade listing - Renken
1912.09.27 - Ö-UM - Prag: Grand Kinematograf Orient - Renken
1912.10 - FRA - TR-PR: Catalogue Pathé - Bousquet
1912.11.22 - FRA - Paris: Omnia Pathé - Bousquet

Archives: FRA-CML; FRA-CNC-Par; FRA-Lob-Par

Note: re-released 9,5mm Pathé-Baby nr 440 DEUX COQS VIVAIENT EN PAIX, notches 20 m (2 cassettes).

1912-27
MAX VEUT GRANDIR
405 m = 1329 ft = 0:19:41 if at 18 fps
b&w

Max veut grandir - French release title (original - FRA) - Bousquet
Max will größer werden - German release title (DEU+Ö-UM) - Renken
Max's Efforts to Grow - English release title (GBR) - Renken
Max Joins the Giants - English release title (USA) - Renken

Max's latest love, Barcord's daughter, craves a giant for her future spouse, and declares she will wed no other. Max essays to become one by assuming a pair of stilts. His efforts to walk on them result, however, in the ruining of his apartment and the despoiling of his immaculate attire. The advertisement of a Professor Rotte quickens his flagging hopes. This gentleman has a machine which, if the hand be placed on figure 1 increases the width, if on figure 2 the height. The professor gives a practical demonstration, and Max carries it home. Wishing to demonstrate to the incredulous Barcord his newly acquired ability to increase his inches, he places the machine in position, in his excitement putting the hand on figure 1. Immediately Max is reduced to a grotesquely shortened and much distended figure and is ignominiously ejected by Barcord. Max is wrapped in gloomy reflections when his friend Service calls. Service comes to his aid by suggesting that, carried on his shoulders and hidden by a long cloak, Max will present the appearance of a giant. Barcord welcomes him warmly this time, but Service, who has an appointment with his fiancée, Betty, hurries Max into the hall, where she is waiting. Service explains matters to the astonished Betty, and Barcord learns how he has been deceived. The two conspirators make a somewhat undignified exit, and Max then seeks Professor Wires, who claims to lengthen people by electricity. Max at last realizes his ambition, and when quite 7 ft. in height, he hurries to Barcord's house to claim Betty and the parental blessing. *(The Bioscope, 1912.10.17, in Renken)*

1912.10 - FRA - TR-PR: Catalogue Pathé - Bousquet
1912.10.11 - Ö-UM - Prag: Grand Kinematograf Orient - Renken
1912.12.06 - FRA - Paris: Omnia Pathé - Bousquet

Archives: CAN-CQ-Mon; DNK-DFI-Køb; FRA-CF-Par; FRA-CNC-Par; FRA-GPA-Par; FRA-CML

1912-28
L'ENLÈVEMENT EN HYDROAÉROPLANE
255 m = 837 ft = 09:17 if at 18 fps
Pathécolor - 220 m in colours

Enlèvement en hydroaéroplane, L' - French release title (original - FRA) - Bousquet
Liebespaar im Hydro-Aeroplan, Das - German release title (DEU+Ö-UM) - Renken
Waterplane Elopement, A - English release title (GBR) - Renken
Enlèvement en hydroplane, Un - French listing title (attribution) - Mitry
Enlèvement par hydroaéroplane - French listing title (attribution) - Ford

Max and Kiddie are in love with each other, but Kiddie's guardian persists in being jealous of all his charming ward's suitors and forbids them his house. Kiddie eventually whispers from her window the one word, "elope", to Max in the garden below. Her lover enters into a pact with his sweetheart's music master, to take his place for an hour in order to arrange the details of the plan. Max is, unhappily, discovered. He gathers his courage together and arrives once more beneath Kiddie's window. He carries the girl off and installs her comfortably in his waterplane. The start is made, and the lovers leave the guardian and bolts and bars far behind them. The flight is a delightful one, but Max grows negligent of his steering, and the hydroplane overturns and falls to earth, crashing on its way through the roof of a tall house. The wreckage and the lovers land at the feet of a startled-looking clergyman, and Max and Kiddie turn to this gentleman with the words: "Sir, we have fallen from Heaven for you to marry us." *(The Bioscope, 1912.11.07, in Renken)*

1912.10.17 - DEN - København: Palats-Teatret - Renken
1912.11 - FRA - TR-PR: Catalogue Pathé - Bousquet
1912.12.27 - FRA - Paris: Omnia Pathé - Bousquet

Archives: no film print known to this date

1912-29
PETIT ROMAN
160 m = 525 ft = 0:07:46 if at 18 fps
b&w

Petit roman - French release title (original - FRA) - Bousquet
Max in der Sommerfrische - German release title (DEU+Ö-UM) - Renken
Affinity - English release title (GBR) - Renken
Dos pares de zapatos - Spanish archive title [attribution] - FIAF TFA db
Roman de Max, Le - French listing title (attribution) - Mitry

Max Linder is spending a holiday at the seaside and reaches his hotel at the same time as a charming unknown. Their respective rooms adjoin. They put their footgear outside their doors at the same moment. The boots, during the night, change places, and, when sought by their owners in the morning, Max's left boot is by the side of his fair neighbor's, and vice versa. Max and the lady go for an early constitutional, and Max sits down to sketch on the rocks, while the lady, engrossed in a book, sits on a seat above; their boots, however, persist in playing uncanny pranks. At last Max's left boot, without any help, leaves him altogether, and goes scampering up the rocks, with Max climbing wildly after it. At the same moment the charming stranger's left boot mysteriously leaves her, and runs gaily down the path, with the owner in excited pursuit. Finally, the boots and their owners meet, and, wondering much, the latter sit down to put the former on again. Then Max and the lady exchange a smile, and the next moment they exchange a kiss. Cupid scores, for the result is a wedding a few months later. *(The Bioscope, 1912.10.31, in Renken)*

1912.10.18 - Ö-UM - Wien: Arkaden-Kino - Renken
1912.11 - FRA - TR-PR: Catalogue Pathé - Bousquet
1912.12.20 - FRA - Paris: Omnia Pathé - Bousquet

Archives: FRA-CF-Par; FRA-CML; FRA-CNC-Par; URY-ANIP-Mon

1912-30
JALOUSIE
225 m = 738 ft = 0:10:56 if at 18 fps
b&w

Jalousie - French release title (original - FRA) - Bousquet
Eifersucht - German release title (DEU+Ö-UM) - Renken
Green-Eyed Monster, The - English release title (GBR) - Renken

Max becomes a benedict, and we are introduced to him and his charming bride, Jane, in the first hours of their honeymoon. After the honeymoon is over, Jane frets so much over Max's undemonstrativeness that she consults the family doctor, to whom she pours out her grievance. This worthy gives her a prescription, which has, in similar cases, been the means of quickening a flagging affection. Jane must make herself look pretty again, have mysterious appointments, and pretend to have a lover - in short, make Max jealous. Jane, delighted with the plan, proceeds to put it into execution. Max's jealousy is thoroughly aroused. The next day Max finds a note on the floor (carefully placed there by Jane) in which the writer plans to meet his wife that evening, adding that he will enter by the window. Jane has arrayed herself in some of her husband's clothes, and when Max looks through the keyhole into his wife's room, he sees a stranger enter, and ostensibly make love to his wife. He bursts into the room, and seizing a pair of swords, hands one to his betrayer, and insists on having his honor vindicated on the spot. Jane takes the sword, and after a few thrusts she discloses her identity. Max embraces her affectionately. *(The Bioscope, 1912.12.05, in Renken)*

1912.11.22 - Ö-UM - Wien: Kinoplastikon - Renken
1912.11.30 - DEU - TR-PR: Erste Internationale Film-Zeitung - Renken
1912.12 - FRA - TR-PR: Catalogue Pathé - Bousquet
1913.01.24 - FRA - Paris: Omnia Pathé - Bousquet

Archives: FRA-CF-Par; FRA-CNC-Par

1912-31
LA PEUR DE L'EAU
300 m = 984 ft = 0:14:34 if at 18 fps
b&w

Peur de l'eau, La - French release title (original - FRA) - Bousquet
Max ist wasserscheu - German release title (DEU+Ö-UM) - Renken
Water-Funker, The - English release title (GBR) - Renken
Max a peur de l'eau - French listing title (attribution) - Mitry

Max and Dora, his fiancée, are together with some friends, playing at tennis. Dora wearies of this, and, dilating on the pleasures of a dip in the briny, leaves the tennis court, and makes Max accompany her to the shore. Here they enter two bathing machines, and both emerge attired in bathing dress. Dora plunges into the sea with delight, but Max, who has a dread of water, lingers at the edge of the waves. In vain Dora urges him to join her. He remains on the shore until she returns to the bathing machine. Dora expresses her contempt of his conduct in no uncertain terms; further, she attaches one of her rings to a piece of ribbon and throws it into the sea, vowing she will not marry Max until he brings it back to her. Max makes valiant attempts to conquer his aversion to water, both on the shore and later, on returning home, by experiments with a homemade shower bath; but his efforts are fruitless. He is dining that evening with some friends. Fish is served, and the host comes upon a ring suspended from a ribbon. Max, greatly excited, snatches it from his host, empties the contents of the water decanter on his own head, and, after embracing his friends, takes his departure. Max seeks Dora and presents her with the ring. He recounts his imaginary adventures, and she embraces him warmly. *(The Bioscope, 1912.12.19, in Renken)*

1912.12 - FRA - TR-PR: Catalogue Pathé - Bousquet
1912.12.06 - Ö-UM - Wien: Kino Theater Mizzi Schäffer - Renken
1913.02.07 - FRA - Paris: Omnia Pathé - Bousquet

Archives: FRA-CML; FRA-CNC-Par; GBR-BFI-Lon

Note: re-released 28mm Pathé-Kok nr 834-835 LA PEUR DE L'EAU 224 m (= 284 m in 35mm).

1912-32
MAX ET L'INAUGURATION DE LA STATUE
290 m = 951 ft = 0:14:05 if at 18 fps
b&w

Max et l'inauguration de la statue - French release title (original - FRA) - Bousquet
Max und die Denkmalsenthüllung - German release title (DEU+Ö-UM) - Renken
Living Statue, The - English release title (GBR) - Renken
Max et la statue - French re-release title (9.5mm) - Poisson
Inauguration de la statue, L' - French listing title (attribution) - Maud Linder
Max and the Statue - English listing title [attribution] - FIAF TFA db
Max y la inauguracion de la estatua - Spanish [release or archive] title (MEX) - FIAF TFA db

Max, arrayed in the disguise of a knight in armor, is preparing to attend the opera ball, where he is to meet a fair admirer, disguised in a blue domino. The knight appears in the midst of the gay crowd, and, spying Blue Domino, makes his way to her side. Later he takes her to Maxim's, and makes love to her, in spite of his costume. Time flies, and at 5 a.m. we see Max, alone, asleep at the table in the restaurant. The waiter, arousing him, presents the bill, but the knight's suit contains no pockets, therefore there is no money forthcoming, and Max is deposited on the pavement outside. It happens that a statue of Bayard is that day to be unveiled at one of the galleries, and some apaches stealthily enter the gallery and remove the statue. When its loss is discovered the police set off in search of it. Seeing Max's prostrate figure clad in amour, they believe him to be the missing statue, and pick up his inert body and carry it to the pedestal, where it is installed. The unveiling takes place a little later amid complimentary speeches and the singing of the Marseillaise. This interesting ceremony over, two other apaches, learning that the unveiling has taken place, seek to emulate their predecessors, and once more the statue is carried off. They convey it to one of their haunts, where they begin to disrobe it. To this the knight forcibly objects, and the apaches rush into the street, and into the arms of the police! The whole party then return to the cellar, but the statue has vanished. Presently the knight appears playing a guitar, and all fly precipitately out of the cellar. *(The Bioscope, 1913.01.02, in Renken)*

1912.12.20 - Ö-UM - Wien: Imperial Kino - Renken
1913.01 - FRA - TR-PR: Catalogue Pathé - Bousquet
1913.02.21 - FRA - Paris: Omnia Pathé - Bousquet

Archives: ARG-FCA-Bue; AUT-ÖFM-Wie; ESP-FE-Mad; FRA-CF-Par; FRA-CNC-Par; FRA-GPA-Par; FRA-CML; FRA-Lob-Par; ITA-CdF-Gem; MEX-FUNAM-Méx; USA-BkHk; USA-GEM-Roc; USA-UCLA-Los

Note: re-released 9,5mm Pathé-Baby MAX ET LA STATUE whole length titles 100 m (1 reel).

1912-33
LE RENDEZ-VOUS
285 m = 935 ft = 0:13:51 if at 18 fps
b&w

Rendez-vous, Le - French release title (original - FRA) - Bousquet
Verlorene Adresse, Die - German release title (DEU+Ö-UM) - Renken
Max Linder's Appointment - English release title (GBR) - Renken
Rendez-vous de Max, Le - French listing title (attribution) - Mitry
Max et le rendez-vous - French listing title (attribution) - Ford

Max becomes enamored of a girl whom he meets in the park, and, making an appointment with her, scribbles her address on one of his cuffs. The next morning his man-servant, failing to arouse him when the laundry maid arrives, collects the linen and sends it to the laundry, including the shirt with the fair one's address. When Max awakes, he dwells with pleasurable anticipation upon his forthcoming meeting until he bethinks himself of the address. His shirt is not to be seen, and Max strews the floor with the contents of his wardrobe. He learns the fate of the address, and, clad in his night attire, rushes into the street. The laundry van is at the door, and Max goes hurriedly through all the bags of linen, until the roadway is strewn with garments of every description. Unable to find his property, he departs, with the laundryman in pursuit. He next visits a laundry, where his exploits among the clean garments arouse the forewoman's indignation. The pursuing laundryman's entry, and his subsequent retaliation, causes Max to beat a retreat. He reaches the river, where a girl is washing some linen, and he upsets her into the water. With apologies he fishes her out, and makes another appointment, scribbling the address on his hat lining. Her name is Marie, and she is no other than the first one's maid! Max calls upon her, when the sudden return of her mistress causes her to hide him in the piano. The mistress seats herself at the piano, but soon finds that something is wrong, and on opening it discovers Max. Having almost given up hope of seeing him, she is delighted, when Marie enters and claims him as hers. Both ladies go off into hysterics, whilst Max hurriedly retreats in dismay. *(The Bioscope, 1913.01.16, in Renken)*

1912.12.26 - DEN - København: Kosmorama - Renken
1913.01 - FRA - TR-PR: Catalogue Pathé - Bousquet
1913.03.07 - FRA - Paris: Omnia Pathé - Bousquet

Archives: BEL-CRB-Bru; CZE-NFA-Pra; DEU-DK-Ber

Note: in the English contents summary (The Bioscope, 1913.01.16), Max writes the second address on his hat lining; in the French contents summary (Bousquet nr 5655) he writes it on his pajama cuff. It is not known if one of the two is mistaken, or if the versions differ.

1913-01
JOCKEY PAR AMOUR
365 m = 1198 ft = 0:17:44 if at 18 fps
b&w

Jockey par amour - French release title (original - FRA) - Bousquet
Jockei aus Liebe - German release title (DEU+Ö-UM) - Renken
Double Event, A - English release title (GBR) - Renken
Jockey for Love, A - English release title (USA) - Renken
Max jockey par amour - French listing title (attribution) - Mitry

Max falls in love with Mdlle. Dulcienne, owner of "Kismet", favourite for the Chantilly Grand Steeplechase. The lady views Max coldly. She is preoccupied on account of the forthcoming race. A disappointment awaits her. Her jockey falls ill, and it looks as if the favorite would have to be scratched. Max volunteers to ride Kismet to victory and commences to get down weight by strenuous exercises. He fades away visibly under the treatment. The great day comes at last, and Max mounts Kismet. He has a fall, but, sustained by love, remounts, and comes in first. Emboldened by his success, he dares to speak of his love to Kismet's owner and is told by that lady that she can never marry a thin man. Max starts from that day to fatten himself up. He eats and drinks prodigiously, but no sign comes to cheer his spirits, and his cheeks remain haggard and drawn. Eventually he fakes a little embonpoint. At this juncture the lady changes her mind and declares that she will have Max thin and slender. Max, eagerly reducing his bulk, goes to his lady love, all elegance, charm and gaiety. *(The Bioscope, 1913.01.30, in Renken)*

1913.01.17 - Ö-UM - Wien: Wiener Lichtspiel-Theater - Renken
1913.02 - FRA - TR-PR: Catalogue Pathé - Bousquet
1913.03.21 - FRA - Paris: Omnia Pathé - Bousquet

Archives: CZE-NFA-Pra; FRA-CF-Par; FRA-CNC-Par

1913-02
LES DÉBUTS D'UN YACHTMAN
300 m = 984 ft = 0:14:34 if at 18 fps
b&w

Débuts d'un yachtman, Les - French release title (original - FRA) - Bousquet
Max wird Segler - German release title (DEU+Ö-UM) - Renken
Max Becomes a Yachtsman - English release title (GBR) - Renken
Max Debut as Yachtsman - English archive title [attribution] - GBR-BFI
Debuts of a Yachtsman, The - English archive title [attribution] - GBR-BFI

Max is in love with Maud, but she can only love a sailor. Max buys a yacht, and a kit of clothes, then sends a message, carried by his dog to Maud telling her that he will be competing in the annual regatta. Max, his attire complete down to a smelly pipe which he pretends to enjoy, sets sail in great style, with two crewmen. However, a sudden squall overturns the boat, and while the crew swim for shore, Max is left yelling on the upturned hull. Maud rows to the rescue, and they embrace happily. *(GBR-BFI 54252)*

1913.03 - FRA - TR-PR: Catalogue Pathé - Bousquet
1913.04.10 - Ö-UM - Czernowitz/Chernivitsi: Kinotheater Cinephon - Renken
1913.05.23 - FRA - Paris: Omnia Pathé - Bousquet

Archives: FRA-CML; FRA-CNC-Par; FRA-Lob-Par; GBR-BFI-Lon

Note: re-released 28mm Pathé-Kok nr 788-789 LES DÉBUTS D'UN YACHTMAN 225 m (= 286 m in 35mm).

1913-03
MAX EST CHARITABLE
245 m = 804 ft = 0:11:54 if at 18 fps
b&w

Max est charitable - French release title (original - FRA) - Bousquet
Max als Wohltäter - German release title (DEU+Ö-UM) - Renken
Fool and His Money, A - English release title (GBR) - Renken
Max inima larga - Romanian title - FIAF TFA db

Max develops exaggerated bumps of benevolence. He stops a crowd of children on their way to school, and, mounting on a tub, he distributes his surplus wealth. On his way home he sees a crowd of beggars outside a church. Max cannot resist their appeals for charity. Having already come to an end of his money, he now gives away coat and hat, and even boots. A little farther on he sees a fisherman caught by a fish. He saves the unfortunate and seeing that the man's clothes are drenched with water, he gives him as many of his own as he can possibly spare. It happens that Max meets his banker. He tries to borrow this gentleman's coat, but the businessman refuses to be generous, and informs poor Max that his account at the bank is overdrawn. Our hero is now in despair. How can he gain more money? As he ponders, a note arrives inviting him to attend a dance. Each guest is requested to come dressed as an apache. Max has an idea. On the day of the ball he pretends to forget the regulation regarding costume. All the other guests are in apache garb. Stealing into another room, he rings up the police. "Quick, my house is attacked by desperadoes." While his host and friends are being conducted to prison. Max disguises himself as the banker and proceeds to rob the safe. Hearing a sound, he rushes to the ballroom, and twisting a rope round his hands, pretends he has been attacked. The merry revelers soon reveal their true identity to the police. They return home to find Max almost purple in the face with his sufferings. The next morning Max takes his morning walk. Armed with a fresh supply of banknotes, he again visits his beggar friends. *(The Cinema, 1913.04.02, in Renken)*

1913.03.15 - Ö-UM - TR-PR: Oesterreichischer Komet - Renken
1913.03.29 - LUX - Lëtzebuerg/Luxemburg: Marzen's Cinéma Parisiana - Renken
1913.04.18 - FRA - Paris: Pathé Palace - Renken
1913.06 - FRA - TR-PR: Catalogue Pathé - Bousquet

Archives: CZE-NFA-Pra; FRA-CF-Par; FRA-CML; FRA-CNC-Par; ROU-ANF-Buc

1913-04
MARIAGES IMPRÉVUS
210 m = 689 ft = 0:10:12 if at 18 fps
b&w

Mariages imprévus - French release title (original - FRA) - Bousquet
Liebesheirat, Die - German release title (DEU+Ö-UM) - Renken
Wife of His Choice, The - English release title (GBR) - Renken
Mariage imprévu, Un - French listing title (attribution) - Mitry

Through the garden hedge, Mr. Reverdi and his son Max court a charming widow, Mrs. de

Sassetasse, and her daughter Coralie. Very soon, they trade notes: "Dear Madam, you have a daughter. I have a son. You're a widow. I am a widower. Could we meet?" "I agree" answers Mrs. de Sassetasse. However, Max found Coralie too thin and Mr. Reverdi judged Mrs. de Sassetasse too stout. They did a direct exchange: Mr. Reverdi married young Coralie; Max married the inviting widow. *(Translation DD from Bousquet nr 5737)*

1913.04.17 - Ö-UM - Czernowitz/Chernivitsi: Kinotheater Cinephon - Renken
1913.05 - FRA - TR-PR: Catalogue Pathé - Bousquet
1913.06.27 - FRA - Paris: Omnia Pathé - Bousquet

Archives: FRA-CNC-Par; FRA-CML

1913-05
MAX LINDER PRATIQUE TOUS LES SPORTS
400 m = 1312 ft = 0:19:26 if at 18 fps
b&w

Max Linder pratique tous les sports - French release title (original - FRA) - Pathé dépôt légal
Max pratique tous les sports - French listing title (attribution) - Bousquet
Max als Sportsmann - German release title (DEU+Ö-UM) - Renken
Complete Sportsman, The - English release title (GBR) - Renken
Max Wins a Widow - English re-release title (GBR - 1917) - Renken
Max fait du sport - French listing title (attribution) - FRA-CNC
Max et le(s) sport(s) - French listing title (attribution) - FRA-CNC

Gladys Maxence, a charming lady from New York, puts an ad in the newspapers: "Rich American lady would be honored to marry any young man who can practice every sport". Every kind of champion (boxing, swimming, tennis, golf, racing, aviation) applies: Mac Aron from Ireland, a black man named Hipiphongrah, Sam Botte from USA, Couchetoilawa from Romania, Willy from England, and Max Linder from France, champion among the champions. Hesitating between them all, the young American woman organizes a multi-sport challenge. Winner takes it all. Max wins the equestrian and fencing events. But Willy, the Englishman, beats him at skating. Max is the best at pole vaulting, winning with 4 meters 50. Unfortunately, he is disqualified at boxing due to foul play. He is much better flying his plane, beating everybody else. In the end, only Max and Willy stay in the race for the last contest: the car racing. A tough fight ensues. Unable to keep Willy's pace, Max is too imprudent and his car runs off the road. He's safe, though much disappointed. He therefore decides to feign an injury in order to gain the young American woman's sympathy. He is thus declared the winner. *(Translation DD from Bousquet nr 5776)*

1913.04.26 - LUX - Lëtzebuerg/Luxemburg: Marzen's Cinéma Parisiana - Renken
1913.05 - FRA - TR-PR: Catalogue Pathé - Bousquet
1913.07.06 - FRA - Paris: Olympia - Renken

Archives: BEL-CRB-Bru; FRA-CF-Par; FRA-CNC-Par; FRA-CML

FILMOGRAPHY

1913-06
RIVALITÉ
310 m = 1017 ft = 0:15:04 if at 18 fps
b&w

Rivalité - French release title (original - FRA) - Bousquet
Max hat Konkurrenz - German release title (DEU+Ö-UM) - Renken
I Fear No Foe - English release title (GBR) - Renken
Rivalité de Max, La - French listing title (attribution) - Mitry

Marcelle has two suitors: Robert Dubelair and Max Linder. She is unable to make a decision. However, being a great sportswoman, she clearly states that she will marry no other champion than a boxing or a skating one. The problem is that neither Max nor Robert know anything about boxing or skating's subtleties. However, a lady's heart being at stake, the two lovers take it upon themselves. They both choose skating. A fierce battle ensues, despite the uncertainty of the field. Marcelle acts as referee, however, considering her two suitors' cowardice, she decides to let them settle the dispute by themselves. *(Translation DD from Bousquet nr 6002)*

1913.05.17 - LUX - Lëtzebuerg/Luxemburg: Marzen's Cinéma Parisiana - Renken
1913.06 - FRA - TR-PR: Catalogue Pathé - Bousquet
1913.08.01 - FRA - Paris: Omnia Pathé - Bousquet

Archives: NLD-EFM-Ams

1913-07
MAX ET LES CRÊPES
210 m = 689 ft = 0:10:12 if at 18 fps
b&w

Max et les crêpes - French release title (original - FRA) - Bousquet
Max auf der Brautschau - German release title (DEU+Ö-UM) - Renken

Max and the Pancake - English release title (GBR) - Renken
Max et Jane font des crêpes - French listing title (attribution) - Mitry

Uncle Mauroc wants his niece to take a husband. That very evening, while having dinner, he intends to introduce Max, the fiancé he wants her to marry. While Mrs. Durand and her daughter are preparing nice dishes with the cook, the latter quits, leaving Colette and her mother managing with the dinner. That is the time Max chooses to come in. The house is empty. Finally, he finds Colette, who wears a white apron, and misidentifies her as the cook. Because he finds her quite cute, he begins to court her, while helping her to make pancakes. He questions her about his future fiancée. Astute Colette displays a picture of her mother. Horrified, Max is about to take the French leave when he comes across his mother-in-law to be. Fortunately, everything becomes clear and Max doesn't think about running away anymore. *(Translation DD from Bousquet nr 6060)*

1913.05.24 - LUX - Lëtzebuerg/Luxemburg: Marzen's Cinéma Parisiana - Renken
1913.07 - FRA - TR-PR: Catalogue Pathé - Bousquet
1913.08.15 - FRA - Paris: Omnia Pathé - Bousquet

Archives: FRA-CF-Par; FRA-CNC-Par; FRA-CML

1913-08
MAX TORÉADOR
580 m = 1903 ft = 0:28:11 if at 18 fps
b&w

Max toréador - French release title (original - FRA) - Bousquet
Max als Torero - German release title (DEU+Ö-UM) - Renken
Max as a Toreador - English release title (GBR) - Renken
Max als Stierkämpfer - German listing title (attribution) - FIAF TFA db

In France, Max attends a bull fight. He is so enthusiastic that he wants to become a bullfighter. He even buys a cow to practice in his apartment. The cow is not a bull: it remains unimpressed by the bullfighter and his gesticulations. In Barcelona, a bull fight is organized, whose benefits will help the poor of the city. Max, very popular in Spain, is invited. Toreros pick him up to bring him to the arena, where he is welcomed by charming Spanish young women, elegantly dressed with mantillas. Max fights the bull, kills him with bandoleros, and is triumphantly cheered by the crowd. *(Translation DD from Bousquet nr 6103)*

1913.06.14 - ESP - Barcelona: Gran Cine Eldorado - Renken
1913.07.06 - FRA - Paris: Olympia - Renken
1913.08 - FRA - TR-PR: Catalogue Pathé - Bousquet

Archives: AUT-ÖFM-Wie; CZE-NFA-Pra; FRA-CF-Par; FRA-CML; FRA-CNC-Par; GBR-BFI-Lon

Note: re-released 28mm Pathé-Kok nr 706-707-708 MAX TORÉADOR 356 m (= 452 m in 35mm). Re-released 9,5mm Pathé-Baby 1925 nr 811 MAX TORÉADOR, notches 20 m (2 cassettes). The [1921] re-release appears to have a different ending: "He raises his sword to answer the crowd's cheers… and wakes up in his bed, facing the cow who quietly stares at him" (Lé-Than-Tuong, L'Écho annamite, 1921.10.27, in Renken).

1913-09
LES VACANCES DE MAX
375 m = 1230 ft = 0:18:13 if at 18 fps
b&w

Vacances de Max, Les - French release title (original - FRA) - Bousquet
Maxens Sommerreise - German release title (DEU+Ö-UM) - Renken
Max and the Portmanteau - English release title (GBR) - Renken
Max's Vacation - English release title (USA) - Renken
Vacances de Max Linder, Les - French listing title (attribution) - Maud Linder
Max part en vacances - French listing title (attribution) - Mitry
Max en vacances - French listing title (attribution) - Ford

Max is invited by his uncle to spend some days in his countryside home. But the uncle doesn't know that Max has married Pierrette. The latter cries many tears, so Max accepts not to go alone to the railway station. So heartbreaking is the separation that Pierrette jumps into the train as it leaves. Max doesn't want her to meet his uncle and thus tries to send her back to Paris. But he surrenders once more. Pierrette enters the uncle's house hidden in Max's suitcase. Max struggles to keep his wife hidden but his uncle finally finds her in the bathtub where she had sought refuge. All is well that ends well: Uncle forgives Max after scolding him for keeping such a pretty niece hidden for so long. *(Translation DD from Bousquet nr 6329)*

1913.07.11 - FRA - Paris: Olympia - Renken
1913.10.31 - DEU - Berlin: U.T.-Unter den Linden - Renken
1913.12 - FRA - TR-PR: Catalogue Pathé - Bousquet

Archives: BEL-CRB-Bru; CAN-CQ-Mon; FRA-CNC-Par; FRA-CML

Note: Maud Linder claimed to have found two different versions of this film with two different partners for Max.

1913-10
MAX N'AIME PAS LES CHATS
295 m = 968 ft = 0:14:20 if at 18 fps
b&w

Max n'aime pas les chats - French release title (original - FRA) - Bousquet
Max ist ein Katzenfeind - German release title (DEU+Ö-UM) - Renken
Love Me, Love My Cat - English release title (GBR) - Renken
Max's Cat-Astrophe - English re-release title (GBR - 1917) - Renken
Max en de katten - Dutch re-release title (9.5mm) - NLD-EFM

Max is engaged to a young woman, whose greatest interest in life is her cat. Max is married in due course, but, as a husband, finds himself even less able to cope with pussy's influence. He protests, he storms, but always comes off second best. He orders the servant to hide pussy in the piano. After a feverish search, Mrs. Max is obliged to leave without her. They return home after a delightful visit to their relatives. Max thinks he will try a little music. He tests himself at the piano, then opens the lid of the instrument. Oh, heavens! Pussy is still there and is surrounded by a progeny that is both numerous and varied. Max hears some unexpected feline airs, and once more has to give way to his wife's pets. *(The Bioscope, 1913.08.13, in Renken)*

1913.07.12 - LUX - Lëtzebuerg/Luxemburg: Marzen's Cinéma Parisiana - Renken
1913.08 - FRA - TR-PR: Catalogue Pathé - Bousquet
1913.09.26 - FRA - Paris: Omnia Pathé - Bousquet

Archives: CAN-CQ-Mon; FRA-CNC-Par; FRA-GPA-Par; FRA-CML; NLD-EFM-Ams

Note: re-released 28mm Pathé-Kok nr 752-753 MAX N'AIME PAS LES CHATS 229 m (= 291 m in 35mm). Re-released 9,5mm Pathé-Baby nr 743 MAX N'AIME PAS LES CHATS, notches 20 m (2 cassettes).

1913-11
LE DUEL DE MAX
960 m = 3150 ft = 0:46:39 if at 18 fps / 1300 m = 4265 ft = 01:03:11 if at 18 fps
b&w

Duel de Max, Le - French release title (original - FRA) - Bousquet
Max und die Liebe - German release title (DEU+Ö-UM) - Renken
Max and His Rival - English release title (GBR) - Renken
Max on the Road to Matrimony - English part title (GBR) - Renken
Last Laugh, The - English release title (AUS) - Renken
Bonne farce, Une - French re-release title (9.5mm) - Poisson
Good Joke, A - English re-release title (9.5mm) - Newnham www.pathefilm.uk

Exhausted by a long day of hunting, Max comes back home. The shortest way takes him across Baron Fritz's domain. A guard sees him and, taking him for a thief, decides to chase him. Frightened, Max jumps over a wall, over a balcony fence, and entering by an open window, he finds himself in the bedroom of Baron Fritz's daughter, Lily. Woken up with a jolt, the young woman is terrified, but she quickly realizes that there is no danger and she offers to hide Max under her mattress. Before leaving, Max asks Lily for her portrait because he has been very impressed by her beauty. The following day, reading the newspapers, Max learns that a very expensive miniature has been stolen from Baron Fritz's castle. A large reward will be granted to the one who'll bring the portrait back. Max considers this a good opportunity to get in touch with Lily's family. He writes to the Baron, explaining he is a great detective, with a very capable dog, and that he will find the miniature. Unfortunately, Max's maid has been unable to find a German shepherd dog. Instead, she presents Max with a miserable trembling pooch. Max is furious but nevertheless pulls the dog to the spot where the miniature has been hidden. Max is the winner. However, the Baron's nephew is skeptical, so he decides to keep an eye on Max. A dispute ensues, followed by the promise of a duel. But Lily prevents the fight. Her father finds in a newspaper the perfect idea for a duel. Each fighter riding a donkey, the first one who'll succeed in stealing the other man's hat will be declared the winner. Max is defeated. Never mind. He succeeds in proving his honesty and finally wins. *(Translation DD from Bousquet nr 6169)*

1913.07.19 - DEU - TR-PR: Erste Internationale Film-Zeitung - Renken
1913.07.25 - FRA - Paris: Olympia - Renken
1913.08 - FRA - TR-PR: Catalogue Pathé - Bousquet

Archives: BEL-CRB-Bru; FRA-CF-Par; FRA-CML; FRA-CNC-Par; FRA-Lob-Par; GBR-BFI-Lon; NLD-EFM-Ams

Note: re-released 9,5mm Pathé-Baby nr 625 UNE BONNE FARCE / A GOOD JOKE, notches 20 m, (2 cassettes). There appears to be two versions of this film, one without the broken mirror skit (ca 960 m) for countries where the copyright claim of Carl and Camillo Schwarz for the skit applied (France, Germany, Spain) and one containing the skit (1300 m) for countries where the claim couldn't be enforced (United Kingdom, the Netherlands, Australia and Brazil), see Renken.

1913-12
LE BILLET DOUX
265 m = 869 ft = 0:12:52 if at 18 fps
Pathécolor - 224 m couleurs

Billet doux, Le - French release title (original - FRA) - Bousquet
Liebesbrief, Der - German release title (DEU+Ö-UM) - Renken
Max and the Love Letter - English release title (GBR) - Renken
Love Letter, The - English release title (USA) - Renken
Max et le billet doux - French listing title (attribution) - Mitry
Max, hoofdinspecteur van de gasfabriek - Dutch archive title (attribution) - NLD-EFM

A young dandy flirts with a pretty young woman and follows her home. She shuts the door in his face but tosses him a note out the window. The wind catches it up and blows it into another window of another apartment. To get into this place and secure the note, Max, the dandy, poses as the Chief Gas Inspector. A poodle, however, has carried the note out into the street again, although the beau is not aware of this. While he is searching for his letter, a neighbor complains to him of his exorbitant gas bill of $15. This Max remedies by making it 15 cents. At last he learns the dog carried off the note, follows and captures it, only to find it written in a foreign language.

Nothing daunted he carries it to a translator, who interprets it as follows: "Sir. I am an honest woman, and I beg of you to cease your attentions. Otherwise, I shall tell my husband. X.Y.Z."
(The New York Dramatic Mirror, 1913.08.20, in Renken)

1913.08.02 - USA - TR-PR: Moving Picture News - Renken
1913.08.09 - LUX - Lëtzebuerg/Luxemburg: Marzen's Cinéma Parisiana - Renken
1913.09 - FRA - TR-PR: Catalogue Pathé - Bousquet
1913.10.24 - FRA - Paris: Omnia Pathé - Bousquet

Archives: DEU-DK-Ber; NLD-EFM-Ams

1913-13
LE CHAPEAU DE MAX
213 m = 699 ft = 0:10:21 if at 18 fps
b&w

Chapeau de Max, Le - French release title (original - FRA) - Bousquet
Maxens Hut - German release title (DEU+Ö-UM) - Renken
Chapeau de Max Linder, Le - French re-release title (9.5mm) - Poisson
Hoed van Max Linder, De - Dutch re-release title (9.5mm) - print at NLD-EFM

Max is renowned as one of the smartest men in Paris, especially thanks to his legendary top-hats. He is invited to Chardin's, an immensely rich businessman whose charming daughter Max would like to marry. The daughter and her mother have been impressed by Max's refinement. He has therefore dressed himself with the most careful attention, and he is wearing his most elegant top hat. Unfortunately, fate is against him, and he has to replace his hat four times. Finally, he arrives safely at the Chardin's and, refusing that his hat be handled by a servant, he places it in a remote part of the living room. A disrespectful poodle lifts its leg...When Mr. Chardin shows how elegant Max's hat is, he is showered. That unexpected misadventure puts a pitiful end to Max's visit. *(Translation DD from Bousquet nr 6210)*

1913.08.23 - LUX - Lëtzebuerg/Luxemburg: Marzen's Cinéma Parisiana - Renken
1913.09 - FRA - TR-PR: Catalogue Pathé - Bousquet
1913.11.07 - FRA - Paris: Omnia Pathé - Bousquet

Archives: AUT-ÖFM-Wie; BEL-CRB-Bru; CAN-CQ-Mon; ESP-FdC-Bar; FRA-CNC-Par; FRA-GPA-Par; FRA-CML; FRA-Lob-Par; NLD-EFM-Ams

Note: re-released 9.5mm Pathé-Baby nr 627 LE CHAPEAU DE MAX LINDER, notches 10 m (1 cassette).

1913-14
MAX FAIT DE LA PHOTOGRAPHIE
305 m = 1001 ft = 0:14:49 if at 18 fps
Pathécolor - 78 m in colours

Max fait de la photographie - French release title (original - FRA) - Bousquet
Max will sie knipsen - German release title (DEU+Ö-UM) - Renken
Max, the Snapshooter - English release title (GBR) - Renken
Max fait de la photo - French listing title (attribution) - Mitry

Max Linder, amateur photographe - French re-release title (9.5mm) - Pathé-Baby catalogue 1923
Max amateur photographe - French cassette title (9.5mm) - on cassette 9,5mm CC
Max Goes in for Photography - English listing title (attribution) - GBR-BFI
Amateur Photographe - English listing title (attribution) - FIAF TFA db

Vacationing in Luc-sur-Mer, Max lazily rolls onto the sand when a young woman arrives and opens the bathing cabin in front of him. She seems perturbed by his presence. Hesitating, she tells him: "Pardon me, Sir, as I'm used to swimming in a very skin-tight bathing suit, I would appreciate if you could close your eyes when I go swimming". Max obeys, putting his hand in front of his eyes, which allows him to have a look through his fingers. As soon as she is in the water, Max takes his camera and waits for the young woman to exit the sea to take a snapshot. The bather protests. Max argues that he has promised not to look at her when she enters the sea, but not when she returns to the shore. The bather then dives into the waves. Max is amazed because the young woman doesn't reappear. The mermaid has gone! Thinking that she has drowned, Max searches for her in the whole ocean, requisitioning small boats and divers. Nothing! In the meantime, the young bather, an accomplished swimmer, has exited the waves on the opposite side of the beach. When she leaves her cabin, she sees a crowd surrounding Max who mourns his mermaid. It's impossible to describe his joy when he realizes she is still alive.
(Translation DD from Bousquet nr 6250)

1913.09.13 - LUX - Lëtzebuerg/Luxemburg: Marzen's Cinéma Parisiana - Renken
1913.10 - FRA - TR-PR: Catalogue Pathé - Bousquet
1913.11.28 - FRA - Paris: Omnia Pathé - Bousquet

Archives: CAN-CQ-Mon; FRA-CF-Par; FRA-CNC-Par; FRA-GPA-Par; FRA-IJV-Per; FRA-CML; FRA-Lob-Par; GBR-BFI-Lon; ITA-FCI-Mil; NLD-EFM-Ams

Note: re-released 28mm Pathé-Kok nr 755-756 MAX FAIT DE LA PHOTOGRAPHIE 239 m (= 303 m in 35mm) - re-released 9,5mm Pathé-Baby MAX LINDER, AMATEUR PHOTOGRAPHE, notches 10 m (1 cassette).

**1913-15
MAX VIRTUOSE
335 m = 1099 ft = 0:18:19 if at 16 fps
b&w**

Max virtuose - French release title (original - FRA) - Bousquet
Max am Klavier - German release title (DEU+Ö-UM) - Renken
Max as a Musician - English release title (GBR) - Renken
Max's Musical Masterpiece - English re-release title (GBR - 1917) - The Bioscope

Back from a tour in America, the famous pianist Panilewski finds out that his daughter has fallen in love with Max during his absence. However, Paulette has been imprudent because she has not inquired about Max's musical abilities before giving him her heart. Max is a complete amateur, totally unable to make the difference between a crotchet and a minim. As he doesn't want to be turned down, he decides to learn how to play the piano. Unfortunately, a monkey would be better at learning Paderewsky and Pugno's art. His professor advises him to buy a player-piano, which convinces his future father-in-law to give Max his daughter's hand. However, when the betrothal is celebrated, Palinewski asks Max to play the piano. Without his player-piano, Max has no other choice than entirely disassembling his father-in-law's Pleyel, on the pretext of searching for his fallen glasses. He has worked so well that reassembling the piano is impossible, which puts an end to Max's marriage plans. *(Translation DD from Bousquet nr 6285)*

1913.10.03 - DEU - Berlin: Kammer-Licht-Spiele - Renken
1913.11 - FRA - TR-PR: Catalogue Pathé - Bousquet
1913.12.12 - FRA - Paris: Omnia Pathé - Bousquet

Archives: BEL-CRB-Bru; FRA-CF-Par; FRA-GPA-Par; FRA-CML; ITA-CdF-Gem

1913-16
MAX FAIT DES CONQUÊTES
250 m = 820 ft = 0:12:09 if at 18 fps
b&w

Max fait des conquêtes - French release title (original - FRA) - Bousquet
Maxens Verehrerinnen - German release title (DEU+Ö-UM) - Renken
Max, the Ladies' Man - English release title (GBR) - Renken
Max, the Lady Killer - English release title (USA) - Renken

During school holidays, Max does homework with his nephew Jacques. Jacques cannot be called a model pupil: instead of learning his lessons, he pins a tag on his professor's back that reads "I love you. Kiss me". The first victim is Pulcherie, the maid. Then three women: a neighbor, the janitor and a passerby. Max, who is on his way to his fiancée's, is chased by a feminine crowd. To escape it, he jumps into a cab, but his pursuers follow him and everybody arrives at the fiancée's house. The latter fires Max, totally dumbfounded. Fortunately, the fiancée sees the tag and, understanding the bad joke, calls Max back. In front of the embracing couple, all the ladies leave, offended, disappointed and furious. *(Translation DD from Bousquet nr 6300)*
1913.10.05 - Ö-UM - TR-PR: Pathé Woche - Renken
1913.10.15 - LUX - Esch-Uelzecht/Esch sur Alzette: Pariser Kinema - Renken
1913.11 - FRA - TR-PR: Catalogue Pathé - Bousquet
1913.12.26 - FRA - Paris: Omnia Pathé - Bousquet

Archives: DEU-DK-Ber; FRA-CF-Par; FRA-CNC-Par; FRA-CML

1913-17
LA MÉDAILLE DE SAUVETAGE
300 m = 984 ft = 0:14:34 if at 18 fps
b&w

Médaille de sauvetage, La - French release title (original - FRA) - Bousquet
Max und die Tochter des Kapitäns - German release title (DEU+Ö-UM) - Renken
Max to the Rescue - English release title (GBR) - Renken
Max sauveteur - French listing title (attribution) - Mitry

On the beach, Max meets a cute sunbather whose only flaw is her father, a veteran of the sea who kicks him in the bottom when he finds him posted in front of his daughter's cabin. Paradoxically, that kick turns into love at first sight: Max immediately asks for the girl's hand in marriage. The old man accepts, setting only one condition: that Max gets a lifesaving medal, like the one he got himself in his youth. Max is quite embarrassed. Fortunately, a friend of his comes to the rescue. His plan is very simple: while swimming in the waves, he'll simulate drowning, and Max will rescue him. Max is delighted, just forgetting one point: he cannot swim. What was bound to happen happened: supposed to be the rescuer, Max becomes the rescued, dragged by the hair to the shore. The old sailor and his daughter arrive. The rescuer is immediately granted the daughter's hand, while Max, shameful and pitiful, remains alone on the sand. *(Translation DD from Bousquet nr 6346)*

1913.11.08 - LUX - Lëtzebuerg/Luxemburg: Marzen's Cinéma Parisiana - Renken
1913.12 - FRA - TR-PR: Catalogue Pathé - Bousquet
1914.01.23 - FRA - Paris: Omnia Pathé - Bousquet

Archives: FRA-CNC-Par; FRA-CML

1913-18
MAX COLLECTIONNE LES CHAUSSURES
290 m = 951 ft = 0:14:05 if at 18 fps
b&w

Max collectionne les chaussures - French release title (original - FRA) - Bousquet
Max als Stiefelsammler - German release title (DEU+Ö-UM) - Renken
Max's Latest Hobby - English release title (GBR) - Renken
Max collectionneur de chaussures - French listing title (attribution) - Ford

While vacationing on the French Riviera, Max idles on a beach when he notices a cute bather, dressed as a prawn fisherwoman. He decides to follow her. While she takes off her lovely shoes, Max takes the opportunity to steal one of them. That infuriates the young lady. Imitating her, Max throws the shoe at the sea. Believing that a game is on, Max's dog brings back the shoe to his master. The latter kisses it tenderly then falls asleep. In the meantime, the dog, persuaded that his master has begun a collection of shoes, brings him back every shoe he can find, on the beach, at the hotel, in a second-hand goods store, and so on. When the cute prawn fisherwoman comes back, she finds her fervent admirer buried beneath a mountain of shoes of every kind. Her gaiety wins over her resentment. The two young people make up and become very good friends. *(Translation DD from Bousquet nr 6371)*

1913.11.23 - Ö-UM - TR-PR: Kinematographische Rundschau - Renken
1913.11.28 - DEU - Berlin: Passage Theater - Renken
1914.01 - FRA - TR-PR: Catalogue Pathé - Bousquet
1914.02.09 - FRA - Paris: Omnia Pathé - Bousquet

Archives: FRA-CF-Par; FRA-CNC-Par; FRA-CML

Note: re-released 28mm Pathé-Kok nr 766-767 MAX COLLECTIONNE LES CHAUSSURES 232 m (= 295 m in 35mm).

1913-19
MAX ILLUSIONNISTE
220 m = 721 ft = 0:10:40 if at 18 fps
b&w

Max illusionniste - French release title (original - FRA) - Bousquet
Max als Zauberkünstler - German release title (DEU+Ö-UM) - Renken

Max as a Conjurer - English release title (GBR) - Renken
Max illusionniste - French re-release title (28mm) - Catalogue Pathé-Kok
Max Linder illusionniste - French re-release title (9,5mm) - Poisson
Max the Magician - English archive title (attribution) - GBR-BFI

Being an absolute Robert Houdin's fan, Max is determined to become a magician. The audience is captivated when freshly hatched chicks are sent back into their egg, and the egg into the hen. When he has successfully performed various acts of the same kind, Max addresses his audience telling them that he will throw a pigeon at the most unfaithful woman present. The room clears instantly. Only two young people remain: they have married the day before. *(Translation DD from Bousquet nr 6397)*

1913.11.29 - DEU - TR-PR: Erste Internationale Film-Zeitung - Renken
1913.12.06 - LUX - Lëtzebuerg/Luxemburg: Marzen's Cinéma Parisiana - Renken
1914.01 - FRA - TR-PR: Catalogue Pathé - Bousquet
1914.02.20 - FRA - Paris: Omnia Pathé - Bousquet

Archives: AUS-NFSA-Can; AUT-FAA-Wie; CZE-NFA-Pra; FRA-CML; FRA-Lob-Par; GBR-BFI-Lon

Note: re-released 28mm Pathé-Kok nr 593 MAX ILLUSIONNISTE 120 m (= 152 m in 35mm). Re-released 9,5mm Pathé-Baby nr 46 MAX LINDER ILLUSIONNISTE / MAX LINDER ILLUSIONNIST, notches 10 m (1 cassette).

**1913-20
N'EMBRASSEZ PAS VOTRE BONNE
590 m = 1936 ft = 0:28:40 if at 18fps
b&w**

N'embrassez pas votre bonne - French release title (original - FRA) - Bousquet
Küsse nie die Magd zum Scherz! - German release title (DEU+Ö-UM) - Renken
Max Wishes He Hadn't - English release title (GBR) - Renken
Max et la bonne à tout faire - French listing title (attribution) - Mitry

Max is so imprudent that when he sees Marie, the maid, breaking a plate, his first reflex is to comfort her with a kiss. This is too good an opportunity: the maid, breaking plate after plate, becomes Max's lover. At the same time, Max's betrothal is announced. When the wedding day comes, Max hasn't been courageous enough to break with Marie. Of course, he truly wants to get married. However, how could he cheat a jealous woman? Marie is perfectly aware of the situation. She therefore voluntarily forgets to wake up her master, delaying his alarm clock by two hours. In the end, while the bride is still waiting for the groom, the latter, unaware, is quietly having breakfast in his bed. The groomsman is sent. In the meantime, Max tries to get rid of the maid, pretending he has swallowed a spoon, sending her to the doctor. But she has taken Max's suit with her. Trapped, Max convinces the groomsman to take his place in the bed, he dresses with the naive man's clothes and arrives on time for the wedding ceremony. Later, Marie bursts into the room where dinner is served. Max leaves discreetly with his wife while Marie has a violent dispute with the in-laws in front of a bewildered crowd. *(Translation DD from Bousquet nr 6448)*

1913.12.16 - DEU - Berlin: Lichtspiele "Mozartsaal" - Renken
1914.02 - FRA - TR-PR: Catalogue Pathé - Bousquet
1914.03.06 - FRA - Paris: Pathé Journal - Renken

Archives: no film print known to this date

1913-21
L'ANGLAIS TEL QUE MAX LE PARLE
285 m = 935 ft = 0:13:51 if at 18 fps
b&w

Anglais tel que Max le parle, L' - French release title (original - FRA) - Bousquet
Wie Max englisch spricht! - German release title (DEU+Ö-UM) - Renken
Max and the Daughter of Albion - English release title (GBR) - Renken
Amour mouillé, L' - French re-release title (9.5mm) - Poisson
Damped Love - English re-release title (9.5mm) - Newnham www.pathefilm.uk
Max spricht kein Englisch - German archive title [attribution] - AUT-FAA

Miss Williams is on her way to Paris to visit her father, a rich sanitary appliances manufacturer. She travels with Max, who tries unsuccessfully to start a conversation. The problem is that Miss Williams only speaks English, whereas Max only speaks French. But Max is resourceful and he uses drawings to communicate. A railroad followed by a question mark means "Where are you going?" The young woman draws a city map, showing a street close to the Eiffel Tower. Max draws a bunch of flowers, then a heart that he gives her. Miss Williams pretends to tear it but she changes her mind and places it against her own heart. In Paris, Max goes in search of the young lady. He finds her in her father's shop. As he tries to tell her the three words of English he has learned, "I love you", a customer enters. Max is obliged to hide in a shower. When his future father-in-law finds him, Max is soaked. Fortunately, the salesman doesn't mind, and the story will end with a marriage. *(Translation DD from Bousquet nr 6414)*

1913.12.20 - LUX - Lëtzebuerg/Luxemburg: Marzen's Cinéma Parisiana - Renken
1914.02 - FRA - TR-PR: Catalogue Pathé - Bousquet
1914.03.06 - FRA - Paris: Omnia Pathé - Bousquet

Archives: AUT-FAA-Wie; AUT-ÖFM-Wie; FRA-CML; FRA-CNC-Par; NLD-EFM-Ams;

Note: re-released 28mm Pathé-Kok nr 603-604 L'ANGLAIS TEL QUE MAX LE PARLE 224 m (= 284.5 m in 35mm). Re-released 9,5mm Pathé-Baby nr 483 L'AMOUR MOUILLÉ / DAMPED LOVE, notches 10 m (1 cassette).

1913-22
MAKS LINDER I G-ZHA PROKHOROVA
n/a

Maks Linder i g-zha Prokhorova - Russian release title (transliteration) - Renken
Max Linder et Mme Prokhorov - French title (translation) - Renken
Maks i kupchikha - Russian alternative title (transliteration) - Renken
Max and the Merchant's Wife - English title (translation) - Renken

Max [falls] in love with Moscow merchant Prokhorov's wife. After a series of qui pro quo Max escapes from jealous Prokhorov's place and everything ends in a common scuffle. *(Translation Renken from Stol. Molva, 1913.12.22)*

1913.12.21 - RUS - Moskva/Moscow: Teatre Zona - Renken

Archives: no film print known to this date

Note: reference to this film has been found by Georg Renken in the Russian press: "On the screen was a picture "MAX LINDER AND MRS PROKHOROV", newly acted out by Max in Moscow" (Stol. Molva, 1913.12.22, in Renken). It was shown in Russia while Max Linder was touring the country. It seems safe to assume that the production company is Pathé, since Max Linder was under contract with them.

1913-23
MAKS I KURSISTKA
n/a

Maks i Kursistka - Russian release title (transliteration) - Renken
Max et l'étudiante - French title (translation) - CC

A Muscovite student girl sees Max Linder at his arrival at the station and throws flowers at him. In order to get into the theater where Max Linder plays, she cuts and sells her braid. After the theater Max is enjoying himself with the company in a restaurant. The student girl finds her way in. Some drunks insult her. Of course, Max "saves" the girl. She thanks Max and says that he can demand from her everything he wants. Max is humble and gracious. He asks only: "Show me Moscow". After sightseeing of the ancient Russian capital, Max Linder is leaving.

The student girl is crying on the bridge. *(Adaptation CC from translation Renken from Russkoye Slovo, 1913.12.19)*

1913.12.19 - RUS - PR: Russkoye Slovo - Renken
1914.01.02 - RUS - Rīga: Teatris "Zeppelins" - Renken

Archives: no film print known to this date

Note: reference to this film has been found by Georg Renken in the Russian press (Russkoye Slovo, 1913.12.19). It was shown in Russia while Max Linder was touring the country. It seems safe to assume that the production company is Pathé, since Max Linder was under contract with them.

1914-01
MAX PROFESSEUR DE TANGO
325 m = 1066 ft = 0:15:47 if at 18 fps
b&w

Max professeur de tango - French release title (original - FRA) - Bousquet
Max als Tangolehrer in Berlin - German release title (DEU+Ö-UM) - Renken
Leçon de tango, La - French listing title [attribution] - FRA-CNC

While he is enjoying some days in Berlin, Max goes to a fashionable night-club. He invites a young woman to tango. The audience applauds. Prince Stadtwarter notices his performance and asks him to teach that modern dance to his family. However, Max has drunk too much Rhine wine and falls asleep on the table. Very early in the morning, he finds himself in the streets of Berlin. He gets lost, which gives the audience an opportunity to visit the main spots of the capital like the Reichstag, the zoo, and so on. Quite drunk, Max finally arrives at the Prince's house but the steps he teaches to his pupils prove very unconventional. In the end, he loses one shoe, puts it inside his pocket and looks for it on the floor, helped by the Prince's eldest daughter. Max pinches her calf, so he is strongly slapped in the face and kicked out of the house without really understanding what is happening. *(Translation DD from Bousquet nr 6626)*

1914.01 - FRA - TR-PR: Catalogue Pathé - Bousquet
1914.02.06 - FRA - Marseille: Eden Cinema Pathé - Bousquet
1914.03.14 - DEU - Offenbach: Schwan-Lichtspiele - Renken

Archives: CUB-CdC-LaH; FRA-CF-Par; FRA-CNC-Par; FRA-CML

1914-02
MAX PÉDICURE
335 m = 1099 ft = 0:16:16 if at 18 fps
b&w

Max pédicure - French release title (original - FRA) - Bousquet
Max als Hühneraugen-Operateur - German release title (DEU+Ö-UM) - Renken
Max as a Chiropodist - English release title (GBR) - Renken
Max callista - Italian title - FIAF TFA db
Pedicure, The - English listing title (attribution) - GBR-BFI

Lili is walking her dog when mischievous boys steal it. Max hears her screaming. He runs after the boys and brings the dog back to Lili. The following day, Max pays a visit to Lili, considering she is in debt to him. She has an appointment with a chiropodist. She tells the latter to wait in an adjacent room while she receives Max. When Lili's father comes in, Max panics and decides to introduce himself as the chiropodist. But the father wants his corns to be cut. Max has no idea about how to use the chiropodist's tools. He therefore acts very unconventionally before running away. In the second room, the father finds his daughter with a man at her feet. He kicks him out by the window, misidentifying him as a vulgar seducer. The chiropodist falls on Max's back, which puts an end to his adventures. *(Translation DD from Bousquet nr 6488)*

1914.01.31 - LUX - Lëtzebuerg/Luxemburg: Marzen's Cinéma Parisiana - Renken
1914.03 - FRA - TR-PR: Catalogue Pathé - Bousquet
1914.03.20 - FRA - Paris: Pathé Journal - Renken

Archives: BRA-CMAM-Rio; FRA-CF-Par; FRA-CML; FRA-CNC-Par; FRA-Lob-Par; GBR-BFI-Lon; ITA-CdF-Gem; ITA-CN-Rom; USA-GEM-Roc

1914-03
MAX DÉCORÉ
240 m = 787 ft = 0:11:39 if at 18 fps
b&w

Max décoré - French release title (original - FRA) - Bousquet
Max und sein Orden - German release title (DEU+Ö-UM) - Renken
Max's Decoration - English release title (GBR) - Renken
Max Knighted - English re-release title (GBR - 1917) - Renken
Max cavaliere - Italian title - FIAF TFA db
Max decorat - Romanian title - FIAF TFA db
Max est décoré - French listing title (attribution) - Renken

Everybody in France, cinematographers, artists, writers, have been pleased to learn that the great Max Linder will receive the Legion of Honor very soon. Journalists have even wondered why the genius of the screen had not been decorated long ago, given that the incomparable artist, also a true pacifist, has made the whole world laugh. Being very modest, the new knight insists on celebrating the event with a huge party. Everybody sings, laughs, dances, drinks. At 4 am, Max, together with another joyful guest, is presented with the bill. He has drunk too much, which prevents him understanding why he should pay that much. As he cannot agree with the waiter, the party ends at the police station, where the Chief of Police settles the dispute. *(Translation DD from Bousquet nr 6536)*

1914.02.14 - LUX - Lëtzebuerg/Luxemburg: Marzen's Cinéma Parisiana - Renken
1914.02.14 - DEU - TR-PR: Pathé Woche - Renken
1914.04 - FRA - TR-PR: Catalogue Pathé - Bousquet
1914.05.08 - FRA - Paris: Omnia Pathé - Bousquet

Archives: FRA-CML; ITA-CN-Rom

Note: re-released 28mm Pathé-Kok nr 761-762 MAX DÉCORÉ 204 m (= 259 m in 35mm).

**1914-04
MAX, MAÎTRE D'HÔTEL
305 m = 1001 ft = 0:14:49 if at 18 fps
b&w**

Max, maître d'hôtel - French release title (original - FRA) - Bousquet
Max als "Stütze der Hausfrau" - German release title (DEU+Ö-UM) - Renken
Max, the New Butler - English release title (GBR) - Renken
Max's Flurried Flirtation - English re-release title (GBR - 1917) - Renken

Lili has married Sir Williams, an immensely rich American cattle producer who works in Buenos Aires, but she has refused to leave Paris. During her husband's absence, Lili entertains herself by flirting with Max. However, Sir Williams comes back unexpectedly: surprised, Lili introduces her lover as the butler. Max, who is now obliged to work in the house, is pained by the husband's marital enthusiasm, and interferes every time Sir Williams tries to kiss his wife. He must also go shopping with his master, carrying loads a mule would refuse to bear. Max cannot stand it anymore: he sends a letter that reads: "Buenos Aires. Cattle ill with appendicitis. Come back at once." Sir Williams is fooled, and Max can take his revenge. *(Translation DD from Bousquet nr 6567)*

1914.03.21 - LUX - Lëtzebuerg/Luxemburg: Marzen's Cinéma Parisiana - Renken
1914.03.21 - DEU - TR-PR: Pathé Woche - Renken
1914.05 - FRA - TR-PR: Catalogue Pathé - Bousquet
1914.05.29 - FRA - Paris: Omnia Pathé - Bousquet

Archives: GBR-BFI-Lon

**1914-05
MARI JALOUX
330 m = 1083 ft = 0:16:02 if at 18 fps
b&w**

Mari jaloux - French release title (original - FRA) - Bousquet
Max und seine Film-"Kollegen" - German release title (DEU+Ö-UM) - Renken

Max Cures Cinemania - English release title (GBR) - Renken
Max et le mari jaloux - French listing title (attribution) - Mitry
Max jaloux - French listing title (attribution) - Ford
Jealous Husband, The - English listing title (attribution) - GBR-BFI
Max inszeniert einen Film - German archive title [attribution] - DEU-DK

Madame and Monsieur meet Max Linder at the Alhambra theatre. They invite him to have tea the next day at 5 pm. Max agrees. However, Monsieur begins to worry about his wife's growing interest in Max. Asked by Monsieur for a piece of advice, his friend the director of the theatre has recommended that he put a laxative in Max's cup of tea. But the cups are involuntarily switched by the maid, and Monsieur drinks the laxative. Madame tells her guest that she would like to be an actress, which is confirmed by Monsieur. Max asks them to play in his next movie, a drama of jealousy where the wife is in love with the servant. Monsieur will be the servant, Madame the unfaithful wife and Max will play the jealous husband. In the studios, Max directs: the husband comes unexpectedly and surprises his wife embracing the servant. He kills the servant first, then his wife and finally himself! While recording, the gun doesn't work, so Max cannot "kill" his wife. He throws at the unfaithful couple every object he can get his hands on. Terrified, the couple runs away as rapidly as they can. *(Translation DD from adaptation CC from Erste Internationale Film-Zeitung, 1914.03.28, in Renken)*

1914.03.28 - DEU - TR-PR: Erste Internationale Film-Zeitung - Renken
1914.04.11 - DEU - Berlin: U.T.-Unter den Linden - Renken
1914.05 - FRA - TR-PR: Catalogue Pathé - Bousquet
1914.06.19 - FRA - Paris: Omnia Pathé - Bousquet

Archives: DEU-DK-Ber; FRA-CF-Par; FRA-CML; FRA-CNC-Par; GBR-BFI-Lon

Note: re-released 28mm Pathé-Kok nr 650-651 MARI JALOUX 238 m (= 302 m in 35mm).

1914-06
MAX ET LA DOCTORESSE
350 m = 1148 ft = 0:17:00 if at 18 fps
b&w

Max et la doctoresse - French release title (original - FRA) - Bousquet
Max und die Doktorin - German release title (DEU+Ö-UM) - Renken
Max and the Lady Doctor - English release title (GBR+USA) - Renken
Max e la dotoressa - Italian title - FIAF TFA db

Max discovers that in the same apartment house with him lives a most charming woman doctor. To meet her he fakes a sickness and calls upon her for professional advice. She thumps him, puts her little ear down to his chest, diagnoses his case and prescribes for him. Max departs so full of happiness that he finds difficulty in walking as a sober man should. The days pass and, winning the lady's love, Max becomes married to her. On the wedding night just as they have reached the seclusion of their own room and Max has started to pour out his rapture into her willing ear, the servant hammers at their door. They find that the bride is called out upon a case, so in wedding gown and orange blossoms she leaves the despondent Max to await her return. The time passes and finally she returns, but only for a moment. The servant raps at the door again, and again she must go out to see a patient. The unhappy bridegroom protests in vain. He is sleeping uneasily in his chair when she finally comes back. As they are embracing, the servant raps at the door again, announcing another call for the doctor. The now infuriated Max rushes upon the disturber of his happiness, throws him out of the room and locks the door. A year later the happy husband, bearing a baby in his arms, wanders into the reception room of his wife's office. He finds it filled with waiting patients, all men. He steps into the office and sees the wife of his bosom, with her head at a man's chest listening to his heart. Filled with rage he deposits the baby in the arms of the man nearest him and proceeds to drive every patient out of the house. Thus, he is convinced that from henceforth his wife must cease to be an "M. D.", and become more of a wife and mother. *(Moving Picture World, 1914.12.05, in Renken)*

1914.04.18 - DEU - TR-PR: Pathé Woche - Renken
1914.04.25 - LUX - Lëtzebuerg/Luxemburg: Marzen's Cinéma Parisiana - Renken
1914.06 - FRA - TR-PR: Catalogue Pathé - Bousquet
1914.07.10 - FRA - Paris: Omnia Pathé - Bousquet

Archives: BEL-CRB-Bru; CAN-CQ-Mon; FRA-CNC-Par; FRA-GPA-Par; FRA-CML; ITA-CN-Rom; USA-AFA-Los; USA-BkHk

1914-07
LE PENDU [1914]
305 m = 1001 ft = 0:14:49 if at 18 fps
b&w

Pendu, Le - French release title (original - FRA) - Bousquet
Max will sterben - German release title (DEU+Ö-UM) - Renken
Max's Persuasive Suicide - English release title (GBR) - Renken

Max has fallen in love with May. He decides to ask for her father's blessing. Baron Lebourru ["Gruffy"] replies that his daughter will never marry a movie actor. Max leaves, desperate. Resolving to commit suicide, he chooses to hang himself in the park. Seeing him, the servant and the gardener alert the other servants, who alert the local authorities, who alert the Police Commissioner. The latter unties Max who explains the reasons for his act. The Police Commissioner meets the Baron and asks his daughter's hand on Max's behalf. The proposal is rejected once again. Max hangs himself on the chandelier. The Baron finally relents. *(Translation DD from Bousquet nr 6699)*

1914.05.23 - LUX - Lëtzebuerg/Luxemburg: Marzen's Cinéma Parisiana - Renken
1914.07 - FRA - TR-PR: Catalogue Pathé - Bousquet
1914.08.28 - FRA - Paris: Omnia Pathé - Renken

Archives: CZE-NFA-Pra

1914-08
MAX JOUE LE DRAME
165 m = 541 ft = 0:08:01 if at 18 fps
b&w

Max joue le drame - French release title (original - FRA) - Bousquet
Max als Tragöde - German release title (DEU+Ö-UM) - Renken
Max's Melodrama - English release title (GBR) - Renken
Max Plays the Drama - English release title (USA) - Renken

Max Faces the Footlights - English re-release title (GBR -1917) - Renken
Max Acts in a Drama - English listing title (attribution) - FIAF TFA db
Max juega al drama - Spanish [release or archive] title - FIAF TFA db

Standing in the center of a living room, Max recites a monologue whose effect is unexpected. Angry, Max tells the audience: "I swear to make you cry with a drama I'll write myself". The bet is accepted. The day of the performance arrives. Max bows and announces: "A 3-act and 5-scene drama during Louis 13th's reign. Direction: Max Linder; the Marquis de Monpitchoune: Max Linder; the Marchioness: Miss Fabris; The Duchess des Haussaie: Maphalda; a servant: Scapini". Costumes, sets, wigs, furniture and props provided by the "Comédie Française". The audience laughs. First act: Max hangs up the phone and is speaking as his wife enters and hears: "Allo? Is that you, Duchess? Very well, we'll go to the airplane meeting together. I'll wait for you in my car. I love you." His wife is so furious that Max loses his wig, putting it back on his head backwards. Roars of laughter. Second act: Max's wife enters and has a dispute with the Duchess, asking for reparations. Third act: the duel. The Duchess is fatally injured. Max erupts onto the scene and throws himself at the dead woman's feet, putting his wig backwards. The audience laughs. Max throws away his wig, takes a small bottle filled with poison and drinks it, kneeling alongside the corpse. The audience anxiously waits. Max acts as if he had really been poisoned. The female spectators can't stand the performance anymore and become hysterical. Max dies in horrible seizures, falling on the Duchess' body. The whole audience faints. Nobody moves anymore. Max stands up, very satisfied with his success. He takes a hose and showers the spectators, who run away. Max can be proud of himself. *(Translation DD from Bousquet nr 6727)*

1914.06.03 - DEU - TR-PR: Pathé Woche - Renken
1914.06.06 - LUX - Lëtzebuerg/Luxemburg: Marzen's Cinéma Parisiana - Renken
1914.07 - FRA - TR-PR: Catalogue Pathé - Bousquet
1914.12.04 - FRA - Paris: Tivoli-Cinéma - Renken

Archives: AUT-ÖFM-Wie; FRA-CML; GBR-BFI-Lon; ITA-CdF-Gem; ITA-CN-Rom; MEX-FUNAM-Méx USA-BkHk; USA-UCLA-Los

Note: re-released GBR 1917 MAX FACES THE FOOTLIGHTS; listed as 740 ft (225 m) in The Bioscope, 1917.06.21 (in Renken) and is therefore is consequently longer than the original release. Re-released 9,5mm Film Office MAX JOUE LE DRAME, full length titles 100 m (1 reel).

1914-09
MARIAGE FORCÉ
510 m = 1673 ft = 0:24:47 if at 18 fps
b&w
Mariage forcé - French release title (original - FRA) - Bousquet
Maxens Hochzeit - German release title (DEU+Ö-UM) - Renken
Max's Chosen Bride - English release title (GBR) - Renken

Uncle Gaston demands that Max get married, otherwise he will cut him off. He shows Max the photos of two charming ladies. Taking the photos with him, Max first visits the blonde lady. While she is looking for a larger picture, Max contemplates the second photo and decides to meet the other young woman. He thus visits the brunette lady, playing the game again. In the meantime, Max's servant is given by his girlfriend a complete lady outfit that he intends to wear at a masked ball. Max then decides to introduce his disguised servant as his fiancée. He'll then marry "her", which will save the day. Jean is convinced with some banknotes. The marriage is celebrated. Satisfied, the uncle gives 20 000 Francs to Max. Jean elopes, followed by Max. They arrive at Max's home, immediately followed by the uncle who understands he has been fooled. Max runs away once more, laughing and raising the twenty 1000-Franc banknotes. *(Translation DD from Bousquet nr 6760)*

1914.06.27 - LUX - Lëtzebuerg/Luxembourg: Marzen's Cinéma Parisiana - Renken
1914.08 - FRA - TR-PR: Catalogue Pathé - Bousquet
1914.12.18 - FRA - Paris: Le Colisée - Renken

Archives: FRA-CF-Par; FRA-CNC-Par; FRA-CML

1914-10
MAX À MONACO
340 m = 1115 ft = 0:16:31 if at 18 fps
b&w

Max à Monaco - French release title (original - FRA) - Bousquet
Max in Monaco - German release title (DEU+Ö-UM) - Renken
Max on the Briny - English release title (GBR+USA) - Renken

Max is going to Monaco to visit the English battleship "Good", anchored in the port. He hesitates to board a rowboat, then he changes his mind with the help of a bottle of whisky. He drinks heavily during the short journey. He's so drunk that he needs help to board the cruiser, where he behaves very eccentrically. Thanks to a high-powered telescope, he can see the young woman he was flirting with being kissed by another man. Max is so furious that he wants to fire a canon at them. Though he is forced to calm down, he nevertheless succeeds in firing, thus wounding a sailorman. In the end, Max falls overboard, and hangs by the seat of his pants. *(Translation DD from Bousquet nr 6797)*

1914.07.11 - LUX - Lëtzebuerg/Luxembourg: Marzen's Cinéma Parisiana - Renken
1914.09 - FRA - TR-PR: Catalogue Pathé - Bousquet
1915.01.01 - FRA - Paris: Ciné Max Linder - Renken

Archives: BEL-CRB-Bru; CAN-CQ-Mon; CZE-NFA-Pra; FRA-CF-Par; FRA-CNC-Par; FRA-GPA-Par; FRA-CML; ROU-ANF-Buc

1914-11
MAX ASTHMATIQUE
355 m = 1165 ft = 0:17:15 if at 18 fps
b&w

Max asthmatique - French release title (original - FRA) - Bousquet
Max in den Alpen - German release title (DEU+Ö-UM) - Renken
Max's Marvellous Cure - English release title (GBR) - Renken

Max, who has difficulties breathing, consults his doctor who prescribes a stay in the Alps above 3000 meters. Back home, Max goes to bed. He's so worried by the prescription that he begins to dream of his trip. He arrives in a sled, then enters the hotel lobby. He dresses as the perfect Alpine tourist and goes out. He climbs the mountain higher and higher. Cold air anesthetizes him. Awakened, he goes back to his hotel, shivering. He wants to check his breathing: he makes balls of paper, puts them on the table and blows... The balls and the table are blown away! Max goes out, blows on a skid that begins to move. A busy sled passes by. He blows and the sled moves backwards. Max goes skating. He blows and all the skaters fall. Then he dances on the ice. He takes part in a skiing competition. He starts from the top of the hill, flies over the mountains, crosses the sea, flies over a city. He then hits a roof, and, passing through it has the ceiling fall on the head of people who were having dinner. But Max awakes; he has just fallen out of his bed. He stretches, breathes with difficulty and finally goes back to bed. *(Translation DD from Bousquet nr 6818)*

1914.07.27 - Ö-UM - Wien: Hotel Monopol "Trade Shows" - Renken
1914.08.28 - Ö-UM - TR-PR: Trade listing - Renken

1914.09 - FRA - TR-PR: Catalogue Pathé - Bousquet
1915.02.26 - FRA - Paris: Ciné Max Linder - Renken

Archives: FRA-CF-Par; FRA-CNC-Par; FRA-CML

1914-12
MAX ET SA BELLE-MÈRE [1914]
590 m = 1936 ft = 0:28:40 if at 18fps
b&w

Max et sa belle-mère - French release title (original - FRA) - Bousquet
Max und seine Schwiegermutter - German release title (Ö-UM) - Renken
Max's Mother-in-Law Loves Sport - English part title (GBR) - Renken
Max Gets Too Much Mother-in-Law - English part title (GBR) - Renken
Max's Revenge - English part title (GBR) - Renken
Max and His Mother-in-Law - English release title (USA) - Renken

Max, a recently married man, cannot stay alone with his wife because his mother-in-law is always present, in the bedroom, in the dining-room, in the kitchen, on the stairs, on the platform of the station, so much so that Max stays alone in the carriage while his wife and his mother-in-law stand on the platform. At the next station, Max gets off the train and comes back following the rails. He is obliged to take his mother-in-law with him because his wife doesn't want to part with one or the other. They arrive in Chamonix. The next day at skating lesson, Mother-in-law and Max fall very often. The following day, sled lesson! Mother-in-law falls on her bottom. Same result with a pair of skis. She even disappears in a hole, her feet only visible out of the snow.

Max rescues her. Everything returns to order and they all go back to Paris. *(Translation DD from Bousquet nr 6847)*

1914.08.31 - ITA - Torino: Cinema Splendor - Renken
1914.09 - FRA - TR-PR: Catalogue Pathé - Bousquet
1915.01.08 - FRA - Paris: Ciné Max Linder - Renken

Archives: FRA-CNC-Par; FRA-CML

1914-13
CUISINIER PAR AMOUR
330 m = 1083 ft = 0:16:02 if at 18 fps
b&w

Cuisinier par amour - French release title (original - FRA) - Bousquet
Max Becomes a Cook - English release title (GBR) - Renken
Max cuisinier par amour - French listing title (attribution) - Ford

Max and Lili are very much in love. However, Lili's father wants her to marry a Mr. van den Houye, an old but rich man. Max nevertheless asks for Lili's hand, which is denied. He then concocts an idea to take the cook's place. Unfortunately, he has absolutely no skills in cooking. He prepares the meal in an unconventional way. The father makes a face, while Lili pretends that everything is excellent. The father wants to speak to the cook, but Lili arrives first. They are caught kissing. Max is fired. Fortunately, the maid gets an idea. When Mr. van den Houye comes in, she declares that he courts and kisses her every day. Poor Mr. van den Houye is dismissed. Max comes back, now accepted. *(Translation DD from Bousquet nr 6879)*

1914.10 - FRA - TR-PR: Catalogue Pathé - Bousquet
1914.10.30 - ITA - Torino: Cinema Splendor - Renken
1915.02.05 - FRA - Paris: Ciné Max Linder - Renken

Archives: FRA-Lob-Par; GBR-BFI-Lon; USA-AFA-Los

Note: re-released 28mm Pathé-Kok nr 813-814 CUISINIER PAR AMOUR 239 m (= 303 m in 35mm).

1914-14
MAX AU COUVENT
700 m = 2297 ft = 0:34:01 if at 18 fps
b&w

Max au couvent - French release title (original - FRA) - Bousquet
Max im Klöster - German release title (Ö-UM) - Renken
Max's Elopement - English release title (GBR) - Renken
Max in a Convent - English listing title (attribution) - GBR-BFI
Max im Mädchenpensionat - German listing title (attribution) - Renken

Max is in love with Lily, but her father doesn't want to hear about him. In order to prevent the two young persons from dating, he sends Lily to a convent. Thanks to Lily, Max finds the address of the convent she is resides in. Max goes there by car with his chauffeur. He simulates an accident and asks for the sisters' hospitality for the night. They let him enter. In the early hours of the morning, and after a hectic night, Max succeeds in eloping with his fiancée and in marrying her. *(Translation DD from Bousquet nr 6909)*

1914.11 - FRA - TR-PR: Catalogue Pathé - Bousquet
1914.11.13 - ITA - Torino: Cinema Splendor - Renken
1915.03.12 - FRA - Paris: Ciné Max Linder - Renken

Archives: AUT-FAA-Wie; CAN-CQ-Mon; FRA-CNC-Par; FRA-GPA-Par; FRA-IJV-Per; FRA-CML; FRA-Lob-Par; GBR-BFI-Lon

Note: re-released 28mm Pathé-Kok nr 655-656-657 MAX AU COUVENT 361 m (= 458 m in 35mm).

1914-15
DICK EST UN CHIEN SAVANT
185 m = 607 ft = 0:08:59 if at 18 fps
b&w

Dick est un chien savant - French release title (original - FRA) - Bousquet
Mean Trick on Max, A - English release title (GBR) - Renken
Dick, de slimme hond - Dutch release title (NLD) - NLD-EFM

Max and his friend fall in love with a charming blind woman whose dog is so clever that she has taught it to read! Both suitors get the same idea: each one informs the dog that the other wants to kill it. Dick reads Max's friend's letter first, and chases Max up to the roof. The latter struggles to convince Dick that his adversary wants to poison it. Finally, he takes a well-deserved revenge. *(Translation DD from Bousquet nr 6936)*

1914.12 - FRA - TR-PR: Catalogue Pathé - Bousquet
1914.12.25 - ITA - Torino: Cinema Splendor - Renken
1915.04.09 - FRA - Paris: Ciné Max Linder - Renken

Archives: FRA-GPA-Par; NLD-EFM-Ams

1914-16
COIFFEUR PAR AMOUR
310 m = 1017 ft = 0:15:04 if at 18 fps
b&w

Coiffeur par amour - French release title (original - FRA) - Bousquet
Friseur aus Liebe - German release title (Ö-UM) - Renken
Max, Hairdresser - English release title (GBR) - Renken
Max als Friseur - German release title (CHE) - Renken

Max and a friend of his are riding their horses when they meet two young ladies and a man. Max goes back home, one of the two ladies still in his mind. He concocts an idea to enter his sweetheart's home by taking the hairdresser's place. The latter accepts, persuaded by financial compensation. Max first combs the mother's hair in a bun secured with a fork. Then he shampoos the husband's hair with glue, before shaving one half of his head. Finally, he knocks everything down and is chased by the husband armed with a gun. He runs away, dives into the river, then climbs out of it to push his adversary into the water. *(Translation DD from Bousquet nr 6941)*

1914.12 - FRA - TR-PR: Catalogue Pathé - Bousquet
1914.12.31 - ITA - Torino: Cinema Splendor - Renken
1915.04.16 - FRA - Paris: Ciné Max Linder - Bousquet

Archives: FRA-CF-Par; FRA-CNC-Par; FRA-CML

1914-17
TRÈS MOUTARDE
575 m = 1886 ft = 00:20:57 if at 18 fps
b&w

Très moutarde - French release title (original - FRA) - Bousquet
Max ist schüchtern - German release title (CHE) - Renken
Max Sees Life - English release title (GBR) - Renken
Max Hits the High Spots - English release title (USA) - Renken

The subject opens by showing Max in a very unfamiliar role, that of a young man who it too shy to make any progress in paying addresses to desirable members of the fair sex. To overcome this shyness, Max's uncle takes him to a night club, where there is a tango supper and a galaxy of gilded beauty. In this atmosphere Max soon loses his bashfulness. Being somewhat "elevated" by champagne, Max and his uncle take possession of a taxi-cab with intent to drive themselves home. They are hailed by a sedate, elderly couple, and accept them as fares to the Gare du Nord. It is a very adventurous journey, and the luggage is the cause of much trouble. Collisions with other vehicles and all sorts of thrills end in the car being driven over the edge of a pit and wrecked. We need hardly say that this is not the end of Max; he and his companions crawl out from the wreckage quite happily, and Max is certainly entitled to say that he has seen life this time, if never before. *(The Bioscope, 1915.04.08, in Renken)*

1914.12.18 - FRA - Paris: Ciné Max Linder - Renken
1915.04 - FRA - TR-PR: Catalogue Pathé - Bousquet

Archives: no film print known to this day

1915-01
LE BAROMÈTRE DE LA FIDÉLITÉ
235 m = 771 ft = 0:11:25 if at 18 fps
b&w

Baromètre de la fidélité, Le - French release title (original - FRA) - Bousquet
Max and the Flirtometer - English release title (GBR) - Renken

Madam, does your Lord and master's fidelity worry you? Quick, ask your barometer, a new invention from Chicago, it will tell you how his heart oscillates between sincere fidelity and tempestuous passion. Jane begins to ask the precious tool, thus learning her misfortune. Forewarned is forearmed: Jane astutely brings her unfaithful husband home. *(Translation DD from Bousquet nr 6961)*

1915.01 - FRA - TR-PR: Catalogue Pathé - Bousquet
1915.01.11 - ITA - Torino: Cinema Splendor - Renken
1915.05.07 - FRA - Paris: Ciné Max Linder - Renken

Archives: FRA-CF-Par; FRA-CML; FRA-CNC-Par; FRA-Lob-Par

Note: re-released 28mm Pathé-Kok nr 598 LE BAROMÈTRE DE LA FIDÉLITÉ 125 m (= 159 m in 35mm). Re-released 9,5mm Pathé-Baby nr 670 LE BAROMÈTRE DE LA FIDÉLITÉ, notches 40 m (4 cassettes).

**1915-02
LE SOSIE
765 m = 2510 ft = 27:53 if at 18 fps
b&w**

Sosie, Le - French release title (original - FRA) - Bousquet
Max Linders Doppelgänger - German release title (CHE) - Renken
Max's Double - English release title (GBR) - Renken
Ringer for Max, A - English release title (USA) - Renken
Sosie de Max, Le - French listing title (attribution) - Maud Linder

Albert Obry, a gentleman who lives by his wits, is down to his last jitney and his room rent is due. He is at a loss as to his next move when a friend writes him advising that he make up like Max Linder, since he looks so much like the great comedian, and pass off as Max. He finds a picture of his double and determines to follow his friend's advice. Accordingly, he rushes into the apartment of Max and starts to change his clothes for some of the fine raiment of the comedian. The valet of the real Max is somewhat put out, but the remark "I was hit by an auto", and the fact that his boss sometimes changes his clothes many times a day, makes it appear all right to the servant. But the return of Max makes it necessary for the imposter to connive to get him out of the way again. He does this by sending a telegram saying that his mother is ill and advising him to come at once. The real Max goes at once to the side of his "sick" mother and is dumbfounded when he learns that she is well. While away, the spurious Max again takes possession of the apartment of his more fortunate double and receives an invitation to tea at the home of the real Max's sweetheart. He accepts and is there eating his fill when Linder comes on the scene. The faker again makes his getaway. Some remarks made by the valet lead Max to suspect something is wrong and it worries him. But to cap the climax the impostor answers a note from Pathé Frères telling Max to come and call for his quarterly check. So perfect is the likeness that the cashier of the motion picture concern pays the fake Max the money. However, even the best laid plans go astray sometimes, and finally the two Maxes come together, head-on. A battle ensues and they are arrested. But the fake Max makes such a fuss and so indignantly denounces the comedian that the authorities hold the real one. At the trial Max is about to be condemned when he suggests that he be allowed to do his famous boxing act which he did for Pathé in the film "Max Has the Boxing Fever". This is a "scream" and it was easy to see which is the real comedian. The imitation is then taken off to jail and Max is acclaimed a free man. *(Moving Picture World, 1915.09.11, in Renken)*

1915.02 - FRA - TR-PR: Catalogue Pathé - Bousquet
1915.03.10 - ITA - Torino: Cinema Splendor - Renken
1915.05.21 - FRA - Paris: Ciné Max Linder - Bousquet

Archives: FRA-CF-Par

**1915-03
LA TULIPE MERVEILLEUSE
250 m = 820 ft = 0:12:09 if at 18 fps
b&w**

Tulipe merveilleuse, La - French release title (original - FRA) - Bousquet
Max's Marvellous Tulip - English release title (GBR) - Renken

Max is a happy husband. He shares with his wife a passion for flowers, and both look for exotic specimens. In the woods, Max finds an extraordinary tulip that he is sure his wife would love to own. He decides to wait for the flower to blossom. Meanwhile, he must keep the secret. The most difficult task is to protect the flower so that nobody can pick it. He writes to a friend, asking if he could borrow his dog to guard the tulip night and day. Finally, when the flower has blossomed, Max writes a letter to his friend. He is very enthusiastic, but also quite ambiguous. Unfortunately, Max's wife comes upon the letter. She understands why her husband was often out, ignorant that he simply checked how the tulip went. She becomes jealous, and an argument ensues. Max has great difficulty convincing his wife of his innocence. He has to take her to the woods to show her the wonderful tulip and convince her that he had interest in a flower, and not in another woman. *(Translation DD from Bousquet nr 7043)*

1915.03 - FRA - TR-PR: Catalogue Pathé - Bousquet
1915.03.22 - ITA - Torino: Cinema Splendor - Renken
1915.07.02 - FRA - Paris: Ciné Max Linder - Renken

Archives: FRA-CNC-Par; FRA-CML

1915-04
LE HASARD ET L'AMOUR
650 m = 2133 ft = 0:31:35 if at 18 fps
b&w

Hasard et l'amour, Le - French release title (original - FRA) - Bousquet
Max is Love Sick - English release title (GBR) - Renken

Lili's father has a permanent cold. He therefore swears to marry his daughter only to a doctor. Max, Lili's fiancé, pretends to be a doctor when the malicious young woman feigns unconsciousness. The imaginary invalid takes this opportunity to have himself examined by the so-called specialist. However, he is quickly exasperated by the baffling consultation he undergoes, so Max, whose scheme failed, is kicked out of the house. Alas! The two lovers cannot stand the separation and they become neurasthenic. They are dying of love. Fortunately, Max is not satisfied with that sordid end and he finds a better one. When he is about to kill himself on a shore, he notices a dog swimming in his direction. The animal carries a note: a young woman named Lili is lost at sea. Max is sure that his sweetheart is the young lady. He flies to rescue her in his brand new waterplane. Lili is adrift at sea, due to an engine failure of her motorboat. She is rescued thanks to her dog's amazing ability. Now that he has been reunited with his sweetheart, Max doesn't want to die anymore. *(Translation DD from Bousquet nr 7242)*

1915.08 - FRA - TR-PR: Catalogue Pathé - Bousquet
1915.09.27 - ITA - Torino: Cinema Royal - Renken
1915.12.24 - FRA - Paris: Ciné Max Linder - Renken

Archives: FRA-CF-Par; FRA-CNC-Par; FRA-CML

1916-01
DEUX AOÛT 1914
305 m = 1001 ft = 0:14:49 if at 18 fps
b&w

Deux août 1914 - French release title (original - FRA) - Bousquet
Max Linder am Vorabend des Krieges - German release title (Ö-UM) - Renken
Max Linder Joins the Colours - English release title (GBR) - Renken
Max partae para a guerra - Portuguese release title (BRA) - Renken
2 août 1914, Le - French listing title (attribution) - Mitry

All the newspapers announce terrible things to come. Everyone is worried, except Max who wants to continue working as usual. He is shooting a film where, invited to a recital, he tries to escape the terrible performance of the lady singer and stumbles upon the flirtation of a young couple. He walks away with the young lady, but his rival, hidden behind a curtain, spoils the courting until the young lady comes back to him. It is now Max's turn to interfere with the flirtation and, incidentally, with the recital. Max and his rival fight back and forth and each in turn can enjoy the tenderness of the fickle young lady. They would have come to hands, but a newspaper seller announcing the general mobilization interrupts their rivalry. Women cry, men take leave of each other shaking hands. Only Max appears to have some doubts. He goes to see his mother, who faints when she sees she cannot hold him back. The doctor announces a fragile heart, so Max stays with her, but she eventually accepts his decision. Max dressed as a solider takes leave of his mother near the station, and boards a train compartment with four other

soldiers. He is somber, worried about his mother, but the patriotic singing and drinking of his companions light up his enthusiasm. *(CC from file on www.gaumontpathearchives.com)*

1916.04.14 - FRA - Paris: Ciné Max Linder - Renken
1916.04 - FRA - TR-PR: Catalogue Pathé - Bousquet

Archives: FRA-FJSP-Par

1916-02
MAX VICTIME DE LA MAIN QUI ÉTREINT
355 m = 1165 ft = 0:17:15 if at 18 fps
b&w

Max victime de la main qui étreint - French release title (original - FRA) - Bousquet
Max in der Schweiz - German release title (CHE) - Renken
Max and the Clutching Hand - English release title (GBR) - Renken
Max Wins and Loses - English release title (USA) - Renken
Max et la main qui étreint - French listing title (attribution) - Ford
Main qui étreint, La - French listing title (attribution) - Maud Linder

Max and his fiancée enjoy winter sports in the Alps, skiing, skating, snowballing, mountaineering. Max imagines he is a great crime detector; bets his prospective father-in-law he will catch a master criminal known as "Clutching Hand". He has some fine chances of doing this but muddles them all until he finally discovers the "Clutching Hand" is his sweetheart playing a series of hoaxes on him. *(The Bioscope, 1917.01.04, in Renken)*

1916.09.30 - FRA - TR-PR Hebdo-Film - Renken
1916.10 - FRA - TR-PR: Catalogue Pathé - Bousquet
1916.11.17 - NL - Rotterdam: Tivoli Bioscope - Renken
1917.01.26 - FRA - Paris: Ciné Max Linder - Renken

Archives: FRA-CML; FRA-CNC-Par; USA-UCLA-Los

Note: in this film Max is wearing the same clothes as in the films shot in Chamonix during the winter 1913-1914.

1916-03
MAX ET L'ESPION
590 m = 1936 ft = 0:28:40 if at 18fps
b&w

Max et l'espion - French release title (original - FRA) - Bousquet
Max und die Spione - German release title (Ö-UM) - Renken
Max als Spion - German release title (CHE) - Renken
Max and the Spies - English release title (GBR) - Renken
Max Plays Detective - English release title (USA) - Renken
Max und die Schäferin - German listing title (attribution) - Renken

After having brilliantly fought on the front lines and suffered a glorious injury, Max is forced to rest. But he doesn't want to stay inactive. The spies' hidden maneuvers burn him up, so he volunteers to catch them on behalf of the government. The question is why so many boats are sunk when they sail out of the port. Simply because enemy submarines receive signals. The solution is to find out and stop the persons who send those signals. Max hits the road in his car. He is intrigued by a fire burning near the shore. He is about to extinguish it when an armed hand appears above a rock. Max is brave, but he acts carefully. He moves back behind another rock and there meets a charming shepherdess and her herd. Instantly he forgets the aim of his mission. Boats would remain in great danger if it were not for an old picturesque shepherd who advises the young woman: "How can a true patriot like you let her be courted by a man who is not even a soldier!". The chastisement is effective: the shepherdess rejects her lover who resumes his work, now fully conscious of his duty. The old shepherd's suspect attitudes intrigue Max who begins to follow him, thus finding the entire gang's lair. Max proves extremely resourceful in preventing them from acting and he succeeds in foiling their plans thanks to highly hazardous efforts. After he has thrown the old shepherd away from a crenellated tower, Max can resume his pastoral idyll.
(Translation DD from Bousquet nr 7738)

1916.11.16 - FRA - TR-PR: Le Film - Renken
1916.12 - FRA - TR-PR: Catalogue Pathé - Bousquet
1917.02.16 - CH - Lausanne: Cinéma Palace - Renken
1917.06.22 - FRA - Paris: Artistic Cinéma - Renken

Archives: CZE-NFA-Pra; FRA-CNC-Par; FRA-CML

1916-04
C'EST POUR LES ORPHELINS: À L'IMPROVISTE
n/a

C'est pour les orphelins: À l'improviste - French release title (original - FRA) - Renken
À l'improviste - French part title - Renken

Great goodwill film in two parts: one prologue, nine scenes, one episode, created by Roger Lion and the most important production companies, for the benefit of goodwill organisations. [...] Scene nr 9: [UNEXPECTED ARRIVAL] Huguette Duflos; Raphael Duflos; Max Linder; Stacia Napierkowska. *(Renken)*

1916.12.19 - FRA - Paris: Cinéma des Folies Dramatiques - Renken
1917.01.19 - FRA - Paris: Ciné Max Linder - Renken

Archives: no film print known to this day

Note: holdings at FRA-LOB-Par do not contain the scene with Max Linder.

1917-01
MAX ET LE SAC
220 m = 721 ft = 0:10:40 if at 18 fps
b&w

Max et le sac - French release title (original - FRA) - Bousquet
Max sucht die Damentasche - German release title (CHE) - Renken
Max und das Handtäschchen - German release title (Ö-UM) - Renken
Max Bags the Bloomer - English release title (GBR) - Renken
Max, on vacation, is about to cross the Channel to visit the English coasts. As soon as he has boarded, he notices a charming passenger and rapidly decides to court her. Suddenly, the young woman yells: "I've forgotten my bag!". Immediately, Max understands the young woman's critical situation, arriving in a foreign country without any money and papers. "For heaven's sake, delay the departure!", says Max to the captain who orders to moor. Max hurries to the hotel. No bag! "Have a look in the cabins, on the beach". Max redoubles his efforts, even triples them. However, the ship captain is getting more and more impatient. He has already ordered three times to "Raise the anchor" … "Full steam ahead". Even the young woman must ask him to be patient. Her nice blue eyes convince him, and Max, at last, brings the bag back. Without even thinking about thanking her fervent admirer, she removes from her bag a powder puff brush, a red lipstick, a vanity mirror, and contemplating her own image, she begins to spruce herself up. Max, stunned, examines the bag again and again: it is empty, apart from those precious vanity toiletries. The captain takes advantage of the young lady's restored mood to court her, whereas poor Max lies in some other part of the ship, furious, jealous, devastated. *(Translation DD from Le Film 1917.05.02, in Renken)*

1917.02 - FRA - TR-PR: Catalogue Pathé - Bousquet
1917.02.16 - FRA - Paris: Ciné Max Linder - Renken

Archives: CZE-NFA-Pra; FRA-CNC-Par; FRA-CML

1917-02
MAX COMES ACROSS
0:30:00 = [2025 ft if at 18 fps] = [617 m if at 18 fps]
b&w
Production: Essanay Film Manufacturing Company, USA

Max Comes Across - English release title (original - USA) - USA Copyright Office
Max part en Amérique - French release title (FRA) - Renken
Max Linder geht nach Amerika - German release title (Ö-UM) - Renken
Max Linder Goes to America - English release title (GBR) - Renken
Max Goes to America - English listing title (attribution) - Maud Linder

[Max Linder is going to the United States of America] to join the Essanay forces. Accompanied by his friend Maupain the voyage is made, although Max is badly frightened by an item of war news which states that twelve more ships of the Entente have just been sunk by German submarines. He orders a life belt placed in every trunk and a life belt with every meal taken on board! He mistakes the play of two dolphins for an approaching torpedo one day and stirs his co-passengers into a frenzy of fear. The attack of seasickness which seizes his friend Maupain and himself results in uproarious fun for the spectator. In the search for his own cabin he enters that of a passenger and his wife, which leads to another paroxysm of mirth. The services of Max as pianist at a special concert given aboard ship affords one of the most mirthful incidents during the voyage. A storm comes up and the piano slides backward and forward across the salon, with Max either in hot pursuit or in quick retreat; but he always contrives to stick to the piano stool, although in its mad gyrations it is sometimes turned upside down. To get even on his friend, Maupain, Max induces the captain to have an attendant shout at his cabin door that the ship is sinking, not knowing that Maupain had already won over that officer to play the same trick on himself, at the very same hour. Then an actual collision takes place in mid ocean, and the cry, "Everybody on deck, the ship is sinking", arouses the passengers from their slumbers. Max and his friend smile, each to himself, as the cry is heard, ignorant of danger. But when an officer tells them of the accident there is wild scampering and a desperate fight between them for a life belt. Max discovers that the ship is out of danger, and seating himself at the piano in his saloon plays an inspiriting selection. The captain and passengers rush in, marveling at the nerve of the hero, who on being questioned modestly answers, "I was playing the piano to give the passengers courage!" *(Moving Picture World, 1917.02.24, in Renken)*

1917.01.30 - USA - CR: Copyright - USA-LoC
1917.02.18 - USA - New York: The Strand - Renken
1919.10.10 - FRA - Paris: Salle Marivaux - Renken

Archives: ESP-FdC-Bar

1917-03
MAX WANTS A DIVORCE
0:30:00 = [2025 ft if at 18 fps] = [617 m if at 18 fps]
b&w
Production: Essanay Film Manufacturing Company, USA

Max Wants a Divorce - English release title (original - USA) - USA Copyright Office
Max veut divorcer - French release title (FRA) - Renken
Max muss sich scheiden lassen - German release title (AUT) - Renken
Max Divorces - English listing title (attribution) - Ford
Max divorteaza - Romanian title - ROU-ANF-Buc

[Max] on his wedding day receives word that an uncle has left him $3.000.000 on condition that he remains a bachelor. After a lot of argument his wife agrees that he shall get a divorce, and after the legacy is safe in hand they will be remarried at once. He is to flirt with a girl, his wife is to catch him at it, have a detective handy, and let that settle it. He hires an apartment, makes a date with a charmer to meet him there, and his wife in disguise is sent in by the agent to take the place of the maid who has suddenly left. An alienist, with a large following of "nuts", has also hired the apartment from another agent. It takes in both sides of the hall, and his offices are away from the living rooms, where the plot is being worked out. The "nuts" come to the doctor, and are "shooed" into another room where their fancies may have free play, and when Linder begins making love to the charmer, and the detective has failed to arrive on schedule time, his wife breaks up his sport, and a young riot results in the doctor's helpers taking them all across the hall, where they are put into the room with the rest of the looney folks. The detective comes, the mixup is straightened out, and the young couple are surprised by a dispatch from the lawyer saying that his first message was an error - it should have been that the nephew to win the legacy should not remain a bachelor. *(Variety, 1917.03.23, in Renken)*

1917.03.07 - USA - CR: Copyright - USA-LoC
1917.03.18 - USA - New York: The Strand - Renken
1919.11.25 - FRA - Paris: Salle Marivaux - Renken

Archives: CZE-NFA-Pra; FRA-CF-Par; FRA-CML; ROU-ANF-Buc; USA-LoC-Was

1917-04
MAX IN A TAXI
2 reels [= 2000 ft = 609 m = 00:29:37 if at 18 fps]
Production: Essanay Film Manufacturing Company, USA

Max in a Taxi - English release title (original - USA) - USA Copyright Office
Max et son taxi - French release title (FRA) - Renken
Max im Taxi - German release title (AUT) - Renken
Max and His Taxi - English listing title (attribution) - Ford
Feiner Chauffeur, Ein - German listing title (attribution) - AUT-FAA
Max in Amerika - English listing title (attribution) - ROU-ANF-Buc

Max gets on a little "bun" in celebration of his birthday. He and his friends find a cab horse and hitch it backwards to a cab. Thus, they drive nonchalantly down the boulevard. Arriving at home, Max's irate father orders him "never again to darken his door." Cut off thus without a penny, Max tries to hang himself. The rope breaks. Then Max lies down in front of an onrushing express train. The engine reaches within a few feet of Max's neck, then suddenly switches off to another track. Max finds he cannot die. He goes to an exclusive ball, instead. Here he meets the real girl of his dreams. He invites her and her mother for a taxi ride, but the machine gets out of order and won't stop. Breathlessly they plunge down a hill and wind up with a terrific explosion against a telegraph pole. The girl and her mother are buried beneath the wreckage. Max is hurled high into the air and, descending, escapes death by lighting on some telegraph wires. The women, who have been uninjured in the accident, stand one on the other's shoulders and onto this human stepladder Max alights from his perilous position. The comedy ends with Max, his girl, and her mother – the latter a fat lady – doing a somersault to the ground and bowing gracefully. Aside from this Max performs the gastronomic feat of eating 16 cream puffs at one sitting. He extinguishes a fire in the trousers leg of one of his guests at the party with champagne and falls out of a third-story window onto the back of another guest. *(Evening Tribune, 1917.05.20, in Renken)*

1917.04.16 - USA - CR: Copyright - USA-LoC
1917.04.23 - USA - Chicago: Pastime - Renken
1920.03.19 - FRA - Paris: Salle Marivaux - Renken

Archives: AUT-FAA-Wie; AUT-ÖFM-Wie; CZE-NFA-Pra; FRA-CML; ROU-ANF-Buc

1917-05
MAX ENTRE DEUX FEUX
580 m = 1903 ft = 0:28:11 if at 18 fps
partially toned

Max entre deux feux - French release title (original - FRA) - Bousquet
Zwischen zwei Feuern - German release title (Ö-UM) - Renken
From Frying Pan Into the Fire - English release title (GBR) - Renken
Max, the Heartbreaker - English release title (USA) - Renken
Max entre deux femmes - French listing title (attribution) - Ford

Tired of his ongoing success, Max hopes to spend some days in Switzerland unnoticed. As soon as he arrives, two joyful young women, a blonde and a brunette, call out: Hey! Hey! Max Linder! But their laughs are disrespectful. Max feels insulted so he passes, full of dignity and disdain. Disappointed, the young girls try to seek common ground, so Max can take his revenge. However, he is unable to ignore them too long. Both of them are too pretty. But the situation is embarrassing for Max who is caught in the middle. He decides to court sometimes the brunette, sometimes the blonde. One day, Dora and Maud realize Max's double-dealing and swear to have their revenge taken. Max is sure that a drama is going to happen that will cause casualties: the young girls are going to fight to the death in a duel. But the totally unexpected end of the story will leave our hero confused, and he will perhaps enjoy the salutary effect of that lesson of modesty. *(Translation DD from Bousquet nr 7727)*

1917.05 - FRA - TR-PR: Catalogue Pathé - Bousquet
1917.05.04 - FRA - Paris: Omnia Pathé - Bousquet
1919.06.20 - ÖST - Wien: Imperial Kino - Renken

Archives: BEL-CRB-Bru; CAN-CQ-Mon; FRA-CF-Par; FRA-CNC-Par; FRA-CML

Note: re-released 9,5mm [Film Office] MAX ENTRE DEUX FEUX, full-length titles, [100 m or 200 m].

1917-06
MAX, MÉDECIN MALGRÉ LUI
660 m = 2165 ft = 0:32:04 if at 18 fps
b&w

Max, médecin malgré lui - French release title (original - FRA) - Bousquet
Max wird Arzt wider Willen - German release title (Ö-UM) - Renken
Signor Dottore, Il - Italian release title (ITA) - Renken

Max falls in love with a dancer named Lili. But Lili is not a fancy woman. Max is desperate and becomes ill with neurasthenia. He goes to see a doctor he is friends with. The doctor recommends some distraction. He therefore offers Max a ticket to attend a play. That ticket belongs to the theater's physician on duty. By chance, a spectator falls ill that very evening. Max then improvises an unconventional therapy that leads to the final scene of Max and Lili's loving embrace. *(Translation DD from Bousquet nr 7963)*

1917.09 - FRA - TR-PR: Catalogue Pathé - Bousquet
1917.09.21 - FRA - Paris: Omnia Pathé - Renken
1919.10.31 - ÖST - Wien: Kino Schwarzenbergplatz - Renken

Archives: AUT-FAA-Wie; BEL-CRB-Bru; FRA-CNC-Par; FRA-Lob-Par;

Note: this film could be a release of cut-off scenes: the critic of Le cinéma et l'écho du cinéma réunis, 1917.08.24, states: "surprisingly, as generally Max Linder's films have very elaborate scripts, this comedy is full of directing mistakes."

1917-07
MAX DEVRAIT PORTER DES BRETELLES
505 m = 1657 ft = 0:24:32 if at 18 fps
b&w

Max devrait porter des bretelles - French release title (original - FRA) - Bousquet
Max ohne Hosenträger - German release title (CHE+Ö-UM) - Renken
Max's Camera Calamity - English release title (GBR) - Renken
Max Should Wear Braces - English archive title [attribution] - GBR-BFI

Max leaves for Italy in order to make a sensational picture with his state-of-the-art camera. The reward will be a 100 000-French-Franc prize. Attracted by a genre scene, Max photographs some charming Italian young boys. Delighted and certain to be the winner, he comes back to Paris. But the contest organizers remind him that only landscapes and still life photos are accepted, not people. Max leaves. When he is about to take a picture of a lovely place, an old lady and her dog stand in front of the camera. The same event happens once more, which infuriates Max and forces him to leave. On the beach, Ginette's lovely face improves his mood, especially when she comes out of the sea to pick some flowers. Ginette accepts the idea of introducing Max to her father. Max dresses up but his shoes hurt. He unbuttons them and hides them with his pants. Unfortunately, what had to happen finally happens in front of Ginette and her father: Max's pants go lower and lower, leaving him in underpants. Poor Max is taught a well-deserved lesson.
(Translation DD from Bousquet nr 8006)

1917.11 - FRA - TR-PR: Catalogue Pathé - Bousquet
1917.11.09 - FRA - Paris: Omnia Pathé - Bousquet
1917.05.17 - Ö-UM - Graz: Bioskop Theater Annenhof - Renken

Archives: FRA-Lob-Par; GBR-BFI-Lon; USA-AFA-Los; USA-BkHk; USA-GEM-Roc

Note: this film could be a release of cut-off scenes: the critic of Hebdo Film, 1919.10.13 (in Renken), states: "this film looks like it has been made of old scenes haphazardly put together".

1919-01
LE PETIT CAFÉ
1800 m = 5905 ft = 1:27:28 if at 18 fps
Production: Films Diamant, Henri Diamant-Berger, France,

Petit café, Le - French release title (original - FRA) - Bousquet
Kleine Kaffeehaus, Das - German release title (AUT) - Renken
Little Café, The - English release title (GBR+USA) - Renken

Max obtains a job in a little café as a waiter and is contented. In his childhood, he lived with a rich uncle, who frequently went mountain climbing. During his uncle's absence, an old family servant made life miserable for the boy. The uncle disappeared mysteriously, and after enduring the abuse of the servant for some time, Max ran away and forgot his past. In the meantime, his uncle was legally proven dead and his attorneys searched for Max to turn the fortune over to him. The old servant located Max and in conspiracy with Max's employer, influenced him to sign a contract with the café to continue to wait on table for twenty years or forfeit a large sum of money. Max, not knowing of his inheritance, signed. He was then apprised of his fortune. To save making the forfeit, he continued to wait on table during the day and lived like a millionaire at night. In the end, the employer relented and tore up the contract, and Max married his employer's daughter. *(Exhibitors Herald, 1920.05.06, in Renken)*

1919.11.15 - FRA - Paris: Ciné Max Linder "Trade Show" - Renken
1919.12 - FRA - TR-PR: Catalogue Pathé - Bousquet
1920.12.14 - ÖST - Wien: Imperial Kino - Renken

Archives: BEL-CRB-Bru; CZE-NFA-Pra; FRA-CdT-Tou; FRA-CML; FRA-CNC-Par; ITA-CdF-Gem; RUS-GFF-Mos

1921-01
SEVEN YEARS BAD LUCK
5 reels [= 5000 ft = 1524 m = 01:00:36 if at 22 fps]
Production: Max Linder Productions Co., USA

Seven Years Bad Luck - English release title (original - USA) - USA Copyright Office
Sept ans de malheur - French release title (FRA) - Mitry
Sieben Jahre Pech - German release title (DEU+AUT) - Renken
Max Linder heeft zeven ongelukkige jaren - Dutch release title (NLD) - www.cinemacontext.nl

Returning from his last bachelor supper somewhat inebriated, Max goes to bed. In a chase for a kiss, his valet and parlor maid break a cheval glass and try to conceal the loss. When a new glass arrives, Max, afraid he is "seeing things", throws his shoe at the mirror and the bad luck begins: his fiancée abandons him, and his efforts to leave town are thwarted by a mad mishmash of adventures in which policemen, railroad employees, burglars and wild beasts conspire to make life miserable for him. Finally, matters are adjusted, and Max wins back his sweetheart. *(AFI nr F2.4923)*

1921.02.06 - USA - CR: Copyright - USA-LoC
1921.02.19 - USA - Chicago: State-Lake - Renken
1921.11.25 - FRA - Paris: Cinéma Demours - Renken

Archives: BEL-CRB-Bru; BRA-CMAM-Rio; DEU-DFF-Fra; FRA-CML; FRA-CNC-Par; FRA-Lob-Par; ITA-CdF-Gem; ITA-FCI-Mil; NLD-EFM-Ams; USA-AFA-Los; USA-BkHk; USA-GEM-Roc; USA-UCLA-Los

1921-02
BE MY WIFE
5 reels 4650 ft (= 1417 m = 56 min if at 22 fps)
Production: Max Linder Productions Co., USA

Be My Wife - English release title (original - USA) - USA Copyright Office
Soyez ma femme - French release title (FRA) - Mitry
Max heiratet sein Weibchen - German release title (DEU) - Renken

Sei mein Weibchen - German release title (AUT) - Renken
Siate mia moglie - Italian title (ITA) - FIAF TFA db
Who Pays My Wife's Bills? - English work title - Renken
Too Much Pep - English work title - Renken

Max, the fiancé, after he is accepted by his sweetheart, successfully obstructs the machinations of a rival for the girl's favor but has great difficulty in winning over her aunt to his side. After the wedding, when a divorce is pending, he accomplishes the latter feat and at the same time causes his wife to respect him the more. *(AFI nr F2.0298)*

1921.11.06 - USA - Sacramento: Godard's Theater - Renken
1921.11.23 - USA - CR: Copyright - USA-LoC
1923.04.27 - FRA - Paris: Cine Magic Palace - Renken
Archives: CZE-NFA-Pra; FRA-CML; FRA-CNC-Par; FRA-Lob-Par; ITA-CdF-Gem; ITA-FCI-Mil

1922-01
THE THREE MUST-GET-THERES
5 reels, 4900 ft (= 1494 m, 0:59:23 if at 22 fps)
b&w
Production: Max Linder Productions Co., USA

Three Must-Get-Theres, The - English release title (original - USA) - USA Copyright Office
Etroit mousquetaire, L' - French release title (FRA) - Mitry
Max und die drei Musketiere - German release title (DEU) - Renken
Drei Muskrepiere, Die - German release title (AUT) - Renken
Knockout-held, Der - German listing title (attribution) - NLD-EFM
Vingt ans avant - French title (alternative) - Maud Linder

On his way to Paris, Dart-in-Again loses a duel to the Man of Meung, challenges each of the Three Must-Get-Theres, then joins the trio in routing the Duke of Rich-Lou's soldiers. Asked by Connie, the queen's seamstress, to recover from the queen's lover, Bunkumin, a brooch given to her by the king, Dart-In-Again travels to England and has many adventures while accomplishing his task. The king rewards him for "finding" the brooch by making him a full member of the Three Must-Get-Theres, giving him permission to marry Connie, and allowing Dart-In-Again to give a "present" to the Duke of Rich-Lou. *(AFI nr F2.5666)*

1922.08.26 - USA - New York: The Strand - Renken
1922.09.01 - USA - CR: Copyright - USA-LoC
1923.01.26 - FRA - Paris: Ciné Max Linder - Renken

Archives: BEL-CRB-Bru; BGR-BNF-Sof; BRA-CMAM-Rio; CAN-CQ-Mon; CAN-LAC-Gat; CZE-NFA-Pra; DEU-B/F-Ber; DEU-DFF-Fra; DEU-DK-Ber; FRA-CF-Par; FRA-CML; FRA-Lob-Par; GBR-BFI-Lon; ITA-CdF-Gem; NLD-EFM-Ams; ROU-ANF-Buc; USA-GEM-Roc; USA-LoC-Was; USA-UCLA-Los

**1924-01
AU SECOURS!
1500 m shortened to 900 m (4921 ft shortened to 2952 ft) = 0:59:38 / 0:35:46 if at 22 fps
Production: Films Abel Gance**

Au secours! - French release title (original - FRA) - Bousquet
Zu Hilfe - German release title (DEU) - Renken
Maxens Wette - German release title (AUT) - Renken
Seine fürchterlichste Stunde - German release title (AUT) - Renken
Haunted House, The - English release title (GBR) - Renken
Max Linder en het spookslot - Dutch release title (NLD - 1928) - www.cinemacontext.nl
Max Linder in het spookkastel - Dutch re-release title (NLD - 1933) - NLD-EFM
Ajutor! Ajutor! - Romanian title - FIAF TFA db

Max bets he can spend a whole night in a house that might be haunted, according to its landlord. In spite of frightening and incredible phenomena, Max stands firm until his fiancée calls him by phone to rescue her. Defeated, he rings the bell and gives the amount agreed, 100 gold coins, to the laughing and slightly mocking bettor who had imagined that fraudulent scheme. *(Translation DD from Chirat nr 60)*

1924.02.23 - AUT - TR-PR: Der Filmbote - Renken
1924.03.21 - HUN - Prag: Sans Souci - Renken
1924.06.17 - FRA - Paris: Gaumont Palace - Renken

Archives: CZE-NFA-Pra; DEU-B/F-Ber; DEU-DK-Ber; FRA-CF-Par; FRA-GPA-Par; GBR-BFI-Lon; NLD-EFM-Ams; ROU-ANF-Buc; SWE-SFI-Sto; USA-LoC-Was; USA-MoMA-New

**1924-02
DER ZIRKUSKÖNIG
1700 m = 5577 ft = 1:07:36 of at 22 fps
Production: Vita-Film, Austria**

Zirkuskönig, Der - German release title (original - DEU+AUT) - Renken
Roi du cirque, Le - French release title (FRA) - Mitry
Circusmania - English release title (GBR+USA) - Renken
Max, der Zirkuskönig - German listing title [attribution] - Renken
Clown aus Liebe - German work title - Renken
King of the Circus - English title - FIAF TFA db

Count Max de Pompadour, a drunken and worthless young fool, is offered marriage or disownment by his guardian. He has three choices of a bride and desires to marry the one whose photograph he hits first with a revolver bullet. He misses all three but frightens a pretty girl into a fainting fit. She makes an appointment to meet him at the Cirque Buffalo the following night. He goes with his uncle, looks in vain for her in the auditorium and eventually finds she is a trapeze artist. His ardor is increased but receives a severe shock when her burly father says she can only marry "in the profession". The girl gives him a book "How to Become an Acrobat" but his studies prove disastrous. He assays to become a flea-tamer with even more disastrous results and loses his troupe. His future father-in-law, however, provides him with lions. Things are awkward but a friendly clown agrees to see him through. His rival foils this attempt and things get worse but ultimately he wins the day and the girl. *(Variety, 1924.06.25, in Renken)*

1924.09.12 - NL - Rotterdam: Rotterdam: Cinema Royal / Cinema Thalia - www.cinemacontext.nl
1925.02.19 - FRA - Paris: Aubert-Palace - Renken

Archives: AUT-FAA-Wie; BEL-CRB-Bru; CZE-NFA-Pra; ESP-FE-Mad; FRA-CML; FRA-CNC-Par; FRA-Lob-Par; GBR-BFI-Lon; ITA-FCI-Mil; NLD-EFM-Ams; RUS-GFF-Mos; SWE-SFI-Sto

Titles Cross-referenced:

2 août 1914, Le	Deux août 1914	1916-01
Absent-Minded Max	Max est distrait	1910-19
Ach diese Schwiegermütter	Obsession de la belle-mère, L'	1908-10
Adventures of a Madman	Exploits d'un fou, Les	1907-17
Adventures of Tartarin the Younger	Exploits du jeune Tartarin, Les	1909-16
Aeronaut's First Appearance, The	Débuts d'un aéronaute, Les	1907-13
Affectionate Pets	Trop aimée	1910-22
Affinity	Petit roman	1912-29
Ah les femmes!	Oh! les femmes	1912-15
Ahoreado, El	Pendu, Le [1906]	1906-04
Ah! Quel malheur d'avoir un gendre	Ah! Quel malheur d'avoir un gendre	1907-03
Aimé par sa bonne	Aimé par sa bonne	1909-02
Ajutor! Ajutor!	Au secours!	1924-01
À l'improviste	C'est pour les orphelins: À l'improviste	1916-04
All for a Necklace	Pour un collier	1907-04
All's Well That Ends Well	Tout est bien qui finit bien	1910-12
Ama secca por necessidade	Nourrice par nécessité	1907-05
Amateur Acrobat	Obsession de l'équilibre, L'	1908-04
Amateur Photographe	Max fait de la photographie	1913-14
American Marriage, An	Mariage américain, Un	1909-06
Amerikanische Hochzeit	Mariage américain, Un	1909-06
Amme aus Not	Nourrice par nécessité	1907-05
Amour de toréador, Un	Drame à Séville, Un	1907-16
Amour et fromage	Amour et fromage	1910-14
Amoureux de la femme à barbe	Amoureux de la femme à barbe	1909-04
Amoureux de la teinturière	Amoureux de la teinturière	1912-03
Amour mouillé, L'	Anglais tel que Max le parle, L'	1913-21
Amour tenace	Amour tenace	1912-22
Âne jaloux, L'	Âne jaloux, L'	1912-09
Anglais tel que Max le parle, L'	Anglais tel que Max le parle, L'	1913-21
Ansteckendes Nervenzucken	Tic nerveux contagieux, Un	1908-15
À qui mon cœur?	À qui mon cœur?	1909-09
Armoire, L'	Armoire, L'	1907-18
Artful Husband	Ruse de mari [1907]	1907-06
Artist Max	Peintre par amour	1912-18
Attempted Suicide	Pendu, Le [1906]	1906-04
At the Cinematograph Theatre	Représentation au cinéma, Une	1910-10
At the Music Hall	Au Music-hall	1907-01
Auf der Hochzeitsreise	Voyage de noces	1912-21
August geht zum Ball	Julot va dans le monde	1906-02
Au Music-hall	Au Music-hall	1907-01
Au secours!	Au secours!	1924-01
Avant et... après	Avant et... après	1909-14
Baffles, Bandit	Kyrelor, bandit par amour	1910-13
Bandit par amour	Bandit par amour	1912-05
Baromètre de la fidélité, Le	Baromètre de la fidélité, Le	1915-01
Bashful Young Man, A	Jeune homme timide, Un	1908-16
Bébé encombrant, Un	Bébé encombrant, Un	1908-17
Before and After	Avant et... après	1909-14

Beginning of the Serpentine Dance	Création de la serpentine	1908-23
Bella professora de piano, A	Maîtresse de piano, La	1908-13
Be My Wife	Be My Wife	1921-02
Bet, The	Pari original, Un	1912-17
Billet doux, Le	Billet doux, Le	1913-12
Bill Goes to a Party	Julot va dans le monde	1906-02
Bobo mal placé, Un	Bobo mal placé, Un	1909-01
Bonne bonne, Une	Aimé par sa bonne	1909-02
Bonne farce, Une	Duel de Max, Le	1913-11
Bonne pour Monsieur, un domestique pour Madame, Une	Bonne pour Monsieur, un domestique pour Madame, Une	1910-02
Bootmaker's Revenge, The	Vengeance du bottier, La	1909-13
Boxer aus Liebe	Boxeur par amour	1912-24
Boxeur par amour	Boxeur par amour	1912-24
Busy Fiancé, The	Fiancé trop occupé, Un	1908-19
By the Doctor's Orders	Max prend un bain	1910-31
Cacoete contagioso	Tic nerveux contagieux, Un	1908-15
Case of Lumbago, A	Bobo mal placé, Un	1909-01
C'est Papa qui a pris la purge	C'est Papa qui a pris la purge	1906-05
C'est pour les orphelins: À l'improviste	C'est pour les orphelins: À l'improviste	1916-04
Champion Boxer, A	Champion de boxe	1910-24
Champion de boxe	Champion de boxe	1910-24
Chapeau de Max, Le	Chapeau de Max, Le	1913-13
Chapeau de Max Linder, Le	Chapeau de Max, Le	1913-13
Chaussure trop étroite	Chaussure trop étroite	1907-08
Cheese and Kisses	Amour et fromage	1910-14
Chien qui rapporte, Un	Mon chien rapporte	1910-27
Circusmania	Zirkuskönig, Der	1924-02
Clever Dog, A	Mon chien rapporte	1910-27
Clown aus Liebe	Zirkuskönig, Der	1924-02
Coiffeur par amour	Coiffeur par amour	1914-16
Comment Max fait le tour du monde	Comment Max Linder fait le tour du monde	1910-29
Comment Max Linder fait le tour du monde	Comment Max Linder fait le tour du monde	1910-29
Comment on fait le tour du monde	Comment Max Linder fait le tour du monde	1910-29
Complete Sportsman, The	Max Linder pratique tous les sports	1913-05
Conjurer's Triumph, The	Succès de la prestidigitation, Le	1912-08
Conquest, A	Conquête, Une	1909-05
Conquête, Une	Conquête, Une	1909-05
Consulta improvisada	Consultation improvisée	1908-26
Consultation improvisée	Consultation improvisée	1908-26
Contagious Nervous Twitching	Tic nerveux contagieux, Un	1908-15
Country Lad, A	Vertueux jeune homme, Le	1908-25
Coup de foudre, Le	Coup de foudre, Le	1908-22
Coup d'œil à chaque étage	Max se trompe d'étage	1910-21
Création de la serpentine	Création de la serpentine	1908-23
Cross-country	Cross-country original, Un	1910-26
Cross-country original, Un	Cross-country original, Un	1910-26
Cuisinier par amour	Cuisinier par amour	1914-13

Cumbersome Baby	Bébé encombrant, Un	1908-17
Cupboard, The	Armoire, L'	1907-18
Cure for Cowardice, A	Timidité guérie par le sérum, La	1910-01
Cure for Timidity, A	Timidité guérie par le sérum, La	1910-01
Daarlig Mave	C'est Papa qui a pris la purge	1906-05
Damped Love	Anglais tel que Max le parle, L'	1913-21
Débuts au Cinématographe	Débuts de Max Linder au cinématographe, Les	1910-28
Débuts de Max au cinéma	Débuts de Max Linder au cinématographe, Les	1910-28
Débuts de Max au cinématographe, Les	Débuts de Max Linder au cinématographe, Les	1910-28
Débuts de Max Linder au cinématographe, Les	Débuts de Max Linder au cinématographe, Les	1910-28
Débuts d'un aéronaute, Les	Débuts d'un aéronaute, Les	1907-13
Débuts d'un patineur	Débuts d'un patineur	1907-07
Débuts d'un yachtman, Les	Débuts d'un yachtman, Les	1913-02
Debuts of a Yachtsman, The	Débuts d'un yachtman, Les	1913-02
Defekte Gasleitung, Die	Fuite de gaz, La	1912-20
Dem ersten das Herz, dem letzten die Hand	À qui mon cœur ?	1909-09
Deux août 1914	Deux août 1914	1916-01
Deux coqs vivaient en paix	Entente cordiale	1912-26
Deux grandes douleurs	Deux grandes douleurs	1908-14
Dick, de slimme hond	Dick est un chien savant	1914-15
Dick est un chien savant	Dick est un chien savant	1914-15
Diener als Hypnotiseur, Der	Domestique hypnotiseur, Le	1907-14
Dienstmädchen für den Herrn, einen Diener für die Frau, Ein	Bonne pour Monsieur, un domestique pour Madame, Une	1910-02
Difficult Task, A	Épreuve difficile, Une	1910-15
Doings of a Maniac	Exploits d'un fou, Les	1907-17
Domestique hypnotiseur, Le	Domestique hypnotiseur, Le	1907-14
Dos pares de zapatos	Petit roman	1912-29
Double Event, A	Jockey par amour	1913-01
Double Sight, A	Mauvaise vue	1910-08
Drama in Sevilla, Ein	Drame à Séville, Un	1907-16
Drama in Seville, A	Drame à Séville, Un	1907-16
Drame à Séville, Un	Drame à Séville, Un	1907-16
Drei Muskrepiere, Die	Three Must-Get-Theres, The	1922-01
Duel de Max, Le	Duel de Max, Le	1913-11
Duel de Mr Myope, Le	Duel de Mr Myope, Le	1910-16
Duel du monsieur myope, Le	Duel de Mr Myope, Le	1910-16
Duel d'un Monsieur Myope, Le	Duel de Mr Myope, Le	1910-16
Duelista por amor	Max a un duel	1911-06
Effets des pilules, Les	Effets des pilules, Les	1910-20
Effets des pilules de Max, Les	Effets des pilules, Les	1910-20
Ehemann der Pech hat, Ein	Mari peu veinard, Un	1908-24
Eifersucht	Jalousie	1912-30
Eifersüchtige Esel, Der	Âne jaloux, L'	1912-09
Empoisonneuse, L'	Empoisonneuse, L'	1907-02
En bombe	En bombe	1909-12
En el café concerto	Au Music-hall	1907-01

Enlèvement en hydroaéroplane, L'	Enlèvement en hydroaéroplane, L'	1912-28
Enlèvement par hydroaéroplane	Enlèvement en hydroaéroplane, L'	1912-28
Ensimäinen kosintaretki	Premier rendez-vous, Le	1909-15
Entente cordiale	Entente cordiale	1912-26
Épreuve difficile, Une	Épreuve difficile, Une	1910-15
Erbneffe, Der	Tribulations d'un neveu, Les	1908-27
Erfolg des Gaukelspiels, Der	Succès de la prestidigitation, Le	1912-08
Erlebnisse eines Narren	Exploits d'un fou, Les	1907-17
Erlebnisse eines Verliebten	Péripéties d'un amant, Les	1907-12
Erste Rendez-vous, Das	Première sortie	1905-01
Erste Rendez-vous, Das	Premier rendez-vous, Le	1909-15
Erster Versuch eines Schlittschuhläufers	Débuts d'un patineur	1907-07
Erste Zigarre des Primaners, Die	Premier cigare d'un collégien, Le	1908-03
Escape of Gas, An	Fuite de gaz, La	1912-20
Escarpins de Max, Les	Chaussure trop étroite	1907-08
Es lebe das Junggesellenleben	Vive la vie de garçon	1908-07
Espinha mal collocada, Uma	Bobo mal placé, Un	1909-01
Eternal Woman	Oh! les femmes	1912-15
Etroit mousquetaire, L'	Three Must-Get-Theres, The	1922-01
Étudiants de Paris, Les	Étudiants de Paris, Les	1906-01
Exploits du jeune Tartarin, Les	Exploits du jeune Tartarin, Les	1909-16
Exploits d'un fou, Les	Exploits d'un fou, Les	1907-17
Fake Doctor, The	Consultation improvisée	1908-26
Farm-House Romance, A	Idylle à la ferme	1912-16
Feiner chauffeur, Ein	Max in a Taxi	1917-04
Femme sandwich, La	Femme sandwich, La	1908-06
Feu sacré, Le	Max veut faire du théâtre	1911-08
Fiancé trop occupé, Un	Fiancé trop occupé, Un	1908-19
First Cigar	Premier cigare d'un collégien, Le	1908-03
First Night Out	Première sortie	1905-01
Flûte merveilleuse, La	Flûte merveilleuse, La	1910-25
Fool and His Money, A	Max est charitable	1913-03
For Love of a Maid	Bandit par amour	1912-05
Friseur aus Liebe	Coiffeur par amour	1914-16
From Frying Pan Into the Fire	Max entre deux feux	1917-05
Fuite de gaz, La	Fuite de gaz, La	1912-20
Furchtsamer junger Mann, Ein	Jeune homme timide, Un	1908-16
Gatte der Frau Doctor, Der	Mari de la doctoresse, Le	1907-19
Geldnot macht erfinderisch	Ingénieux attentat, L'	1910-11
Gelegenheitsarzt, Der	Consultation improvisée	1908-26
Gentleman als Dieb, Der	Voleur mondain, Le	1909-11
Gentleman Thief, The	Voleur mondain, Le	1909-11
Geprüfte Heiratskandidat, Der	Petite rosse	1909-08
Geschichten über Hanswurst	Légende de Polichinelle, La	1907-11
Gestörtes Rendez-vous, Ein	Péripéties d'un amant, Les	1907-12
Giftmischerin	Empoisonneuse, L'	1907-02
Glorious Start, A	Débuts d'un aéronaute, Les	1907-13
Glück des Buckligen, Das	Veine de bossu, Une	1908-11
Gnädige Frau bei schlechter Laune, Die	Madame a ses vapeurs	1907-10
Gobbo portafortuna, Il	Veine de bossu, Une	1908-11
Good Chance Lost, A	Max manque un riche mariage	1910-35
Good Joke, A	Duel de Max, Le	1913-11

Green-Eyed Monster, The	Jalousie	1912-30
Grünschnabel, Ein	Petit jeune homme, Le	1909-03
Hängelampe, Die	Suspension, La	1908-05
Hanging Lamp, The	Suspension, La	1908-05
Hapless Hubby, The	Mari peu veinard, Un	1908-24
Harlequin's Story, A	Légende de Polichinelle, La	1907-11
Hartnäckige Liebe	Amour tenace	1912-22
Hasard et l'amour, Le	Hasard et l'amour, Le	1915-04
Haunted House, The	Au secours!	1924-01
His First Air Trip	Débuts d'un aéronaute, Les	1907-13
His First Cigar	Premier cigare d'un collégien, Le	1908-03
His First Night Out	Première sortie	1905-01
Hoed van Max Linder, De	Chapeau de Max, Le	1913-13
Hooligan Idea, A	Idée d'apache	1907-09
How Max Linder Traveled Round the World	Comment Max Linder fait le tour du monde	1910-29
How Max Went Around the World	Comment Max Linder fait le tour du monde	1910-29
Hubby Cures His Wife of Flirting	Ruse de mari, Une [1910]	1910-09
Hühneraugenoperateur aus Liebe	Pédicure par amour	1908-12
Hunchback Brings Luck	Veine de bossu, Une	1908-11
Hurrah for Bachelorhood	Vive la vie de garçon	1908-07
Husband's Trickery	Ruse de mari [1907]	1907-06
Ich möchte ein Kind	Je voudrais un enfant	1910-06
Idée d'apache	Idée d'apache	1907-09
Idylle à la ferme	Idylle à la ferme	1912-16
Idyll im Gutshofe, Ein	Idylle à la ferme	1912-16
Idyll on a Farm, An	Idylle à la ferme	1912-16
I Fear No Foe	Rivalité	1913-06
Im Musik-Hall	Au Music-hall	1907-01
Impossible Rest	Mes voisins me font danser	1908-18
Impossible to Get Sleep	Mes voisins me font danser	1908-18
Improvised Consultation	Consultation improvisée	1908-26
In a Difficult Position	Mon pantalon est décousu	1908-01
Inauguration de la statue, L'	Max et l'inauguration de la statue	1912-32
In eine bärtige Frau verliebt	Amoureux de la femme à barbe	1909-04
Ingénieux attentat, L'	Ingénieux attentat, L'	1910-11
In Love with the Bearded Woman	Amoureux de la femme à barbe	1909-04
Jalousie	Jalousie	1912-30
Jealous Husband, The	Mari jaloux	1914-05
Jeune fille romanesque	Jeune fille romanesque	1910-03
Jeune homme timide, Un	Jeune homme timide, Un	1908-16
Je voudrais un enfant	Je voudrais un enfant	1910-06
Jockei aus Liebe	Jockey par amour	1913-01
Jockey for Love, A	Jockey par amour	1913-01
Jockey par amour	Jockey par amour	1913-01
Joe Teaches Max a Lesson	Âne jaloux, L'	1912-09
Johann als Kindermädchen	Pitou, bonne d'enfants	1907-15
Joined Lips	Lèvres collées	1906-03
Jongleur im Restaurant	Obsession de l'équilibre, L'	1908-04
Jongmensch heeft zich ophangen, Een	Pendu, Le [1906]	1906-04
Joys of Tight Boots, The	Chaussure trop étroite	1907-08

Julot va dans le monde	Julot va dans le monde	1906-02
Junggesellenleben Lebe Hoch! Das	Vive la vie de garçon	1908-07
Kasperles Erlebnisse	Légende de Polichinelle, La	1907-11
King of the Circus	Zirkuskönig, Der	1924-02
Kirelor, bandit par amour	Kyrelor, bandit par amour	1910-13
Klavierlehrerin, Die	Maîtresse de piano, La	1908-13
Kleine Kaffeehaus, Das	Petit café, Le	1919-01
Kleine Schlaumeier, Der	C'est Papa qui a pris la purge	1906-05
Kleine Störenfried, Der	Nuit agitée, Une	1912-07
Knockout-held, Der	Three Must-Get-Theres, The	1922-01
Kurzischtige Max, Der	Duel de Mr Myope, Le	1910-16
Küsse nie die Magd zum Scherz!	N'embrassez pas votre bonne	1913-20
Kyrelor, Bandit aus Liebe	Kyrelor, bandit par amour	1910-13
Kyrelor, bandit par amour	Kyrelor, bandit par amour	1910-13
Lady Doctor's Husband	Mari de la doctoresse, Le	1907-19
Lady-Killer Foiled	Coup de foudre, Le	1908-22
Last Laugh, The	Duel de Max, Le	1913-11
Leçon de tango, La	Max professeur de tango	1914-01
Légende de Polichinelle, La	Légende de Polichinelle, La	1907-11
Legend of Ponchinella	Légende de Polichinelle, La	1907-11
Leggenda di Pulcinella, La	Légende de Polichinelle, La	1907-11
Lehrzeit eines Luftschiffers	Débuts d'un aéronaute, Les	1907-13
Lèvres collées	Lèvres collées	1906-03
Liebesbrief, Der	Billet doux, Le	1913-12
Liebesheirat, Die	Mariages imprévus	1913-04
Liebespaar im Hydro-Aeroplan, Das	Enlèvement en hydroaéroplane, L'	1912-28
Liebe und Käse	Amour et fromage	1910-14
List des Gatten	Ruse de mari, Une [1910]	1910-09
Little Café, The	Petit café, Le	1919-01
Little Vixen, The	Petite rosse	1909-08
Living Statue, The	Max et l'inauguration de la statue	1912-32
Lost Baby, The	Bébé encombrant, Un	1908-17
Love and Boxing	Boxeur par amour	1912-24
Love and Cheese	Amour et fromage	1910-14
Love and Goodfellowship Pills	Effets des pilules, Les	1910-20
Loved by his Servant	Aimé par sa bonne	1909-02
Love Letter, The	Billet doux, Le	1913-12
Love Me, Love My Cat	Max n'aime pas les chats	1913-10
Lover's Ill Luck	Péripéties d'un amant, Les	1907-12
Love's Surprises	Surprises de l'amour, Les	1909-07
Love Unconquerable	Amour tenace	1912-22
Macht des Revolvers, Die	Revolver arrange tout, Le	1910-17
Madame a ses vapeurs	Madame a ses vapeurs	1907-10
Madam's Tantrums	Madame a ses vapeurs	1907-10
Magic Flute, The	Flûte merveilleuse, La	1910-25
Main qui étreint, La	Max victime de la main qui étreint	1916-02
Maîtresse de piano, La	Maîtresse de piano, La	1908-13
Maks i kupchikha	Maks Linder i g-zha Prokhorova	1913-22
Maks i Kursistka	Maks i Kursistka	1913-23
Maks Linder i g-zha Prokhorova	Maks Linder i g-zha Prokhorova	1913-22
Mal de mer, Le	Mal de mer, Le	1912-13
Maler aus Liebe	Peintre par amour	1912-18

Malle au mariage, La	Malle au mariage, La	1912-10
Ma montre retarde	Ma montre retarde	1908-02
Maniac Juggler, The	Obsession de l'équilibre, L'	1908-04
Man Who Hanged Himself, The	Pendu, Le [1906]	1906-04
Mariage à l'américaine, Un	Mariage américain, Un	1909-06
Mariage américain, Un	Mariage américain, Un	1909-06
Mariage au puzzle, Un	Mariage au puzzle, Un	1910-23
Mariage au téléphone	Mariage au téléphone	1912-25
Mariage de Max, Le	Max se marie	1911-02
Mariage forcé	Mariage forcé	1914-09
Mariage imprévu, Un	Mariages imprévus	1913-04
Mariage par téléphone, Un	Mariage au téléphone	1912-25
Mariages imprévus	Mariages imprévus	1913-04
Mari de la doctoresse, Le	Mari de la doctoresse, Le	1907-19
Marido caipora	Mari peu veinard, Un	1908-24
Mari jaloux	Mari jaloux	1914-05
Mari peu veinard, Un	Mari peu veinard, Un	1908-24
Match de boxe entre patineurs à roulettes	Champion de boxe	1910-24
Mauvaise vie, Une	Mauvaise vue	1910-08
Mauvaise vue	Mauvaise vue	1910-08
Max Acts in a Drama	Max joue le drame	1914-08
Max aéronaute	Débuts d'un aéronaute, Les	1907-13
Max a la richerca di una fidanzata	Max cherche une fiancée	1910-33
Max a le feu sacré	Max veut faire du théâtre	1911-08
Max als Anfänger in der Kinematographie	Débuts de Max Linder au cinématographe, Les	1910-28
Max als Boxer	Champion de boxe	1910-24
Max als circus artist	Amoureux de la femme à barbe	1909-04
Max als Friseur	Coiffeur par amour	1914-16
Max als Hühneraugen-Operateur	Max pédicure	1914-02
Max als Modekönig	Max lance la mode	1911-09
Max als Opfer des Bordeaux-Weines	Victime du quinquina	1911-07
Max als Spion	Max et l'espion	1916-03
Max als Sportsmann	Max Linder pratique tous les sports	1913-05
Max als Stiefelsammler	Max collectionne les chaussures	1913-18
Max als Stierkämpfer	Max toréador	1913-08
Max als „Stütze der Hausfrau"	Max, maître d'hôtel	1914-04
Max als Tangolehrer in Berlin	Max professeur de tango	1914-01
Max als Torero	Max toréador	1913-08
Max als Tragöde	Max joue le drame	1914-08
Max als Wohltäter	Max est charitable	1913-03
Max als Zauberkünstler	Max illusionniste	1913-19
Max amateur photographe	Max fait de la photographie	1913-14
Max am Klavier	Max virtuose	1913-15
Max à Monaco	Max à Monaco	1914-10
Max amoureux de la teinturière	Amoureux de la teinturière	1912-03
Max and Dog Dick	Max et son chien Dick	1912-02
Max and His Duel	Max a un duel	1911-06
Max and His Mother-in-Law	Max et sa belle-mère [1911]	1911-03
Max and His Mother-in-Law	Max et sa belle-mère [1914]	1914-12
Max and His Prescription	Victime du quinquina	1911-07
Max and His Rival	Duel de Max, Le	1913-11

Max and His Taxi	Max in a Taxi	1917-04
Max and the Clutching Hand	Max victime de la main qui étreint	1916-02
Max and the Daughter of Albion	Anglais tel que Max le parle, L'	1913-21
Max and the Donkey	Âne jaloux, L'	1912-09
Max and the Flirtometer	Baromètre de la fidélité, Le	1915-01
Max and the Fowl	Max reprend sa liberté	1912-01
Max and the Lady Doctor	Max et la doctoresse	1914-06
Max and the Love Letter	Billet doux, Le	1913-12
Max and the Maid	Malle au mariage, La	1912-10
Max and the Merchant's Wife	Maks Linder i g-zha Prokhorova	1913-22
Max and the Pancake	Max et les crêpes	1913-07
Max and the Portmanteau	Vacances de Max, Les	1913-09
Max and the Spies	Max et l'espion	1916-03
Max and the Statue	Max et l'inauguration de la statue	1912-32
Max and the Telephone	Marriage au telephone	1912-25
Max a peur de l'eau	Peur de l'eau, La	1912-31
Max a peur des chiens	Trop aimée	1910-22
Max as a Chiropodist	Max pédicure	1914-02
Max as a Conjurer	Max illusionniste	1913-19
Max as a Musician	Max virtuose	1913-15
Max as a Toreador	Max toréador	1913-08
Max as Cab Driver	Max cocher de fiacre	1912-14
Max assassin	Quel est l'assassin?	1910-30
Max assassiné	Quel est l'assassin?	1910-30
Max asthmatique	Max asthmatique	1914-11
Max a trouvé une fiancée	Max a trouvé une fiancée	1911-01
Max a trovato una fidanzata	Max a trouvé une fiancée	1911-01
Max au couvent	Max au couvent	1914-14
Max auf dem Wege zur Genesung	Max en convalescence	1911-05
Max auf der Brautschau	Max et les crêpes	1913-07
Max au Music-Hall	Au Music-hall	1907-01
Max a un duel	Max a un duel	1911-06
Max aviateur	Débuts d'un aéronaute, Les	1907-13
Max Bags the Bloomer	Max et le sac	1917-01
Max bandit par amour	Bandit par amour	1912-05
Max Becomes a Cook	Cuisinier par amour	1914-13
Max Becomes a Yachtsman	Débuts d'un yachtman, Les	1913-02
Max beim Diner	Que peut-il avoir?	1912-06
Max bleibt ledig	Max ne se mariera pas	1910-36
Max Boxer	Boxeur par amour	1912-24
Max boxeur	Boxeur par amour	1912-24
Max boxeur par amour	Boxeur par amour	1912-24
Max Callista	Max pédicure	1914-02
Max cavaliere	Max décoré	1914-03
Max célibataire	Vive la vie de garçon	1908-07
Max champion de boxe	Champion de boxe	1910-24
Max cherche une fiancée	Max cherche une fiancée	1910-33
Max cherche un emploi	Max a trouvé une fiancée	1911-01
Max cocher de fiacre	Max cocher de fiacre	1912-14
Max collectionne les chaussures	Max collectionne les chaussures	1913-18
Max collectionneur de chaussures	Max collectionne les chaussures	1913-18
Max Comes Across	Max Comes Across	1917-02

Max Comes Home	Max se trompe d'étage	1910-21
Max cuisinier par amour	Cuisinier par amour	1914-13
Max Cures Cinemania	Mari jaloux	1914-05
Max dans l'armoire	Armoire, L'	1907-18
Max dans les airs	Débuts d'un aéronaute, Les	1907-13
Max dans les Alpes	Épreuve difficile, Une	1910-15
Max dans sa famille	Max en convalescence	1911-05
Max Debut as Yachtsman	Débuts d'un yachtman, Les	1913-02
Max decorat	Max décoré	1914-03
Max décoré	Max décoré	1914-03
Max, der Zirkuskönig	Zirkuskönig, Der	1924-02
Max devrait porter des bretelles	Max devrait porter des bretelles	1917-07
Max distrait	Max est distrait	1910-19
Max diventa alto	Veine de bossu, Une	1908-11
Max Divorces	Max Wants a Divorce	1917-03
Max divorteaza	Max Wants a Divorce	1917-03
Max duelliert sich	Max a un duel	1911-06
Max e la dotoressa	Max et la doctoresse	1914-06
Max e l'aperitivo	Victime du quinquina	1911-07
Max Embarrassed	Max cherche une fiancée	1910-33
Max émule de Tartarin	Max émule de Tartarin	1912-23
Max en Amérique	Max Comes Across	1917-02
Max en convalescence	Max en convalescence	1911-05
Max en de katten	Max n'aime pas les chats	1913-10
Max Engaged	Max a trouvé une fiancée	1911-01
Maxens Bad	Max prend un bain	1910-31
Maxens Duell	Duel de Mr Myope, Le	1910-16
Maxens Hochzeit	Mariage forcé	1914-09
Maxens Hut	Chapeau de Max, Le	1913-13
Maxens Pillen	Effets des pilules, Les	1910-20
Maxens Sommerreise	Vacances de Max, Les	1913-09
Maxens Verehrerinnen	Max fait des conquêtes	1913-16
Maxens Wette	Au secours!	1924-01
Max entre deux femmes	Max entre deux feux	1917-05
Max entre deux feux	Max entre deux feux	1917-05
Max en vacances	Vacances de Max, Les	1913-09
Max en voyage de noces	Voyage de noces	1912-21
Max équilibriste	Obsession de l'équilibre, L'	1908-04
Max escamoteur	Succès de la prestidigitation, Le	1912-08
Max est charitable	Max est charitable	1913-03
Max est décoré	Max décoré	1914-03
Max est distrait	Max est distrait	1910-19
Max et Jane en voyage de noces	Voyage de noces	1912-21
Max et Jane font des crêpes	Max et les crêpes	1913-07
Max et Jane veulent faire du théâtre	Max veut faire du théâtre	1911-08
Max et la belle négresse	Max et sa belle-mère [1911]	1911-03
Max et la bonne à tout faire	N'embrassez pas votre bonne	1913-20
Max et la doctoresse	Max et la doctoresse	1914-06
Max et la fuite de gaz	Fuite de gaz, La	1912-20
Max et la main qui étreint	Max victime de la main qui étreint	1916-02
Max et la statue	Max et l'inauguration de la statue	1912-32
Max et la teinturière	Amoureux de la teinturière	1912-03

Max et le billet doux	Billet doux, Le	1913-12
Max et l'edelweiss	Épreuve difficile, Une	1910-15
Max et le mari jaloux	Mari jaloux	1914-05
Max et l'entente cordiale	Entente cordiale	1912-26
Max et le papier tue-mouche	Max ne se mariera pas	1910-36
Max et le quinquina	Victime du quinquina	1911-07
Max et le rendez-vous	Rendez-vous, Le	1912-33
Max et le sac	Max et le sac	1917-01
Max et les crêpes	Max et les crêpes	1913-07
Max et les femmes	Oh! les femmes	1912-15
Max et l'espion	Max et l'espion	1916-03
Max et le(s) sport(s)	Max Linder pratique tous les sports	1913-05
Max et le téléphone	Mariage au téléphone	1912-25
Max et l'étudiante	Maks i Kursistka	1913-23
Max et l'inauguration de la statue	Max et l'inauguration de la statue	1912-32
Max et sa belle-mère [1911]	Max et sa belle-mère [1911]	1911-03
Max et sa belle-mère [1914]	Max et sa belle-mère [1914]	1914-12
Max et sa belle négresse	Max et sa belle-mère [1911]	1911-03
Max et sa voisine	Voisin, voisine	1911-04
Max et son âne	Âne jaloux, L'	1912-09
Max et son bon chien Dick	Max et son chien Dick	1912-02
Max et son chien Dick	Max et son chien Dick	1912-02
Max et son taxi	Max in a Taxi	1917-04
Max Faces the Footlights	Max joue le drame	1914-08
Max fait de la photo	Max fait de la photographie	1913-14
Max fait de la photographie	Max fait de la photographie	1913-14
Max fait des conquêtes	Max fait des conquêtes	1913-16
Max fait du cinéma	Débuts de Max Linder au cinématographe, Les	1910-28
Max fait du patinage	Débuts d'un patineur	1907-07
Max fait du patinage à roulettes	Vengeance du bottier, La	1909-13
Max fait du ski	Max fait du ski	1910-18
Max fait du sport	Max Linder pratique tous les sports	1913-05
Max fait le tour du monde	Comment Max Linder fait le tour du monde	1910-29
Max Fears the Dogs	Trop aimée	1910-22
Max fiancé	Max a trouvé une fiancée	1911-01
Max Fights a Duel	Max a un duel	1911-06
Max Foils the Police	Kyrelor, bandit par amour	1910-13
Max Gets Married	Max se marie	1911-02
Max Gets the Reward	Max Linder contre Nick Winter	1912-04
Max Gets Too Much Mother-in-Law	Max et sa belle-mère [1914]	1914-12
Max Goes in for Photography	Max fait de la photographie	1913-14
Max Goes Skating	Débuts d'un patineur	1907-07
Max Goes Ski-ing	Max fait du ski	1910-18
Max Goes to America	Max Comes Across	1917-02
Max, Hairdresser	Coiffeur par amour	1914-16
Max ha le scarpe strette	Vengeance du bottier, La	1909-13
Max Has the Boxing Fever	Champion de boxe	1910-24
Max Has to Change	Revolver arrange tout, Le	1910-17
Max Has Trouble With His Eyes	Duel de Mr Myope, Le	1910-16
Max hat eine Braut gefunden	Max a trouvé une fiancée	1911-01

Max hat Konkurrenz	Rivalité	1913-06
Max hat neue Stiefel an	Soulier trop petit, Le	1910-32
Max hat sich in der Etage geirrt	Max se trompe d'étage	1910-21
Max heeft een bruid gevonden	Max a trouvé une fiancée	1911-01
Max heiratet	Max se marie	1911-02
Max heiratet sein Weibchen	Be My Wife	1921-02
Max Hits the High spots	Très moutarde	1914-17
Max, hoofdinspecteur van de gasfabriek	Billet doux, Le	1913-12
Max hypnotisé	Max hypnotisé	1910-34
Max Hypnotized	Max hypnotisé	1910-34
Max illusionniste	Max illusionniste	1913-19
Max im Klöster	Max au couvent	1914-14
Max im Mädchenpensionat	Max au couvent	1914-14
Max im Taxi	Max in a Taxi	1917-04
Max in a Convent	Max au couvent	1914-14
Max in a Dilemma	Pacte, Le	1910-04
Max in a Taxi	Max in a Taxi	1917-04
Max in a Wardrobe	Armoire, L'	1907-18
Max in den Alpen	Max asthmatique	1914-11
Max in den Lüften	Débuts d'un aéronaute, Les	1907-13
Max in der Schweiz	Max victime de la main qui étreint	1916-02
Max in der Sommerfrische	Petit roman	1912-29
Max inima larga	Max est charitable	1913-03
Max in Monaco	Max à Monaco	1914-10
Max in Search of a Sweetheart	Max cherche une fiancée	1910-33
Max inszeniert einen Film	Mari jaloux	1914-05
Max in the Alps	Épreuve difficile, Une	1910-15
Max is Absent Minded	Max est distrait	1910-19
Max is Almost Married	Trop aimée	1910-22
Max is Convalescent	Max en convalescence	1911-05
Max is Forced to Work	Max a trouvé une fiancée	1911-01
Max is Love Sick	Hasard et l'amour, Le	1915-04
Max is Stuck Up	Max ne se mariera pas	1910-36
Max ist ein Aufschneider	Max émule de Tartarin	1912-23
Max ist ein Katzenfeind	Max n'aime pas les chats	1913-10
Max ist hypnotisiert	Max hypnotisé	1910-34
Max ist schüchtern	Très moutarde	1914-17
Max ist wasserscheu	Peur de l'eau, La	1912-31
Max jaloux	Mari jaloux	1914-05
Max jockey par amour	Jockey par amour	1913-01
Max Joins the Giants	Max veut grandir	1912-27
Max jongleur	Obsession de l'équilibre, L'	1908-04
Max jongleur par amour	Petite rosse	1909-08
Max joue le drame	Max joue le drame	1914-08
Max juega al drama	Max joue le drame	1914-08
Max Knighted	Max décoré	1914-03
Max lance la mode	Max lance la mode	1911-09
Max la schi	Max fait du ski	1910-18
Max Leads Them a Novel Chase	Voleur mondain, Le	1909-11
Max Learns to Skate	Débuts d'un patineur	1907-07
Max lernt Skilaufen	Max fait du ski	1910-18
Max liebt seine Freiheit	Max reprend sa liberté	1912-01

Max Linder, amateur photographe	Max fait de la photographie	1913-14
Max Linder am Vorabend des Krieges	Deux août 1914	1916-01
Max Linder contre Nick Winter	Max Linder contre Nick Winter	1912-04
Max Linder en het spookslot	Au secours!	1924-01
Max Linder et Mme Prokhorov	Maks Linder i g-zha Prokhorova	1913-22
Max Linder gaat uit rijden	Ah! Quel malheur d'avoir un gendre	1907-03
Max Linder gegen Nick Winter	Max Linder contre Nick Winter	1912-04
Max Linder geht nach Amerika	Max Comes Across	1917-02
Max Linder Goes to America	Max Comes Across	1917-02
Max Linder heeft zeven ongelukkige jaren	Seven Years Bad Luck	1921-01
Max Linder illusionniste	Max illusionniste	1913-19
Max Linder in het spookkastel	Au secours!	1924-01
Max Linder ipnotizzato	Max hypnotisé	1910-34
Max Linder ipnotizzato dal domestica	Domestique hypnotiseur, Le	1907-14
Max Linder Joins the Colours	Deux août 1914	1916-01
Max Linder pratique tous les sports	Max Linder pratique tous les sports	1913-05
Max Linder's Appointment	Rendez-vous, Le	1912-33
Max Linder's Big Family	Je voudrais un enfant	1910-06
Max Linder's Debut as a Cinematograph Artist	Débuts de Max Linder au cinématographe, Les	1910-28
Max Linders Doppelgänger	Sosie, Le	1915-02
Max Linder v. Nick Winter	Max Linder contre Nick Winter	1912-04
Max, maître d'hôtel	Max, maître d'hôtel	1914-04
Max maîtresse de piano	Maîtresse de piano, La	1908-13
Max Makes a Movie	Débuts de Max Linder au cinématographe, Les	1910-28
Max Makes a Touch	Ingénieux attentat, L'	1910-11
Max Makes Music	Flûte merveilleuse, La	1910-25
Max manque un riche mariage	Max manque un riche mariage	1910-35
Max, médecin malgré lui	Max, médecin malgré lui	1917-06
Max Misses Another Good Chance	Max ne se mariera pas	1910-36
Max muss sich scheiden lassen	Max Wants a Divorce	1917-03
Max n'aime pas les chats	Max n'aime pas les chats	1913-10
Max negro	Amoureux de la teinturière	1912-03
Max ne se mariera pas	Max ne se mariera pas	1910-36
Max ne veut pas se marier	Max veut faire du théâtre	1911-08
Max ohne Hosenträger	Max devrait porter des bretelles	1917-07
Max on the Briny	Max à Monaco	1914-10
Max on the Road to Matrimony	Duel de Max, Le	1913-11
Max on Tour	Comment Max Linder fait le tour du monde	1910-29
Max partae para a guerra	Deux août 1914	1916-01
Max part en Amérique	Max Comes Across	1917-02
Max part en vacances	Vacances de Max, Les	1913-09
Max pédicure	Max pédicure	1914-02
Max peintre par amour	Peintre par amour	1912-18
Max Plays Detective	Max et l'espion	1916-03
Max Plays the Drama	Max joue le drame	1914-08
Max pratique tous les sports	Max Linder pratique tous les sports	1913-05
Max prend un bain	Max prend un bain	1910-31
Max professeur de tango	Max professeur de tango	1914-01

Max reprend sa liberté	Max reprend sa liberté	1912-01
Max sauveteur	Médaille de sauvetage, La	1913-17
Max's Camera Calamity	Max devrait porter des bretelles	1917-07
Max's Cat-Astrophe	Max n'aime pas les chats	1913-10
Max's Chosen Bride	Mariage forcé	1914-09
Max's Debut as a Cinematograph Artist	Débuts de Max Linder au cinématographe, Les	1910-28
Max's Decoration	Max décoré	1914-03
Max's Divorce	Max se marie	1911-02
Max's Double	Sosie, Le	1915-02
Max Sees Life	Très moutarde	1914-17
Max's Efforts to Grow	Max veut grandir	1912-27
Max's Elopement	Max au couvent	1914-14
Max se marie	Max se marie	1911-02
Max se trompe d'étage	Max se trompe d'étage	1910-21
Max Serves as a Soldier	Soldat par amour	1910-05
Max Sets the Fashion	Max lance la mode	1911-09
Max Sets the Style	Max lance la mode	1911-09
Max's Feet are Pinched	Soulier trop petit, Le	1910-32
Max's First Efforts	Débuts de Max Linder au cinématographe, Les	1910-28
Max's First Job	Débuts de Max Linder au cinématographe, Les	1910-28
Max's Flurried Flirtation	Max, maître d'hôtel	1914-04
Max Should Wear Braces	Max devrait porter des bretelles	1917-07
Max slachtoffer van de Bordeaux-wijn	Victime du quinquina	1911-07
Max's Latest Hobby	Max collectionne les chaussures	1913-18
Max's Marvellous Cure	Max asthmatique	1914-11
Max's Marvellous Tulip	Tulipe merveilleuse, La	1915-03
Max's Melodrama	Max joue le drame	1914-08
Max's Mother-in-Law Loves Sport	Max et sa belle-mère [1914]	1914-12
Max's Musical Masterpiece	Max virtuose	1913-15
Max soldat	Soldat par amour	1910-05
Max soldat de 2eme classe	Soldat par amour	1910-05
Max Soldier, 2nd Class	Soldat par amour	1910-05
Max's Persuasive Suicide	Pendu, Le [1914]	1914-07
Max spricht kein Englisch	Anglais tel que Max le parle, L'	1913-21
Max's Revenge	Max et sa belle-mère [1914]	1914-12
Max Starts the Fashion	Max lance la mode	1911-09
Max's Tragedy	Max veut faire du théâtre	1911-08
Max sucht die Damentasche	Max et le sac	1917-01
Max sucht eine Braut	Max cherche une fiancée	1910-33
Max's Vacation	Vacances de Max, Les	1913-09
Max Takes a Bath	Max prend un bain	1910-31
Max Takes Tonics	Victime du quinquina	1911-07
Max, the Heartbreaker	Max entre deux feux	1917-05
Max the Juggler	Obsession de l'équilibre, L'	1908-04
Max, the Ladies' Man	Max fait des conquêtes	1913-16
Max, the Lady Killer	Max fait des conquêtes	1913-16
Max, the Magician	Succès de la prestidigitation, Le	1912-08
Max the Magician	Max illusionniste	1913-19
Max, the New Butler	Max, maître d'hôtel	1914-04

Max, the Snapshooter	Max fait de la photographie	1913-14
Max toréador	Max toréador	1913-08
Max to the Rescue	Médaille de sauvetage, La	1913-17
Max Tries Ski-ing	Max fait du ski	1910-18
Max trouve une fiancée	Max a trouvé une fiancée	1911-01
Max und das Edelweiss	Épreuve difficile, Une	1910-15
Max und das Handtäschchen	Max et le sac	1917-01
Max und der spiellustige Schwiegervater	Mariage au puzzle, Un	1910-23
Max und die Denkmalsenthüllung	Max et l'inauguration de la statue	1912-32
Max und die Doktorin	Max et la doctoresse	1914-06
Max und die drei Musketiere	Three Must-Get-Theres, The	1922-01
Max und die Liebe	Duel de Max, Le	1913-11
Max und die Schäferin	Max et l'espion	1916-03
Max und die Spiöne	Max et l'espion	1916-03
Max und die Tochter des Kapitäns	Médaille de sauvetage, La	1913-17
Max und Jane wollen Schauspieler werden	Max veut faire du théâtre	1911-08
Max und seine Film-"Kollegen"	Mari jaloux	1914-05
Max und seine Schwiegermutter	Max et sa belle-mère [1911]	1911-03
Max und seine Schwiegermutter	Max et sa belle-mère [1914]	1914-12
Max und sein Hund	Max et son chien Dick	1912-02
Max und sein Orden	Max décoré	1914-03
Max und sein Rivale	Entente cordiale	1912-26
Max verfehlt eine reiche Heirat	Max manque un riche mariage	1910-35
Max veut apprendre à patiner	Débuts d'un patineur	1907-07
Max veut divorcer	Max Wants a Divorce	1917-03
Max veut faire du théâtre	Max veut faire du théâtre	1911-08
Max veut grandir	Max veut grandir	1912-27
Max veut patiner	Débuts d'un patineur	1907-07
Max victime de la main qui étreint	Max victime de la main qui étreint	1916-02
Max victime du quinquina	Victime du quinquina	1911-07
Max virtuose	Max virtuose	1913-15
Max Wants a Divorce	Max Wants a Divorce	1917-03
Max will größer werden	Max veut grandir	1912-27
Max will sie knipsen	Max fait de la photographie	1913-14
Max will sterben	Pendu, Le [1914]	1914-07
Max Wins and Loses	Max victime de la main qui étreint	1916-02
Max Wins a Widow	Max Linder pratique tous les sports	1913-05
Max wird Arzt wider Willen	Max, médecin malgré lui	1917-06
Max wird Droschkenkutscher	Max cocher de fiacre	1912-14
Max wird Segler	Débuts d'un yachtman, Les	1913-02
Max Wishes He Hadn't	N'embrassez pas votre bonne	1913-20
Max y la inauguracion de la estatua	Max et l'inauguration de la statue	1912-32
Mean Trick on Max, A	Dick est un chien savant	1914-15
Médaille de sauvetage, La	Médaille de sauvetage, La	1913-17
Meine Hose ist geplatzt	Mon pantalon est décousu	1908-01
Meine Uhr geht zu spät	Ma montre retarde	1908-02
Mein Hund ist ein Genie	Mon chien rapporte	1910-27
Mes voisins me font danser	Mes voisins me font danser	1908-18
Meus visinhos dansam	Mes voisins me font danser	1908-18
Miss Moneybags Wishes to Wed	Mariage américain, Un	1909-06
Moço timido, Um	Jeune homme timide, Un	1908-16

Moço virtuoso	Vertueux jeune homme, Le	1908-25
Moderne Schaukelpartie	Pendu, Le [1906]	1906-04
Mon chien rapporte	Mon chien rapporte	1910-27
Mon pantalon est déchiré	Mon pantalon est décousu	1908-01
Mon pantalon est décousu	Mon pantalon est décousu	1908-01
Mort d'un toréador, La	Drame à Séville, Un	1907-16
Mother-in-Law's Visit	Ah! Quel malheur d'avoir un gendre	1907-03
Motor Boat Trip, A	Mal de mer, Le	1912-13
Music Teacher, The	Maîtresse de piano, La	1908-13
My Neighbours are Giving a Dance	Mes voisins me font danser	1908-18
My Watch is Slow	Ma montre retarde	1908-02
Nachbar und Nachbarn	Voisin, voisine	1911-04
Nach dem glücklich bestandenen Abiturienten Examen	En bombe	1909-12
Nächtliche Bummelei	Première sortie	1905-01
Neighbours	Voisin, voisine	1911-04
N'embrassez pas votre bonne	N'embrassez pas votre bonne	1913-20
Nervous Twitching is Catching, A	Tic nerveux contagieux, Un	1908-15
Noisy Neighbors	Mes voisins me font danser	1908-18
Noivo occupadissimo	Fiancé trop occupé, Un	1908-19
Nourrice par nécessité	Nourrice par nécessité	1907-05
Nuit agitée, Une	Nuit agitée, Une	1912-07
Nur keinen Schwiegersohn	Ah! Quel malheur d'avoir un gendre	1907-03
Obsessão da Sogra	Obsession de la belle-mère, L'	1908-10
Obsession de la belle-mère, L'	Obsession de la belle-mère, L'	1908-10
Obsession de l'équilibre, L'	Obsession de l'équilibre, L'	1908-04
O' diese Frauen	Oh! les femmes	1912-15
Of the Deepest Dye	Amoureux de la teinturière	1912-03
Oh! les femmes	Oh! les femmes	1912-15
On a Racket	En bombe	1909-12
Oncle à héritage, L'	Oncle à héritage, L'	1908-20
On demande un gendre à l'essai	On demande un gendre à l'essai	1908-21
One Can't Believe One's Eyes*	Mauvaise vue	1910-08
One on Max	Vengeance du bottier, La	1909-13
On the Honeymoon	Voyage de noces	1912-21
Op des ververs dochter verliefd	Amoureux de la teinturière	1912-03
Original Cross-Country Running, An	Cross-country original, Un	1910-26
Originelles Wettlaufen, Ein	Cross-country original, Un	1910-26
Originelle Wette, Eine	Pari original, Un	1912-17
Over the 'Phone	Mariage au téléphone	1912-25
Pact, The	Pacte, Le	1910-04
Pacte, Le	Pacte, Le	1910-04
Pari original, Un	Pari original, Un	1912-17
Pariser Studenten	Étudiants de Paris, Les	1906-01
Paris Students	Étudiants de Paris, Les	1906-01
Pech des Gatten, Das	Mari peu veinard, Un	1908-24
Pedicure, The	Max pédicure	1914-02
Pedicure for Love	Pédicure par amour	1908-12
Pédicure par amour	Pédicure par amour	1908-12
Pediscuro por amor	Pédicure par amour	1908-12
Peintre par amour	Peintre par amour	1912-18
Pendu, Le [1906]	Pendu, Le [1906]	1906-04

Pendu, Le [1914]	Pendu, Le [1914]	1914-07
Peregrinação de uma pulga	Pérégrinations d'une puce, Les	1908-08
Pérégrinations d'une puce, Les	Pérégrinations d'une puce, Les	1908-08
Péripéties d'un amant, Les	Péripéties d'un amant, Les	1907-12
Péripéties d'un amoureux, Les	Péripéties d'un amant, Les	1907-12
Perseverance Rewarded	Tout est bien qui finit bien	1910-12
Persuasive Powers of a Revolver, The	Revolver arrange tout, Le	1910-17
Petit café, Le	Petit café, Le	1919-01
Petite rosse	Petite rosse	1909-08
Petit jeune homme, Le	Petit jeune homme, Le	1909-03
Petit roman	Petit roman	1912-29
Peur de l'eau, La	Peur de l'eau, La	1912-31
Pfiffige Gate, Der	Ruse de mari [1907]	1907-06
Phial of Poison, The	Empoisonneuse, L'	1907-02
Pitou, bonne d'enfants	Pitou, bonne d'enfants	1907-15
Plaisirs du soldat, Les	Plaisirs du soldat, Les	1907-20
Pleasant Side of a Soldier's Life, The	Plaisirs du soldat, Les	1907-20
Poison, Le	Empoisonneuse, L'	1907-02
Poor Pa Pays Again	Ingénieux attentat, L'	1910-11
Pour un collier	Pour un collier	1907-04
Prahlhansens Heldentaten	Exploits du jeune Tartarin, Les	1909-16
Precisa-se de um genro	On demande un gendre à l'essai	1908-21
Premier cigare, Le	Premier cigare d'un collégien, Le	1908-03
Premier cigare de Max	Premier cigare d'un collégien, Le	1908-03
Premier cigare d'un collégien, Le	Premier cigare d'un collégien, Le	1908-03
Première sortie	Première sortie	1905-01
Première sortie d'un collégien, La	Première sortie	1905-01
Premier rendez-vous, Le	Premier rendez-vous, Le	1909-15
Prima ascensione di un aeronauta, La	Débuts d'un aéronaute, Les	1907-13
Primeiro rendez-vous, O	Premier rendez-vous, Le	1909-15
Primera Salida	Première sortie	1905-01
Prince of Worth, A	Serment d'un prince, Le	1910-07
Prince's Honour, A	Serment d'un prince, Le	1910-07
Private Atkins Minds a Baby	Pitou, bonne d'enfants	1907-15
Prospective heirs	Oncle à héritage, L'	1908-20
Puzzle, The	Mariage au puzzle, Un	1910-23
Quel est l'assassin?	Quel est l'assassin?	1910-30
Que peut-il arriver?	Que peut-il avoir?	1912-06
Que peut-il avoir?	Que peut-il avoir?	1912-06
Qui a tué Max?	Quel est l'assassin?	1910-30
Qui est l'assassin?	Quel est l'assassin?	1910-30
Rache des Schuhhändlers, Die	Vengeance du bottier, La	1909-13
Raio, O	Coup de foudre, Le	1908-22
Râtelier de la belle-mère, Le	Avant et... après	1909-14
Reklamefrau, Die	Femme sandwich, La	1908-06
Rencontre imprévue	Rencontre imprévue	1905-02
Rendez-vous, Le	Rendez-vous, Le	1912-33
Rendez-vous de Max, Le	Rendez-vous, Le	1912-33
Repos impossible	Mes voisins me font danser	1908-18
Représentation au cinéma, Une	Représentation au cinéma, Une	1910-10
Représentation au Cinématographe	Représentation au cinéma, Une	1910-10
Retour inattendu	Retour inattendu	1908-09

Revolver arrange tout, Le	Revolver arrange tout, Le	1910-17
Ringer for Max, A	Sosie, Le	1915-02
Rivale im Koffer, Der	Malle au mariage, La	1912-10
Rivalité	Rivalité	1913-06
Rivalité de Max, La	Rivalité	1913-06
Robo de la Giaconda, El	Max Linder contre Nick Winter	1912-04
Roi du cirque, Le	Zirkuskönig, Der	1924-02
Roman de Max, Le	Petit roman	1912-29
Romantic Girl, A	Jeune fille romanesque	1910-03
Romantic Young Lady, A	Jeune fille romanesque	1910-03
Romeo als Dieb	Roméo se fait bandit	1909-10
Roméo se fait bandit	Roméo se fait bandit	1909-10
Romeo Turns Bandit	Roméo se fait bandit	1909-10
Romeo Turns Brigand	Roméo se fait bandit	1909-10
Ruse de mari [1907]	Ruse de mari [1907]	1907-06
Ruse de mari, Une [1910]	Ruse de mari, Une [1910]	1910-09
Sad Dilemma, A	Que peut-il avoir?	1912-06
Sandwich Woman	Femme sandwich, La	1908-06
Scéance de cinématographie, Une	Représentation au cinéma, Une	1910-10
Schlaue Erbonkel, Der	Oncle à héritage, L'	1908-20
Schlecht belohnter Verehrer, Ein	Conquête, Une	1909-05
Schlechte Augen	Mauvaise vue	1910-08
Schöpfung des Serpentintanzes	Création de la serpentine	1908-23
Schrank, Der	Armoire, L'	1907-18
Schwärmerisches Mädchen, Eine	Jeune fille romanesque	1910-03
Schwiegersohn auf Probe verlangt	On demande un gendre à l'essai	1908-21
Schwur eines Fürsten, Der	Serment d'un prince, Le	1910-07
Seekrankheit, Die	Mal de mer, Le	1912-13
Sehnsucht nach einem Kind	Je voudrais un enfant	1910-06
Sei mein Weibchen	Be My Wife	1921-02
Seine fürchterlichste Stunde	Au secours!	1924-01
Sept ans de malheur	Seven Years Bad Luck	1921-01
Serment d'un prince, Le	Serment d'un prince, Le	1910-07
Serum gegen Schüchternheit, Ein	Timidité guérie par le sérum, La	1910-01
Servant Hypnotist, The	Domestique hypnotiseur, Le	1907-14
Servants and Masters	Bonne pour Monsieur, un domestique pour Madame, Une	1910-02
Servant's Good Joke, The	Domestique hypnotiseur, Le	1907-14
Servant's Good Joke, The	Aimé par sa bonne	1909-02
Seven Years Bad Luck	Seven Years Bad Luck	1921-01
Shame on Max	Max manque un riche mariage	1910-35
Short-Sighted Duelist, A	Duel de Mr Myope, Le	1910-16
Shy Fellow, A	Jeune homme timide, Un	1908-14
Siate mia moglie	Be My Wife	1921-02
Sieben Jahre Pech	Seven Years Bad Luck	1921-01
Signor Dottore, Il	Max, médecin malgré lui	1917-06
Smitten	Fuite de gaz, La	1912-20
Soldat aus Liebe	Soldat par amour	1910-05
Soldatenvergnügen	Plaisirs du soldat, Les	1907-20
Soldat par amour	Soldat par amour	1910-05
Soldier and the Baby, The	Pitou, bonne d'enfants	1907-15
Sonderbare Erlebnisse eines Babys	Bébé encombrant, Un	1908-17

Sosie, Le	Sosie, Le	1915-02
Sosie de Max, Le	Sosie, Le	1915-02
Soulier trop petit, Le	Soulier trop petit, Le	1910-32
Soyez ma femme	Be My Wife	1921-02
Strange Bet, A	Pari original, Un	1912-17
Streich des Dieners, Der	Vengeance du domestique, La	1912-19
Student aan de Boemel, Een	En bombe	1909-12
Studenti di Parigi, Gli	Étudiants de Paris, Les	1906-01
Student on the Spree, A	En bombe	1909-12
Succès de la prestidigitation, Le	Succès de la prestidigitation, Le	1912-08
Surprise inattendue, Une	Péripéties d'un amant, Les	1907-12
Surprise Package	Tribulations d'un neveu, Les	1908-27
Surprises de l'amour, Les	Surprises de l'amour, Les	1909-07
Surprises of a Flirtation, The	Surprises de l'amour, Les	1909-07
Suspension, La	Suspension, La	1908-05
Tantalising Young Lady, A	Petite rosse	1909-08
Tanzvergnügen bei den Nachbarn, Ein	Mes voisins me font danser	1908-18
Telephonische Verbindung	Mariage au téléphone	1912-25
Their Common Destiny	Max veut faire du théâtre	1911-08
Three Must-Get-Theres, The	Three Must-Get-Theres, The	1922-01
Tic nerveux contagieux, Un	Tic nerveux contagieux, Un	1908-15
Timidez curada, La	Timidité guérie par le sérum, La	1910-01
Timidez curada pelo serum, La	Timidité guérie par le sérum, La	1910-01
Timidité guérie par le sérum, La	Timidité guérie par le sérum, La	1910-01
Timidité vaincue, La	Timidité guérie par le sérum, La	1910-01
Tommy Atkins Minds a Baby	Pitou, bonne d'enfants	1907-15
Too Much Pep	Be My Wife	1921-02
Tormented by His Mother-in-Law	Obsession de la belle-mère, L'	1908-10
Torn Trousers, The	Mon pantalon est décousu	1908-01
Tout est bien qui finit bien	Tout est bien qui finit bien	1910-12
Travels of a Flea, The	Pérégrinations d'une puce, Les	1908-08
Très moutarde	Très moutarde	1914-17
Tribulations d'un neveu, Les	Tribulations d'un neveu, Les	1908-27
Tribulations of a Nephew, The	Tribulations d'un neveu, Les	1908-27
Tricking his Wife	Ruse de mari [1907]	1907-06
Triumph der Liebe, Der	Bandit par amour	1912-05
Trop aimée	Trop aimée	1910-22
Troubles of a Grasswidower	Vive la vie de garçon	1908-07
Tugendhafter junger Mann, Ein	Vertueux jeune homme, Le	1908-25
Tulipe merveilleuse, La	Tulipe merveilleuse, La	1915-03
Two Great Griefs	Deux grandes douleurs	1908-14
Um ein Halsband	Pour un collier	1907-04
Uncle's Will	Oncle à héritage, L'	1908-20
Unerwartete Rückkehr	Retour inattendu	1908-09
Unforeseen Meeting, An	Rencontre imprévue	1905-02
Ungeschickte Equilibrist, Der	Obsession de l'équilibre, L'	1908-04
Unskillful Skater, The	Débuts d'un patineur	1907-07
Unvorhergesehene Begegnung	Rencontre imprévue	1905-02
Unwilling Chiropodist	Pédicure par amour	1908-12
Vacances de Max, Les	Vacances de Max, Les	1913-09
Vacances de Max Linder, Les	Vacances de Max, Les	1913-09
Veine de bossu, Une	Veine de bossu, Une	1908-11

Vengeance du bottier, La	Vengeance du bottier, La	1909-13
Vengeance du domestique, La	Vengeance du domestique, La	1912-19
Verbrecher-Idee	Idée d'apache	1907-09
Verbundene Lippen	Lèvres collées	1906-03
Verliebte Max, Der	Tout est bien qui finit bien	1910-12
Verliebte Max, Der	Amoureux de la teinturière	1912-03
Verliebte Max und seine Hunde, Der	Trop aimée	1910-22
Verlorene Adresse, Die	Rendez-vous, Le	1912-33
Verrassing, Een	Max veut faire du théâtre	1911-08
Vertrag, Der	Pacte, Le	1910-04
Vertueux jeune homme, Le	Vertueux jeune homme, Le	1908-25
Victime du quinquina	Victime du quinquina	1911-07
Vie de Polichinelle, La	Légende de Polichinelle, La	1907-11
Vielbeschäftigter Bräutigam	Fiancé trop occupé, Un	1908-19
Vingt ans avant	Three Must-Get-Theres, The	1922-01
Virtuous Young Man, A	Vertueux jeune homme, Le	1908-25
Vive la vie de garçon	Vive la vie de garçon	1908-07
Voisin, voisine	Voisin, voisine	1911-04
Voleur mondain, Le	Voleur mondain, Le	1909-11
Vom Dienstmädchen geliebt	Aimé par sa bonne	1909-02
Von Amor Pfeil getroffen	Coup de foudre, Le	1908-22
Vorher und Nachher	Avant et... après	1909-14
Vorstellung im Kinematograph	Représentation au cinéma, Une	1910-10
Voyage de noces	Voyage de noces	1912-21
Voyage de noces (en Espagne)	Voyage de noces	1912-21
Wanderung des Flohs, Die	Pérégrinations d'une puce, Les	1908-08
Wanderungen eines Floh's	Pérégrinations d'une puce, Les	1908-08
Wanted: a Bearskin	Max émule de Tartarin	1912-23
Wanted a Son-in-Law	On demande un gendre à l'essai	1908-21
Wanted, a Son-in-Law on Trial	On demande un gendre à l'essai	1908-21
Was Liebe zusammenbringt	Surprises de l'amour, Les	1909-07
Water-Funker, The	Peur de l'eau, La	1912-31
Waterplane Elopement, A	Enlèvement en hydroaéroplane, L'	1912-28
Wer ist der Täter	Quel est l'assassin?	1910-30
When the Shoe Pinches	Soulier trop petit, Le	1910-32
Who Did the Deed	Quel est l'assassin?	1910-30
Who Killed Max?	Quel est l'assassin?	1910-30
Who Pays My Wife's Bills?	Be My Wife	1921-02
Who Will Win My Heart	À qui mon cœur?	1909-09
Wie Max eine Weltreise macht	Comment Max Linder fait le tour du monde	1910-29
Wie Max englisch spricht !	Anglais tel que Max le parle, L'	1913-21
Wife of His Choice, The	Mariages imprévus	1913-04
Willyboy Gets His	Petit jeune homme, Le	1909-03
Wirkung der Pillen	Effets des pilules, Les	1910-20
Would-be Juggler, The	Obsession de l'équilibre, L'	1908-04
Wrong Floor, The	Max se trompe d'étage	1910-21
Wunde an schlechter Stelle, Eine	Bobo mal placé, Un	1909-01
Wunderbare Flöte, Die	Flûte merveilleuse, La	1910-25
Young Lady-Killer, A	Petit jeune homme, Le	1909-03
Zauberflöte, Die	Flûte merveilleuse, La	1910-25
Zerstreute Max, Der	Max est distrait	1910-19

Zirkuskönig, Der	Zirkuskönig, Der	1924-02
Zu enge Schuhe	Chaussure trop étroite	1907-08
Zu Hilfe	Au secours!	1924-01
Zu viel beschäftigte Bräutigam, Der	Fiancé trop occupé, Un	1908-19
Zwei Untröstliche	Deux grandes douleurs	1908-14
Zwischen zwei Feuern	Max entre deux feux	1917-05

www.ingramcontent.com/pod-product-compliance
Lightning Source LLC
Chambersburg PA
CBHW050329230426
43663CB00010B/1786